WOMEN
IN THE
LINE OF
FIRE

What You Should Know
About Women in
the Military

ERIN
SOLARO

SEAL PRESS

WOMEN IN THE LINE OF FIRE
What You Should Know About Women in the Military

Copyright © 2006 by Erin Solaro

Cover photo courtesy of the Department of Defense. Airman Anne C. Lane (Moor), 24th Security Police Squadron, Howard AFB, Panama Branch, United States Air Force (1994-2004)

Published by
Seal Press
An Imprint of Avalon Publishing Group, Incorporated
1400 65th Street, Suite 250
Emeryville, CA 94608

ISBN-13: 978-1-58005-174-3
ISBN-10: 1-58005-174-X

9 8 7 6 5 4 3 2 1
Library of Congress Cataloging-in-Publication Data

Solaro, Erin.
Women in the line of fire : what you should know about women in the military / Erin Solaro.
p. cm.
Includes bibliographical references and index.
ISBN-13: 978-1-58005-174-3 (alk. paper)
ISBN-10: 1-58005-174-X (alk. paper)
1. United States—Armed Forces—Women. I. Title.

UB418.W65S66 2006
355.0082'0973—dc22
2006012044

Cover and interior design by Domini Dragoone
Printed in the United States of America by Malloy
Distributed by Publishers Group West

For James, who made this book possible

And for Philip, who makes everything possible

The American Army really is a people's Army in the sense that it belongs to the American people who take a jealous and proprietary interest in its involvement. . . . In the final analysis, the American Army is not so much an arm of the Executive Branch as it is an arm of the American people.

—GENERAL FRED C. WEYAND,
former Chief of Staff, United States Army

Current Supreme Court doctrine on military service turns the Constitution on its head. The Court has held that citizens may be conscripted into the armed forces at any time and for any purpose; yet citizens who wish to join the armed forces have no constitutional right to do so. Such an approach might make sense in an authoritarian regime; in a regime based upon popular sovereignty, it is perverse.

—AKHIL REED AMAR AND ALAN HIRSCH,
*For the People: What the Constitution
Really Says About Your Rights*

CONTENTS

FOREWORD

In the following pages, Erin Solaro carefully destroys, one by one, many of the long-standing shibboleths erected to exclude women from serving in combat arms. When serving as the commander of the 9th Infantry Division and of Ft. Lewis in the mid-1970s, I was asked by the Pentagon, "What are your views about placing women in combat arms units?" I responded, "Use nukes first."

As post commander, when women arrived in Ft. Lewis in large numbers, I worried about the cost of building new barracks and modifying existing post facilities to accommodate women.

Battalion commanders asked whether women should be positioned in the front or rear ranks during four-mile runs and parades. Squad leaders asked how they should react when women cried in ranks upon being corrected for "hair not up under steel helmet."

Meanwhile, male soldiers saw the arrival of females as a great opportunity for marriages of convenience, which would allow them separate rations and permission to live off-post.

Now, all these questions have been answered, and women are indeed serving with distinction in an Army that simply cannot function without them.

The military world is changing at a rapid rate, as Solaro points out, but as a combat infantry soldier in two wars, I simply cannot change with it. Combat is killing. And I firmly believe that women are better at giving life than taking it. Having said that, I could not be more proud of the fact that two of my granddaughters decided to serve their country as soldiers "in the line of fire."

As for me, I would be more comfortable if the American people decided that the law excluding women from serving in combat arms should be changed, and that the draft should be reinstituted to ensure sufficient numbers of soldiers for continuing the global war on terrorism.

—GENERAL VOLNEY F. WARNER,
U.S. Army, Retired
August 2006

INTRODUCTION

Women in the Line of Fire is about the increasing participation of American women in combat as regular troops. Some argue that women's participation in combat is an advance for women; others that it is the end of civilization. Many, perhaps most, people hold both viewpoints to a greater or lesser degree. I believe we are at the end point of American women's struggle for citizenship, a struggle that predates the Civil War and that is, in fact, almost as old as the Republic itself. I think we are on the threshold of the only civilization that a free people should cherish: one that men and women create and defend together, as public and private equals.

This book is also about the final changes that must be carried out in order to make this participation in the U.S. military de jure, as well as de facto. Women's expanding role in the military is an enormous military, political, and cultural achievement, and it is happening now, in the midst of a highly questionable war. This achievement has been wrought by hundreds of thousands of servicewomen—and -men—in the U.S. Army and, to a lesser extent, Marine Corps. What it amounts to is a fundamental change in the concept of war as a primarily male activity in which women participate only in times of utmost desperation, a notion that has carried its own political and cultural consequences. And yet, despite considerable if sporadic media attention, this achievement and its consequences remain largely out of the national consciousness.

This book examines how and why the last great barrier to women's full equality of citizenship, equal participation in the common defense at all levels and in all ways, is ending. It is ending because the U.S. Army can no longer fight without women. And it is ending because women are fighting well.

This book does not celebrate war. I admire those who cultivate the martial virtues, and believe those virtues to be not only the common human heritage of both men and women, but part of civilization itself. But the "ground truth" of war ought never to be celebrated. David Fraser, a retired British officer and military historian whom I particularly admire, writes, "War can be a gruesome business. Its incidentals are mutilation, death and destruction, its atmosphere is one of violence and pain, its consequences are suffering and bereavement, and it generates—although not necessarily among the fighting troops—casual brutality at best, vicious cruelty at worst."[1]

Nor is this book an apologia for the current war in Iraq, a war that I oppose precisely *because* I take certain threats, including the rise of militant Islamic fundamentalism, seriously. This war has come close to breaking the U.S. Army as a force capable of doing much beyond rotating units into and out of Iraq. The costs have been horrific. And one does not impress—or deter—one's enemies by pouring the nation's military and economic strength into a sand pit

8

But the accomplishments of American military women since September 11, 2001, especially on the ground in Afghanistan and Iraq, must not be denigrated, ignored, or denied because of the current political context or divided support from the citizenry back home. To understand the magnitude of the U.S. Army's accomplishment (for it is, in the end, the Army's and the nation's accomplishment) we have to know something of the history of the wars that preceded the current one.

The U.S. Army's long history of systemically and systematically devaluing servicewomen began even before we became a republic. The British practice, which American colonists continued, was to allocate women to the army's basic combat unit, the infantry regiment, to perform their work as cooks, laundresses, and nurses. Britain initially sent eight regiments, each mustering 677 men and 67 women, to put down the Revolution. George Washington's orders permitted one woman for every fifteen men in his regiments to draw rations. No one knows how many women there were, but several thousand probably served at one time or another during the Revolution. Few of these women were prostitutes. Most were the wives and sometimes mothers of soldiers. Many did laundry and other chores and sold the soldiers everything from snuff to whiskey to clothing. Although they were noncombatants, they lived under the same brutal conditions as the men. They also understood that if the Revolution failed, they, too, could face the gallows. Since these women were not officially considered soldiers, very few of them had any right to veterans' pensions or benefits, no matter how many lives they saved and no matter if they died of their service in the field, or of diseases, injuries, or wounds incurred in the line of duty.[2]

In truth, the United States did not start doing right even by its male veterans until after World War II, and until very recently, women veterans have remained unrecognized or been treated as second-class.

The devaluation of servicewomen begun in the American Revolution continued for the next two centuries. During the Civil War, thousands of women shifted between civilian and military life. Some cross-dressed to serve as regular soldiers, including line infantry. Others engaged in spying and sabotage; still others in cooking and laundering. Many thousands, black and white, worked as nurses in the military hospitals of the Union and the Confederacy. We'll never know how many were killed or wounded or died of disease, or how many spent the rest of their lives afflicted with post-traumatic stress disorder (PTSD) or, as it was known then, "soldier's heart."

More than 20,000 women served as nurses in the American Expeditionary Force of World War I. Thousands more served as physicians and telephone operators, and in other support roles. They were subject to court-martial authority, although they had no rank or military status. After the war, when American military nurses finally achieved rank, it was only relative. A woman captain, for example, would always be outranked by a male captain even if her date of rank preceded his.[3]

World War II was the pivot: Nearly 400,000 women are estimated to have served in the U.S. military. These were huge numbers, small only in the context of the wartime mobilization of a large nation (about sixteen million men and women wore a uniform in some capacity). Though women were recognized for their contributions, the implications of their capacity for solid, hard work were ignored. The national assumption, by men and often women, was that after the war was over, women would return home from the military and the factories (where jobs were considered the rightful due of male veterans). The best these women could expect was to be considered noble aberrations who'd done a fine job on a one-time basis. And frankly, after sixteen years of suffering and stress, between the Great Depression and the Japanese surrender, most men and women were grateful to settle in with their families and concentrate on domestic tranquility.

In 1948, as the cold war yielded up the Berlin blockade and the United States became aware of how its defenses had evaporated, Congress passed the first law allowing women to serve in regular peacetime forces. However, they could make up no more than 2% of the total force. Women officers could make up no more than 10% of the total number of women, and their promotions were capped above the pay grade of O3, or captain (there are eleven officer pay grades, from second lieutenant to five-star general). Captain in the Army, Air Force, and Marine Corps, and what the Navy calls a lieutenant, is the cutoff point for junior officers to transition into mid-career professionals. There could be any number of O3s, but promotions to O4 and O5 were very carefully managed, and generally reflected disproportionately fewer than the number of female O3s would indicate. There were no female O6s, with one statutory exception: The director of each service's women's branch could rise to the O6 level (Army or Air Force colonel, Navy captain), or halfway up the male hierarchy. For men, reaching O6 was not only the culmination of a twenty-plus-year career that provided professional and intellectual growth; it also provided them with a very comfortable retirement income. Women were barred from all ships except hospital ships and Navy transports, and from duty on combat missions. Women had no command authority over men. As for family, when they were allowed to marry at all, women were denied spousal benefits for their husbands unless they could prove their husbands depended on them for more than 50% of their support.[4] Women could be, and usually were, discharged for marrying, getting pregnant—regardless of marital status or cause—and having abortions.

Korea provided servicewomen with additional opportunities. Approximately 120,000 women served.

But Vietnam and the post-Vietnam era proved to be the real turning point. Seven thousand servicewomen served in Vietnam,[5] a drop in the bucket compared to the three million men who passed through, or the 58,000 who died there, and yet more than twice as many as the 3,250 men who went to prison for draft-related offenses, including conscientious refusal to accept induction. Thousands more women who served in Vietnam as civilians sometimes got much closer to combat than their uniformed sisters were permitted.

Though the post-Vietnam military saw the integration of women, the 1970s was a bad time all around. A confluence of forces ranging from the social and cultural to the military and political guaranteed turmoil. Coming out of Vietnam, all the military services, but the Army in particular, were exhausted and demoralized. True, the Army never lost a major battle in Vietnam. But it emerged from that war scarred in body and spirit, and the North Vietnamese victory in 1975 didn't help. The weary and disgruntled veterans, still reeling from the racial tension of those years, were in no mood for any further experiments in social engineering.

But the Army had no choice. The draft was gone and recruiting "sucked," to use the proper military/managerial expression. American society of the so-called Me Decade provided few incentives to serve. Those who joined during the 1970s tended to be less amenable to discipline and less willing to shed their civilian bad habits. Mixing these people in with a lot of weary veterans and a lot of good professionals whose minds were on institutional resurrection was not exactly a recipe for cohesion and tolerance.

Further, the military is the only large organization, apart from hierarchical Christianity, that cannot draw its middle management from outside its ranks. This is a fact whose implications are not often understood by civilians. Your privates and lieutenants today will be your senior sergeants and colonels in twenty years. Inevitably, cohorts that enter the military during hard times (and this was especially true in the aftermath of Vietnam) acquire bad habits that stay with them throughout their careers. Obviously, an individual can transcend his or her personal and historical circumstances and go on to excellence; many who joined during the 1970s did. But it was not a particularly auspicious group of people. To this day, few veterans who served in the operating forces during those years care to talk about their service, or have much positive to say about it when they do.

So why did the military decide to increase the numbers of women in the aftermath of Vietnam? In a word: because of the men who weren't there to take up the slack. The Army planned to use women, with their better education levels, test scores, and discipline, to help it transition from a conscript to a volunteer force. Some among the senior leadership may have seen it as a temporary measure, pending the (very unlikely) resumption of conscription. Others better understood the rationale and the long-term ramifications, but chose not to draw conclusions.

Two vital policies should have been implemented then by those conscientious enough to understand the forces at play. These forces would ultimately lead to great shifts in the way the military operated and defined itself.

First, in introducing women into a poorly disciplined force, they should have set and enforced stern standards regarding how those women were treated. The military chose not to, for reasons ranging from active hostility to the weak defense that "boys will be boys." They also chose to ignore a vital truth: Problems tend to cluster in units. Outfits that tolerate sexual malfeasance usually have other defects as well. With its institutional tolerance of sexism and institutional failure to treat sexual assault and harassment as the crimes they are, the military opened itself up to decades of assault by a feminist movement less concerned with national security than with bringing down the presumed last bastion of machismo through scandal, lawsuits, and legislation. Once the extent and intent of the assault became clear, the military's response was, by and large, bureaucratic self-protection, gamesmanship to appease the feminists and the politicians, idiotic micromanagement of individual behavior, and the occasional sacrifice of innocent victims on the altar of political expediency. The result was the worst-case scenario of three worlds colliding in conflict. Men grew resentful and unaccepting. Women, for all the furor, did not receive equal treatment or opportunities. And the national defense suffered.

Second, even though women were being actively recruited, they were, legally and by policy, banned from going into combat, the military's core function. But combat could not be banned from coming to women. Vietnam had shown that in an insurgency, there are no front lines and few secure rear areas. Further, war planners had long known that in any Soviet invasion of Western Europe, the entire continent would quickly become a battlefield. Still, the Army, knowing where so much crucial fighting would be, persisted in the fiction that it could keep women out of combat. In peacetime, this meant leaving them untrained and unprepared—soldiers upon whom, in a fight, their male counterparts could not depend.

In sum, it took thirty years, from Vietnam to Iraq, to achieve the almost de facto full integration of women into the U.S. military. For most of that time, the military chose to engage in a set of self-deceptions, a complex pretense shattered first by civilian feminist assault and then—and now—by the performance of military women themselves.

Those self-deceptions had terrible consequences. The young men and women who entered the military during its post-Vietnam resurrection and who served through the 1980s and 1990s can tell stories of injustices and crimes that were badly handled. But that forced, awkward, faux integration was the fault of the midlevel, now senior officers who helped resurrect the Army after Vietnam. Some of these men failed to set and enforce standards because, to put it kindly, they were pigs. Many more were noble. But among the nobler ones, most of them were simply too old, and were of a culture and a generation where men and women were reared almost entirely separately. Very few of them could imagine that the challenges they loved, the risks they accepted, and the ideals they valued might speak to women as truly as they spoke to men. As much as they loved their mothers, wives, sisters, and daughters, they simply could not imagine them as equals. How do we judge their failings against the service they rendered their nation? We can only judge them as what they were (and the living still are): good men who did great service for the country, but who were flawed and limited by their times—as are we all.

I hope they will read this book, if only as a meditation upon their own experiences, for this book does not regard the failures and limitations of other generations as a personal insult, or as a means of deriving unearned moral authority.

A new generation of military leadership is now rising, for whom the 1970s are at best a dim bad memory, and Vietnam ancient history. They're not the senior leadership quite yet, but neither are they the young soldiers they command. Sometimes they toss small bouquets of praise to the younger generation of men and women who are doing things their elders once thought impossible, at least for men and women to do *together*. More often, the senior leadership just lets this battlefield integration happen. They know that the role of women in the military, especially in the Army, has far outstripped law and custom and tradition. But in standing passively by and letting the cards of consequence fall where they may, they too are failing to consider the implications of their inaction. The existing senior leadership has not taken steps to legitimatize women's roles as the soldiers—and in wartime this always means combat—they are proving themselves to be. In a way few civilians can understand, the increasing legitimacy of requiring servicewomen to put themselves on the line in combat makes it all the more profoundly shameful to then withhold from them the recognition they're due. There was a time when ethnic men, Jews and blacks especially, were regarded less as combatants than as auxiliaries, if not menials. It is no less shameful to treat women this way. Furthermore, this refusal to legitimate servicewomen's status as combatants lends support to those men who feel that women should not be in the military at all, and sometimes regard their opinion as a license to try to drive women out.

Nevertheless, I hope these men will read this book, too. For they are, in many ways, a generation between two norms, that of segregation with exceptions, and that of full equality. Perhaps this book will help them to understand their own confusions.

This book explains the considerable unheralded accomplishments of female soldiers, which, it must be said, they could never have achieved without the quiet support of their brothers-in-arms. The U.S. Army is undergoing an extraordinary cultural change. As of 30 September 2004, women constituted 14.6% of the 413,515 enlisted soldiers and 15.3% of the 80,776 officers in the U.S. Army.[6] Men and women are serving together under combat and near-combat conditions in huge numbers. Between September 2001 and March 2006, 143,381 female soldiers, sailors, airmen, and Marines, and nearly 70,000 from the Regular Army, or Army National Guard and Army Reserves, had deployed to Operation Iraqi Freedom or Operation Enduring Freedom, out of a total of 1,312,221. That number will probably have risen to approximately 170,000 by the time this book is published.

Often these men and women live in very intimate proximity. That old canard, "Familiarity breeds contempt," is proving untrue. Familiarity can also breed discovery and respect. Since the 1940s, one of Hollywood's standard war-movie offerings has been the story of the small unit whose members (black, white, Jewish, gentile, whatever, and there's always a guy named "Ski") discover each other's humanity and value. Now it's happening between men and women. Men are appreciating women's rightful equality and innate capability, something all the more valued as a result of the military's confrontation with the Arab and Muslim worlds. I've never met a serviceman who liked the way he saw Arab women being treated. "It breaks your heart" was a comment I heard frequently in Iraq. The degraded status of those women often makes those same servicemen take a hard and critical look at the way they treat American servicewomen.

Much of this phenomenon, of course, is being driven by young men and women who have grown up in a society increasingly accepting of female equality and increasingly intolerant of fuss, by men or women, over this issue. Especially in Iraq and Afghanistan, young soldiers are making up rules as they go along, often by necessity running in advance of the military's policies about the combat employment of women, policies set (and increasingly ignored) by their elders in the faraway Pentagon and Congress.

There has recently been scattered publicity about women in combat: media coverage of everything from medals won to wounds received. There are books out by female soldiers, such as General Janis Karpinski's self-serving memoir *One Woman's Army,* and Kayla Williams's *Love My Rifle More Than You,* described by *The New York Times* as a "chick-lit sensibility" on war. Like most books written during or shortly after a war, they'll prove ephemeral.

This book, however, aims for a bit more permanence. In it, I place personal experience and academic research about servicewomen in their historical and political context.

Starting in the 1980s as an Army ROTC cadet, I grew convinced that in the event of the next war, whatever that war was, servicewomen would serve in direct ground combat. I was interested in the military implications of what it meant for women to be citizens, and for half a polity's citizens to be women.

I discussed these thoughts at length with one of my ROTC instructors, a graduate of one of the last all-male classes at West Point. He was the sort of man who had not liked the integration of the Military Academy, but who refused to go back for a visit until he'd made peace with the idea because he didn't think the female cadets should have to endure his attitude. But in the atmosphere of the mid-1980s, with feminism having abandoned Betty Friedan's enduring and still vibrant contribution to American political and personal life for the dead end of sexual politics and consciousness-raising, those conversations went nowhere. It was simply the wrong historical moment. Still, the discussions we had were serious conversations between citizens. We were not arguing, but discussing serious practical and political issues from profoundly different perspectives. I would keep our mutual civility in mind as a moral imperative.

I became an officer, but served very little. In 1987, I married an active-duty Marine captain and the following year allowed myself to be commissioned into the Army's Individual Ready Reserve. The cold war was ending; the demand for second lieutenants was waning. After some desultory reserve duty, commissioning, and six months of training as an ordnance officer, I abandoned my Army career to become a full-time military wife. It was a profoundly wrong decision.

In 1996, as my marriage was disintegrating, I met James N. Pritzker thanks to our shared interest in military history. The Pritzker family of Chicago is well known for its philanthropic activities, and I knew Jim was a trustee on the board of Norwich University. Jim is a classic citizen-soldier who served as an enlisted paratrooper in the 1970s and later retired as a colonel in the Illinois National Guard. He's a friend of the military who supports many activities. When I was living in the Washington, DC, area, he encouraged me to return to graduate school via Norwich University's online program for a master's in military science and diplomacy.

Three very rough years later, in the winter of 1999, I was working as a secretary for the National Society of The Colonial Dames of America and absolutely desperate to find a way to get back to dealing with military issues. Belatedly, I took Pritzker's advice and enrolled in Norwich University. I wrote my master's thesis on a World War II National Guard infantry regiment, the 127th Infantry, drawn primarily from Wisconsin and Michigan, and what happened to it during the Buna campaign in New Guinea.

It was an attempt at serious military history and operational analysis. I worked from primary sources, especially the unit's morning reports, and even interviewed a few members of the regiment. I wanted to examine the fabled connection between cohesion—the emotional bonding of soldiers in a unit—and combat effectiveness. That connection has served the military for decades as an excuse to exclude whomever it didn't think belonged in the service. Once it was black men who "disrupted" cohesion. Later, many of the same arguments were used against women and gays. In fact, I learned what Hollywood has been telling us for ages: that the cohesion produced by social homogeneity was no match for the cohesion produced by hard training and shared perils. I also revalidated another common-sense notion: that cohesion is not the same as combat effectiveness, and indeed can undercut it. Supposedly "cohesive" units can also kill their officers, mutiny, evade combat, and surrender as groups. It was a thesis that drew some attention inside the Beltway, and also upset a lot of people beyond it. I suspect my thesis committee was among them.

As I faced my uncertain future, I was groping, first, for a way to return, even if tangentially, to a profession I had given up for marriage; and second, toward the very important conclusion that cohesion is only one factor in producing combat effectiveness. In an era obsessed with buzzwords like "asymmetric warfare," "fourth-generation warfare," and "maneuver warfare," I unfashionably asserted that attrition, the accumulation of casualties over time, is a permanent factor in all combat operations, and that the wise commander will not only plan for attrition, but also attempt to use it against the enemy. As we have seen in Iraq, the deliberate use of attrition as an operational concept is valid today.

It was a growing experience in many ways. But it was a surreal experience in others. No one wanted to hear what I had to say. Not at a Wednesday night roundtable I attended at the Fort Myers officers' club; not on the military, academic, and feminist lists I belonged to; and especially not as the United States moved closer to war with Iraq. It wasn't that I was a prophet without honor; it was that I had been typecast. I was a woman, a returning student, a secretary, and I had questioned one of the fundamental myths about combat effectiveness, which had profound implications for both the current war and the sexual integration of the military. I seemed to be pissing off everybody, especially my thesis board. Apparently their expectation had been that I would write a glorified book report.

They passed me. Barely. I added a note to the final copy of my thesis, protesting some of the changes they'd forced me to make. They refused to bind it unless I took the note out. I refused to take the note out. They did, however, cash the $55 check for the binding fee. Someday I may ask for a refund.

Soon enough, however, I had other things to think about. A few months after 9/11, it became clear that the Bush administration was using the slaughter in New York as an excuse to settle scores in Iraq. Rather quickly, the invasion of Iraq became a foregone conclusion, within the administration and among its neocon cheerleaders. Unfortunately, those who reached that conclusion had not the faintest idea that the real question was not "Would the Iraqis fight for Saddam?" but "What would they fight for, or against, after his deposition?" Sadly, the answer has been that a great many do not value what we value, and they have only spurned the Western-style freedom we've tried to impose on them. Alas, Saddam Husscin was authentically Iraqi. Prior to the invasion, the administration and the neocons failed to listen to experts who could read maps and ledgers and a troop basis (a kind of spreadsheet telling you how many troops are in combat units, how many in support and service units, and how many in training camps). These experts were simply not in demand at the onset of the war. In fact, they, and the conclusions they would have mandated, were actively spurned. America, we were told over and over, was rich enough to do whatever it wanted. And anyway, we were also told, everybody yearns for the same basic freedoms we do.

I am, as my partner, Philip Gold, another former Marine (it's a hard habit to break), likes to remind me, blessed with a keen grasp of the obvious. Like many people, I understood that a civil war was the likely outcome if the United States was in Iraq for any length of time. I also knew that if precedent were any guide, the military, especially the Army and Marine Corps, which still close the vast majority of their combat positions to women, would face enormous operational pressure to erode the combat exclusion rule that bars women from the infantry, armor, and artillery. For one thing, they would need the women: Male troops searching Afghan or Iraqi women would need-lessly frighten and humiliate them, thus provoking their menfolk. This is, in fact, where women first started getting publicity as combat troops, although no one in the media was drawing the obvious con-clusion that these women were with combat units, going into combat situations. I knew that as casualties mounted and people did not, for many reasons, enlist or reenlist, good women would be wanted, and good men wouldn't care that they were women.

In the spring of 2004, having completed my thesis, and still desper-ate to be involved in a war I thought was a thoroughly bad idea, I received a grant to travel to Iraq for a month, and later to Afghanistan for another month, as a freelance writer accredited by the *Seattle Post-Intelligencer* and embedded with Army and Marine combat troops, as well as with an Air Force unit.

I went to Iraq, and then to Afghanistan, where I was treated with great kindness and courtesy by the combat units that embedded me, and by the vast majority of support units; the few exceptions, mostly public affairs officers, I will discuss later.

I went looking for what I would find. In Iraq, I was curious about how the Army was handling casualties. In Afghanistan, I was interested in what the United States was doing to raise the standards by which Afghans treated each other. But primarily, I wanted to write a book about the changing roles of female soldiers, so I was particularly interested in what they were doing, though I was very low-key about it. I wrote one article about women in combat titled "Lionesses of Iraq," which appeared in the 6 October 2004 issue of the *Seattle Weekly*. To my knowledge, it was the first significant article on female soldiers' increasing participation in combat in the nonmilitary press. But the two series I wrote for the *Post-Intelligencer,* and then a final piece that contrasted my observations in Iraq and Afghanistan, were more concerned with cultural and political issues than with military operations.

I also went on those embedments to break out of my past and change my life. I knew we were in the Islamic world to stay, regardless of what happened in Iraq; and as Africa falls apart, we will probably intervene there as well.

My experiences in Iraq and Afghanistan convinced me that women are now firmly part of the American military, in all its aspects, and that it's time to drop all remaining combat exclusion policies and procedures as a matter both of military necessity and of equality of obligation in citizenship. But I also saw how much it mattered to the Iraqi and Afghan women, especially the Afghan women I saw, that American women were in the military. And it matters to American women that they participate in the common defense of the Republic. Make no mistake. We live in a violent era, and Islamic fundamentalism is only the leading edge of the threats our nation faces.

Not everyone, of course, agrees with me. Many of the opponents of women in combat, indeed of women in uniform, have great vested interests, both personal and professional, in maintaining their opposition. Many have done so for decades; some have made careers of it. Not so long ago, they could make their case without confronting much resistance. Right up until 2001, critics of servicewomen could deride them as an experiment in social engineering, selectively gathering evidence to ignore anything that didn't fit their preconceptions. But social engineering is what our species does, and once an experiment succeeds, it's no longer an experiment. Women serving in the military in previously male-only jobs, it turns out, is an experiment that has proven successful in the crucible of war, amid all the predicted disasters that haven't happened. Those who continue to oppose women's equal status find themselves relying on past and future hypotheticals (since women "couldn't" do Verdun or D-Day or Heartbreak Hill, they "can't" do Ramadi or Fallujah or Tora Bora), outdated studies, faith-based arguments, and simple bigotry. Increasingly, these critics, many of them political and cultural conservatives, do to women veterans what the Left once did to Vietnam vets: deny their honor, scorn their valor, and dismiss or ignore their accomplishments.

We will not turn back on what's been gained. These last few years, there has been on-again, off-again talk of restoring the draft. Most often, this comes from advocates of "national service" with military and nonmilitary "options." There is an expectation that men will be drafted for the military (for which women can volunteer), while the women will be channeled into nonmilitary national service. This is a false expectation based upon a misunderstanding of the legal status of conscription and of the military. In the past, courts, including the Supreme Court,

WOMEN IN THE LINE OF FIRE

have not mandated the drafting of women because Congress deferred to the military's judgment that women conscripts were neither necessary nor desirable. The legal system deferred to the military because, as a unique institution with unique functions and needs, the military is usually deemed the best judge of its own needs. The military can no longer make the case that women are not needed, or that the continued denial of women's full equality under arms has any rational relationship to national security. Such arguments are now, to put it mildly, OBE. Overtaken By Events.

Sadly, however, we're left with harsh memories of another struggle, the culture wars of the late twentieth century, which so often trumped military reality, at least in the popular imagination. Yes, to a great extent, it was the man-hating, antimilitary feminista (a word I use to distinguish them from those passionate women, the feminists of all eras who dared and bore so much to make it possible for women to live full lives as citizens and humans) who opened the doors to servicewomen, who often regarded their support as a distasteful way, at best, of gaining their rightful access. You don't criticize the people who are helping you, even though they hate the institution and values you love. You try to sort it out later. Many have. Today you won't find too many American servicewomen running around with NOW buttons on their body armor.

American women are serving, fighting, killing, and dying in combat at an unprecedented rate. As of March 2006, about 2% of all deaths and wounds were to women. More servicewomen died in World War II, but the rate was about 0.2% of the dead. At this point, the deployment of servicewomen into combat is the norm, not the exception, while the line between combat and noncombat has blurred into invisibility. Now the combat exclusion serves only as a divisive social distinction between men and women. Whatever the positive effects of excluding women from combat service during the early years of the All-Volunteer Force (AVF), they were probably outweighed by the negative, even then. We now know enough to say definitively that the combat exclusion is a purely social distinction that serves only to keep good women out of combat jobs, while making it harder for their male comrades to depend upon them in the combat that inevitably comes their way. The final test of female soldiers and Marines will occur when women serve in (relatively) large numbers in combat units that are formally integrated, and take sustained casualties that add up to heavy losses over time.

As for the American people, while they do not seem to be quite aware of the magnitude of the deployment of U.S. servicewomen into combat and near combat, there has been no public outcry over the deaths, wounding, or capture of servicewomen. Nor has there been any public outcry over the taking of female journalists hostage, even when they are American citizens. This may indicate indifference; more likely, it indicates an acceptance that people have yet to articulate. For like all societies everywhere, Americans have always been willing to countenance the death and suffering of women as part of the duties they owe to their husbands. (Consider those long centuries when childbed was more dangerous than the battlefield.) In stark contrast, the military service of women, even unto combat, is a natural evolution of our lives as citizens, as individuals who owe responsibilities to our political community and who have rights that that community is obligated to uphold and enforce.

I wrote this book as an invitation to all Americans who care about their nation's military and the women who have served, are currently serving, or will serve in it, alongside the men. That's quite a lot of folks.

But this book is also an attempt to make moral sense of this profound evolution of citizenship, and what it might mean for the nation and the planet in this violent age.

—ERIN SOLARO
Mercer Island and Shelton, Washington
August 2006

Chapter 1

A KNIFE
UNDER MY
PILLOW

The Roman god Janus, the two-faced, presides over beginnings and endings: birth and death, adolescence and marriage, sowing and harvest. God of gateways and doors, Janus also watches over the transition from barbarism to civilization, the passage between country and city, war and peace. Life and death, walls and gateways. To the Greeks, civilization began with the walling off of a polis, the creation of bounded political space. And yet, this dividing of human habitation from the land around it preceded the Greeks by millennia; in fact, it's always been vital to human survival. With our soft skin, only two legs, and nontactical teeth and nails, humans have always needed protected space. How we must have been preyed upon until we learned to build walls and defend them. Then we learned to prey upon each other. And some of the worst of this has been the predation of men upon women.

In shelters, as in civilization generally, there are rules for conduct. One of the traditional rules has been the subordination of women to men. And whenever the issue of women's equality is raised, you can always find someone (usually a man, surprisingly often a woman) to tell you that equality isn't sameness. Well, none of us can be good at everything, as anyone who cooks well but can't garden will tell you. But these people always package hierarchy as difference, and then use the word *difference* to mean *hierarchy*. They certainly don't mean that because most men aren't mathematical geniuses, no man should be a mathematician. They mean that male dominance and female subordination are natural differences, and equality means male dominance and female submission. In the United States, these beliefs still exist, but the people who hold them are increasingly recognized as fools (or worse) once they open their mouths. In the Muslim and African worlds, these beliefs are still prominent.

During my time in Iraq and Afghanistan, and my passages through Kuwait and Dubai, I confronted the question of whether dominance and subordination or equality is the more natural way for the two sexes to live together. Those who have opposed women's rights have historically argued that male dominance is natural, that it takes enormous force to impose female equality; they deride the attempt to do so as a feminist social experiment. It seems important to answer the question of whether subordination or equality is more natural before turning to the military and political implications of the answer. My impressions were that equality between men and women was natural, and that it takes an enormous amount of death for inequality between men and women to be the norm. It takes great violence to impose that inequality, and it takes a profound distortion of intellect and emotion to justify women's subordination. These were my impressions. But then, *impression* can be another word for *experience,* and there are mistakes so ridiculous that only experts can make them.

In June 2004, I took four weeks' leave from my job as an administrative assistant to embed with U.S. troops in Iraq as a freelance writer accredited by the *Seattle Post-Intelligencer*. I spent most of my time with the Army's First Brigade Combat Team, First Infantry Division (the "Big Red One"), at Camp Junction City, near Ramadi in the Sunni Triangle, capital of Al Anbar Province and one of Iraq's flash point cities (although Fallujah gets most of the attention). I was hosted by 2/4 Marines (Second Battalion, Fourth Marine Regiment), an infantry battalion, in Ramadi itself, at a location called Camp Hurricane Point, which is right on the Euphrates, and by Echo Company of 2/4 at the battalion's combat outpost inside Ramadi. I passed in and out of Camp Junction City through Al Taqaddum Airbase, where I was hosted by the Marine Corps' First Service Support Group; I flew out of Iraq from Al Taqaddum to Al Asad Airbase, and from Al Asad to the military side of Kuwait International Airport.[1]

For years, my daily commute was a half-hour walk to work, rain or shine, in hot weather or cold, so it didn't much trouble me to go from the heat and humidity of a Washington, DC, summer to the dry heat of Iraq. My dry cleaner was accustomed to very nice dresses with salt stains across the backs. Even wearing body armor in 120-degree heat, I found Iraq to be comfortable, because the heat was dry. I'd sweat, and within a few seconds the gentle wind would dry me. Never having had the misfortune of being caught in a sandstorm, I found Iraq's climate quite pleasant.

When you are at the Army post of Camp Junction City, you are met by a countryside green with crops and grazing for fattening sheep and goats when you go out on patrol. Even at midsummer, at Camp

Hurricane Point (when I was there the headquarters of 2/4 Marines, and formerly one of Saddam's palaces, the workmanship unbearably gaudy and cheap), I could walk along the green banks of the blue Euphrates and smell the water.

But stand out in the dry wind of the lunar landscape at Al Taqaddum Airbase, and you can feel your own sweat cooling you as it evaporates. You understand the centrality of water to life, whether in the great sprawling metropolis that is Baghdad or the small villages in the countryside. Green is the sacred color of Islam, sacred because green represents vegetation: water, and thus life. As far as the eye can see, there is nothing green at Al Taqaddum, not even camel thorn. Your body is 60% water, and that water is being sucked out of you at an alarming rate. You must stay hydrated. Water, along with shelter, is life. Shelters protect from the sun and the wind, but they also have rules to keep the peace. In those shelters, which for me were moments of transition from the American and European worlds into the Islamic worlds, or from the control of one unit to another, I came face to face with those rules. And in the process of comparing them, I was able to confirm that my initial impressions were right, that men and women are naturally equal.

On my trip into Iraq from Kuwait International Airport through the U.S. Army base at Camp Doha to Al Taqaddum to Camp Blue Diamond to Camp Junction City, I had been handed from one group of armed men—everyone is armed virtually all the time—almost always Marines, to another. I was one of very few women I saw, the only civilian woman and the only unarmed person. I slept in a variety of interesting places, including in a hangar full of male Marines, my helmet for a pillow, and at the desk of another Marine while I waited for him to return. I spent a lot of time with armed male U.S. troops, usually infantrymen on patrols, talking, taking notes, and trading ideas and observations, but sometimes just the two of us behind a closed door. In all that time, no one assaulted or raped or threatened me. No one ever made advances toward me, and the one guy who unambiguously wanted to was embarrassed because he *wanted* to, not because he *did*. I did see a number of male troops watch out for their sisters-in-arms, informally and formally, just out of the knowledge that there are real predators out there. I noticed it, stored it up, and took it for granted, even though I was wary of making a mistake.

Finally, on my trip out of Iraq in early July 2004, I got a chance to think about my experiences as an unarmed civilian woman in the company of so many armed male soldiers. I had ridden into Al Taqaddum the previous night with some Army cavalry scouts from Camp Junction City. Captain Joseph Jasper, an extremely thoughtful cavalry officer who had been assigned public affairs duty after two successful company commands, drove me to their rally point and turned me over to the convoy commander. Jasper's most recent command had been of the Brigade Reconnaissance Troop; I suspected these had been his soldiers. If so, they'd left their marks on each other, for Jasper had the gentleness I have come to expect in good combat soldiers. In their turn, each of the three soldiers the convoy commander turned me over to were funny, profane, and genuinely sweet men who also had the smooth feel of very good soldiers.

I learned the name only of the vehicle commander, a Sergeant Clark. With him were his driver and machine gunner. While we were waiting for the operations order, we heard helicopters from Blue Diamond overhead, while Ramadi's bright lights glowed in the darkness beneath the moon and the stars.

"Why aren't you flying out?" a staff sergeant from another vehicle asked me.

"I flew in," I replied, "so I thought I should convoy out."

It seemed such an obvious thing to do that I was a little surprised by his response, a soft "Hooah," an all-purpose Army word denoting various shades of approval and respect.

We listened to the operations order, and afterward I told Sergeant Clark that, if necessary, I would take the machine gunner's secondary weapon and use it at his direction. One thing about scouts: They're very versatile, and casually but extremely competent soldiers. Being "squared away" in the Army sense of the phrase, they assume you are, too. If you're not, they either help you square yourself away or send you on to where you can do no harm. In that spirit, Sergeant Clark handed me his machine gunner's M16 on the spot. It had been a long time since I'd handled an M16, so I ran my hands over the weapon in the dark of the Humvee: trigger, fire-selector switch, magazine release; I mentally rehearsed clearing a misfed round. It was a rough ride, and for most of it the tension level in the vehicle was very high; when the scouts finally relaxed, I let Sergeant Clark know I was going to doze. I slept no more than fifteen or twenty minutes, but it helped. The scouts had changed over their internal clocks to sleep during the day so they could travel at night, but I had not.

That was the first time I really considered the implications of sleeping with a bunch of strange men I'd never seen before. Men who also trusted a woman they'd never seen before with a rifle. But I didn't pursue these thoughts then; I wouldn't until the next night, at Al Asad.

I didn't know it then, as I looked around Al Taqaddum Airbase one last time, but that night and into the next morning, I would have more opportunity to think about the consequences of sleeping in proximity to strange armed men. Since Al Asad was a major transit hub into and out of Iraq, I simply expected that they would have segregated sleeping quarters. Not that I was thinking about it as I got ready to leave Al Taqaddum.

I had about one hundred pounds of gear with me, including body armor and helmet, items whose purpose was unchanged since the time of Alexander the Great's hoplites, who wore them as they strode in triumph through Babylon on their way to conquer the rest of the Persian Empire. (Modern Iraq was once part of the Persian Empire, and if few Americans spend much time thinking about it, Iranians are proud of their history. They were Persia once, and are likely to be so again.) Two Marines picked up my purple backpack and black deployment bag and threw them into the back of the Humvee, a courtesy that never failed to embarrass me. I'd made certain I could carry all my gear in one lift, and had done it plenty of times. But it was rude to reject courtesy, so I made a point of returning it by lending a hand whenever it was needed. We drove out to the flight line and the driver turned to me and said, "This is an angel flight."

I must have looked a question at him, for in his face I saw the answer.

We got out and rendered honors to the five flag-draped coffins as they were loaded aboard the C-130. Except for an infantryman from the First Brigade and two Medical Service Corps officers, I was the only living passenger. I would later look up the names of the dead. One was from 2/4 Marines. Their self-chosen nickname is the Magnificent Bastards, something that always made me think, whenever I heard it, *Magnificent, yes, but don't they like their parents?* The battalion had incurred the highest losses in the Marine Corps to that date. They had fought the enemy very aggressively whenever they encountered them, shocking the insurgents when they moved into fire. But those Marines had also treated enemy prisoners with a mercy that they knew the insurgents would not return, and the conquered populace with dignity. All the more reason that hearing such men call themselves bastards was so jarring.

When I was with 2/4 in Ramadi, I tried to take as many of the logistics convoys between the battalion at Camp Hurricane Point and their combat outpost, which was in Ramadi itself. The convoys contained Echo and Golf companies, and these were some of my few chances to see Ramadi. I was lucky that nothing went *boom* on any of the convoys I rode on, but the last one slowed to a crawl, then a stop, in Ramadi's souk to accommodate Iraqi foot traffic. Without a word between us, without any kind of indication from the Iraqis, the Marines I was riding with and I suddenly became *extremely* tense. It was one of those moments that happens routinely in a combat situation; it was not the tension I had experienced in the past when convoys had slowed down in the souk. It was *far* higher. We *knew* we were under hostile observation, probably by someone who regretted being unable to detonate the Iraqi fuel tanker next to us, regardless of the many Iraqis who would also have been killed.

The next morning, the day I left Camp Hurricane Point, the very next convoy that went out to the combat outpost was hit. Seven Marines were wounded, and one of them would die of his wounds. I did not know his name, and I did not recognize his face from the photograph I would later find on the *Washington Post* website, but he was black—and there aren't too many black guys in the Marine Corps, let alone in the infantry. I wondered if he was one of the two young men whose music and trash talking I'd heard one day on the other side of the plywood partition of the battalion visitors' room. I was typing up my notes on my laptop while listening to bad, violent rap and profanity when I suddenly had to sneeze. My sneezes are rather loud, and this one was no exception; out of habit, I said, "Excuse me." The rap was instantly turned down, followed by a few seconds of silence and then first one, and then another, abashed young male voice saying, "Bless you!"

"Thank you, gentlemen."

There was no more rap, no more profanity. I mentioned the incident to the female Marine combat correspondent who shared the room with me that night, and she replied, "Most of the guys go out of their way not to be offensive, and those who don't usually have the bad reputations and the nasty nicknames."

I didn't need to know the names of the dead men in the plane with me to know that if they were anything like the soldiers and Marines I'd lived and worked among for the past weeks, they had hoped to leave Iraq a better place than they found it. They'd had doubts about American strategy, they'd cared for Iraqi lives and dignity, and they'd loved their families and their nation. I knew that the world was a poorer place for their deaths. I wiped my eyes and blew my nose and hoped the Marines with me thought it was because of the dust.

We landed at Al Asad with the flight crew rendering honors to the dead men while their coffins were unloaded. Al Asad is actually much farther from Kuwait than Al Taqaddum, but the runways at Al Asad are longer, enabling it to handle larger aircraft. Once there, I got on the passenger manifest for a space-available flight to the military side of Kuwait International Airport, then went into transient billeting.

In the military, if you're not with your assigned unit, you are very much an orphan. Everywhere else I'd been, I'd been shown the latrines and showers and mess hall, and then someone had always found a place for me to sleep, even if it was in her own bed while she was on duty. Not here. In the summer of 2004, except for some sleeping huts and port-a-potties, there were no facilities for troops and civilians transiting through at Al Asad. I had to fend for myself.

Al Asad offered transients only MREs ("meals ready to eat"), the military's field ration, also known as "meals rarely eaten" and occasionally described as "three lies for the price of one." In truth, they weren't *that* bad. Certainly, no veteran of the Vietnam-era field chow, the C ration, would ever complain about MREs. (According to legend, "C rats" were some of the few items that you could leave unguarded in Vietnam and not have stolen. The early M16 rifle may have been another.) But I opted for the permanent mess hall/dining facility, strode in as though I belonged there, and dined. What could they do? Charge me the $3.50 my meal cost them? Send me back to the Army at Camp Junction City or the Marines in Ramadi? I walked out with a cup of coffee.

Transient billeting was several air-conditioned plywood huts, each divided into three bays, about ten cots to a bay. There were no doors between bays, no bays marked off for women. Pick a cot, ground your gear, try to get some sleep.

I found an empty cot between two male Marines' cots. In the Sunni Triangle, I had gotten used to being the only unarmed civilian woman. But there, I was always working with a formed unit, and I never worried about the soldiers or Marines I was around. This collection of strangers was different. When most of the men you deal with are decent, it is all too easy to forget the small percentage of real criminals and their active and passive collaborators. Some are simply monsters. Others think that their manhood depends upon women's subordination—that women have no place in the military except as menial service personnel (or perhaps as "comfort girls"), and that their opinions give them license to harass, even rape. I knew that many of the men and the two women in the transient hut were from units I'd been with over the past several weeks, but this was still a different situation. Every unit has its percentage of dirtbags and criminals. *Every unit.* In good units, they don't dare misbehave. But free from the force field of authority and peer pressure that good officers and sergeants use to keep their troops doing the right thing, even when unsupervised, they can be a problem. Especially because strangers can't necessarily recognize what a danger they are until too late. So I put my knife, an elegant dagger that went everywhere with me, under my pillow before starting to chat with the Marine aviator on my right.

Later that evening, as I read on my cot before turning in, I noticed that the Marine between me and the door was a very young man—a boy, really—headed for Fallujah. Unlike the rest of us, who were talking or playing cards or reading and swapping books in turn, he kept to himself, playing a handheld video game. As near as I could tell, his only interaction with the rest of us was to sneak a peek at me, look at his *Maxim* with its scantily clad cover girl, and then sneak another peek at me. It was a jarring sensation. I'd seen a total of three cover girl pictures and calendars—none of which anyone seemed to really look at—in my entire time with the First Brigade and 2/4 Marines. Both services had an extremely strict no-porn rule, and not just because Iraq is an Islamic country. Even in the United States, and increasingly in combat units, male officers ban porn from their areas. Porn increases the risk of sexual harassment and thus rape for women, and a lot of men object to it. Some demur on religious grounds, others because they understand that porn exploits men as well as women. Some just plain don't like it.

I thought of a line from David Shoup, a Marine who'd won the Medal of Honor during the ferocious battle of Tarawa during World War II. Shoup hated "swagger sticks," the "troop alignment tools" that officers once carried. One of his first acts upon becoming commandant under President John F. Kennedy was to put out a message stating, in effect, "If you must carry a swagger stick to feel like a Marine officer, by all means do so." *If you must use porn to feel like a man . . .* Since I was a civilian and the boy was bothering no one, I stifled my impulse to say something to him.

Instead, I stared back at him, then at his *Maxim,* then at him again, whereupon he looked away. I felt bad for him and hoped that when he got to his unit, his platoon sergeant would square him away. He looked so isolated and friendless; nevertheless, he was an armed young man with an attitude that pegged all my warning indicators. I deliberately let him see me adjust my sleeping bag and pillow, let him see me place my knife beneath my pillow where it would rest comfortably in the hollow of my neck.

This barracks, thousands of miles from home, could have been a real war zone for us women. But there were boundaries of respect and mutual regard of Americans for each other that were as effective as any real doors. Maybe more so. The stoutest door can be battered down by those inclined to breach it, just as others will respect the flimsiest screen. Those boundaries starkly delineated appropriate and inappropriate behavior, closed off the places that in some men conflate sex and violence, so that those men, like my young barracks mate, didn't dare enter them outside his thoughts, and maybe not that often even then. Civilization means that the best of us rule the worst, both inside our heads and outside in the world we share, because of the people we want to be, to ourselves and each other and those we love, whom our behavior shames or honors.

I didn't sleep well that night, near the door with people coming in and out, and with aircraft, especially helicopters, taking off and landing at all hours. The lights stayed on for what seemed like forever. At one point, a staff sergeant came in looking for people to put on a flight to Camp Blue Diamond, the First Marine Division headquarters, across the Euphrates from Ramadi. I poked my head out of my sleeping bag and asked him if he'd turn out the light. He shook his head, afraid, I think, that I might be assaulted. It couldn't have been much past midnight, and by that time I felt his concern was excessive.

Not long after that, someone with more sense, or at least with more faith in American men, did turn out the light, and I dozed for a little while. I spent until early evening the next day, 7 July 2004, talking with people or reading on my cot until several Navy doctors came in looking for some space to hang out together for a few hours. If you weren't in the transient hut when they called you, you missed your flight and had to wait for another.

"That your book?" one asked.

Sadly, it was. There on my cot, at nine-hundred-plus densely packed pages, was Ira Lapidus's definitive *History of Islamic Societies,* so heavy that only a recovering grad student like myself would haul it around Iraq, or anywhere else for that matter. "I thought it would be a good idea to understand what I was getting myself into."

"Journalist?"

"I call myself a military critic." The "critic" moniker was in reference to Hanson Baldwin, a gifted defense analyst for *The New York Times* for many years. Even today, it's hard to read Baldwin's early analyses of the Vietnam War without thinking, *He warned us.* In this context, the self-conferred title made me sound like I knew more than I did. At least that's what I was going for. "What do you do?"

"We're epidemiologists. Want to talk about diarrhea?"

"I'd love to," I laughed. "How bad·a problem is it?"

"It makes a lot of people sick and miserable, but short of dysentery, which can really put people down, we've never had anyone tell us it stopped them from doing their jobs. It's pretty easy to keep people healthy. There's adequate water for drinking and bathing, and it's not a nasty environment."

We talked about nasty environments and disease before our conversation turned to the long war with a violent, fundamentalist Islam that the West is facing. We speculated that the United States' war in Iraq was more than likely only the opening campaign. And like most opening campaigns, it wasn't going very well. We talked, too, about the status of women both in the West and under Islam, and what the *jihadi* wanted women to be, or to remain. Our conversation was easy and natural, and I understood myself to be in an outpost of the type of civilization we should strive for, one in which men and women share their lives as equals in public and in private, and defend together as equals.

While we bantered, the surly young Marine, like us waiting for a flight he dared not miss, kept peeking at us. I think he was trying to figure out what men and women who had no sexual or social interest in each other had to say to each other. Or perhaps he did understand but found it distressing. Shortly after the Navy docs were called for their flight to Qatar, one of the Gulf states, the young Marine was called to Fallujah. I hoped he figured out that those docs, their female chief petty officer, and I had, as citizens, both our polity and the entire world in common. Hoped he'd figure it out soon, because in a very real way, that was what he was going to Fallujah to fight for.

Later that evening, I flew out to Kuwait on the same C-130 with the same flight crew and the same coffins I'd flown in on; this time it was packed with Marines coming back from Fallujah. Many of them put their rifles muzzle-down on the decking, rested their heads on the butts and slept. I envied them and tried to get comfortable in my nylon-strap webbing seat, but gave it up when a Marine said she'd flown to Afghanistan like this and it never got better.

Worrying about Kuwait during the flight took my mind off the seats. I was much more afraid of spending a day there alone than I had been of going on combat patrols. In combat, you might be killed, you might be hurt very badly, but everyone with you runs the same risks, and no one has any intention of being taken alive. My prepatrol preparations had always included mentally rehearsing not only how to respond to contact, but a quick way out at the end, if it came to that. Now I was going back to civilization.

Or was I?

I was nervous, for reasons ranging from the political to the personal and back again. It wasn't just that the United States has no Islamic friends in the Middle East. We have allies and then we have hookups with governments who hide their cooperation from their people and whose intentions we can only guess. Who knows what they hide from us? It isn't even that the region is one vast slave market for foreign men, women, and children, often imported from Asia with the tacit support of governments, as the State Department's 2005 *Trafficking in Persons Report* makes clear. It is the totality of how men treat women; indeed, of how everyone treats everyone else, from governmental oppression to the casual brutalities of everyday routine. There are *jihadi* and insurgents who promote violent behavior among their own peoples. There are men who loathe American freedom because they think it symbolizes things to come, including the ways in which their daughters and sisters will be more easily sexually degraded. (Sadly, the first thing many men in extremely repressive countries go for, once the repression is off, is Western-style pornography. The men who don't go for it often know well the danger it poses to their women kin and friends. While the *jihadi* blame the West, especially the United States, for pornography, others understand that there's plenty of blame to go around.)

Everything being for sale, or at least for rent, in much of the Islamic world, it is assumed that Americans, too, must be for sale. Regardless of national interests and economic and military realities, we are perceived as selling ourselves to Israel, to do Israel's bidding. We're perceived as being for sale to Arabs whenever they find it useful to have us defend them.

But, I thought to myself, this was Kuwait. Civilization. A friendly place we'd liberated once from Saddam. Of course, we rarely mention that we did so while a very large chunk of Kuwait's military-age male population was hanging out in the nightclubs of Cairo and elsewhere, waiting for the Americans whom they considered their hirelings to free their land. And those who stayed when they could have left, especially those who resisted the invaders, met with scorn and discrimination from those who chose to leave. After they returned from their partying, that is.

The safest and quickest way to get to my hotel, I thought, would be to cross from the military to the civilian side of Kuwait International, then call the Sheraton and ask them to send a car for me.

I had not counted upon the bureaucratic mentality that insisted that I get from the military side to the civilian side via Camp Doha, for no reason I could determine other than That's The Way We Do It. Over my protests—I did not dare wander about the flight line alone—I was loaded onto a bus with the Marines I had flown in with and driven to Camp Doha. We got on the bus at 10 PM and waited for "shooters," or armed U.S. troops in civilian clothes who would provide security, before we left on the half-hour drive. And waited and waited. The Marines, whom I've always suspected are only happy when they're grumbling, were grumbling unhappily. If it was shooters they wanted, they had plenty of ammo; all they had to do was open the windows and port their weapons. We waited until 11:30 PM, when the shooters arrived, before departing for Camp Doha. Once there, at midnight, I learned that a shuttle bus would be available to take me back to the airport at 2 AM. A former Special Forces soldier, now a Department of Defense civilian who worked with contractors, and was thus used to people incoherent with fatigue, lent me his cell phone so I could call my hotel, then fed and watered me. The shuttle bus showed up at 2:15 AM and we sat for another hour and a quarter waiting for the shooter, a female soldier in civilian clothes, to show up. We finally made it back to the Kuwait airport at 4 AM on 8 July. Six hours to get back to where I'd started.

One of the public affairs officers I dealt with, Captain Randall Baucom, told me, "There are many reasons why we, the military, are so diligent with our force protection, and very few of those reasons are based on the actual threats facing our troops. We tend to be overcautious and [err] on the side of safety. Additionally, it keeps our soldiers in the proper mindset as they travel to and from Iraq."[2]

Possible translation: *We just do this for fun.*

Possible response: *Sure hope to run into you again someday.*

All militaries are bureaucracies. Bureaucrats and service members, despite the fact that they wear the same uniform, wage ceaseless war on each other. Regardless of what their actual positions are, the bureaucrats are concerned with procedures; soldiers and sailors and Marines and airmen, with the enemy. Certainly, the diminutive female shooter who'd protected our bus proved herself a bureaucrat rather than a soldier. Back at Kuwait International, I told her I wanted to go back inside the airport and go to the Sheraton's reception kiosk so they could call their vehicle for me, but she flagged down a taxi instead. Too tired to object, I obediently loaded my gear into the trunk while the Kuwaiti driver, a small, slim man with no muscle tone, went to great lengths to avoid touching me. I would quickly find our great disparity in strength to be of little comfort.

As soon as I was in the backseat, I knew that I had made a potentially serious mistake, one that could quite literally cost me my head. My body armor and knife were in the trunk. My only weapon was a heavy wooden hair stick, crowned with malachite, which I wore to pin my long hair up into a bun. I bought it after 9/11 because it was heavy enough to use as a weapon and innocuous enough to pass through every airport screening without even a glance of suspicion. But it was still a hair stick. Who brings a knife to a gunfight? Or a hair stick? Still, even though wooden weapons went out with the Stone Age, it was all I had. I sat rigid in the backseat, paying very close attention to the Arabic/English road signs. I knew the general direction of my hotel, and I contemplated climbing over the front seat to be in better control of my situation should anything unexpected arise.

I found myself planning to take control of the vehicle were my taxi driver to make a sudden move, such as veering off the road or joining a convoy of *jihadi* terrorists. Overpowering him would be easy, but I didn't think I could control him and drive at the same time. I could reach across him quickly, open the door, and kick him out of the vehicle; there were no seat or shoulder belts in the cab. I could drive my hair stick up underneath his chin and then kick him out the door; that would be much better. Then the car would be mine—a heavy, gassed-up battering ram. At worst, I would make an escape attempt and die in the car as I made my getaway. I knew exactly what my body would look like. The insurgents had taken to incorporating gasoline into their roadside bombs so they could have the pleasure of watching Americans burn to death. I'd seen the photos. But it would be a lot less painful and humiliating than anything the driver, or the vast conspiracy that might soon encircle me, would have in mind.

As I planned a brutal response to brutality, we arrived without incident at the hotel. I checked in, exhausted, and waited while my bags were scanned. I had to open my rucksack to show them that my vest held rifle plates, not blocks of explosives.

"Soldier?" they wanted to know, purple rucksack notwithstanding.

"No." I was sliding rapidly into utter paranoia, a mixture of decompression from Iraq as an unarmed civilian in the midst of a war zone and the strain of being a woman in a society where many consider a lone woman, by virtue of her solitude, available for whatever any man may conjure up. All I could think of at that moment was that I didn't want these men Googling my name and reading the articles I'd written. I simply answered, "I don't work for the government." I didn't want them thinking I worked for the CIA, although my travel-stained clothing, body odor, dry, frayed hair, and worn desert boots, not to speak of that vest and those plates, all said I hadn't been playing tourist since the Kuwaiti visa had been entered into my passport. In the end, they probably just wrote me off as one more crazy American and, as a woman, not worth the bother unless somebody with money took a personal interest.

Once in my room, I called my partner, Philip, himself a former Marine intelligence officer. He seemed more concerned about my emotional state than my immediate safety, but he commanded: "Put a chair against the door, and something heavy on it. Now. Before we talk more."

This despite the locks. I did it. "My knife is already under my pillow," I told him when I picked up the receiver again.

"Good. Young, pretty, obviously single women draw attention in hotels. Anywhere."

I spent most of that day, still 8 July, in my room. My cold room. My very cold room. The air-conditioning was impossible to turn off, and even with it turned all the way down, I had to sit next to the open window for any degree of comfort. Air-conditioning is one of the many displays of the prodigious wealth that enables Kuwait to subsist on an enormous amount of foreign wage labor. The glossy official guidebook to Kuwaiti society that I leafed through in my hotel room said that female domestics have eased life for Kuwaiti women—who often have many children—but that their presence has also caused serious family tensions. A euphemism. Some of these domestics might, at least while young and on good behavior, enjoy the status of a well-treated concubine. Others would be slaves, forced to work without pay, perhaps also starved, beaten, and raped repeatedly by employers who hold their passports. That some Gulf state employers treat foreign domestics as respected employees, and give them fair value for fair value received, does not make such treatment anything more than a matter of luck rather than law. Law that is not enforced is merely a matter of opinion.

My flight back to the States wasn't until the next morning, and I did not leave the hotel once until then. At Camp Junction City, I had walked alone at night without much concern. I thought about the metal detectors I had passed through at the entrance to the Sheraton and realized that getting out with a knife was one thing, but getting back in would be something else entirely. Especially as a foreign civilian.

I'd showered only every other day and washed my hair only twice a week. Camp Junction City and Al Taqaddum had adequate water for sanitation and cleanliness, and not much else. Full-length mirrors were nonexistent, so I was a little surprised to find myself *covered* with bruises I didn't remember acquiring. Now that I didn't have to worry about whether the soldier behind me would have enough water for her shower, I took advantage and showered for a long time, washing and conditioning my hair, then soaking the soreness out of my muscles. After a nap and breakfast, I felt normal enough to get my hair trimmed and have a manicure and pedicure in the salon downstairs. As a courtesy to the beautician, I scrubbed my feet and my shower shoes alike before sliding my feet into them and shuffling down to her.

There were a half-dozen young women in the salon preparing for a wedding. I quickly discovered that their *abayas* of fine, light fabrics, sometimes beautifully embroidered, concealed apparel that few young American adolescent female mall rats would care to sport: skimpy skirts and scandalously tight blouses. They wore ornate makeup and had teased hair; the bride-to-be's makeup and hairstyle were the most elaborate. They were fragile and slender and physically vulnerable, a type of woman I had forgotten existed after my month with strong, competent women soldiers. I wished them long lives, happy marriages, many children, and better taste.

I spent my time in Kuwait reading and writing, getting restless and walking around the hotel with my knife in my belt, hidden by my shirt, feeling like a barbarian until I realized it was the response of a civilized woman to the barbarism of a society that considers women fair game. American entertainment is coarse and degrading, and parts of the United States, parts you don't always find on a map, haven't quite gotten the word yet. But as I restlessly paced the hotel, the hilt of my knife rubbing against my ribs, I realized that I had been safer as a lone, unarmed woman sleeping in an open-bay barracks among armed soldiers and Marines than in Kuwait, with all its luxurious shopping.

In strictly material terms, I suppose you could call Kuwait civilized: safe water, flush toilets, air-conditioning, expensive stores. But if you define civilization as people, men and women alike, being able to safely assume they can trust each other with their lives and honor, Kuwait, like much of the Arab world, is not civilized. Arabs are infamous for not trusting each other. Men do not trust men, women do not trust women, and men and women certainly do not trust each other. The most basic trust is hard-earned, rarely extended outside family, clan, or tribe, and *never* assumed. And alas, the virtues of those Arabs who are instinctively, reflexively trustworthy are private, not public. No societal assumptions may be safely drawn from their personal conduct, even when it is of the highest standard, even if they are widely respected for it.

Is my assessment harsh? Several Iraqis—translators and a judge with enormous moral authority among both Americans and other Iraqis—told me in separate, serious conversations that lack of trust was a fundamental problem in Iraqi society. Part of that was thirty years of Baathist tyranny, which Saddam Hussein deliberately modeled on Stalinism. But he built upon that old Arab cliché: "Me against my brother, my brother and me against our cousin; my brother, my cousin, and me against the world." A cliché because, unfortunately, it is true. For Coalition forces, this means that information on insurgent activity may be a serious tip, the preliminary of an ambush, or the means of settling scores between individuals, factions, or tribes. As for the Iraqi Police and National Army, neither the Coalition nor the Iraqis knew how many Iraqi soldiers and police were insurgents who had infiltrated, equipped, armed, and trained at the government's expense, until they were presented with an opportune moment to kill Americans or other Iraqis. I was once escorted around an Iraqi National Army barracks by two male U.S. Army drill instructors who were training the Iraqi recruits: They were armed, magazines in the wells of their rifles, their fingers on the trigger guards, and their eyes alert. This would have been an unthinkable occurrence in any American basic training barracks.

Chapter 2

CHOOSING
SIDES

I made up my mind to go to Iraq on 11 March 2004, the day an al-Qaeda franchise, the Moroccan Islamic Combatant Group, bombed the Madrid subways, resulting in a horrendous loss of life. My decision was complex but also inevitable. I wanted to write, to say what needed to be said. I was not in the position to be hired as a full-time journalist because I didn't have the experience, but without the experience I couldn't be hired as a full-time journalist. In order to get out of that catch-22, I had to put together my own package of funding and stringer accreditation, then publish enough articles to be credible, then get an agent. (I went through five before finding Mr. Right. One agent was so hot for a personal "How I Fucked My Way Through the Sunni Triangle" approach that I briefly considered inventing a paramour, a James Bond–type, pro-American, undercover Iraqi nicknamed "Genital Ali," until I realized I'd probably be believed.)

But the principal reason I wanted to go was that I was one of the few people talking about the fact that this odd war we were fighting against radical fundamentalist Islam profoundly engages the interests of American women. This problematic war is about the kind of world we want to live in. Given that most women, worldwide, live under conditions of poverty and oppression extreme even by the standards of men in those societies, the outcome of this war has vastly different implications for men and women. I wanted to write about the Iraq War in a way that would speak to American citizens of both sexes, regardless of their views. I felt a moral obligation to go there. Beyond that, anyone who presumes to write about war ought to find a way to experience it. Good journalists, like good soldiers, head for the sound of the guns.

Finally, I was going to keep faith with the little girl I had once been. Perhaps, after a detour of a decade and a half, I could become something of the woman that little girl should have grown into. My earliest memory is of watching, at age two, the 1968 Tet Offensive on television, seeing the Marines fighting in Hue City, and thinking, at some preverbal level, *Those are my people. I ought to be with them.* Now I would go be with them, at least for a while, for the purpose of returning and telling my people about these servicemen and -women and what they were doing together.

The belief that women are "naturally" more peaceful than men cuts across the ideological spectrum. Certainly, testosterone makes its own complex contribution to aggression. But there is a tendency to forget all the women who are not naturally peaceful, an inexcusable tendency since such women both fill and transcend history. The Greeks had Medea, the Amazons, and a pantheon full of goddesses you didn't want to piss off—myths and legends that did not achieve such status because they were unrelated to human experience. The Norse, the Teutons, and most everyone else had the same. The Bible speaks both of violent women and of peaceable women who took up arms. The line from the prophet Deborah to the French general Joan of Arc is a long, straight one. The American heritage is filled with tough frontier women, as well as stories, many true, of the ferocity of Native American women. In his poem "The Young British Soldier," Rudyard Kipling wrote of female cruelty:

When you're wounded and left on Afghanistan's plains,
And the women come out to cut up what remains,
Jest roll to your rifle and blow out your brains
An' go to your Gawd like a soldier.

More recently, there were the Rwandan women who voluntarily participated in the Hutu slaughter of 800,000 Tutsis, and the now infamous gals of Abu Ghraib and Guantanamo. That we should hear so much more about the militarily idiotic, self-indulgent sexual abuses by these American servicewomen than about real genocide, or than about the vastly more prevalent mistreatment of Iraqis by Iraqi security forces, perhaps says things about the United States and its culture that we might wish to ponder. Lynndie England and her ilk may not have been very good soldiers, but they sure knew how to make porn flicks.

In equal measure, women have for much of recorded human history been advocates of male violence. Not all societies adopted the Spartan mother's admonition, "Come back with your shield or on it," or the British practice during World War I wherein young women handed white feathers to men they thought should be in uniform (some of whom turned out to be decorated veterans on leave or men invalided out for their wounds). But the rallying of women leading up to and during wartime over the centuries has been nothing short of intense, as has the historical motivation to have lots of male babies for future wars. There have also been women who embraced violence as an acceptable, even righteous means to political ends. The nineteenth-century American abolition movement held its share of such women, as did twentieth-century Zionism and Islamist fundamentalism, to name only a few examples.

Of course, women have also withheld their support from war. Aristophanes's play *Lysistrata,* in which Athenian women join with Spartan and Theban women to engage in a sex strike to end the Peloponnesian War, captured the widespread Athenian disgust with that war. The disgust of women who had seen too many other women widowed, who then had to bury their sons. The disgust of too many men who had been too long from their wives, engaged in a dubious war that had brought Athens nothing but harm. By the 1890s, feminism had begun its long dalliance with sundry "peace" movements—some antimilitarist, some antimilitary, some just antimale. That old line, "There's something about a uniform . . . " often enough collided with that other old line, "I didn't raise my son to be a soldier." Much, much later there was the Vietnam-era slogan, "Girls say yes to guys who say no." (Did they?)

There is little truth to the notion that women and children are often the first victims of war. Far more often, women have been the last victims, after their men have been killed or defeated, after their lands and bodies have been taken by the victors. No one can ponder the execrable history of siege warfare, ancient and modern, without realizing that *vae victis* (woe to the vanquished) holds special meaning for women. Still, it is exceedingly unlikely that female casualties of any war would exceed male casualties. I know of no instance where that has been the case.

Military losses are heavily, and sometimes virtually entirely, male, while civilian losses tend to be a representative cross section of age and sex, excluding military-age males where they are subject to conscription. Between combat losses and collateral damage, it is the historical norm for more men than women to be killed. Certainly, of the European participants in World War II, for example, only German, French, Polish, and Yugoslav civilian losses exceeded their military losses.[1] What those four nations had in common was defeat, although the manner of defeat and the aftermath were very different.

The reality of women's role in wartime is found somewhere among the semitrue caricatures of Woman the Violent, Woman the Peacemaker, and Woman the Victim. Women, like men, have political, military, and moral interests in war and peace, in foreign and defense policy. Different group perspectives reflect different group life experiences, of course. But in war, even different group life experiences can lead to the same conclusions.

A rational European woman of the cold war era might easily have decided that, given the East German and Central European experience of mass rape at the hands of the Soviet Army during the last months of World War II, women should be supporting NATO. This rational European woman might have thought that women had serious contributions to make to their military and foreign policy establishments, both as citizens who cared about such issues and as women with specific interests and expertise in war and foreign policy. She might have found an additional reason to support NATO in comparing how Western European women really lived to how women in the Eastern bloc and the former Soviet Union lived. Such a comparison might have begun with a material standard of living—for example, in the latter countries, the inability to buy fresh fruits and vegetables, meat, and fish because those items were attainable only at special stores reserved for either the *nomenklatura* or those with hard currency. This train of thought might have continued to domestic relations, and might have taken into consideration the routine *need* for Soviet women to use abortion, sometimes without anesthesia, for birth control because decent contraception, even just condoms, was often scarce or nonexistent. And it might have ended with the corrosion of the very idea of friendship due to widespread spying by neighbors on neighbors, colleagues on colleagues, friends on friends, family on family, a legacy from which none of the Eastern bloc countries have yet recovered. Each of these reasons—personal and political—might have led her to conclude that Western European women, as Western European women, should be supporting NATO.

In fact, as feminists, such hypothetical Western European and American women alike might well have considered the gross discrepancy between Soviet and Western Allied treatment of both the liberated and the conquered, especially women and girls, and favored greater defense spending. Reasonable women might even have *insisted* on participating in large numbers in their nations' defenses, including NATO military forces.

Some women, of course, actually did arrive at these conclusions. But the vast majority of these did not call themselves feminists; they called themselves soldiers, sailors, airmen, or Marines. The vast majority of self-professed feminists, especially American feminists, allied themselves uncritically with whatever peace and protest movements came along, usually emphasizing women's status as victims, much as the movement in domestic politics did.

Today, the shelves of university libraries groan under the weight of all the feminist antimilitary publications of the late twentieth century. They sit there weighing down shelves that few people bother to visit anymore. Those who do read them often really do groan, especially when encountering the "postmodern" strain, with its ignorance of reality, impenetrable jargon, and willful irrelevance to real women's interests and lives. Take Jean Bethke Elshtain, a feminist scholar who published her book *Women and War* in 1987, toward the end of the cold war, during the Reagan years; nearly a decade earlier, President Carter had successfully reinstituted selective service registration for draft-age men, and had unsuccessfully attempted to institute it for the first time for draft-age women. That unsuccessful attempt was a signal that the political and military landscape was changing around American women. In the opening paragraph of her preface, however, Elshtain tells us that her title is not straightforward because *women* and *war* are not straightforward words.

> *I am not concerned with origins and standard histories*
> *in taking on war as a theme; rather, I am involved—as a*
> *political theorist, a citizen, and a mother—in what we*
> *continue to make of war. How do we treat the war stories*
> *deeded us?*[2]

She concerned herself with *representations* of war and of women, not with real women preparing for a real war if the late cold war had gone hot. It's a legitimate literary device, provided it doesn't pass itself off as more important than reality; and it was not at all what American women—citizens—needed from a feminist philosopher writing about just war theory.

Such a serious consideration of women and war was also missing from *Loaded Questions: Women in the Military,* an anthology of articles by feminists that appeared in 1981, when the possibility of the cold war turning hot was quite real. In terms of military matters, it might have served as a harbinger for what was to come in the women's movement of the following years. This is the conclusion of Cynthia Enloe's article, "What Is NATO—and Why Should Women Care?"

> *Women have learned how subordination is legitimized by such supposedly functional divisions. Women are skilled in tracking the long-range implications regarding security and liberation that follow out of such divisions of labour. The 1980s is an especially good time for women to focus their feminist analytical sights on Nato* [sic].[3]

Nothing about how Europeans, especially women from a feminist perspective that believes "Women are citizens, not the warrior's prize," should deal with the massive Brezhnev-era military buildup in the heart of Europe during the late 1970s, which would continue all the way through the 1980s.

This intellectual self-indulgence in political and military matters went on, decade after decade. In her 2000 book, *Citizenship Rites,* Ilene Rose Feinman fulsomely congratulates antimilitarist feminists for their contributions to peace in the 1980s. What were their contributions?

> *[W]ebs woven across rivers to filter garbage, and anthologies and articles of ecofeminist perspectives. . . . webs across the doorways . . . animal images such as batik butterflies held on both sides of the fence to connect people committing civil disobedience and those not, animal tunnel/birth canals under the fence, rituals of levitation . . .*[4]

None of this playacting helped women answer the question: How do we, as citizens, help steer our nation through a dangerous time? Granted, the Pentagon might well benefit from levitation, but trying to levitate the Pentagon is a fantasy. And admittedly, Ronald Reagan was trying to achieve a spectacularly dangerous goal, the rollback of the Soviet Union's post–World War II occupation of Eastern Europe. But he was also doing it with a broadly bipartisan consensus, and his modernization of the U.S. military ensured that when that rollback did happen, it was as a Soviet response to East European dissident movements, such as the Polish movement Solidarity. And because the Soviet leadership was unwilling to risk the physical destruction of its homeland, and unwilling to purge the conquered nations of Eastern Europe as Stalin had done after World War II, in the end, that rollback was almost bloodless.

Feinman patted herself and her fellow antimilitarist feminists on the back over a decade after it had become exquisitely clear that they had contributed nothing to peace and nothing to the liberation of Eastern Europe. They had provided no significant support to the Eastern European dissidents who risked so much, suffered so greatly, and in some cases lost their lives in enormous pain. A rational observer might have concluded that the real "feminist peace activists" were American and European servicewomen who took to heart that old adage, "If you wish peace, prepare for war," and who, by their presence, skills, and patriotism, helped end the cold war.

Moreover, when Feinman's book was published, in January 2000, it was a time of rising militant Islamic fundamentalism. Yet Feinman writes as if Islamic fundamentalists had not already bombed the World Trade Center in 1993; as if, when the Murrah Federal Building in Oklahoma City was bombed in 1995, the first immediate and reasonable thought was not "Islamic terrorists" (even though we quickly realized that the perpetrators were native-born, white American terrorists). Nor did she take into account the fact that the Khobar Towers in Saudi Arabia were bombed in 1996. (The USS *Cole* would be bombed in October 2000, less than a year after *Citizenship Rites* was published, and the bombing would be followed by the attacks against the World Trade Center in September 2001.) She ignored the fact that we were locked into a scenario of sanctions enforcement against Saddam Hussein, with no good alternative. Not to mention that the United States had tried to save millions of lives, especially Muslim lives, in the Balkans and Africa. Instead, feminism chose to implode, applauding game-playing and acting-out and indulging themselves with counterproductive jargon and promiscuous condemnation of serious work.

In the nineteen years between Enloe's publication and Feinman's, American feminists dealing with military issues had not learned to understand the military's force structure or to assess the violent threats to this country. In fact, they seemed to be unwilling to do so. The military, of course, has its own jargon. The documents can be boring and disheartening, and, saddest of all, you often learn there are no purely good solutions to anything. There's better and there's worse, and often there's a vast difference between the two. But it is a field where people have to deliberately desensitize themselves to suffering and death in order to provide the better solutions that cause the *least* suffering and death. It's a lot more fun to weave webs and talk about testosterone poisoning than to decide: "This is important to me as a citizen, and interesting to me as an individual, so what can I do to have a positive impact?" and then accept the burdens of making that positive contribution, as so many servicewomen did during the cold war.

Sad, because feminism had done such good work and opened

so many doors in other areas. One woman who walked through these doors, and through others opened by the civil rights movement, was Dr. Condoleezza Rice, ambitious, accomplished, dignified. First as national security advisor to the president, and now as secretary of state, she has spoken movingly, and often reasonably, about the need for the United States to help bring freedom to the Middle East, especially to women. Yet her readiness to compare the democratization of Germany and Japan to the liberation of Iraq bespeaks at best political spin and opportunism, at worst strong evidence that she ought to take a refresher course in history.

Addressing the 104th convention of the Veterans of Foreign Wars in August 2003, Dr. Rice said:

> *There is an understandable tendency to look back on America's experience in postwar Germany and see only the successes. But as some of you here today surely remember, the road we traveled was very difficult. Nineteen-forty-five through 1947 was an especially challenging period. Germany was not immediately stable or prosperous. SS officers—called "werewolves"—engaged in sabotage and attacked both coalition forces and those locals cooperating with them—much like today's Baathist and Fedayeen remnants.*

Unfortunately, this comparison is so far-fetched as to be laughable. We, along with our Soviet allies, did not liberate Germany or Japan as we actually did liberate Iraq—quickly and with due concern for collateral damage. We first pushed German and Japanese armies across three continents and bombed their cities into rubble and ashes, then invaded them. After killing them by the millions, we conquered them beyond all possibility of resistance, forced the submission of their governments, and occupied them indefinitely. The Western allies gave all who thought the old regimes worth fighting for a chance to die for their beliefs, and the Soviets went a good deal further.

We have visited no such catastrophe upon Iraq, nor did we ever intend to, and the Iraqis knew it. Having not been defeated "in detail"— military terminology indicating complete collapse—it's tragically clear that the Iraqis have no intention of behaving as if they had been so defeated. Also importantly, Iraq did not have the tradition, however weak and attenuated, that the Germans and even the Japanese did of a civil society. Additionally, there is now no country threatening Iraq the way the Soviet Union threatened postwar Western Europe. However much the West Germans might have resented American and British bases, the Soviets were a worse threat. Iran is not nearly such a threat to Iraq, and certainly, given Iranian penetration of Iraqi governmental and security organizations in southern Iraq, the Iraqis do not seem to fear the Iranians the same way the Germans feared the Soviets.

Like Enloe and Feinman, Dr. Rice might as well have said, "We don't have to know anything about other people, all we have to know about is ourselves." Between Enloe, Feinman, and Rice, the goals may vary, but they're equally impossible goals because the dynamics of self-delusion are the same.

From the outset I believed, and still believe, that we are fighting a war with militant Islamic fundamentalism, and that the outcome of such a war is important not just to American men, but also to American women. Therefore, logically, women should be part of the military, even if the opening campaign in Iraq has proven ill-advised and poorly executed.

This was the message I wanted, and still want, to convey to my readers. But how? I often feel like the soldier who asks his sergeant where his foxhole is. Replies the sergeant: "You're standing on it. All you have to do is remove the dirt."

So I started to dig. In truth, I had been digging for ages. Before the invasion, I went through a period of wondering if it might, in fact, be possible for an American invasion to ignite a sort of Arab renaissance, especially for women. But then common sense reasserted itself. Common sense, and a lifetime spent with animals who could have told the Bush administration and its neocon cheerleaders that while they were free to believe anything they wanted, they were not free to escape the consequences of their delusions.

———————— ⊕ ————————

As a girl, I worked at a local stable for several summers, and I came to regard myself as having been raised by horses. One of the loveliest things in the world is a horse displaying what is called self-carriage: moving forward freely at the gait asked for, in balance and harmony under the saddle, head down, face almost vertical, neck arched, back full and rounded, hindquarters underneath him. Later, I took up professionally training dogs. I had some idea of what it takes to turn a cur into a trusted and trustworthy companion, how to take an animal from believing he's running the show—an animal who believes he is well within his rights to punish you for disobedience—to a well-mannered and well-intentioned friend. I have the scars on my face and forearms to show for my mistakes.

Force has a place in this kind of training. I had to teach dogs that, although my teeth are indeed puny, and horses that, while I *am* afraid of them (why lie? they know the truth!), they can't push me around. But you can no more force a horse or a dog to develop the self-carriage necessary to become a partner than you can force people to develop the self-carriage necessary to live in freedom.

For humans, self-carriage means living within a fundamental social compact. Freedom means living your life for yourself while meeting your obligations; fulfilling your abilities and desires while harming no one who intends you no harm; and helping those who can't or won't protect themselves from the inevitable bullies, thugs, and brutes. It also means that you choose to live this way not out of fear of punishment if you don't, but out of respect: first for yourself, then for your family, friends, and neighbors, and finally for the civilization that you share, maintain, and protect. Such self-carriage can only develop organically in a society that collectively chooses it and is prepared to deal with those individuals and groups who don't. Self-carriage takes years to develop, whether in dogs and horses, or in humans, generations, and civilizations.

It seems to be a truism that elections and constitutions signify the arrival of a mature society, one in which people share power because they've learned to trust each other through a thousand daily interactions at home, at work, and on the street. In truth, elections and constitutions are only the means. Democracy is the end of political, social, and cultural self-carriage, that elusive and beautiful quality that must be developed voluntarily and over time and can be neither faked nor bestowed.

This, unfortunately, was not how the administration and the neocons viewed Iraq. According to their glib predictions, Iraqis would throw rose petals at us from the rooftops, yank down the statues of Saddam, and then neatly pick up the ruins of their lives from thirty years of Baathist tyranny. Hardly the reality, as we now know. By 2003, millions of Iraqis had been driven in upon themselves by tyranny. Connections outside the family had withered, leaving Iraqis unable to band together to defy Saddam, or defend themselves, much less pick up the pieces afterward. There were countless Iraqi sympathizers, supporters, informers, murderers, and torturers, and thousands upon thousands who profited from him and by him. As I've said, I was against the war in Iraq from its outset for the simple reason that it was a bad idea. I understood that the Iraqi people had suffered terribly under Saddam Hussein, suffering that the United States had tolerated, even intensified. I knew that only an American invasion and occupation would offer Iraqis any real possibility to escape from this particular tyranny, but I knew that interfering in a society we do not understand is not America's responsibility. Like so many others, I did not think that the United States should run substantial military, economic, and political risks to overthrow a monster who posed no imminent threat to us. Once we invaded, however, the question became, "Now what?" Despite all the American babble about "staying the course," the real outcome would be, and still is, a question only the Iraqis can answer.

Now let's be clear: Opposing a particular war does not make me, or anyone else, antimilitary. Among the most rational people against invading Iraq were former military, such as two decorated old Marines, former secretary of the Navy James Webb and retired general Anthony Zinni, the latter a former commander of the U.S. Central Command. In the spring of 2002, as the Bush administration clearly began preparing for war in Iraq, my partner Philip became one of the first mainstream conservatives in the country to oppose the war, costing him his position in a prestigious conservative think tank.

During the buildup to the invasion of Iraq, I did not hear from or of a single active or retired soldier or Marine who thought the invasion was a good idea, although I knew plenty of soldiers who wanted to be part of such an invasion, regardless of how unwise they thought it. These men, who thought the invasion was a bad idea, ranged from public figures like General Eric Shinseki, who presciently warned against trying to implement a twelve-division strategy with a ten-division force, to personal acquaintances. If they took for granted that Iraq had not been behind 9/11, despite some contacts with al-Qaeda (*all* governments have such unsavory contacts), they also accepted that the attack was a legitimate casus belli. Of course, Afghanistan, not Iraq, was sheltering al-Qaeda, but in either case a casus belli does not mandate a full-fledged invasion and occupation of a country that not only poses no strategic threat to yours but is also profoundly different from yours. The United States went into Iraq despite the quiet consensus of much of the active and retired military communities, and of nearly anyone who could foresee that invading Iraq was a bad idea. "Mission Accomplished" segued into an insurgency/civil war that quickly consumed the U.S. Army, Reserves, and National Guard and left the Marine Corps more stretched than normal.

Of the total number of people in the Armed Services, 15% are female. By December 2003, the barriers preventing women from serving in direct ground combat were breaking down under the demands of military necessity and simple, soldierly morality. Servicemen have every right to expect servicewomen to fully participate in military operations, just as the men in their positions do.

Sadly, when we think of American women in combat, especially enlisted soldiers, we are far too likely to think of Jessica Lynch, a private in the 507th Maintenance Company. On 20 March 2003, thirty-three soldiers from her company blundered into the outskirts of An Nasiriyah. Eleven were killed in combat or died of their wounds and injuries; seven were captured; and the remainder retreated to U.S. control. Of the twenty-two soldiers who survived, nine were wounded in action.[5]

Private Jessica Lynch—blond, described often in the media as pretty and waiflike—was at first made out to be a hero by the Pentagon's public affairs machine. She was fighting to the death, we were told; she did not want to be taken alive. The true story turned out to be quite a bit different. Her element of the 507th had careened into a city braced for an American onslaught, and the soldiers quickly found themselves brutally overmatched. Things went from bad to worse when, rather than laagering up on high ground in a defensive perimeter and letting the enemy come to them, they tried to outrun the Iraqis on their home turf. There were soldiers who did fight heroically. Private First Class Patrick Miller received the Silver Star, as did Sergeant Donald Walters (whose award was posthumous; he was taken prisoner and murdered by the Iraqis). Both men fought effectively. Lynch, by her own account, never fired a shot. And even though, in purely literary terms, the story she told to Rick Bragg was hardly worth the million-dollar advance her publisher gave them, her injuries and the dignity with which she comported herself were real. She certainly did not deserve the abuse she received from a good many armchair warriors on their blogs. She was not a hero and she's said so herself. To call her such is to debase the word and thereby insult her. She was simply a private soldier who served without distinction but honorably, and despite the military and the media's initial attempts to turn her into a Barbie doll heroine, she quickly retreated from the limelight.

For far too many Americans, however, Jessica Lynch, and her injuries, is still the face of the American female combat soldier.

Officially, of course, there are no American female combat soldiers. Officially, women are not *assigned* to direct ground combat units below brigade level (currently, a unit of about three thousand to five thousand soldiers). If they're involved with units below this level, they're simply referred to as *attached*. These distinctions, which used to mean a great deal, are in the process of becoming meaningless. Importantly, they have never meant anything to the enemy. They're simply part of a political game and a legalistic facade that is no more than a divisive social distinction between female and male soldiers and Marines.

There are not many female combat soldiers. But there are more than you'd think, and far more than the military or the media acknowledge. Suffice it to say that a soldier, male or female, becomes a combat soldier by serving in combat. Some volunteer. More often, combat comes to them. The enemy doesn't scan for ponytails or buns or braids sticking out of helmets on the occupants of a Humvee before detonating that IED (improvised explosive device) or opening fire when those troops have dismounted.

And for a unit commander who's short of men, the unofficial status of women is nothing short of a headache when he has to play games or skirt the law to attach women to fill positions in combat units they should be assigned to, and therefore be a part of. Remember, in the military, if you're not assigned to a unit, you are an "orphan."

On 29 December 2003, *Time* magazine selected "The American Soldier" as its person of the year. In "Portrait of a Platoon," Romesh Ratnesar and Michael Weisskopf profiled the Tomb Raiders: Survey Platoon, Headquarters Battery, Second Battalion, Third Field Artillery Regiment, First Armored Division. There are women in the field artillery, but they are restricted to corps (a high-level, multidivision echelon) and above. Officially, you're supposed to find these women in high-level headquarters, not in survey platoons serving as dismounted infantry.

But the platoon medic of the Tomb Raiders, attached from another unit, was a woman, Specialist Billie Grimes, from Lebanon, Indiana.

While Ratnesar and Weisskopf were embedded with the Tomb Raiders, Weisskopf had his hand blown off when an Iraqi heaved a grenade into his Humvee. Specialist Grimes, who dashed out of her own Humvee to treat Weisskopf, was one of the soldiers on the cover. A very bad painting of the soldiers accompanied the article; in it, a wisp of hair floating free from Grimes's helmet signifies her womanhood.

Neither in the article nor on the Department of Defense website (www.defenselink.mil), which posted the article, was there a hint of concern that Grimes was a bad soldier, or that she hurt the unit's cohesion, its ability to function as a unit. According to the predictions of all those opposed to women in the military, and especially in direct ground combat, the presence of Specialist Grimes should have precipitated a disaster. The men should have raped her, or engaged in fistfights over access to her favors, even if she wasn't dispensing them; she herself could have been expected to engage in promiscuous sex, or at least date one of the guys with no regard to good order and discipline. And she was certainly supposed to be incapable of doing her job because she wasn't physically strong enough, or mentally tough enough, and even if she had been, the men were supposed to abandon their military discipline and mission to protect her under fire.

Instead, this woman was simply a good soldier doing a brutally demanding job alongside the men in her unit, who were also good soldiers.

The *Time* article wasn't the only one I read that hinted at a very quiet and profound change running through the U.S. Army, but it was the most prominent. And while Grimes and the two male soldiers who shared the cover with her to represent the American GI got considerable publicity, the media appeared oblivious of the change. It was as though, having been told for decades that something never should or could happen, no one even noticed when it finally did.

In fact, as near as I can tell, even Elaine Donnelly, who makes her living from fighting any progression of servicewomen into combat roles, has not mentioned Grimes in her organizational publications. Donnelly is the president of the Center for Military Readiness, a tiny operation in Livonia, Michigan. Her board of advisors is composed of senior military officers and various members of the conservative public policy world. Perhaps the most interesting aspect of her board is the men who have remained on it indefinitely—even after their deaths. (Admiral Thomas H. Moorer and Vice Admiral Dudley Carlson both died in 2004.) Her website may be visited at www.cmrlink.org, although her *Notes* and *Reports,* to which I refer, are not accessible without a subscription. She does keep a list of "Issues" on her website, which groups publicly accessible essays under topics. Her response to the harsh fate that befell the element of the 507th Maintenance Company that blundered into An Nasiriyah was to focus luridly on the female soldiers in that unit, especially PFC Lynch: their wounds, the probability of torture, the reality of sexual assault (as if their male comrades did not share their sufferings, likely in every detail).[6] Yet in all Donnelly's *Reports* and *Notes,* she has never mentioned the Tomb Raiders and their female medic. In fact, Donnelly has only grudgingly and in the abstract acknowledged the existence of women serving in combat at all.[7]

It's not that Donnelly doesn't know about servicewomen serving where they "shouldn't." In the past, she denounced the Defense Advisory Committee on Women in the Services (DACOWITS) for "disregarding Army policy" because DACOWITS thought that women should get credit for serving in ground combat positions that were officially male only. "Forget about concepts essential to military discipline, such as honesty and obedience within the chain of command," Donnelly wrote. "The clueless DACOWITS prefers to support practices that violate official directives. This sets a bad example for servicewomen and puts their superiors in an untenable position."[8]

Suffice it to say that women can't serve in all-male combat units without their presence being known and approved of by at least their immediate chain of command. Military units just don't work that way. The chain of command knows when someone is assigned, or even attached, for that matter. And yes, men do notice when one or two women join the unit. Back in the summer of 2001, this business of "illegally" attaching women was a very obscure peacetime practice, but Donnelly knew about such attachments and denounced them. Donnelly's failure to speak about Specialist Billie Grimes's appearance on the cover of *Time* magazine was a harbinger of things to come. As Army recruiting suffers from a war most Americans of military age (and their parents) do not find worth their sweat, and certainly not their blood, sending women into combat has become increasingly common. Yet there is little outcry against this, either inside the Army or in the larger world of U.S. civilian society. It bespeaks both ignorance of just how widespread the practice has become and an uneasy acceptance of the logic of equality that has yet to be articulated.

Chapter 3

THE LIONESSES OF IRAQ

Movement to contact is a military term that means a movement, such as a patrol, that seeks contact with the enemy. My movement to contact in Iraq began when I was a girl of two. My parents, conventionally anti-Vietnam academics, found my enthusiasms, well, disconcerting. I demanded (and eventually got) a GI Joe doll, and displayed an aptitude for taking things apart, figuring out how they worked, and putting them back together. They almost always still worked. As I got older, I read military and diplomatic history voraciously and would have wanted to go to West Point if I'd ever been exposed to the place.

There are women born when I was, in the late 1960s, or even fifteen years earlier, who did the things I dreamed of. Often, but hardly always, they came from more "conservative" families, sometimes from families with strong military traditions. In my "liberal" family, where both parents were literature professors, I had only the dimmest idea of the existence of engineering schools and service academies, much less how to get into them.

I grew up on the fringes of "feminist antimilitarism," and despite other interests (that GI Joe doll among them), I absorbed some of those values. But the summer before I turned fourteen, I did something that crystallized my changing perspective. Like many more conventional teenage girls, I was horse-crazy, and so I found a stable to work in during the summers.

Horses reek of aristocracy, but this aristocracy is far more a matter of understanding, hard work, and skill than of dollars. Humans began domesticating dogs about 15,000 years ago; we began using horses to draft (pull) a mere 5,000 years ago, about the same time we begin to use oxen for drafting purposes (although horses are a vast improvement in terms of speed). The relationship between humans and dogs on the one hand, humans and horses on the other, is so ancient and so profound that we have influenced each other's evolutionary development. This goes far beyond our influence in creating the recognized dog and horse breeds, most of which are fairly recent. It also means that over our histories of providing shelter, food, and protection for each other, we've helped one another become and do things that wouldn't have been possible otherwise. To learn how to seriously work with horses and dogs, then, is to assume partial custody of a body of knowledge that has historically been of central importance to human civilization and even survival.

Those years working in the stables, and the years I spent much later working as a professional dog trainer, have permanently shaped how I think about the world. I have come to view civilization as fragile, dependent upon the transmission of hard skills and coherent ideas. Unless skills are practiced by craftsmen through fine handwork and quality manufacturing, they can be lost; serious ideas that are not

passed on through research and writing that tests them agains
ity, and modifies them, will vanish. To be effective, the transmiss
skills and ideas must not be by expert specialists, but ordinary people
who understand their place in the larger world; who have assumed custody of these skills and ideas, added to them, and passed them on to
subsequent generations. Civilization must be defended from those who
wish to plunder it for its good things rather than share in them, not only
through creation, but through the passing of its traditions and knowledge from one generation to the next.

In college, I joined the Army Reserves and went through enlisted
basic training at Fort Dix, New Jersey. Then I went through the Army's
Reserve Officers' Training Corps (ROTC), sans scholarship, and was
commissioned at the end of the cold war, in 1988. One of many second
lieutenants suddenly rendered surplus, I did six months of training in my
branch, ordnance, then went into the Individual Ready Reserve (IRR).
The IRR consists largely of names in a computer, people to be called to
active duty only after the Pentagon has mucked up a given war so badly
that they've exhausted the regulars and the organized reserves. (In fact,
the Pentagon has abandoned this practice after no one showed up when
called upon for the current war in Iraq.) Being in the IRR wasn't what I
wanted; in fact, it combined with my marriage to be the worst mistake I
ever made. But it was 1988, and women in the military were everyone's
favorite punching bags. The Left considered servicewomen dupes of the
patriarchy or, even worse, responsible for any mistreatment and discrimination they faced because, after all, the military was not only inherently masculine, but misogynistic and homophobic to boot. The "logic"
was: Since servicewomen knew what they were getting into, they all
but deserved anything bad that happened to them. The Right despised
servicewomen as nontraditional, although it occasionally excused them

as the product of "dysfunctional father/daughter relationships." While touting themselves as promilitary, the Right never lost an opportunity to attack and tear down the very women who had helped make possible the military's recovery from Vietnam. And unlike many other women, who to their eternal credit gutted out the difficult decade ahead, I simply could not see a way to be the kind of soldier I wanted to be in a force that recruited, trained, and utilized women as second-class human beings, and not as citizens with equal rights and obligations.

Thirteen years later, in the spring of 2001, I met Philip on a military Listserv. I was beating up on one of his Marine buddies, a decorated Vietnam vet and former college football player who is now a distinguished Naval War College professor, and he felt compelled to come to the rescue. He later confessed that he'd been intrigued by me from the start. Any woman who could tear Marines up one side and down the other, then sign her emails "V/R," or "Very Respectfully," had to be of interest. My initial sense of him was simpler. He was the man I was going to marry. First, however, we were destined to become partners in other ways.

We corresponded for a couple of years, phoned incessantly, coauthored some columns, did not swap photographs. I started writing on my own, seriously, and getting published. I date being sane and at peace from the day in February 2004 that he came walking into my office after a cross-country trip from Seattle to DC on Amtrak that should have been three days but took four due to winter weather delays. Dragging his suitcases behind him, he looked for all the world like a derelict. Having just turned in his manuscript for his latest book (*Take Back the Right*[1]) to his publisher, he was deep into negative stress. It didn't take too long for us to get around to planning the next several years, which for me would include visiting two war zones, quitting my job, selling my house, moving to Seattle, and writing a book.

78

Philip was the one who convinced me to ask Jim Pritzker for a grant, then helped me arrange my accreditation with the *Seattle Post-Intelligencer* and my embedment in Iraq. Since I'd been Army and Jim Pritzker's heart belonged to the National Guard, we agreed that I should find a citizen-soldier outfit to cover. The Eighty-first Brigade Combat Team, a National Guard unit out of Washington State, was getting ready to rotate over. I emailed their public affairs officer, a Captain Anne-Marie Peacock. We corresponded for a few weeks. I sent her my paperwork. She lost my paperwork. I resubmitted it, then heard nothing until she informed me that I couldn't be accommodated during "the time you're requesting." I hadn't requested any dates. Philip suggested that I try the Marines. They took two days to say yes and then referred me to the Army brigade with which they were serving in the Sunni Triangle.

I like Marines.

On 14 June 2004, the day after Philip put me on a British Airways flight to Kuwait via London, I was met by Army public affairs officer Captain Randall Baucom, who took me from Kuwait International Airport to Camp Doha, about half an hour outside Kuwait City, and handed me over to some Marines headed in the same direction I was: Iraq's Al Anbar Province, which includes the cities of Fallujah and Ramadi, and my destination, Camp Junction City. I was the only civilian woman all the way from Kuwait to Camp Junction City, in a pale peach polo shirt and jeans, showing the effects of two nearly sleepless nights, an intercontinental flight, and a couple of missed meals. I was, for all practical purposes, unarmed. I saw one or two women; in fact, I spent a few hours sleeping in a tent of female Marines at Al Taqaddum en route to Camp Junction City.

From the military side of Kuwait International Airport to Al Taqaddum Airbase to Camp Blue Diamond, First Marine Division

Headquarters, to Camp Junction City, my final destination and home of the First Brigade Combat Team of the U.S. Army's First Infantry Division, one group of armed male Marines handed me off to another. Never was there any problem; in fact, I took for granted that there would be no problem with American GIs.

Some eighteen hours later, I staggered into Camp Blue Diamond and was shown the desk of Marine combat correspondent Gunnery Sergeant Mark Oliva. I grounded my gear, found a chair, folded up my arms on the desk, and went to sleep. A little while later, Gunny Oliva found me and took me to breakfast, where I asked about Ramadi and the use of human shields. He confirmed that the insurgents used Iraqi noncombatants, especially women and children, as human shields, although the Marines did not react as the insurgents hoped. "Makes the grunts want to kill the insurgents all the more," I recall him saying. And they did.

After breakfast, Gunny Oliva handed me off to two U.S. Army officers, both men, both armed, who drove me across the Euphrates to Camp Junction City, my new home for the next three weeks. One of them was Captain Joseph Jasper, a cavalry officer and brigade public affairs officer (PAO); another was Captain Moses Scheinfeld, who wore a Pathfinder badge in addition to the Ranger and Airborne patches you usually see on a good infantry officer's uniform. The Pathfinders are the guys who go in first to secure a drop zone for follow-on paratroops. He was from New York, an observant Jew who was trying to keep kosher as well as he could. Scheinfeld was the S-1, or administrative officer, of 1-16 Infantry Battalion, one of the First Brigade's subordinate elements.

Captain Jasper had made arrangements for me to be temporarily housed with some women of the 101st Forward Support Battalion (FSB), First Brigade's maintenance element: Chief Warrant Officer

Parker, an older woman and widow; Sergeant Gomez, from the Dominican Republic; PFC McIntosh, married, with a six-month-old daughter living with her mother-in-law. Also, Specialist Vickers, a Bradley maintenance tech and squad automatic weapon (SAW) gunner. Some units billet men and women who work together in the same squad bays; some don't. Clearly, the 101st FSB billeted women with women and not with their male workmates, which did not please many of the women billeted separately from their workmates.

The SAW is an M16 on steroids; back in the mid-1980s it replaced the M60 machine gun, which fired heavier rounds (7.62 millimeters in diameter). The SAW fires 5.56-millimeter rounds, about the same size as a .22 caliber varmint round. No one considers the SAW a good trade for the M60, but every maintenance team has to have two gunners, and Vickers's team split their SAWs between one man and one woman. "To be fair," they told her. As in: If a man has to carry one of those beasts—the old M60 was nicknamed "the pig" because it was so heavy—a woman should have to, too. Since Vickers was the only woman in the shop, she got her own SAW. She told me that after four years of carrying it, it didn't weigh any more to her than an M16 did to other women. And, all arguments about round caliber aside, she preferred the SAW to the M16 out here in Iraq. Firepower's nice.

PFC McIntosh lent me her bed to take a nap, and I took her up on the offer after a shower. After my nap, I made the deliberate decision to downplay the research I was doing on servicewomen. I certainly didn't hide my interest, let alone lie. However, I knew that in the past the sporadic but intense media focus on servicewomen had disturbed many of the women and alienated some of the men. I also knew the issue had once been radioactive and could be again. Besides, the real story was less what the women were doing than the fact that men and women aging in the traditionally all-male domain of offensive combat and increasingly as equals.

...haps this wouldn't be so if combat in Iraq was a matter of extended trench warfare, as we saw during World War I, or of the sustained ferocity characteristic of World War II, and of much of the wars in Korea and Vietnam. Those wars were fought by young men who were far more accustomed to death and hardship on the farm, at work, while hunting, and during childhood than the young men and women who were raised in our relatively hardship-free society. Every nation fights in ways that reflect its values, and values are constantly shifting. Among our current values is the all-important value of equality, and it's much more visible now than it was during previous American wars. And despite what soldiers are accustomed to at home, let's face it: The U.S. Army lives better than any other. The privations of the field, though often intense, are temporary. This eases acceptance.

After a few days with the 101st Forward Support Battalion, I was billeted just down the street, joining up with the First Engineer Battalion, the Army's oldest and most decorated engineer battalion, which was another element of the First Brigade also at Camp Junction City. Most other units in Iraq had women who engaged in whatever combat came their way. But the First Engineers went further. The unit sent its own women, known as "Lionesses," to other units, including combat units. Their mission was to attach to these units at the most basic level of the infantry platoon or squad, and interact with Iraqi women and children on combat missions. The presence of these women soldiers reassured Iraqi women, who could not fathom Iraqi soldiers searching their homes without raping them. Unless American women were present, they feared even worse from American men, who were, after all, foreign conquerors. The habit of fear dies hard.

On 19 June 2004, I went out on two missions. I walked across the road from my barracks to those of Coldsteel "C" Company, First Engineers, and joined Second Lieutenant John Johannes, a West Point graduate, and his First Platoon to search for buried explosives. We were operating in an area where, the day before, a patrol of dismounted tankers from Bravo Company, 1-34 Armor Battalion, had found the body of a 155-millimeter shell, minus its warhead. A warhead can do a lot of damage if it's used as an IED.

The tankers had gotten a little nervous and had asked the engineers, who had specialized training and equipment, to come back and do a thorough search for that warhead. Of course, the engineers were nervous, too. Like all the lettered companies of the First Engineer Battalion, Coldsteel is a line company. In traditional terms of a front line, line companies are just that. They're on the line, or in Iraq, where there is no "line" demarcating friendly from enemy territory, they're the ones who do the most patrolling outside the wire, supported by a variety of specialized elements in the rear or inside the wire. For a battalion, those elements include a headquarters company with maintenance and medical personnel. The engineers, like aviation, are a combat arm in which women are allowed to serve because women supposedly will not engage in direct ground combat in these units.

To generalize, there are not supposed to be women in line companies, even in the engineers. But in fact, the exclusion of women from direct ground combat was not strictly held to, so my patrolling with them, even as a journalist, was not unusual. Their medic, Sergeant Norwood, was a woman. She was also the smallest person I ever saw patrolling with them, and she carried by far the heaviest load, a medical pack that weighed fifty pounds. This was in addition to her individual body armor of Kevlar helmet, vest, rifle plates, and load-bearing equipment. The men typically carried just their individual loads of armor, weapons, and ammo.

In M113 armored personnel carriers, we approached two houses that we presumed belonged to whoever owned the land upon which the shell casing had been found. The idea was to talk to the landowner before searching; not surprisingly, he agreed to the search. He wasn't going to disagree, not with armored vehicles with machine guns in his driveway, regardless of how politely he was asked. One of the houses was still under construction. There was a Mercedes in the driveway and some cows, vastly more elegant than their American cousins, tethered by their lyre-shaped horns and gleaming as if they'd been washed and waxed. There were also two horses, the only ones I'd ever see in Iraq. In the courtyard of the property were some women in black who became visibly nervous when they saw the soldiers, but who relaxed when they saw me accompanying them. (My hair is long. I'd originally gone out on missions with my braid tucked up in my helmet in deference to military regulations, even though I was not a soldier. But for comfort, and because I noticed how the women and girls would relax as soon as they spotted me, I started to let my braid fall straight down my back.)

The soldiers found nothing on the premises, so we got back in the M113s and drove down the road to the village of Bu Zhyahb, hoping to find that warhead or a weapons cache. We dismounted and walked past a girls' school. Men and women, boys and girls, were working in the fields. Despite the work women do bearing children—the most dangerous work of all—women and girls in Iraq also tend to do the harder work of agricultural labor, while the men and boys do the lighter work of herding. The sheep and the cows, complacent around their Iraqi caretakers, became agitated by our presence. In our helmets and body armor we must have looked like space aliens to them. I edged nervously by a cow that had, minutes earlier, calmly let a woman in a billowing black *abaya* pass by. The animal lunged to her feet, eyes rolling anxiously at me. I held my breath, hoping she wouldn't kick, and jumped when a nearby calf licked me. Soldiers of many other nations would have vented tension by shooting the cattle, but I watched as the GIs tried to feed them. You're considered to have scored a social coup if local cows will eat from your hand.

Bu Zhyahb turned out to be a dry hole, too, so we returned to base before the full, brutal heat of the afternoon kicked in. Even so, when I stripped off my body armor, I was absolutely soaked. Wicking under-shirts help, but not enough. I drank vast amounts of water to replace what I'd sweated out. After dinner, I went to meet up with the Lionesses, and to prepare for my first Lioness mission.

Some women volunteered for Lioness missions, others didn't; but I never met a woman who felt free to decline one, because that meant someone else would have to go in her place, and if no women went, the mission was more dangerous than it otherwise would have been. This is because the presence of women and children normally deescalates tension, and without that, fighting can rise to a fever pitch of ferocity. The killing of women who have taken up arms is well within the bounds of war. The killing of noncombatant women and old men, much less children, however, signals not war but massacre. The Iraqis viewed the presence of female soldiers not only as a sign of respect, for it meant that Iraqi women would be searched by female, not male, soldiers, but also as a guarantee that any violence would be kept within the realm of what is referred to in the Western tradition as civilized warfare.

The women with whom I would engage in my first mission

included my roommate, Captain Anastasia Breslow. She was the First Engineer Battalion's signals officer and a second-generation soldier. By ancestry, she was half-Russian, half-Chinese, and, as her Eighty-second Airborne Division combat patch from Afghanistan indicated, all-American. Another Lioness was one of Breslow's soldiers, PFC Jennifer Acy—young, small, not quite certain that she was up for combat. Her first Lioness mission had involved a firefight at a traffic control point, and she hadn't been able to fire back for fear of hitting Marines. She and Captain Breslow did what they could to keep terrified Iraqi women who bolted into the fields of fire between the Marines and the insurgents from being killed. People get disoriented and actually do this. Additionally, many Iraqi civilians expected American troops to have the same bad marksmanship and undisciplined fire as Iraqis. The U.S. military is one of the few in the world that emphasizes marksmanship in all ranks of all the armed services. There are some fine Arab marksmen, but in general, Arabs are bad marksmen, not by U.S. (or for that matter British) standards, but by world standards. And it's not simply that Arabs are poorly trained; it's that they frequently fire up into the air or in a variety of directions away from the target area, regardless of whom their rounds might hit. As might be expected, the consequences were sometimes tragic. The Iraqi approach to combat was so casual that U.S. soldiers engaged in a firefight with insurgents would sometimes see Iraqis who, to the Americans' knowledge, were uninvolved in the firefight drive up, collect the bodies of dead insurgents for immediate burial, and drive off. The experience of being under fire, Breslow told Acy to stiffen her up, is one very few American men, and still fewer American women, have had.

The three of us joined up with Lieutenant Colonel Michael Cabrey, commander of 1-5 Field Artillery Battalion, and his Alpha

Battery. Cabrey is a West Pointer, not tall, with a wrestler's speed and stocky build, green eyes, and a bold, honest way about him. That night he was planning a "knock and greet," and he needed Lionesses to deal with the women. He had received information that a man had sold a vehicle to a maker of vehicle-borne IEDs (VBIEDs, as the military calls them). They cause horrendous damage. A VBIED can be hidden among any of the many abandoned cars that litter the streets of Ramadi and its suburbs, including this one, Tamim, quite close to Camp Junction City.

Except for a few modern touches, such as cars parked in front and electrical wires running out of them, the homes in the area looked as if they were thousands of years old. With their low square or rectangular buildings with thick walls, constructed from dun-colored bricks, often with a walled courtyard fronting them, a resident of Sumer would have recognized the homes. It was a poor neighborhood, but the genuine damage of tyranny and a dozen years of sanctions, during which the UN systematically looted Iraq under the guise of the Oil-for-Food Program, had been made worse by the Iraqis' resolute refusal to pick up after themselves. Frequently, roadside landscaping consisted of trash out to the horizon. Neighborhood streets were often filled with trash that the children played in. When Americans asked Iraqi men, "Why don't you police this up so your kids have a place to play?" they were told, "No one pays us to." It was a pervasive attitude that would defeat even the most civic-minded Iraqi.

The yard of the house we approached for the knock and greet was ankle deep in car parts and feces, by their appearance children's. There was an old blue Volga sedan in front. According to the interpreter, in the house were two men, the homeowner's son and cousin, along with their wives, daughters, and grandchildren. The homeowner himself was not there. The Lionesses were a little slow going in. Cabrey's policy was that they never be first in a stack, because they didn't have the extensive training combat arms soldiers get. However, as soon as the Iraqis saw the women soldiers, men and women alike visibly relaxed. The Americans were still foreigners, still armed—Iraqis know the women will use their weapons—but the presence of women reassured them that any violence would be military, not criminal. Captain Breslow and PFC Acy were very gentle with the women, and gave candy and pens to the children, but they also listened to and watched them carefully. Were they talking among themselves? Were they hiding papers or ammunition? They talked to them through the two interpreters about school and the elections and the forthcoming handover of sovereignty. (The First Brigade had been easing off combat operations for weeks, trying to accustom the Iraqi National Guard, now the Iraqi Army, into doing for themselves.)

A search turned up four magazines of ammo for an AK assault rifle, an SKS carbine, and RPG (rocket-propelled grenade) sights in a safe belonging to the cousin's wife. She was given a receipt for the lock the soldiers cut off the safe, as well as for the RPG sights kept in it, to claim reimbursement from the Americans. The homeowner's son told Lieutenant Colonel Cabrey that the AK assault rifle had been sold to finance "home construction," although there was no evidence of said construction. As for his father, the homeowner himself, who had supposedly sold the car to the maker of the VBIEDs, he was in Samarra for three days for his daughter's wedding. Since each family was authorized one weapon per adult for self-defense, Cabrey left him the carbine and SKS, along with three of the AK magazines.

The patrol was leaving as the father pulled up in a white Volga. Like the blue Volga, the condition of this one—filth included—was unimaginable. The soldiers reacted promptly, swarming the Volga before the father could get out and coordinate stories with his son. But the father was straightforward and apparently honest with Cabrey. "I wasn't in Samarra; I went to a mechanic to get my car fixed. You can talk to him."

Cabrey, an artillerist, not an intelligence or police officer, was impressive in his questioning of the son, who had lied and kept trying to change the subject. Standing outside in the yard between father and son, carefully, courteously, Cabrey boxed the son in. The son's lies did not add up, but rather contradicted both each other and what his father had said. They went back and forth through the interpreter. What kind of car, what colors, to whom did you sell it, where does he live? Finally, Cabrey's exasperation showed and he said—politely—"Don't lie to me. There's no reason to lie."

It was this courtesy, from a man who clearly had enormous fire-power at his command, that finally broke the son—and it was fascinating to watch him respond.

"I sold the car for a hundred dollars."

"What color is the car?"

"Taxi colors, white and orange. It's a Toyota Cressida. I sold it to a guy. He sells black market fuel."

Under the former regime, telling the truth did not pay; lying was a habit born of moral degradation. As Soviets would tell you, you did one thing, said another, and thought yet another on the same subject.

"Where does he live?" Cabrey continued.

The son started to give directions, then said, "I'll take you there. Just follow my car."

No one in my line of sight said a word, fidgeted, or so much as adjusted a rifle sling as the two continued to converse. And yet we might as well have shouted our thoughts. *Ambush! What if the man has a cell phone?* Who was this second man the son was offering to take us to, after all? The man to whom the father had sold the orange-and-white Cressida, possibly for a VBIED, was already on Cabrey's list. A setup in which we might well have been massacred was all too real a possibility. We were in the Sunni Triangle. We all knew what had happened in Fallujah, not long ago, where four contractors had been butchered, their charred and mutilated bodies hung from a bridge to be photographed. I'd seen the photos; probably everyone there had. And yet, Cabrey and his team got back in the vehicle, and I got in with them. There was a mission to be accomplished, and we had enough firepower, both in the heavy .50 caliber machine guns and on call, that any ambusher would have paid a high price.

It turned out there was no ambush. I have no idea whether the son ran the risk of being seen as a collaborator because, this once, he opted not to lie. But people are willing to die for such things as the respect of others and themselves.

We drove through the evening streets of Tamim to a second house. Even in comparison with the first house, this one was squalid. The walls had not been painted, or even washed, in years. There was a pot of rotting tomatoes on the stairs. Garbage, parts of . . . things . . . were everywhere. There were no books. There appeared to be no electricity, and don't blame it on the Americans for not providing power. The Iraqis maintain their own power stations, with a lot of money from the United States. I saw no light fixtures or wiring, even though the Iraqi practice is to run the wiring on the outside of walls rather than inside. No candles, no oil lamps. This was not poverty; this was despair.

This landowner was not at home, either, but a thorough search turned up three rifles. I had heard that the allowance was one rifle and three magazines per adult male in the house, but the troops I dealt with interpreted it as per adult in the house. The usual assorted women and children, including a teenage boy who was clearly the eldest son, sat in the courtyard under a lean-to of some sort. Breslow and Acy again watched them closely without staring at them, talking with the women through interpreters about education and voting in the upcoming elections. Benign conversation, meant to put these women at ease, to try to make some sort of human connection with them. The female soldiers had scarcely more in common with the Iraqi women they encountered than their male counterparts did. As Americans, these female soldiers lived in a different moral universe from the Iraqi women, a universe where women are citizens, not virtually lifelong minors and wards, first of their fathers and then of their husbands. But they were able to find common ground with them, woman to woman, in speaking to them about their local schools and politics.

When he learned that the man of the house was not home, Lieutenant Colonel Cabrey asked to speak to the woman of the house. The presence of the Lionesses notwithstanding, she came out, terrified, wringing her hands. What else could it mean, but that he was going to rape her? Saddam's Mukhabarat, his intelligence service, often raped women they interrogated; furthermore, she risked the wrath of her husband, or even her son, for being raped. If she were to become pregnant (contraceptive use is uncommon) from such an encounter, either an abortion or pregnancy would have been life-threatening, and any child born of the rape would likely be killed in the unlikely event that the woman herself were not murdered. Since women do not generally bear arms, they are to a certain degree culturally immunized from being directly killed. The Mukhabarat deliberately used the cultural meaning of rape as a fate that is "worse than death," common in many societies, but uncommonly intense in Arab society, as a means of inflicting shame and dishonor on the victim's family. The Mukhabarat relied on the woman's family to cripple themselves by murdering her.

Layers upon layers of cruelty, and the American troops I encountered were extremely aware of these cultural complexities.

I stepped up toward the woman to listen more closely, smiled at her, and put my arm around her daughter, who had come up to inspect me and presumably to keep an eye on her mother. Because I am a woman, and despite the fact that I was part of a foreign occupation, the girl put her arm around my waist. I made certain I knew where her hand was, just in case she started to feel for my knife, but kept myself relaxed. Cabrey went much further to put the mother at her ease, since you can't talk with someone who's that afraid of you. First he took off his helmet and ballistic goggles, and then he knelt before her in the courtyard, ensuring that his weapon was pointed down, making gentle small talk, asking about her daughter, until she relaxed and began to talk to him. During Cabrey's careful, polite cross-checking, her husband came home. It turned out that he had indeed bought the car for his son to use to sell black market fuel. He himself sold vegetables, as well as fuel. Cabrey admonished him that his son needed to be in school, along with his daughters, then asked him which weapons he'd like to keep. "Pick two," Cabrey encouraged him. "One for you, one for your wife, so you can protect your family."

In short, another dry hole. We went home to bed.

Two days later, four Marines were killed at an observation post in Ramadi, sending rumors flying around Camp Junction City. The base communications package was promptly shut down so that the dead

Marines' next of kin could be properly notified. I coordinaᵗ
out with 1-5 again, this time on a raid to a suspected safe hou
eign fighters, likely Syrians. The original plan was for me to acc⁙
pany the Lionesses, who would go in on the lead vehicle. But here
was where different unit styles came into play. The artillery wants
women in two-women teams because searching people takes two soldiers—one to search, one to cover; on the other hand, the infantry
"spread-loads" the women so that if they lose one, they can still carry
out their mission.

I was extremely nervous. Whose fucking idea was it to go off
to a fucking war zone without a fucking weapon? But many of the
soldiers I rode with were equally nervous. We all had the dead men on
our minds. They were good Marines. Marines put into words the way
all the U.S. troops I saw behaved: "No better friend, no worse enemy,
do no harm." The enemy were not soldiers, but a mélange of foreign
jihadi, former regime elements, criminals, and poor people paid by
rich people with a vested interest in instability. They hid among civilians whom they tried to provoke Americans into killing. The classic tactic of the terrorist is to provoke the enemy into unnecessary or
misplaced violence, thus turning the local populace into sympathizers
with, or members of, the group that furnished the provocations. It was
critical to strike the right balance when raiding the suspected safe
house: hard and correct, not brutal. Nothing the United States was
willing to do could possibly match what Saddam Hussein would have
done, but there was no need to encourage the enemy by being soft, and
no need to make enemies needlessly by humiliating people.

I rehearsed with 1-5, and it occurred to someone that I didn't have
a weapon, at which point I was shifted back with Lieutenant Colonel
Cabrey. My door in the back of the armored Humvee refused to open

from the inside. I am a strong woman, but I couldn't budge the door latch. So part of the rehearsal involved him letting me out.

Specialist Key, Cabrey's driver, told me by way of explanation: "The colonel ripped his hand trying to get out once."

I stopped fighting the latch and eyed the radios between me and the front seat. There was enough room for me to crawl over them if I had to.

Cabrey must have seen me eyeing the radios, because he said, "I promise, if the door doesn't open, I'll pull you out over the radios."

Perfect, I thought. "I'll be pushing with my feet," I told him.

Other parts of the rehearsal involved troops being shot and evacuated to the rear. At one point, a man bearing a stretcher went down with such force, and made such noise, that I was sure he had broken his ankle. The medic, a small Hispanic man, very emphatically told the soldiers, "Do not re-wound my patients! If you drop them, it will only hurt them more. If they can't live for a few more seconds after they get to me, I can't save them."

The emphasis on overwhelming speed and force was Cabrey's. He didn't want to give whoever was in a given house any time to think about fighting back. His philosophy was, *If they don't fight back, you don't have to kill them.* By that time, he had mounted thirty such raids in which not a single soldier had fired a single round. That's not being lucky; that's being good.

After rehearsal, I spent a few hours catnapping, checking my watch, and napping again. It was a surprisingly easy sleep. At 3 AM I woke and dressed in the dark, then walked over to 1-5 with two Lionesses, Specialists Michele Perry, softly pretty and plump, a wife and a mother who was a fine soldier, and Rebecca Nava, a tiny Puerto Rican spitfire who did her best in tough situations.

The objective had been under continuous observation; Cabrey had learned that there was no one on the roof of the house, no cars parked before the gate. Good news. I hated being unarmed. And I wondered what was waiting for us in the house.

We went in hard, breaking down the gate. I jogged beside Cabrey to keep up as he headed to the front of his column of vehicles. The two most dangerous words in the English language? *Follow me!* The infantry motto. For this was pure dismounted infantry work, whether the soldiers were engineers or artillerists. I tucked up beside Perry and Nava against the home's courtyard wall, which we hoped would provide cover if the mission went bad, and tried to keep my feet out of the sewer.

The clearing team went in and came back out with seven Iraqi men, including two who were neither related to, nor close friends of, the family. They were cuffed, blindfolded, and told to keep silent. The team made them kneel against the courtyard wall, and I watched as they handled them more gently than the GIs had handled each other during the practice. Only a few hours ago, four Marines had been killed. And yet I watched American troops submit themselves willingly to a rigorous discipline, maintained by self-respect, self-interest, and not a little empathy for those who have lived through the unimaginable. They did not act out of fear of punishment.

There were also women and children in the house: the mother, two of her daughters-in-law, and what looked to be a granddaughter and two babies. One of the babies was left up in his room, which upset the women terribly. A male soldier brought the child down as fast as he possibly could, calling for a Lioness; Perry grabbed the child and immediately handed him to his mother. It was this presence of women and children that made the unrelated males of fighting age in the house such a warning sign. It would be in any culture, but in Iraq, where women and children are segregated from the male world, it was deeply unnerving.

I was very careful to stay out of the GIs' fields of fire, to let them know when I was entering a room, to be no more than a room away from them at any given time (and I was almost always close enough to touch a GI), to let them know when I was using a flash to take photographs. The one time I didn't, I thought to myself while the dazzle faded from my eyes, *So this is how reporters get shot* . . . At least I remembered to stay off the roof. Unlike the soldiers, I had no glint tape on my shirt or helmet cover, and we had guardian angels overhead: the U.S. Air Force. I didn't know whether they were cleared to fire, and I didn't care to find out.

I came down the stairs from the second story of the house, and Cabrey's interpreter, an American citizen who took a pay cut to come to Iraq because he thought the U.S. military was Iraq's best hope for civilization, asked me to accompany him. He returned a purse to the woman of the house; I was there to witness that he'd stolen nothing.

There were several $100 bills in it, and the older woman seemed more worried about it than the children. Her daughter kept saying, across the interpreter's questioning, "We're women, we don't know anything." The interpreter asked the younger woman to let the older one answer for herself, but she refused. The Lionesses promptly offered their interpretation of what was going on. They thought the Iraqi women were trying to cover for the men.

As the conversation with the interpreter continued, we learned that the first car in the driveway, the deepest in, had supposedly been driven up from Baghdad that day, but it was coated with dust, and the women couldn't find the keys. That made no sense. We found a little cash and some gold jewelry, which were returned, and only one chrome-plated pistol, though most houses had at least one automatic rifle per adult, or at least per adult male. There was also an address book with Syrian phone numbers in it.

We were home by breakfast, and afterward I talked with the brigade S-1, Major Thomas Trazcyk, a powerfully built infantryman a little taller than me, very freckled, and like Lieutenant Colonel Cabrey, a man whose longing for his family was stamped all over him. Our conversation ranged from how the Army likes to develop its infantry officers (light infantry first, so they develop the physical and interpersonal skills before they have to deal with the tactical speed and logistical complications of mechanized infantry) to casualties and retention. Then I suddenly recalled that he was, indeed, an infantryman. "It must feel strange that there are women who have more combat time than you do."

He gave me a wry smile. "It does!"

I never learned what happened to those Iraqi and Syrian detainees. They were handed over to the brigade's intelligence shop for further interrogation at Camp Junction City, perhaps to be released, perhaps to be sent to the prison at Abu Ghraib, a step that wasn't taken lightly, because it risked the lives of American troops to transport them there. I had no interest in the fate of these men beyond having extremely strong feelings that if they were indeed insurgents, they ought to face execution, as the Geneva Conventions had permitted before 1979.

The 1949 Geneva Conventions defined legitimate combatants quite broadly. Legitimate combatants included the members of the armed forces of a "party to a conflict," as well as members of a militia, a volunteer corps, and even unorganized civilians spontaneously taking up arms to resist an imminent invasion of their country. Such combatants did not even have to profess allegiance to a government or authority recognized by the enemy party to the conflict. However, these combatants had to abide by the following conditions: They had to be part of a responsible chain of command (a condition that did not apply to civilians spontaneously trying to defend their hearths and homes); They were required to wear some kind of distinctive sign, such as a uniform, or even an armband, that would be recognizable at a distance; They had to conduct their operations in accordance with the laws and customs of civilized warfare; Finally, and perhaps most importantly, they had to bear their arms openly. Those who did not adhere to these rules were subject, after fair trial, to execution. A hard rule made by hard men who had lived through both World Wars. However sympathetic they might have been to people's right to resist, they also knew that combatants who disappeared into the civilian population after trying to kill soldiers placed those civilians at risk. Sooner or later, those soldiers would have their revenge, no matter what the cost to civilians. This is what makes counterinsurgency warfare the most morally corrosive of all forms of warfare. ("Civilized warfare" is not a meaningless phrase.)

By contrast, Protocol 1 (Protocol Additional to the Geneva Conventions of 12 August 1949, and relating to the Protection of Victims of International Armed Conflicts), adopted in 1977 and entered into force in 1979, removed key protections from civilians. By making reference to colonial domination, alien occupation, and racist regimes, Protocol 1 politicized a document that ought to have been universal. It grants to *some* participants to a conflict the extensive rights of prisoners of war *because of their sympathies and causes*, not their organization and conduct. Article 44 requires *any* combatant who falls into enemy hands to be treated as a prisoner of war. Combatants are still obliged to comply with the rules of international law, although no violation of international law suffices to strip a combatant of his right to be a combatant, and to be treated as a prisoner of war. And combatants who jeopardize civilians by hiding amongst them forfeit their right to *be* prisoners of war, but

must be treated *as* prisoners of war. Finally, Protocol 1 plac
of avoiding collateral damage on the attacker, even though the
generally chooses what civilians and civilian objects to endangeɪ
he disposes his forces for battle. This leads to such moral lunacʏ ᴐ
blaming the attackers for striking a hospital that is used for combatant
purposes, such as an anti-aircraft installation.

Protocol 1 was meant to level the battlefield between regular forces,
particularly those of the United States, and terrorists or freedom fighters. In practice, by eroding the consequences for barbarous behavior,
Protocol 1 not only jeopardized the combatants of nations that attempt
to wage war in a civilized manner, but all non-combatants. The United
States is absolutely correct to refuse such illegitimate combatants as
members of al-Qaeda and Iraqi and Afghan insurgents, and to treat such
detainees as prisoners of war or domestic criminals. However, this is
an interim measure. For our own sake, America needs a solution that
will permanently resolve the status of these detainees. Clemency is a
grace not only for those prisoners who deserve it, but also for the jailer
who may reasonably grant it. It would be enough for me that prisoners not be beheaded, as had happened to Daniel Pearl, the *Wall Street
Journal* reporter, in 2002; Nicholas Berg, the tragically benign American businessman, in 2004; and, as we would wake the next morning to
learn, a South Korean translator and would-be missionary, Kim Sun-il,
after his captors forced him to beg for his life. Men who had done their
share of killing in combat spoke to me of their absolute horror at these
beheadings. Beheading someone is physically difficult because you
have to hack through the vertebrae before you can sever the spinal cord,
and while it's one thing to kill someone, it's something else entirely to
kill them that slowly and painfully. But there was a deeper meaning,
a more chilling meaning, other than the obvious symbolism of taking

someone's head as a trophy, or even the pleasure of slowly killing a prisoner. *Halal* and *kashrut* (Muslim and Jewish religiously correct) slaughter call for the cutting of the animal's throat—the jugular vein and carotid artery even more than the windpipe—with a razor-sharp knife. Done well, as an act of piety, halal or kashrut slaughter is a humane death. The throat is not a nerve-rich area, and the immediate loss of vast quantities of blood means that the animal goes into shock probably before it can feel the cut, and is dead within less than a minute. When you see the heads of cattle or goats laid out at a shop to advertise the meat available, you can be sure the animals were killed by being quickly bled to death first. The insurgent use of beheadings without such a merciful preliminary was a clear statement that their prisoners were not even animals to be slaughtered, to whom they had the religious obligation of granting a humane death.

And that's how my time at Camp Junction City went. The small change of soldiering. Patrols and raids, always wondering when you're going to get hit. Straight-up infantry work, military operations in urban terrain. Women medics patrolling with combat units, women second in the stack not only for knock and greets, but for full-up raids. Doing it with less training and indoctrination than the men they were working with—which is a matter of real concern—and doing far better than anyone ever expected.

Cabrey offered his own opinion on the subject of women in combat in an article for the *Marine Corps Times*. "I don't think this is a door-opening experiment, what we've done here," Cabrey told the reporter. "It can't be used as the only case study for women in combat, but it is an interesting chapter."[2]

WOMEN IN THE LINE OF FIRE

I didn't follow up with him on that opinion, because he was ri
There is a tradition, far from universal, but widespread across time
place, of women successfully engaging in combat. They fight, and often
extremely well, but they do so very rarely as line troops. The tradition,
also common across time and place, has been that women fight only in
desperate situations, and as soon as the desperate moment passes, they
leave the front line, and even the military altogether. While the American experiment of using women as regular combat troops is proving that
their involvement is far from a military catastrophe, and in fact adds to
combat capability—more on this later—you make wholesale and immediate changes to such an entrenched tradition only at great peril.

The instinctive refusal of many older men to accept that servicewomen are engaged in combat, are in fact doing infantry work, and so
should be treated as infantry has its own perils. Upon returning home
to the United States in October 2004, I published an article based on my
experiences with the Lionesses entitled "Lionesses of Iraq" in the *Seattle
Weekly*. To my knowledge, it was the first in-depth treatment anywhere
on the growing participation of women in all-male combat units. A male
military-historian acquaintance of mine dismissed my work with the
comment that these were "touching stories that emphasize the common
sense involved in using women in a civil affairs capacity in dealing with
foreign civilian women." It surely did not go beyond that, he wrote. As a
former infantry officer, he should have known better, but if he was waiting for a mass casualty incident to convince him that missions like the
knock and greets and raids I went on were combat missions, he'd get it.

In Fallujah on 24 June 2005, a suicide bomber who had loaded
his car with propane tanks deliberately targeted female Marines. The
Marines were searching women and girls in an effort to reduce tensions
and to keep the insurgents from using women as mules for packing

arms, ammunition, explosives, and documents. Six Marines were killed and thirteen wounded; three of the dead and eleven of the wounded were women.[3]

These women were high-value assets, and as such, high-value targets. They should have been treated as such, or even just as regular line infantry. Instead, the Marine Corps had sent them out in an open-backed cargo truck with steel plating that came up only to their shoulders. Their security element consisted of two Humvees with mounted machine guns; a third Humvee that should have been there had been detailed to another security team. Worst of all, they had to commute back and forth, at about the same times, on the same routes, on a daily basis between their camp and the checkpoints where they searched Iraqi women. James Glanz and John F. Burns of The *New York Times* wrote, "Male marines also worked at the checkpoints, but did not have to face the dangers of the daily commute. They slept at a Marine Corps outpost in downtown Fallujah, but Marine Corps rules barred the women from sharing that space with the men."[4]

The First Brigade's Lionesses are an anecdote in politico-military history. But the plural of anecdote is data. I needed more.

Upon my return to the States, Philip picked me up at Ronald Reagan Washington National Airport and followed me with a certain bemusement as I tried to lead him through the parking garage to the car he had parked. It finally penetrated my stupor that I had no idea where I was going. A month in Iraq, plus a 12,000-mile flight, plus Reagan National's oft-expanded incomprehensibility, will do that to you, especially after you've gotten used to being assertive enough to get done what needed to be done.

In the following months, I got engaged, discovered that a lot of people would no longer talk to me, quit my job, sold my house, moved to Mercer Island, Washington, and kept getting lost until I accepted that it really does matter in which direction you get on Interstate 90. I attended my first-ever high school football game and saw Phillip's son Jonathan play, came away with a chilled and rain-soaked new appreciation for cheerleaders, fell in love with Seattle, shopped majorly, went through a couple more agents, and started preparing to go to Afghanistan. The National Guard public affairs apparatus once again demonstrated its ability to turn friends into enemies. Later, I would file a complaint, still unanswered, with the National Guard Bureau in Washington, DC. But for the moment, I had a far greater crisis. I lost my knife.

This was serious. Actually, I hadn't lost it, just misplaced it somewhere in our condo. I searched. No luck. I searched again. My knife resolutely refused to be found. With only a few days before packing out again, I decided to purchase another. Philip and I headed for Bellevue Square, the local upscale mall, and its overpriced cutlery store. Jonathan tagged along, his fear that his friends might see him on a Saturday night in the company of two people old enough to be his parents (one of whom was) not outweighed by the pleasure of flaunting his football letterman's jacket on an archrival's turf.

We entered the store. A clerk and I began discussing the merits of various brands and forms of fighting knives. Jonathan and Philip headed for the door. Emerging some time later with two new blades, I smiled at Jonathan. "Girls and their toys."

"Only girl I know who plays with knives," he muttered with a shrug.

It may have been a compliment. Then again, maybe not. I discovered my missing knife in a closet ten months later, proving anew that old adage: You'll find it in the last place you look.

Chapter 4

Afghanistan and the Tragedy of Biology

In February 2005, I returned to the Middle East, this time in transit to Afghanistan. On 3 February 2005, a Kam Air flight from Herat to Kabul went missing in a snowstorm shortly before it was to land at Kabul International Airport. Twelve hours later, the Afghan National Army found the wreckage in mountainous terrain northwest of Kabul. Word was that Kam Air used Russian pilots who didn't know the terrain as well as Afghan pilots. But instrument flying—relying on your instruments rather than on what is in front of you—is the most difficult and demanding, flat-out dangerous thing a pilot has to learn. And if your control surfaces ice over, your ability as an instrument-rated pilot is almost meaningless. No one knew what that aircraft was doing taking off in such weather. It was the worst aviation disaster in Afghan history. All of the 104 people aboard were lost.

I was in Paris the day the Kam Air flight went down; I flew into Dubai several days later, very early on the morning of 6 February. There

I learned that Kabul Airport was still closed, and when it remained closed well into the afternoon, it became apparent that there would be no flights into Kabul until at least the following morning. (Kabul Airport does not like to handle nighttime landings because it doesn't have ground control radar, and without it, pilots don't like nighttime landings, either—with good reason, passengers on some of those nighttime landings told me.)

I was stuck, but not entirely without options. Like most minimally prudent travelers, I'd made certain that I had either a visa or transit rights for any country I transited through. Dubai, in the United Arab Emirates, grants Americans transit rights, and I found a reasonably priced room at the Quality Inn Horizon in Dubai's hotel district.

I could not claim my luggage at Dubai International Airport, as it was checked through to Kabul. So all I had were the clothes I was wearing and a carry-on containing my electronics. My helmet, body armor, and knives were packed, of course. When I finally flew out of Dubai two days later, I would have to mount an extensive search in the baggage storage areas of both Terminal 1 and Terminal 2 to make certain the bags were transferred for the Kabul leg of my trip, which was mercifully aboard Ariana, Afghanistan's national airline, flown by Afghans.

At the Quality Inn, the desk clerk wanted to keep my passport. Exhausted but polite, I told him no. "But the government says we must inform them of our guests," he insisted. "It's for your safety."

So that's why employers steal their employees' passports. Holding employees' passports is an endemic practice all over the Middle East. Without them, an employee disgruntled by mistreatment or nonpayment of wages can neither go to another country for work nor return to his or her home country.

"You can copy it," I said. He agreed that that was quite acceptable, and promptly did so. There was another minor discussion about me taking my drink up to my hotel room when I ordered brandy at the bar, but as a single woman I had no intention of drinking alone in that hotel— no matter how cosmopolitan and modernizing Dubai is said to be. I think the bartender reached the same conclusion, because I was allowed to take my brandy up to my room, where I showered and washed my clothes and made some calls to let people know I was alive.

The Middle East, to repeat a point that few Americans like to hear, is one vast slave market. Arab slavers were crucial to the Atlantic slave trade for centuries, and it has never really died out in the region, nor in the parts of Africa where the Arabs have established a strong presence. It's not comforting to know, especially when you're on their turf, and when you have no arms with which to exact the full and proper price for your life: the lives of those who would deprive you of yours, or of your liberty. But despite my uneasiness at being unarmed, the brandy did its job and I slept.

I was back at Dubai International the next morning by six. This time, I was at Terminal 2. Terminal 1 is Dubai's gateway to the developed world, Terminal 2 its gateway to everywhere else. Both terminals were full of people coming back from the hajj, the pilgrimage to Mecca that every devout Muslim should make once in his or her lifetime. Terminal 2 was also full of people trying to get to Kabul. Expatriate Afghans, UN and NGO types, contractors, and myself.

Among those who were clearly not UN or NGO employees were two men about whom I had an indefinable good feeling. I suspected, because it wasn't obvious, that they were in good, hard shape. Not only did they have "American" written all over them; they might as well have had "U.S. Army" stamped on their foreheads. They were, as it turned out, retired, though, and now working as contractors for a private military corporation with an excellent tactical and ethical reputation.

I hadn't planned to spend this kind of time in Dubai, so I introduced myself and asked if I might hang out with them, even though I was a journalist.

Sam and Will[1] were quick to respond yes. Whatever our differences might be, we were Americans together in an uncertain part of the world. So we got rooms in the hotel they had stayed in the night before, and again our passports were taken from us. Sam and Will were content to leave their passports with the front desk. I told them I'd catch up with them, and waited for the desk clerk to return my passport to me after he'd copied it. When he returned it, he gave me theirs as well. When I turned their passports over to them, it was a rather nasty surprise. They asked me how I'd gotten them. "The desk clerk gave them to me." I let them draw their own conclusions about who else their passports might have been given to, and the wisdom of allowing them out of their custody any more than absolutely necessary.

After dropping our bags in our respective rooms, we wandered down the street to the local Starbucks (yes, there is Starbucks in Dubai), where we talked over coffee. They told me everything they could about Afghanistan, and I did the same for them about Iraq. We also talked about our families. They were both married, still to their first wives, a rarity in the military and contracting communities, with their reality of lengthy separations. Both had daughters, Sam's hoping to be able to follow her father into the infantry, then into Special Forces. After coffee, like good Americans, we decided to wander through the local mall. We spent time in the bookstore, curious about what the Emirates were reading, at least in Dubai, popping our heads up over the racks at regular intervals to account for each other. I regretfully did not buy a large, lavishly illustrated book about Arabian horses, simply because I didn't know where I was going to put it.

As we continued along, Sam was particularly struck by the fabric stores. There were easily half a dozen in that mall alone, displaying bolt after bolt of sheer cloth and lavish lace, gorgeously dyed, intricately embroidered, glittering with sequins and metallic thread. Equally stunning were the jewelry stores, with their wide collars of gold and platinum, gems and pearls. But these fabrics and jewels were a glaring reminder of the stark contrast between such beautiful textiles and what the women in the streets actually wore. Although we saw a good many women in Western attire, many, if not most, of the local women were dressed in the traditional manner of head-to-toe black *abayas* and *hijabs* or *yashmaks*. Later, strolling after dinner, we were horrified to see women whose veils covered even their eyes.

The dichotomy between public and private lives was stark. Only the idle rich can afford such a dual existence. But it also hinted at a strict segregation of men and women, a belief that men and women have only sex and reproduction in common, even when their lives belie that dogma. Sam, Will, and I, on the other hand, assumed we had an entire universe in common, and that we could share that universe without compromising their relationships with their wives or my relationship with Philip. When I mentioned what I was thinking about to my new friends, Will told me that if the locals had known the nature of our relationship, they would have thought the three of us were crazy.

There was nothing to keep us from shacking up, after all. There is a saying about journalists—perhaps only among journalists—"Wheels up, rings off." In the military, for many decades, it was WESTPAC rules:

What happens in the WESTern PACific stays in WESTPAC, a slogan now co-opted by the city of Las Vegas. In a foreign land, particularly in a culture where women are too often blamed, and sometimes murdered, for being raped, the normal laws and customs do not apply. There was nothing, save for their own character, values, and sense of the world, to keep Sam and Will from raping me.

But that was not what an American woman who was raised among American men would expect to be the outcome of asking to tag along with two strangers. Quite simply, we had other interests and other priorities than sex. There were things we wanted to be, to ourselves and to our loved ones. Dalliance and violence would harm those things. We treated each other kindly and respectfully; we even taught each other something. I thought about the utter absence of force between us. None was required for us to treat each other as human beings. We needed only the notion of a woman's full human worth, based on the fact that men and women are not separate species, to oppress and be oppressed. And then I compared the gentleness that governed our dealings with the extreme level of violence that the Muslim world uses to segregate men and women.

If you think this segregation is merely custom, consider the possibilities for an average Arab girl to learn to read, to be adequately educated, to choose work she finds interesting without the need for anyone's permission, to marry the man she chooses (not to mention the freedom to explore *anything* that might fall outside of a traditional heterosexual marriage), to be free of the fear of her husband divorcing her simply by saying so. Consider how much danger she may be in for spending time with unrelated males. Her chastity will always be questioned; at a minimum her reputation as a "good," marriageable woman will suffer; she may even be killed. Honor killings are widespread throughout the Arab world, and while sometimes the male offender is also killed, if only one person is killed, it *will* be the female. Nor are these honor killings always instigated by men. Sometimes they are instigated by women who cannot bear the thought that another woman, perhaps especially their daughters, should live a freer life than they do, should suffer less than they have.

The next day, en route to Kabul, I flew alongside two American de-mining specialists, Bill and Matt, and a young Afghan woman named Roxane.[2] A nervous flier under the very best of circumstances, I was scared out of my mind. The only thing that kept me from having a full-blown panic attack was sheer embarrassment. The de-miners coped better. They were drunk. Fairly drunk, as near as I could tell, but also polite and neat. There was nothing uncivil or even sloppy about them. Buffered by the alcohol, they jollied Roxane and me through the landing. We came in over the mountains that ring Kabul, and descended very steeply and quickly into a fast, smooth landing that elicited cheers from everyone aboard the plane.

Roxane helped ease us through immigration, including getting us past a young guard who beckoned to Bill and insisted on smelling his bottle of Pepsi and rum. Bill asked if he was going to be taken out and flogged, but Roxane spoke with the guard and then told us no, he would help us through. The guard made a face, then looked at the aircraft and handed the Pepsi and rum back to Bill with a shrug, as if to say, *No wonder that's what it takes . . .* Roxane was met by her family and the immigration agent waved the drunken de-miners through more quickly than he might have without an upstanding young Afghan woman vouching for them. As for me, I was supposed to check in with Captain Mike

Eckart, and his deputy, Sergeant First Class Darren Heusel, the public affairs officer at the Coalition Joint Civil-Military Operations Task Force (CJCMOTF), known as Kabul Compound, in the heart of that city. Both men were serving in the Army National Guard, and seemed to regard Afghanistan, their jobs, and my existence as personal affronts. They informed me that if they were to meet me, a lone woman, at the airport, they would have to meet every journalist. So their email instructions were clear: "Just take a taxi . . . "

When I mentioned this to Bill and Matt, they were horrified. The de-miners and their Afghan driver/translator/executive assistant thought that taking a taxi was an invitation to disaster for any Westerner, but particularly for a woman traveling alone. The Taliban receive little support from the average Afghan, who is more likely to consider them tools of Pakistan; when I was there, the consensus seemed to be that if we wanted to invade Pakistan, the Afghans would be happy to help because they had real scores to settle about the Taliban—but the airport is a target-rich environment for any Taliban supporter.

On the theory that it takes a lot to scare a de-miner, I accepted their offer of alternative transportation. They and their male Afghan coworker took me to Kabul Compound and waited to make certain that there was a bed for me. If there hadn't been, they had offered to either put me up in their team house and then take me up to Bagram Airfield, my immediate destination, with them the next day, or take me to a hotel. Captain Eckart and Sergeant Heusel, who now added mendacity to their repertoire of sullen apathy and state-of-the-art laziness, told me that they had no place to put me and to please just go back out into Kabul and find a hotel room until they called for me. Their devious plot failed when my airman (the most junior of Air Force enlisted ranks) escort offered me her own bed and Eckart/Heusel suddenly

112

remembered that they did, actually, have a room with four em

When I reported back to the de-miners, still waiting for me ᴜᴜ their battered workaday SUV, they handed me their card. "We'll come get you if you need us!"

In fact, I did visit Bill and Matt at Bagram, where I met their boss, a South African named Mike. Mike, who had the very interesting résumé of many white South Africans who have served in that poor country's defense forces, was equally forthcoming and considerate. I would later spend the better part of a day in Mike's quarters, talking with him about many things, including de-mining and his de-mining dogs, whom he liked and trusted and thought of as full-fledged teammates even though he had never liked dogs before, and the evolution of the South African defense forces after apartheid. Woven in through these many things was a considerable amount of information about the incredible level of sexual violence in South Africa. Because of my awareness of the extreme disparity between my own situation and those of my female Afghan counterparts, I had many moments when I reflected on the fact that anything could have happened to me with these de-miners—American, Afghan, and South African alike. But nothing did—nor, as far as I could tell, did even the thought of anything inappropriate cross their minds. Even when Bill and Matt were very drunk.

My experiences with these and many other situations lead me to believe that the subordination of women to men, and the threat of social ostracism for men who do not subordinate "their" women, cannot possibly be natural to our species. Imposing male dominance and female subordination requires a broad application of violence and social control backed by the threat of violence not only against the vast majority of women, but also against those men who are inclined to treat women as human beings. You have to brutalize people, men

omen alike, to get men to treat women as animals, whether as
ute labor or as pampered pets, and to force women to accept that
treatment. In stark contrast, you can maintain equality between the
sexes also by applying violence and social control, but only against
those men who actively want to subordinate women. And if you apply
that violence and social control rigorously and evenly, you will soon
find you have fewer criminals to deal with.

———————— ⊕ ————————

I spent most of my time in Afghanistan with the Parwan and Ghazni Provincial Reconstruction Teams (PRTs), located at Bagram Airfield and
Ghazni Forward Operating Base (FOB), respectively, which fall under
the Army's Civil Affairs branch. Civil Affairs units are almost entirely
reserve units, so they can draw upon the enormous breadth and depth of
experience available in the civilian world. The branch also has a curious
history. The Army's extensive experience with Civil Affairs grew out of
its occupation of Germany and Japan after World War II; Civil Affairs
was an essential part of military government. As the occupations ended,
this capability was transferred to the reserves, on the presumption that
they would be needed after World War III to govern the Soviet Union.
Not particularly realistic, but over time, and especially after Vietnam,
these officer-heavy units became convenient holding pens for majors
and colonels awaiting retirement, and for politically significant reserv-
ists who weren't much good for anything else. A sinecure, really. Then,
beginning with the Balkan commitments under President Bill Clinton,
these units morphed into some of the finest outfits in the Army reserve,
and have done some of the best work in Iraq and Afghanistan. Indeed,
their importance was recognized when they were placed under the operational control of the U.S. Special Operations Command (SOCOM); the

reserve component civil affairs units, which are in fact the bu branch, recently left SOCOM.

There's only one problem: Women are barred from bein for and assigned to actual special operations units, such as the Army's Special Forces and the Navy's SEALs (although untrained women have been attached to them for actual operations). However, there are women in Civil Affairs, there have been for ages, and no one demurs. Additionally, PRTs have force protection provided by small infantry units, generally platoon size. At the time I was in Afghanistan, Ghazni and Parwan PRTs drew their force protection from the Iowa National Guard. A shortage of qualified men meant that a female communications soldier had to be deployed with each infantry platoon. They did not stay in the rear with the gear, even though, if there is one place American servicewomen aren't supposed to be, it's up front with the infantry platoons.

First Lieutenant Raul Gonzalez, a burly infantryman, commanded the force protection team for Parwan PRT, based out of Bagram Airfield. (He and his troops would kindly drive me from Bagram to the Mustafa Hotel in downtown Kabul when I left Afghanistan.) Gonzalez's troops were also drawn from 1-168 Infantry Battalion of the Iowa National Guard. One of his soldiers was a female communicator, Specialist Hatch, who exercised a time-honored tradition of women everywhere in her attempt to "fit in" in a male-dominated organization. She swore more than all her male comrades combined. Although they gave the distinct impression of not caring for her profanity, they also didn't regard her as "easy" or "loose." After watching the way they treated other female soldiers, I got the impression that the only thing the men expected of women was for them to be good soldiers. If they were, they fit in.

And indeed, one of the most comforting things I had ever heard in my life was Specialist Hatch's voice coming over the radio net into our Bradley one February day: "All weapons, lock and load," followed by the machine gunner chambering a round into his weapon over my head. (Another comforting sound was a .50 caliber machine gun being test-fired right over my head as I was setting out on a convoy.) We were leaving Bagram for Surobi, a village where the path to the girls' school had been mined. It was a long drive through such brutal terrain that I almost felt sorry for the Soviet conscripts who had fought and died there in what is called the Soviet War, the Soviet invasion and occupation of Afghanistan. Almost, but not quite, for I knew that perhaps a million Afghans had died in that war.

Hatch's presence with an infantry platoon was not an aberration. While I was at Bagram, I interviewed two U.S. Army military police (MPs), Sergeants Smith and Jones.[3] In contrast to the military's "party line" that women are not special operations troops per se, there are women who do special operations.

Smith and Jones normally worked customs at Bagram, and it took me a while to get them talking. Soldiers know how often the media embedded among them are looking for scandal or bad news, and how little benefit they'll derive from being "mentioned in dispatches." Why else would I be interested in them?

But I eventually got them talking about their experiences. They certainly hadn't wanted to think of themselves as exceptions. But they were.

Smith is an elegant black woman, nearly six feet tall and strongly built; Jones is white and a half foot shorter, also strongly built, a woman who would have been pretty under less grueling conditions. She wore her long blond hair back in a very tight bun. When you're married and away from your husband in an environment where there are at least seven men to every woman, too pretty isn't necessarily something you strive to be. In fact, pretty was something an awful lot of women— single or married—didn't seem to want to be. I didn't see much makeup on display, even though it's sold at the Base Exchange. In fact, a little pink lipstick or nail polish, even on someone who worked in an office environment, stood out.

You might have called Smith and Jones sisters-in-arms. They were the two go-to women in their MP company any time the combat arms servicemen needed women to interact with Afghan women. Whether Army infantry or Special Forces, Marine infantry, or Navy SEALs, the men who called on them preferred to work with women Army MPs, who are used extensively for light infantry missions. In fact, anyone who goes into the Army's MPs for a law enforcement career, as Smith had, will probably be disappointed. They will more than likely find themselves working as infantry, which can be very disconcerting to people who thought they had to join the infantry to be infantry. But so many women otherwise inclined have joined the MP branch looking for infantry work that the MPs have been nicknamed "chick infantry," although the MPs are proud to tell you that you have to score higher to get into their branch than into the infantry.

After several false starts, I broke the ice with Smith and Jones when I said that in some Arab cultures, women who fulfilled certain expectations were regarded as honorary men. Did they find that true for themselves as well? Perhaps because the term "honorary men" also fit so many American stereotypes of female soldiers, Smith turned to Jones and asked, "Are you an honorary man?" and they both started giggling.

Smith, visibly more comfortable with me than Jones was, gave her impressions about interacting with the Afghans, both the military and police, as well as civilians. "When I first started going outside the wire on missions, the Afghans stared. They weren't used to seeing female soldiers, but once they started working with us, they didn't treat us differently. I don't think they saw me as an honorary man, but they did do what we wanted them to do. When I first started pulling security at the Friday bazaars, and I'd say, 'Move back a bit,' the Afghans would look at me like I was crazy. But that may be simply because the Afghans didn't think they were too close, rather than because I was a female."

Jones added, "I think Afghan females are shocked that American females are treated with respect, because they're not. And of course, one of the reasons American females are treated with respect [in the military] is because we go through the same training as the males."

Jones's comment was a vast oversimplification: Infantry-oriented basic training sets a standard for many male soldiers (and even more so for male Marines) that it does not for female soldiers or Marines, and that specialized MP training certainly does not for female soldiers. This is why, back in the 1990s, many thoughtful men, not just social conservatives, were so distressed by integrated basic training for combat support and service support male soldiers, as well as all Air Force and Navy recruits. (Combat arms soldiers are, by definition, all male; but Marines of both sexes have always attended segregated basic training.) But I certainly was not going to correct Sergeant Jones! And of course, male soldiers working in an attached capacity who had proven themselves as these women had would probably have been encouraged to apply for selection into Special Forces, but such invitations weren't forthcoming for these women. (In fact, civilian males with no military experience may apply right off the street for the qualification process into special operations units.)

"At first the Afghans thought I was a man," Smith tol￼ women would cry when I was going to search them, so I le￼ off my helmet and show them my hair and face." Afghan wom￼ ally do not show their faces to men outside their families; a common saying is that a woman's place is in the home or the grave, and women can be murdered, much less beaten, by their husbands even for visiting their birth families without permission. The women you see shopping on the streets are out because they're *allowed* to be out. Considering that women can be murdered by their families for being raped, it's no wonder that it's more frightening for them to be searched by a man than by a woman. Not to mention that in their cultural and religious traditions it is unimaginably humiliating for a woman to be searched by a man, no matter how respectful he is of her dignity. In the beginning, out of respect for that intense fear and humiliation, American men did not search Afghan women. As soon as the Afghan men learned that, they started hiding documents, explosives, and ammunition on the women. Hence the need for American women to search the Afghan women.

"I think you have to understand and respect this culture, the people, and their religion," Smith said. "Once the females saw I was a female, they'd stop crying and let me search them. We had a Turkish interpreter, a female, and she'd tell the Afghan females, 'These women have come, like the men, all the way from America to free you. But they also came specifically to search you, so you wouldn't have to be searched by men.' We never heard anything negative from these women: They always thanked us, not only for being there to search them, but also for being brave enough to be here."

I asked about the troops they worked with. Sergeant Smith told me that the Marines she'd worked with were pretty squared away. "They've been here nearly a year, so, you know, they know what to do. It's a little unnerving when you're joining an inexperienced infantry unit and tell-ing them how to do things."

I savored a little the image of these women, barred by law from serving in the infantry, telling Marine grunts how to do their work.

Smith continued, "When I first got here, it was, 'Oh, we're going to do a mission'; it was, 'Let's go, let's go.' But now, we're due to leave here in the first week of April and while we'll do what we need to, we want to make it home." She was describing a trajectory, from eager ignorance to cautious experience, that male combat soldiers also learn.

Sergeant Jones spoke again. "I enlisted after 9/11, and expected I would deploy. And while I'm willing to do missions, if you ask me, I'll say I don't want to. I'm willing to die for my country, but I'm not willing to jump in front of a bullet. And to me, that's what volunteering for a mission means.

"I've had some bad experiences in the past, where missions did not go the way they should have. We have gone into hostile villages, and they knew we were coming, they were there and waiting for us. We took fire but weren't allowed to return it because we didn't know who was shooting at us. They were throwing stones at us—not little rocks, but stones that were breaking the heavy armored glass of our vehicles. But we couldn't fire back then, and those very restrictive ROE [rules of engagement] do make a difference in your confidence levels."

Both Smith and Jones had worked with female soldiers whose military jobs were essentially office work, and found those women to be utterly unprepared for missions. They didn't know how to search; they weren't physically hardened to bear the weight of their equipment or mentally prepared for the austere living conditions. It was a real physi-cal strain for these women, and a mental strain for Smith and Jones, who had to be even more concerned for these women than they were for the inexperienced infantrymen, who at least had been trained for the work they were doing.

Smith and Jones had trained with the units they were attached to before they went out with them on missions, which not only boosted the confidence of the men, but also boosted *their* confidence in the men. Smith clarified exactly what that meant, destroying any lingering notions that she was a glorified baby sitter rather than a combat soldier. "When we go out with SF [Special Forces], they cross-train us on weapons: .50 cals [heavy machine guns firing a bullet half an inch in diameter] and C-4 [a military explosive]. They taught us how to use their radios [which would enable the women to call for fire support, a basic skill for military professionals, but one which women are typically not taught because it is combat-related]; and when our medic treated an Afghan with a gunshot wound, or someone who'd blown off his foot stepping on a mine, he showed us what he was doing and why. All that helped me feel safe with the guys I went out with. They're very competent, especially the SF, who are familiar with the language and the terrain. This is their second tour in this area. With the Marines, it's, 'Let's go, let's go.'"

Sergeant Jones laughed and elaborated on Sergeant Smith's description of the Marines. "The Marines are like little kids who need Ritalin." She paused, smiled again, and clarified, "The young ones, who are on their first combat tour."

I asked them about living conditions when they went out on these missions. "When I went out on a month-and-a-half-long mission with the SF, we were living out of the back of a truck," Sergeant Smith told me. "You could put your sleeping bag on a cot, but most people simply used a mat and a bag. Latrines were, 'I'll be behind this rock or this bush, watch your step.' I was wearing Afghan men's clothes for days near Tora Bora, just observing. We lived together, did everything together. But with the Marines, we live separately and they're very careful; they call me 'ma'am.' When they do that, I grab my collar: 'Do you see these? They're sergeant's stripes!'" In the language of the old Army, "Don't call her ma'am; she works for a living."

Sergeant Jones elaborated. "When I did a monthlong mission with NAVSOF [Navy Special Operations Forces], I shared a tent with them. It's much better. You lose privacy, but you gain so much more. You're closer, you're more cohesive, it's easier."

I asked them both, "Would you do this work if you could?" Meaning, *Would you transfer into the infantry or apply for the selection process into special operations units?*

"No," Jones told me. "Well, actually, my husband is a medic assigned to an infantry battalion. If it meant being assigned to his company—yes. But not otherwise."

Smith didn't hesitate. "Yes. One of the guys asked me, 'If you could, would you apply to go through the [Special Forces] qualification course?' And I said yes. I mean, I don't know if I could pass it, but I'd like to at least be able to try for Special Forces."

I sat there, absorbing what these women—Smith, who liked to do combat missions, and Jones, who considered volunteering for them suicidal—had told me. All they had to do to get out of doing hard, dangerous work for which they would not be recognized was do a little less than their absolute best. The standard of Special Forces and SEALs is to be your best. That doesn't mean that you have to have an exceptional physique. Most of the men don't. The last thing you want is for the locals to look at you and think, *Didn't we see you in that Jean-Claude Van Damme movie we bought at the bazaar?* The men are, however, mentally exceptional. Their training has taught them

what their bodies can do if their minds will it, and their physic
ties reflect that mental discipline.

I struggled to hide my anger at the repercussions of what the
responses meant. That Jones, who had given difficult service in some
of the most appalling terrain on the planet, should have been taught to
have so little confidence in her abilities, or that Smith should be denied
the formal opportunity to do the work she had already done informally,
got under my skin.

Jones must have read my face. "There are people who simply
don't understand what we do, don't recognize what we do." These
women had been all over Afghanistan, most often in Nangarhar Province, but there had been times when they hadn't known where they
were going. They'd just climbed onto a helicopter or into a truck or
Humvee, weapons locked and loaded, ready to deal with whatever
and whomever they encountered, wherever they needed to be, to kill
if necessary. "It's totally different from even the MPs who patrol outside the gate on a daily basis. They're just outside the gate. Let alone
sitting at a desk doing paperwork—paperwork is necessary, but it is
not what we do."

I looked at Jones. A small woman, especially sitting there next to
Smith. Not trained, not hardened, not physically developed the way the
men were. As a woman, she wasn't allowed to be trained and hardened
like men who had gone through Special Forces or Navy SEALs, or even
just Marine infantry training. But there she was, working alongside
them, doing combat work she thought was suicidal because her pride
and professionalism wouldn't allow her not to do it.

Jones was good enough to do the brutally demanding work of
long-range missions in Afghanistan to some of the highest standards
in the military, but not good enough to be recognized for it. Not only

would it be contrary to policy to do so, but it messed with too many of the self-perceptions of the men. Perhaps, even more than the men they were serving alongside, women like Jones messed with the self-perceptions of the men they were *not* serving alongside, those whose self-image depended on being thought of as sharing the risk of combat without actually serving in a combat specialty.

A reasonable woman would quit, would simply do less than her best. What could her commander do? Court-martial her for being unwilling to do what the law forbade her to do? But Jones was as reasonable as Smith: She wanted a career in the Army because she loved it. Both of these women, very different from each other, had embraced the profession of arms as their own.

These are not isolated instances. Almost every soldier, male and female, I've talked to has stories of women being where they "shouldn't be," doing things they "shouldn't do." In war, one can generally get leave to do more than one must, even if one is a woman. And as the strain on the U.S. military grows, there will be more and more women with more and more experience of combat, particularly of dismounted infantry combat in cities and special operations in rural areas. This is in addition to the combat women face as MPs used as light infantry, in civil affairs units, on convoys and small bases subject to incessant (if often inept) mortar attacks and infiltration attempts, and in taking their turn at pulling guard or security duty.

President Bush was not (and is not) about to make it clear to the American public what these women were doing (and will continue to do). He was not about to keep faith with them as soldiers, much less as the combat soldiers they are, and he was sending a clear signal to the cultural and religious right that it was open season on female combat troops. At the same time, the senior leadership of the Army and Marine Corps saw little gain and great loss in pushing this issue, even though these women had given them more raw combat power than they ever expected. Many of these men have done astonishing things, but their record on the issue of servicewomen is, to put it charitably, not so admirable.

 ⊕

Leaving Afghanistan, I stayed at the Mustafa Hotel in Kabul, across the street from Shah Mohammad Rais's bookstore, made famous by Asne Seierstad in *The Bookseller of Kabul,* a book that makes clear just how much violence is required to subjugate women. I had my luggage with me, and plenty of space for books. Unfortunately, it was a Friday, the Muslim holy day, so I could not go book-buying. I could, however, go shopping in the bazaar.

In wealthy, developed, cosmopolitan Kuwait City, I wouldn't leave my hotel room. In poor, isolated Kabul, with its primitive construction and buildings powered by their own generators, I tucked a knife into my belt, pinned my hair up with my hairstick, and went shopping on Chicken Street, just down the block. Like every other street, road, or track I saw in Afghanistan, it was both primitive and relatively clean. (In Iraq, trash as far as the eye could see was the usual roadside attraction.) When a man stared me down, I gave him the evil eye right back, my knife warm and comforting against my ribs, my body tautly prepared for violence. Whatever he was thinking, he passed on his way in peace, although at frequent intervals I looked for him or anyone else who might pose a problem.

I bought lapis and shawls and wooden boxes finely painted in the Persian manner, coins from the Soviet era, and a war rug commemorating Afghan victories over both the Soviets and the Taliban. The United States contributed to the former and brought about the latter, but without Afghan courage and strength and endurance, U.S. aid would have been useless, and liberation pointless. These were gifts for my grantor and editors, for Philip, and for Jonathan, who was finishing four years as the smallest offensive lineman in his high school football league. I passed, foolishly, on some beautiful peachy pink tourmalines, and bought instead a lapis necklace for myself.

As I wandered down Chicken Street, there was not a single woman vendor in sight. Nor, as far as I could tell, was there a single Afghan woman shopping. All the Western women wore head scarves, which I refuse to wear as a point of honor. For a woman to cover her head is a sign of submission. Though some women argued with me that it was a matter of cultural understanding, I wondered if they would ever ask American women to do as Paul says in the Bible and cover their heads as a sign of submission to their men and to their god. Americans do not expect Muslim women *not* to wear head scarves in the United States, after all; if a woman wishes to keep her face covered at all times, except for identification purposes, that should be no one's choice but hers. Cultural sensitivity is all well and good, so long as it doesn't become a matter of degrading yourself or others. By the same token, when you draw the line between respect and self-abasement, you need to know what your self-respect will cost you and be prepared to pay the price.

I was also the only American alone on those streets. Even the male GIs walked in pairs. I made a point of making casual contact with them—"Hi, how are you?"—and I made certain that I knew where they were at all times.

I searched for a horse bridle, but had to settle for a pair of bits, an iron curb bit decorated with brass lion heads, and a straight brass Liverpool driving bit. By their size, they looked to have been copied from British originals. Afghan horses are, in the old language of horsemen, clearly blooded. They have a high percentage of Arabian, Barb, or, very rarely, Akhal-Teke ancestry, and are thus quite small and elegantly built.

After dinner at a small, private house serving traditional and delicious (if very rich) Afghan food, where, again, no Afghan women were in evidence, I returned to my hotel. In the bar over a glass of wine, I wrote up my notes until the generator cut out. I was the only woman there, a newcomer, and I was utterly ignored by the male contractors. I have come to regard being ignored that way as the male courtesy of simply assuming that you're there for a drink and a bit of relaxation after work and that you'll appreciate being intruded upon about as much as they will.

In my experience, this is not something Arabs, or many Central Asian Muslims, understand. The male Iraqi and Afghan interpreters whom I talked with both told me separately, in long conversations, how astonished they were by the contrast between our coarse, commercialized, ever more pornographic popular culture and the surprising chastity of the men and women who passively tolerated such entertainment. These interpreters told me that it was not just Afghan and Iraqi girls who are expected to be virgins when they marry, although the consequences for a girl who is not a virgin when she marries (especially if the man she is marrying is not the man who had her maidenhead) are often fatal. A boy with a bad reputation is extremely hard up to find a partner in marriage, if he is not already disowned and ostracized by his father. The interpreters I spoke with did get it when I told them that I thought that the more men and women were allowed to socialize and work together—to be friends—the less likely we were to reduce our sheer human need for each other to sex. But then the pornographicization—a word I just made up—of our popular culture made even less sense to them. They could not understand why people who liked

as much as American men and women seem to could tolerate
nt made for people who viewed "women as animals," as one
l me.

--------------------- ✛ ---------------------

Back in my room with my second glass of wine, I pondered the significance of these two types of relationships that exist between the sexes.
The exterior and hall walls of my room were floor-to-ceiling windows
hung with curtains for both privacy and warmth. The exterior window
faced one of Kabul's hillside residential neighborhoods, the homes built
directly into the hill. I opened the drapes and watched the few cars pass
by on the street and the lighted homes on the hill above me.

Why, I wondered, if equality between men and women is easier to
enforce than dominance and submission, do so many women worldwide
live under conditions of enormous inequality, degradation, and violence? If equality is the state of nature between men and women—and
my experiences as a single, visibly unarmed American woman among
so many armed male American troops, with the odd Iraqi, Afghan,
and South African thrown in, have convinced me it is—why is pervasive, profoundly violent inequality the norm in so much of the world?
In the Middle East and Africa, that violent inequality is so extreme it
has crippled the development of those cultures. Why is the law, with
its formal written precepts of equality and justice, reserved for men,
whereas women are expected to be content with the prejudices and cru-
elties of culture and custom? Why is it so hard for the U.S. Army's
institutional leadership, the product of very different cultural attitudes
toward women, to apply the idea of equality to servicewomen, which, in
contrast, they demanded be applied to black and Jewish men?

I needed an explanation that would transcend time and place.

128

Almost every culture I know of has imposed to a greater or lesser degree legal, social, and economic disabilities upon women that go far beyond a flexible and practical division of labor based upon human physiology. Those cultures that do not impose such disabilities are very much the exception that prove the rule. Some of these disabilities, such as corseting, or far worse, foot-binding, are sadistic. The widespread taboo of women bearing and using arms to deadly effect renders women profoundly vulnerable to those who would take advantage of their generally shorter stature and slighter build. To call a man a woman is almost universally an insult, and there are a great many insults derived from the phrase "to have sexual intercourse with," insults that go far beyond the idea of intercourse being something men do to women.

I examined many possible explanations for this state of inequality, including the generally smaller size of most women as compared to most men, and pregnancy per se, as well as the widespread need for many children to help with family, clan, and chores. None of them were adequate. Edged weapons, which require muscle strength to wield effectively, can be a great equalizer between men and women. But this is not the historical or cultural norm.

Even the much-touted male promiscuity is an inadequate explanation for male dominance and female subordination. Given humans' long gestation period, risks associated with pregnancy, and the need of young humans for prolonged care, an individual man's reproductive success would ultimately be maximized by mating with one woman and helping her raise their children to adulthood within the institution of marriage. On a social basis, polygamy ensures not only that any individual man will have a harder time caring for his young, but that men as a group will be reproductively disadvantaged.

Eventually, I settled on maternal mortality as the root explanation women's low social status. It transcended time and place, and for ually all of human history, it was inherent in both women's biology and reproductive sex.

I knew from my work as a graduate student with The National Society of The Colonial Dames of America that maternal mortality had been widespread in colonial America. Indeed, I talked to older women who knew women who had died or nearly died in childbirth, and who had had their own near misses. And although very few Dames were feminists, their reception of my suggestion that maternal mortality might be the root explanation for male supremacy was very positive. These usually older, often socially conservative, women gave such a warm reception to my idea that maternal mortality was the electrified "third rail" of male-female relationships that I was encouraged to pursue the theme. When I came back from Iraq, the Dames wanted to know what I thought about women in combat. I floated the idea that the nearly universal exemption, not to say exclusion, of women from combat service was an attempt to balance risk for risk. Without exception, the Dames agreed that my reasoning made emotional, intellectual, and moral sense. So I took with me to Afghanistan the seed of an idea that the root cause of male dominance and female subordination lay in high rates of maternal mortality.

According to the CIA *World Factbook,* which I accessed online in February 2005 from Bagram Air Field, the average Afghan woman has 6.78 children, while Afghanistan's birth rate is 47.27 per 1,000 people. I kept those figures with me in my head. So when a nurse in the Salang District Clinic in Parwan Province told me that she currently sees one or two maternal deaths per 100 births, I knew the women whose deliveries she attended ran an average lifetime risk of dying to deliver live children that was between 6.78% and 13.56%. Elsewhere in the same district, it was considerably worse. Just before I left Afghanistan, I joined soldiers of the Parwan PRT, based at Bagram Air Field, in a trip to the district of Shekh Ali, also in Parwan Province. Shekh Ali was sixty miles of mostly narrow, twisting, muddy road up the Ghorban river valley from Bagram. There, the elders said their first need was for a clinic: "One hundred to two hundred of our ladies die every year in childbirth," they told us. I asked them how many children they had and what the district population was. They said the district had about 70,000 people, and that while men normally had only one wife, fifteen or sixteen children was the norm. From the CIA's birthrate figures of 47.27 births per 1,000 people, I was able to calculate a range of 100 and 200 maternal deaths per 3,309 live births per year. That translated to a woman's risk of dying in childbirth in Shekh Ali as falling between 3.02% and 6.04%. Fifteen children times a 3% risk of dying in childbirth per birth equals a 45% lifetime risk; 15 children times a 6% risk equals a 91% lifetime risk. A virtual certainty.[4]

I started to ask the elders, "Do you mean one wife at a time?" and bit my tongue, for I did not dare ask, "How many wives does it take to produce that many children?"

It's often said that one death is a tragedy, but a million deaths is a statistic. Perhaps. But there is a way of putting these statistics into a perspective Americans can grasp. A U.S. Army infantryman in World War II stood a better chance of survival than an Afghan woman does in childbirth today.

And so it was that, driving back to Bagram from Shekh Ali later that February day along the Ghorban Road, I spent four hours passing the wreckage of the Soviet War, unintended memorials silently screaming, *This happened here.* I looked at the women and their daughters, working in the fields, very differently coming out than I had going in. For I was beginning to understand that to be female in Afghanistan is to live under sentence of death, and the shame and honor killings began to make a certain kind of tragic sense when logic is deranged by such extreme grief and guilt.

Afghanistan is an incredibly poor country. The terrain is rugged beyond belief; travel even within a village, or from local farm to local farm, can be difficult. Winters can be very harsh, especially at Afghanistan's elevations. I'd heard of people freezing to death trying to cross from one taxi to another at the crest of a mountain pass. Clan and family peace must be kept at all costs. So when sexual activity threatens the cohesiveness of a clan or tribe existing on the margins of a hostile world, it is the woman who pays the highest price. Why not? She will likely die in childbirth anyway. Her death warrant was signed at birth; it is only being executed a little early. And the obscene tragedy of it all is that such an attitude, necessary as it might be and shared by quite a few women, the world over, only makes things worse. The more violent and cruel male supremacy is, the more women must acquiesce under it. It is easy to put down a man who is merely patronizing or contemptuous. It is easy, too, for men to defend themselves against other men. It is not so easy, however, despite the great differences across cultures in how women are viewed and treated, for women to defend themselves against violent and cruel men. And it's not merely a matter of being told you are inferior, although that does damage enough. It is also the legacy of death in childbirth, and the knowledge that perhaps your own mother died bearing you, or bearing your brother or sister, and perhaps worst of all knowing that they loved and were loved by their husbands.

———————— $\oplus$ ————————

Upon my return to the United States, I would make an effort to quantify, on a provincial and national basis, the anecdotal reports of maternal mortality I had heard in Afghanistan. The World Health Organization's study *Maternal Mortality in 2000* reported that, as a region, the Middle East and North Africa combined have the world's third-highest risk of maternal mortality. (As a region, all of Africa south of the Sahara has the world's highest risk of maternal mortality, about a 6.25% lifetime risk; South Asia has the world's second-highest regional risk of maternal mortality, with a lifetime risk of 2.43%.) The mythical average Middle Eastern or North African woman has a 1% lifetime risk of dying in childbirth. Since some women never bear children, a mother's actual risk is somewhat higher, without even accounting for a variety of social and economic factors that can grotesquely elevate her risk above that baseline. At that time, Afghanistan, as a single country, was estimated to have the world's second-highest lifetime risk of maternal mortality, 16.6%, which, again, given the existence of women who never bear children, means that the rate is higher for actual mothers. By contrast, *Maternal Mortality in 2000* cited the U.S. maternal mortality rate as 17 per 100,000 live births.[5] In fact, since 1996, the American maternal death rate has remained stable at 7.5 per 100,000 live births, while according to the 2006 CIA *World Factbook*, American women average 2.09 births. In 2006, the average American woman runs a .0157% chance of dying in childbirth. In other words, about one out of every 6,396 American women dies in childbirth, compared to 33 out of every 200 Afghan women.

The lower end of the estimated maternal mortality rates in Shekh Ali is not, by the standards of Afghanistan, particularly high. The upper end of 200 women a year dying per 3,300 live births, or 6,060 per 100,000 live births, is. After my return to the United States, I learned that Badakhshan Province, in Afghanistan's mountainous northeast province, has 6,500 maternal deaths per 100,000 live births, the highest maternal death rate recorded in the world.[6]

Since Afghanistan lost both its infrastructure and the knowledge to operate and maintain that infrastructure during two decades of war, first with the Soviets, then with the Taliban, Badakhshan Province's maternal mortality rates are probably close to the historic norm for the human species. Those rates are the context of modern Middle Eastern women's lives.

I then began to research historical American maternal mortality, because Americans across the political spectrum consistently oppose motherhood to military service. There is a deeply rooted, very powerful belief that women are not supposed to be risked in war because most women either have or will have children. Antifeminists consider women's contribution to the common defense to be raising strong sons for military service, and some feminists believe that motherhood gives women special moral insights. To quote one old soldier I won't name, "Just as one buck can service many does, one man can service many women." (A very old man, this soldier also told me that while such proclamations once drew agreement from men and provoked women to fury, now both men and women he shared this little tidbit with looked at him as if he was from another world. In many ways, of course, he is.)

At the other end of the moral spectrum, people struggle to understand why the death of PFC Lori Piestewa, PFC Lynch's buddy from the 507th Maintenance Company, in Iraqi captivity (whether of her wounds and injuries or of torture, in which case she should be understood to have died in combat) was acceptable. She was a mother, and, most emotionally, the single mother of young children. I wondered if the maternal mortality rates in American women were high enough to account for the very strong emotional reaction many people have against women serving in combat. They were.

Table 4.1

AVERAGE AMERICAN WOMAN'S LIFETIME RISK
OF MATERNAL MORTALITY AND MATERNAL LOSSES,
1915–1960[7]

Year	Maternal Deaths per 100,000 Live Births	Risks per Live Birth	Fertility Rate	Children Born to the Average Woman 15-44	Risk of Maternal Mortality	Children Born	Maternal Deaths
1960	37.1	0.04%	118.0	3.54	0.14%	42.57	1580
1959	37.4	0.04%	119.9	3.60	0.14%	42.86	1603
1958	37.6	0.04%	120.0	3.60	0.14%	42.46	1596
1957	41.0	0.04%	122.7	3.68	0.15%	43.0	1763
1956	40.9	0.04%	121.0	3.63	0.15%	42.1	1722
1955	47.0	0.05%	118.3	3.55	0.18%	40.97	1926
1954	52.4	0.05%	117.9	3.54	0.18%	40.71	2133
1953	61.1	0.06%	115.0	3.45	0.21%	39.59	2419
1952	67.8	0.07%	113.8	3.41	0.24%	39.09	2650
1951	75.0	0.08%	111.4	3.34	0.24%	38.2	2865
1950	83.3	0.08%	106.2	3.19	0.25%	36.32	3026
1949	90.3	0.09%	107.1	3.21	0.29%	36.49	3295
1948	116.6	0.12%	107.3	3.22	0.39%	36.37	4241
1947	134.5	0.13%	113.3	3.40	0.44%	38.17	5134
1946	156.7	0.16%	101.9	3.06	0.49%	34.11	5345
1945	207.2	0.21%	85.9	2.58	0.54%	28.58	5922
1944	227.9	0.23%	88.8	2.66	0.61%	29.39	6698
1943	245.2	0.25%	94.3	2.83	0.71%	31.04	7611
1942	258.7	0.26%	91.5	2.75	0.71%	29.89	7733
1941	316.5	0.32%	83.4	2.50	0.80%	27.03	8555
1940	376.0	0.38%	79.9	2.40	0.91%	25.59	9622
1939	493.9	0.49%	77.6	2.33	1.14%	24.66	12180

(continued on next page)

Year	Maternal Deaths per 100,000 Live Births	Risks per Live Birth	Fertility Rate	Children Born to the Average Woman 15-44	Risk of Maternal Mortality	Children Born	Maternal Deaths
1938	493.9	0.49%	79.1	2.37	1.16%	24.96	12328
1937	493.9	0.49%	77.1	2.31	1.13%	24.13	11918
1936	493.9	0.49%	75.8	2.27	1.11%	23.55	11631
1935	493.9	0.49%	77.2	2.32	1.13%	23.77	11740
1934	636.0	0.64%	78.5	2.36	1.51%	23.96	15239
1933	636.0	0.64%	76.3	2.29	1.46%	23.07	14673
1932	636.0	0.64%	81.7	2.45	1.57%	24.4	15518
1931	636.0	0.64%	84.6	2.54	1.62%	25.06	15938
1930	636.0	0.64%	89.2	2.68	1.71%	26.18	16650
1929	668.6	0.67%	89.3	2.68	1.79%	25.82	17263
1928	668.6	0.67%	93.8	2.81	1.89%	26.74	17878
1927	668.6	0.67%	99.8	2.99	2.01%	28.02	18734
1926	668.6	0.67%	102.6	3.08	2.06%	28.39	18982
1925	668.6	0.67%	106.6	3.20	2.14%	29.09	19450
1924	689.5	0.69%	110.9	3.33	2.30%	29.79	20540
1923	689.5	0.69%	110.5	3.32	2.29%	29.1	20064
1922	689.5	0.69%	111.2	3.34	2.30%	28.82	19871
1921	689.5	0.69%	119.8	3.59	2.48%	30.55	21064
1920	689.5	0.69%	117.9	3.54	2.44%	29.5	20340
1919	727.9	0.73%	111.2	3.34	2.44%	27.4	19944
1918	727.9	0.73%	119.8	3.59	2.62%	29.48	21458
1917	727.9	0.73%	121.0	3.63	2.65%	29.44	21429
1916	727.9	0.73%	123.4	3.70	2.70%	29.64	21575
1915	727.9	0.73%	125.0	3.75	2.74%	29.65	21582

total deaths: 525429

In the United States, records of maternal deaths began to be kept in 1915. The year 1940 was the first year maternal mortality dropped below 1% in the lifetime of the mythical average American woman. It's not until 1960 that we saw a tapering off of childbearing by the older women who'd begun to have children under that sword, just as young women who did not grow up under it began to have children. The early 1960s saw the development of a revitalized feminist movement, and it was only in the early 1980s that we started to see young people entering military service who were born to parents whose lives were not shaped by the unconscious knowledge that the mother might die or be crippled in childbed, and that the father would be the sole support for the mother and the children.

Between 1915 and 1960, 525,429 American women died in childbirth. Figure an average of 21,000 maternal deaths per year from 1914 back to 1900 (according to the table above, a reasonable assumption), or a total of 315,000 deaths, and the death toll rises to 840,429 from 1900 to 1960. As shocking as this number is, it also underestimates women's total reproductive risk: Women who died miscarrying, during stillbirths, or due to complications during abortions, and women who were simply terribly injured during childbirth, are not included. I have not even attempted to estimate the women who died in the nineteenth or eighteenth or seventeenth centuries, when access to food, sanitation, and medical care were even more limited than they were in 1900. And due to the lack of reliable contraception, women bore far more children before 1860 than they did after the widespread use of vulcanized rubber in the manufacture of reliable condoms afterward.

I asked myself, *How do maternal deaths compare to American war deaths, both combat and noncombat, through the end of the*

Korean War? (Since the Vietnam War occurred after 1960, its casualties do not figure in this calculation.)

Table 4.2

DEATHS IN MAJOR AMERICAN WARS[8]

Major Wars	Battle Deaths	Total Deaths
Revolutionary War, 1775–1783	4435	4435
War of 1812, 1812–1815	2260	2260
U.S.-Mexico War, 1846–1848	1733	13283
Civil War, Union Forces, 1861–1865	140414	364511
Civil War, Confederate Forces	74524	133821
Spanish-American War, 1898	385	2446
WWI, 1917–1918	53402	116516
WWII, 1941–1946	291557	405399
Korean War, 1950–1953	33741	36574
Total	602451	1079245

The major American wars from the beginning of the Revolutionary War to the end of the Korean War in 1953 (thirty-four years of war in a span of 178 years) account for 602,451 battle deaths, which is just 71.6% of the maternal deaths that took only sixty-one years to accumulate. Account for nonbattle losses, which are usually combat-related, as well as battle losses, and those deaths total 1,079,245, 128.4% of actual and straightline projection of maternal mortality from 1900 to 1960. Now let's use 1940 as a baseline, the year when the average American woman began to run a lower lifetime risk for maternal mortality than the average Middle Eastern and North African woman did in 2000. Between 1900 and 1940, 762,613 American women died in childbirth, while between the Revolution and the end of World War I

(twenty-four years of war spanning 143 years), war lo:
637,272, a figure much lower than losses in childbirth. Ne:
American war losses, 41% of them, occurred during World \
Korea (after 1940), when all but the poorest and most fragil ˯men
stood an excellent chance of surviving childbirth.

The conclusion is inescapable. For most of American history, from the landings at Jamestown until deep into the twentieth century, childbirth was more dangerous than military service, even in the infantry. The very few years when military service, especially in the infantry, was more dangerous than childbirth are concentrated: the great losses of the Civil War that deranged the demographic balance; the shock of World War I, where for the first time battle deaths of most major powers exceeded nonbattle losses; the utter failure of European civilization during World War II. And it is the very shock of these hugely concentrated battle deaths that proves the point. They were an aberration. The steady bloodletting of more than ten thousand women who died each year in childbirth alone was the norm, for all of American history until 1940. And throughout much of the world today.

To a significant extent, the sociocultural meaning of maternal mortality obliterated women's individuality except at the most surface level of dress, hairstyle, and taste in domestic furnishings. American— world—history is filled with men who have survived combat to lead distinguished public lives, but vulnerability to combat and death in it was a function of politics, not biology, especially not reproductive biology. It was an aberration, whereas maternal mortality was a natural constant, natural for women to suffer and men to impose. No wonder so many men felt so strongly that it was their duty to protect women at the same time so many of them also believed deeply in the inferiority of women.

During World War II, Korea, and Vietnam, it was commonly believed that combat service was a duty American men owed to their wives, mothers, and daughters. That looks like an awful lot like a sustained cultural attempt to redeem a blood debt with blood.

You have to look long and hard to find women who survived not merely the tragedy of human reproductive biology but also the judgments it imposed upon female worth. Their brothers learned Greek and Latin and mathematics; they learned needlework. While their needlework was often an artistic achievement that shames even the finest art of the time, it was not the common tongue of scholarship. (And it's still not considered art.) Since these maternal deaths occurred year in and year out, in peace and in war, they must have stood like the very judgment of the gods against the equal human worth of women. As the Judeo-Christian god says: "I will greatly multiply thy pain and thy travail; in pain thou shalt bring forth children; and thy desire shall be to thy husband, and he shall rule over thee."[9]

For however strong women are muscularly or intellectually or emotionally, however great their physical or moral courage, until what was, in historical time, only an eyeblink ago, all women were (and are still in the developing world) in mortal danger through our sex as women, for having sex in the act of reproduction. That knowledge grew between men and women like a cancer, and it still lives in both sexes, despite the fact that the reasons for it have long since been forgotten.

I have delved into maternal mortality as deeply as I have because, while I do not respect the social conservatism that sniffs people's sheets and wants to turn the clock back to the 1950s, or even before the 1850s, I do respect people's powerful emotional reactions to the thought of young women and mothers, as opposed to young men and fathers, being killed and wounded in wars, especially as combatants rather than victims. I have spoken to far too many people who have felt these powerful reactions very sincerely to dismiss the legitimate moral concerns that arise in any discussion of women serving as combatants. As soon as it became clear that the war in Iraq, and, for that matter, Afghanistan, would drag on, I recognized that operational pressure would force the Army and the Marine Corps to relax combat restrictions in practice, if not in law. I knew that the Army and Marine Corps would see only the downsides in pressing for the end of the restrictions on women's combat service, shameful as it is not to, in part because of these deeply felt emotions, which are held by much of the American public. They are emotions that represent a moral balance, regardless of the fact that the balance is outdated. And outdated only very recently at that.

Before I arrived in Afghanistan, the political fight over the issue of women in combat was already brewing. On 11 January 2005, President Bush held an Oval Office press conference. There he announced that there would be "no women in combat" in Iraq or anywhere else. After his pronouncement, he quickly backtracked, noting that women had been serving on warships and combat flight crews for decades, and he was "comfortable" with that. What he would not authorize or condone was women in ground combat, specifically the infantry, artillery, and armor units of the Army and Marines, and the special operations forces of all the services. But of course, he refused to order women out of "illegal" combat and missions, because the military desperately needs them there. However, the press conference was meant to release authority to the Right to start flogging the issue of women in combat, while the president relied upon his allies to carry out his policies.

I don't know what President Bush saw in Iraq on his Thanksgiving

Day trip there in 2003 (or his March 2006 trip to Afghanistan, where he was on the ground for only four hours), or what he'd been told about what women have been doing in both countries for years now. But I do know that what I saw when I was there was less the photo-op scene set for the commander in chief and more of the daily grind that reflects the reality of the roles of women in wartime.

The war in Afghanistan is a different war than the one we're fighting in Iraq. Americans and Afghans are dying there at the hands of the Taliban, who are widely considered to be sponsored by Pakistan. There, combat operations matter, but they are merely a protective screen. Jeopardized by utterly inadequate funding, American service members have nevertheless concentrated on helping Afghans continue to raise the standards by which people live. These things, though influenced by foreign aid, are ultimately in the Afghans' hands.

U.S. servicewomen play an absolutely vital role in this effort. Without them, you cannot reach Afghan women, particularly to help reduce maternal mortality; and if you don't reach half a society, your efforts go less than half as far.

As for Iraq, it is a sand pit into which the United States has poured not only the blood and pain of many good troops, but so much money that it will affect this country's financial stability for decades to come, while straining the military to the breaking point. There's a bad joke making the rounds: The Iraq War is over; Iran won. Indeed, the real question is, did Iran, through agents like Ahmed Chalabi, help sucker the United States into doing what it couldn't during the Iran-Iraq War—destroy the Iraqi Army so Iran could install a theocratic or puppet government? For our invasion of Iraq has not caused an improvement in American security worth the cost, much less the redemption of a people who are being torn to rags by insurgents and separatists. And we certainly don't need

to repeat the experiment of trying to redeem and save peop
very different values than we do, and wouldn't want to be
saved by us even if they wanted the same things we did.

And yet, there is a real issue at the heart of the odd, violent confrontation between the West and Islamic fundamentalism. And that
issue is whether or not men and women will share the world as equals
under the law. That being so, there is a hard question to be asked. How
can American women in good conscience leave it to men to bear the
overwhelming burden of this nation's security? This is not an issue of
numbers and quotas per se. But if you accept the reality of the West's
confrontation with Islamic fundamentalism; the stake American women
have in helping create a world in which women are citizens; that the law
of equality rather than the custom of inferiority should govern our lives,
then the faces of the fallen on the *Washington Post*'s website should
shock your conscience. Nearly all of them are men.[10]

Chapter 5

Pretending
to Integrate
the Military

When the Army began to integrate women after the end of the draft in 1973, it began an experiment in profound bad faith. This was the pretense that female soldiers could be insulated from participation in combat due to enemy action. Combine that pretense with the formal exclusion of women from the combat arms units (had the combat arms been opened to women, most women, *like most men,* would not have opted for them) and you had a recipe for the second-class treatment of female soldiers. By the time the old Women's Army Corps (WAC) was dissolved in 1978, that experiment had become an exercise in self-serving institutional and human blindness. It is ending now, slowly, under the twin pressures of reality and experience. But it is not yet over.

From the birth of the WAC in 1942, women were generally required to be better educated than men in order to enter the military, and, once in it, to be far better behaved. This went far beyond lower tolerance for criminal assault or even drunken and disorderly conduct; it went to the almost pathologically prudish. Writes Colonel Bettie Morden in her history, *The Women's Army Corps, 1945–1978:*

> *WAC entry and retention standards came under examination in 1970. The commander of the Army Recruiting Command, Maj. Gen. Donald H. McGovern, wrote in May 1970, "The movement for more liberal moral standards and the rising emphasis toward equality of the sexes require that this command be prepared to answer an increasing number of questions and charges concerning the validity of allegations of discrimination against female applicants for enlistment." He asked the DCSPER [the Army's deputy chief of staff for personnel, then Lieutenant General Albert O. Connor] why waivers could not be considered for women who had illegitimate children or a record of venereal disease (VD) when these factors did not bar men from enlistment or even require submission of a waiver.*
>
> *The director of the WAC [then Brigadier General Elizabeth P. Hoisington] and the director of procurement and distribution, ODCSPER, Brig. Gen. Albert H. Smith, Jr., prepared the reply to General McGovern. Arguing that American society demanded higher moral character in women, they wrote, "Having a history of venereal disease or having had a pregnancy while unmarried is an indication of lack of discipline and maturity in a woman."*[1]

In theory, if a man acquired VD it was an offense regardless of circumstances. In practice, every commander distinguished (as they should) between the guy who got VD because, well, people do have sex and they don't always use protection, and the dirtbag who needs to visit the medic or corpsman every time he comes off liberty. (I've heard older, now retired male Marines describe their humiliation at being required to take penicillin before they went on liberty, on the assumption that they would have sex with prostitutes.) This sharp cultural distinction between treating male soldiers as individuals and female soldiers as representatives of their sex would follow women out of the WAC and into the larger Army.

Men were presumed to make good soldiers until they proved otherwise, something that has always been measured by their individual achievements and failures. Women, on the other hand, had to prove themselves as individuals and as a group. This was hard, since even after the WAC was disbanded, women were still regarded as convenient temporary help until recruiting picked up again. Their presence was deemed so disruptive that the Army even tried to determine what percentage of women could serve in a unit before they degraded that unit's performance. Common sense might have indicated that no firm number, or any number at all, could be assigned, but the mere fact that it was seriously studied inescapably led to the conclusion that women were inferior troops by nature.

It is a common and reasonable practice for units to test the new men who come in. Women, however, were routinely more harassed than they were tested. They endured everything from crude comments that turned walking past a barracks or eating in a mess hall into ordeals to rape via abuse of rank or pure physical force. Chronic harassment and worse were major factors in women's "get me out of here" pregnancies and decisions not to reenlist. Few men mourned. Men were, after all, the norm against which women were judged and usually (save for a few exceptional individuals who were often then dismissed as "dykes") found wanting. Women's differences, limitations, and needs were all deemed to be more than adequate reasons why they should not be in the service. Furthermore, women were deemed inferior because of their male-imposed exclusion from combat.

From the killing part, that is. Not the dying part. Though they were barred from forward and combat units, servicewomen were concentrated in headquarters and logistics depots that would have stood high on Soviet targeting lists all the way from 1973, the end of the draft, to the end of the cold war in November 1989. Women were given scant combat training, and they would have died wholesale as Warsaw Pact forces and Soviet Operational Maneuver Groups slashed through Europe. The Army knew this, but since nobody seriously believed that NATO could stanch an invasion without the first use of nuclear weapons, it didn't matter. During the late, or post-Vietnam, cold war, the Soviets pledged no first use of nuclear weapons in their courting of the Western European and American peace movements. What most peace activists missed was that the Soviets didn't *need* to use nuclear weapons. Conscription and the traditional precommunist Russian belief that great victories must be paid for by great loss of life meant that the Soviet army could afford the huge casualties inherent in any invasion of Western Europe. Still, imagine an officer saying, "We don't need to seriously train our men in Europe since they're all going to be charbroiled, anyway." Impossible. But that's what was happening.

Throughout the early years of experimenting with women as regular troops, a number of the United States' most distinguished generals and admirals vehemently opposed any serious integration of women into the military, for personal and moral reasons. It was their duty, as they saw it, to protect women as they would the nation, and they did not perceive women as capable of contributing to the common defense. Though I do not share this perspective, I have come to understand it. I realize that the unfortunate attitude of these generals and admirals was not entirely unreasonable given what human and American life was like for women until 1940.

As I mentioned earlier, during my grad school years I supported myself by working as the national secretary for the National Society of The Colonial Dames of America. The NSCDA is a genealogical society, even more exclusive than the better-known Daughters of the American Revolution (DAR). These women trace their roots back to the upper classes of the original thirteen colonies. I was responsible for entering new members into the national database by linking these women to their ancestors. This was my first exposure to the historical reality of widespread maternal mortality, something Americans now associate with underdeveloped nations. It was not always easy to verify lineage, since the ancestors (and many current members) followed the old way of naming. At marriage, Miss Mary Jones became Mrs. John Black. Should she be widowed, she retained her husband's name, but should she divorce, she became Mrs. Mary Black. Should she remarry, she became Mrs. Theobald Smyth.

Since very few women at that time could own property in their own right and name, much less businesses, or participate in the public life of the colony, virtually all of their recorded ancestors were male. Many of these men had two or three wives, and not because they were polygamists. The simple reason was that their previous wives had died. Over time, I became haunted by the names that were not there. Names of children were known from wills, family Bibles, or

leeds. But often all that survived of the mothers was a first
d for many, not even that.

y of the Dames of the NSCDA had grown up in a world
where the tragedy of reproductive biology was real. Quite a few of
the younger Dames I talked to knew women who had almost died;
quite a few of the older Dames I talked to knew women who hadn't
survived a pregnancy. This is the world into which the senior leadership that oversaw the integration of women into the Army was born,
as well. They, too, lost mothers, wives, sisters, and daughters, or knew
men who had. That reality imposed a binding moral obligation upon
men to protect women, though it too often devalued women into weak
and transient creatures rather than full human beings and equal citizens. Further, this protection was all too often contingent upon female
behavior. Good women were expected to stay within the roles pre-
scribed to them by their society, and breaches of sexual mores were
often more forgivable (or easily overlooked) than assertions of intellectual or professional capability and independence. Thus, the Army's
senior leadership unwittingly mandated the simultaneous protection
and disparagement of servicewomen. Their attitude set servicewomen
up for decades of disrespect, harassment, and outright abuse, with
all the attendant damage to military efficiency that that entailed. The
senior leadership was doing what had been done to women for generations—although it became increasingly antiquated in the post-Vietnam
civilian world, a world they regarded with a mixture of bewilderment
and disdain.

These were good men, many of them heroes of the United States'
hot and cold wars from the 1940s through the 1970s. But they were
limited, as are we all, by their own times and experiences. They made
the integration of women far harder than it had to be, sometimes at

WOMEN IN THE LINE OF FIRE

unbearable personal cost to those women. So perhaps the final judgment should be: good men, but they knew not what they did.

———————— ⊕ ————————

Once it became apparent that women were in the Army to stay, it should have also become apparent that there was a way to integrate women properly, effectively, and with due regard for personal and institutional sensitivities. The Army, an institution that values history, could have engaged in a bit of historical analysis and drawn a couple of obvious conclusions. Sadly, it did not.

It's not, as we have seen, that the United States had little experience with women in uniform, or even women in combat. Women had served, in uniform and out, as nurses (and more rarely as doctors), from the Revolutionary War through Vietnam. During World War II, a few Office of Strategic Services (OSS)—the forerunner of today's CIA and Army Special Forces—women served behind enemy lines in Nazi-occupied Europe, and in neutral countries where they were at great risk because they were within easy reach of the German intelligence services. And indeed, the entire history of U.S. westward expansion, from the initial landings on the eastern seaboard in the 1600s to the settlement of the Pacific Coast in the 1890s, speaks of women's ability to fight, often under arduous conditions, sometimes when pregnant or recovering from childbirth.

Compared to the men, women's numbers were small. But in the aggregate, they should have permanently silenced any doubts whatsoever about women's military value. Yet the best women could hope for in the early years of the All-Volunteer Force (AVF) was to be treated as noble aberrations . . . or as dykes. Even well into the early 1970s, the military was, and perceived itself to be, intrinsically and exclusively masculine. War was deemed the most manly of endeavors, not because women were not involved in war, but because most military men simply could not conceive of women as professional subordinates, much less equals, and especially not as superiors.

But if men were blind to women's military history, a history that was being aggressively expanded and updated during the post-Vietnam years, another military experience in integration was being played out at that time, one that offers today's historians a few useful parallels.

I mean the wartime experience of African Americans. Blacks also had a long, too often minimized, dismissed, or forgotten military history. In the aftermath of World War II, neither their accomplishments nor their demands, most of which came out of the growing postwar civil rights movement, could be ignored. Nor could the Army's ongoing need for black men, who, at least in the beginning, were deemed "substitute whites."

After victory in World War II, the Army did not bring entire units home and then disband them. GIs were released as individuals, based on how many "discharge points" they'd earned for time served, overseas duty, combat, wounds, dependents back home, and so on. As a group, black soldiers had fewer discharge points than whites. Further, they were reenlisting at higher rates because they feared returning to a civilian society that they believed, not incorrectly, would be hostile to them. Finally, it was also clear that the draft would soon come to an end. By 1946, the Army needed men desperately for occupation duty and for the demands of the nascent cold war.

But the Army was still segregated, and thus limited in the numbers of black troops it was willing and able to absorb. Many of these black veterans were poorly educated, and in ways that went far beyond limited formal schooling. Most of them had been born and raised in the former Confederacy, "where they had attended segregated sc[...] were limited occupationally largely to farm or menial labor, and li[...] their lives in a rigid culture which constantly emphasized and rein[...] forced their inferior status."[2] Others, products of northern urban ghettos, had grown up with their alleged inferiority drilled into them by a prejudiced society.

The military had to find a way to make use of these troops. In 1945, Lieutenant General Alvan C. Gillem Jr. was charged with formulating a policy for the postwar use of black soldiers. The Gillem Board was in the difficult position of finding short-term ways to reduce military discrimination without advocating permanent integration. Every single factor that the Gillem Board considered pointed toward integration, which neither military nor civilian America was ready to accept. However, the board recognized that black troops had given excellent combat service, and that black soldiers must be treated as individuals. The board may have been fettered, but it stood by two principles from which it did not flinch: Black Americans had a constitutional right to fight, and the Army was obligated to make the best use of every soldier.[3]

The solution, pursued by Lieutenant General Clarence R. Huebner, then deputy commander, later commander of U.S. Army troops in the European theater, was to institute a program of remedial military training and broad-based civilian education for black troops. This program not only raised the soldiers' scores on the Army General Classification Test by an average of twenty points, it also made a major, if unprovable, contribution to the discipline and performance of black troops in the European theater. "'If you're going to make soldiers out of people,' he later explained, 'they have the right to be trained.' Huebner had specialized in training in his Army career, had written several of

ʒ manuals, and possessed an abiding faith in the abil-
ʼange men." He liked to say, "'If your soldiers don't
'''4

ʌrd's two principles and Huebner's experiences,
ʋerved the Army well in integrating women. Constitutional
. aside, women clearly had every soldier's right to be trained. In their
case, the problem wasn't education, but physical capability. A remedial
physical education program could have been designed to dramatically
increase women's capability, but the military chose to ignore the possibility that, like supposed low intelligence in black soldiers, physical
weakness in female soldiers was culturally imposed rather than innate.

From this perspective came two assumptions: that gender was a
bigger obstacle to overcome than race, and that little if any meaningful
parallel could be drawn between blacks and women because, black or
white, men are men and women are not. Differences between the sexes
are perceived to be far deeper, more important, and more intractable
when it comes to aggression and strength than differences between the
races. Sex, in short, is perceived to be a behavioral determinant that
governs how people relate to each other in ways that race never can. Put
differently: People may be educated out of prejudice, but they can never
be educated to put aside gender differences, even when women prove
themselves competent and trustworthy.

Once again, biology is destiny.

A misguided conclusion.

While male or female status is biological, how the sexes relate to
each other is cultural. Sexual activity is only one part of the equation.
Yes, there are physical differences. But only some of these differences
are of possible military significance: women's generally smaller stature, yes, but more crucially their lower weight and higher levels of

154

body fat. In the 1970s, those physical differences were tho[u]
largely innate and definitive. Other differences are practic[a]
ingless, and many—extreme physical weakness, for instance
turally imposed. A society that wants weak women usually manages to
produce them.

But training and respecting women as soldiers hit a roadblock for
a deeper reason—something not often made explicit: the sometimes-
subtle, often-blatant societal oppression of women by men. In the pre-
1960s United States, relationships between the sexes were reaching a
boiling point when Betty Friedan came out with her book *The Feminine
Mystique,* which described the horrifyingly small and circumscribed
lives that even educated middle- and upper-class women were expected
to lead. (The lives of poor women and women of color were often even
more restricted.) Women found themselves in her pages and were suddenly able to define "The Problem That Has No Name." Friedan later
wrote and spoke of her husband's abuse, and many middle-class wives
could certainly relate to that, too. Violence and abuse existed, yes, but,
without minimizing their horrible effect on women, it's important to
note that they did not define women's relationships with men. Social,
often internalized oppression played an insidious and central role in the
lives of women, even those in whose lives violence and abuse played no
role. For too many men, however, who had made it their priority to support their wives and children, the restriction of women to the home did
not seem like oppression at all. Thus, as women's demand for equality
in the armed forces was on the rise, military men, recalling their own
ordeals, wondered why any sane woman would wish to subject herself
to such violence.

Among the many unexpected pleasures of researching and writing this book has been talking with the men of the generation who oversaw the initial integration of women into the military. One man stands out in particular. Although he was not part of the integration process, John Collins, now eighty-five, exemplifies the ambivalent attitudes of his generation toward servicewomen. He was born in 1921, a year in which nearly one American woman in forty died bearing a living child. Collins enlisted in the Army in May 1942, then served in Europe from Normandy to Vienna. After thirty years in the Army, including later wartime duty in Korea and Vietnam, he retired from the infantry in 1972 as a full colonel. He took a four-day weekend, then reported to the Congressional Research Service as the senior specialist in national defense, where he worked for another twenty-four years. Although he signs his emails "Geriatric John," he is taken seriously by all who read him. He's also been married to the same woman for "forever." "I'm of the older generation who has a different view of women than most people do today. I was taught to stand up for women when they entered the room, open the doors for them. I'm from a culture that disappeared a long time ago. It's almost analogous to John Collins being raised in a totally segregated society," he told me.

But Collins is also a man who assessed the Soviet women he saw in Vienna as the capable combat soldiers they were. He extends this respect to the current generation of American servicewomen. "When I look at these women with their machine guns on those Humvees, I think, *They're a better man than I am.* I admire them. That doesn't mean I don't wish they weren't there. [But] those are their lives, their decisions. I wouldn't try to stop them or dissuade them from doing something unless I thought it was really dumb. I do think the Army has made a big mistake, painting itself into a corner, being unable to function without

15% of its members being female. Everyone needs to be deployable, and especially with the kind of combat we're engaged in, where there are no front lines and no flanks. Everyone is subject to armed combat whether they like it or not."

For Collins, the issue is not capability, but a profound emotion that prevents him from accepting his sisters in the Army as combat soldiers no matter how much he respects them. "I like girls, let's put it this way, have liked them for eighty years now. Just the thought of women coming back from combat, either in body bags or mutilated, gives me the shudders. It's bad enough for men to come home like that, but for women, it just gives me the horrors. Because I love women. I can't think of a clearer explanation. I admire the women who are running the risks of combat. But it doesn't change my feelings."

This heartfelt combination of reflexive cultural hierarchy and profound and instinctive love was no doubt the prevailing sentiment of the Army's senior leadership through the 1970s. Still, the military resisted developing a long-range, comprehensive plan for the complete integration of women soldiers out of ingrained prejudice as much as willful ignorance. Did these men devalue women soldiers because they couldn't imagine seeing them coming home from wars in body bags? Did they refuse to train them because that would have constituted an admission of the danger in which *they* were placing women? Were they, in their own way, the military equivalent of the men I saw in Afghanistan, condemning their women to subservience and death in spite of, but also perhaps because of, their love?

Maybe. What is clear is that, out of a mixture of love and male supremacy, plus refusal to acknowledge the obvious risk female soldiers assumed in cold war Europe, the Army's senior leadership could not and did not plan for orderly, long-term, and complete integration of women. As John Collins says, "Integration kind of crept up on me. I never seriously considered combat roles for women until recently. The Army went a lot farther than I ever expected it to, and the end is not yet."

As the Vietnam War wound down and the draft sputtered out, good soldiers, men who might have made the military their lives, left in droves. And in disgust. Disgust over the war, disgust over what the war had done to the Army. Those who proved to be saving remnants were those few men who stayed or joined because they had a calling, and some bad men who joined because they thought the Army could help them become better. In the 1970s, these men did the hard salvage work and the necessary rethinking and retooling. Other lackluster men joined the forces for less than admirable reasons during the graceless early years of the All-Volunteer Force, when the Army's advertising slogan was TODAY'S ARMY WANTS TO JOIN YOU. I remember the photos of the authorized haircuts. Bushy Afros and full, drooping bangs were among the styles the Army permitted, styles that had previously been rejected. Discipline problems followed, endless as the ranks of a demoralized, underfunded, sometimes seemingly purposeless Army filled with those who drifted in, then along, then out. The 1981 Bill Murray movie *Stripes* may have been a fun comedy about a bunch of pre–Desert Storm misfits, slackers, and pussy hounds (traditional Army slang for men who can't keep their hands off women) hitting on female MPs.

But in the real Army, few were laughing. In 1980, President Reagan increased defense spending from $113.6 billion (in 1979, the last year of the Carter administration) to $130.9 billion; by 1984, defense spending was at $220.8 billion.[5] When this "bow wave" of spending hit the Pentagon in the early 1980s, the money was well spent on modernizing equipment from uniforms and rifles to the Bradley fighting vehicle, the Apache helicopter, and the Abrams tank, not to speak (

able ("stealth") technology, which the new generation of

well received. Ultimately, Desert Storm would be their vii

that was still more than a decade off.

———————— ⊕ ————————

An old adage of the civil rights movement held that in the North, white people didn't care how big you got, so long as you didn't get too close, while in the South, white people didn't care how close you got, so long as you didn't get too big.

Through the 1970s and into the 1980s, the Army wanted its women soldiers to be neither too close nor too big. Opening the combat arms to women—or even areas close to the traditional zone of deadly contact, then known as the forward edge of the battle area, or FEBA—was anathema. Women might be treated as equals for the purposes of whatever jobs the military allowed them to do. They might receive recognition and promotion within those parameters. Individual women might earn respect. But women were still far from being full soldiers.

The military focuses on combat. A man may choose a noncombat specialty and be respected as a soldier until he proves he's a bad one because it is expected he will serve as a combatant in a time of need. He's trained and indoctrinated accordingly, or at least he has the right to expect that he will be. But a person who is categorically excluded from combat, whether a male "nondeployable" or a woman, is a second-class member of the most hierarchical organization in the United States. Your legal rank may be worn on your collar or your sleeve, but your actual significance is determined by your branch and your ribbons. And if you hope to reach the top without membership in the combat club—don't even bother.

It's important to be clear about this. Some have derided the quest for full equality in simplistic terms—stating that women merely want to break a "glass ceiling," and that the reality is that few women *really* aspire to break it. In fact, naysayers argue, only a small percentage of men and women actively hope to run corporations, or armies for that matter. Many women, they argue, find extremely rewarding and fulfilling careers doing support work, both in the military and in the civilian world. And this is certainly true in both worlds. Yet the military is fundamentally different from the civilian world. Those who risk their lives and take the lives of others control and determine the future of the institution in ways that no civilian could ever control a business; those who do not, however necessary their skills, remain second-class. Yes, women have attained three-star status in the Army and other services, but they remain, at best, supporting actresses. So severe is this distinction between combat and support that Elaine Donnelly, ever on the alert for reasons to oppose women in combat, has complained that the Army keeps women in Iraq to provide career-enhancing opportunities for the daughters of the generals. An odd and inaccurate cavil, but evocative, to say the least. That such a charge could even be leveled at the Army's senior leadership at least bespeaks some major changes in attitudes.[6]

Then there are those who deride this equality under arms in terms of a woman's equal right to risk death and mutilation. In 2005, Lory Manning, a retired Navy captain with twenty-five years of service to her credit, was interviewed on national television by Tucker Carlson, an anchor who rarely appears without his bow tie and customary sneer. When Carlson referred to women serving in combat as "mutilation as a woman's right," Captain Manning tactfully suggested that he sign up. Carlson immediately terminated their chat. (Go Navy!)

Bow tie and sneer notwithstanding, Carlson missed the point

entirely. The military—the Army and the Marines especially—exist to fight. To be excluded from that core function is to be second-class. To be second-class because, and only because, one is a woman is to invite disrespect, no matter how well one performs one's job. To invite disrespect is to attract the attention of the lowlifes, the predators, the jerks. Even worse, to be second-class is to lead the good soldiers to believe, rightly or wrongly, that in a fight *they can't depend on you.* In the military, there is no worse opprobrium than being deemed someone who can't be trusted in combat. And while many women did prove they could be trusted during the late cold war, just as many men did come to trust them, this trust was always on an individual, not institutional, basis.

And yet, throughout the cold war, the Army knew female soldiers could be counted on to die, if not to fight. In his excellent 1986 book, *The Straw Giant,* Arthur T. Hadley Jr , a respected defense correspondent and decorated World War II tank officer, succinctly explained the consequences of concentrating women in noncombat specialties:

> *If the United States is forced to fight in Europe or elsewhere,*
> *such as the Middle East, death will be an equal opportunity*
> *employer. More female soldiers, sailors, and airmen will*
> *die in the first five minutes in any next war we are forced to*
> *fight than were killed in World War II, Korea, and Vietnam*
> *combined. In fact, since females are clustered in the high-*
> *priority targets, initially women will die all out of proportion*
> *to their numbers in the armed services.*[7]

Was this recognized by the military? Hadley's answer: "Over and over I hear from both high-ranking officers and civilian defense officials some such phrase as, 'Yes, we realize women will die in the next et at the same time, I find everyone hiding behind the rubric that are not in combat jobs."[8] Hadley's observation was prescient, yet no one was willing to admit the facts of war, let alone draw the appropriate conclusions.

To maintain this charade while continuing to assign women where they were needed, the Army played an intricate bureaucratic game, the lineal ancestor of the present pretense that women in Iraq and Afghanistan are not *assigned* to combat units, only *attached*.

Until 1988, the Army used the Direct Combat Probability Code as a guide to assigning women. Positions were coded P1 to P7—P1 having the highest probability of engaging in direct ground combat and P7 having the lowest.[9] Women could be assigned to positions coded P7 through P2, but not P1. All assignments forward of an infantry or armored brigade's rear boundary were coded P1, a technicality that meant more on paper than in reality.

Except for a battalion's infantry and tank system support teams, women could fill jobs in forward support battalions (FSBs), which did provide combat support services forward of the brigade's rear boundary. Those FSBs were created by an Army reorganization designed in part to evade the service's own rules prohibiting the assignment of women to P1 positions. Previously, separate battalions providing medical, maintenance, supply, and transportation services to combat arms battalions had been located behind the brigade's rear boundary. Outside the brigade. Under the Probability Code rating system, women could be assigned to those brigades. Reorganization meant that while some services remained outside the brigade's rear boundary, there were three FSBs *inside* it. On paper, it was a location change; in practice, it meant that women were closer to the possibility of combat.

And that was a contradiction, because all positions in those FSBs were coded as P1, in other words closed to women; but the positions themselves were held by women and there were no men to replace them. There was a solution, according to the General Accounting Office (GAO) report *Combat Exclusion Laws for Women in the Military*, arrived at "with strong support from field commanders." They simply changed the Probability Code, except for the tanks and infantry systems support teams, which were expected to continuously travel with those maneuver battalions and had a high likelihood of routinely engaging in direct combat. As an additional nod to reality, women were allowed to serve in positions that required them to "periodically" be forward of brigade rear, with no limit set on either how often or for how long they could do so.[10]

The curious language of the military bureaucracy, when they're caught doing something, always seems like an attempt to waffle out with the explanation: "Well, yes, but it isn't policy." Recently, we've seen this applied to prisoner abuse at Abu Ghraib and Guantanamo. Here, the Army was placing women ever closer to combat, but, except for a few minor administrative changes to the regulations and procedures here and there, it wasn't *really* happening, because it wasn't *policy*.

Of course, this didn't fool the troops. Jim Kurtz is a retired artillery officer who dropped out of college and traipsed all over Europe and India before requesting accelerated induction as a draftee. He entered the Army in 1966, served two tours in Vietnam, and topped out as a full colonel in 1998. Like John Collins, he has embarked on a successful second career as a very thoughtful defense analyst. Kurtz, who also did two tours in cold war Germany and one at a NATO headquarters in the Netherlands, recalls his sense of utter vulnerability to any Soviet attack. "We had NEO [noncombatant evacuation operations] plans and exercises, but I told my wife, 'Here's your NEO kit: vodka, black negligee,

Russian phrasebook.'" As for the vulnerability of women, he told me: "Position on the battlefield doesn't matter. It didn't matter then. [The combat exclusion] was language used to satisfy political requirements. We'd have women in intelligence, for example, and they'd take their vans very close [to what was in fact the front line of the inter-German border]. They had to." He was very candid about his thoughts on assigning female soldiers. "I'm not prepared to integrate all MOSs [military occupational specialties]; I am prepared to integrate all units. For example, I don't think women should be in the infantry, and I don't think they should be cannoneers. That's a line I draw. I guess it's a cognitive block."

As a bureaucracy, the Army was in no way as honest as Colonel Kurtz.

In February 1988, the Department of Defense abandoned the Probability Code and promulgated the risk rule in the hope of standardizing the rules for assigning, or excluding, women from units and missions. According to the risk rule, women were not supposed to serve if their risk of exposure to direct combat, hostile fire, or capture was equal to or greater than the risk of the men in the combat units they supported. There was some moral logic in the development of the risk rule, but not enough to override its fundamental failings. Every soldier, male or female, who faces the possibility of combat should be trained and prepared for it. This did not happen.

In our current war, for example, female soldiers drive fuel tankers all over Iraq. They are not, however, allowed to crew tanks. A fuel tanker is not a glamorous target, but it is a lucrative one, particularly if it is resupplying tanks or Bradley fighting vehicles. Since it lacks armor, it's far more vulnerable. And of course, if you're near one when it explodes, you stand a good chance of becoming a "secondary casualty."

The engineers, who are a combat arm but do not generally operate as fighting units per se, do frequently operate in advance of the combat troops to prepare the battlefield. Laying bridges for an opposed crossing is almost an exercise in suicide. Women serve as engineers, and in fact a disproportionate number of women serve as bridge crew members, too—one of the heaviest and dirtiest occupational specialties in the Army. They not only go into the specialty, they stay in it. In March 2003, some of these women would have helped bridge the Euphrates under Iraqi fire had it been necessary to force the river.

The risk rule lasted until 1994, at which point Defense Secretary Les Aspin abolished it. Some units enforced it during Desert Storm; others did not. Some might have *preferred* to, but could not because they didn't have enough men to sideline the women. In any event, the war was over so quickly that the risk rule received no serious test. However, what Desert Storm did make clear was that the United States could no longer fight a major war or campaign without women. The 1993 GAO report *Women in the Military: Deployment in the Persian Gulf War* estimated that of the approximately half a million Americans deployed to the Gulf, 7%—or 41,000—were women. Desert Storm witnessed the largest deployment of American women up to that point. Women, like men, died in a variety of ways: when their barracks where hit by a Scud missile, when they flew their helicopters into unlit towers during bad weather. And like men, women were taken prisoner. They flew reconnaissance missions over Iraq and they brought fuel forward to armored and mechanized infantry units. They even shared quarters with men, with surprisingly little trouble. And they learned that, even in a war as "linear" as the Gulf War, weapons such as Scud missiles meant that everyone was at risk.

In the aftermath of Desert Storm, it became clear to anyone who wished to understand it that servicewomen's expectations had changed profoundly. More and more women were joining the service, some with careers in mind, others because they wished to spend three or four years of their youth doing something outside of what would be the mainstream of the rest of their lives: learning discipline or a skill, getting experience that's difficult for women to get in the civilian world, and securing an education to boot. While perhaps only a few hoped to enter the combat arms, most were less and less content to be treated as members of a ladies' auxiliary, with their personal and professional development controlled not by what they *could* do, but by what others *thought* they *should* do. It would be pleasant to report that, after the Gulf War, barriers fell like Saddam's divisions, yielding one after another to the reality of the situation. Unfortunately, this was not to be. Sadly, the next great infusion of equality would come via a sustained civilian feminist assault, a devastating barrage of scandalmongering, lawsuits, lobbying, litigation, and legislation, much of it in the aftermath of the Navy's crisis of leadership at the 1991 Tailhook Convention. Sad, also, was the fact that this assault would drive the military—the Army especially—not toward genuine equality, but toward an ineffectual response that hurt women, men, and the institution.

There is a philosophy of war known as "maneuverism." Based on the work of Colonel John Boyd, a retired Air Force fighter pilot and guru of the 1970s/1980s defense-reform movement, it held that the way to defeat the enemy was to outthink him. You did it by getting "inside his decision cycle," his ability to process information and react effectively. Once the enemy finds that you're moving, hitting, thinking faster than he is, he discovers that he's responding too slowly. After a while, panic sets in. The enemy either goes into spasms of ineffective activity or collapses.

166

The feminista, arrogantly antimilitary and vindictive, spent the 1990s rollicking around inside the Army's decision cycle. The Army (and the other services) responded with bewilderment and panic, hoping that sensitivity training, micromanagement of behavior, occasional witch hunts, and sporadic poster girl campaigns would deflect the assault. It didn't, and a decade that might have worked to both women's and the military's benefit was wasted. The '90s were a decade that could have been spent completing the integration of women into the post–cold war Army and building cohesion between men and women. Instead, it was more often devoted to dealing with sexual harassment and assault by micromanagement and sensitivity training, while aggregate differences in physical capacity were dealt with very gingerly, rather than comprehensively.

The military couldn't say they didn't know that their dependence on women was increasing, or that women's accomplishments were not justifying that dependence. In November 1983, about seven years before the Gulf War, a conference was held at the U.S. Naval Academy to commemorate ten years' experience with an all-volunteer armed force. Stephen E. Herbits, then vice president for corporate development of the food and beverage company Seagram, had served on the 1970 President's Commission on an All-Volunteer Armed Force. During the current Bush administration, he combined gay rights advocacy as a quietly but openly gay man with consulting for Secretary of Defense Donald Rumsfeld. Herbits is currently the secretary general of the World Jewish Congress. In a remarkably prescient speech at that 1983 conference, he was unusually honest about the military's need to deal with servicewomen as professional peers:

Finally, there is the issue of women. The services have made
extraordinary progress in accepting and assimilating women
. . . . But are we ready for the next generation? Are we ready
to press again for a new level of assimilation and comfort and
emotional acceptance (because this issue is more emotional
than anything else) of the role that women can play in the
service? A new major push, talking about 20% levels, not 9 or
10 or 11% levels, is what we should be seeking if we really want
to keep the primary goal in mind of manning and "womaning"
the armed forces in a way which will optimally serve our
defense needs.[11]

Herbits knew what he was talking about. Congress understood the ramifications of his statements, too, or so it might seem. After the Gulf War, the Kennedy-Roth Amendment to the Defense Authorization Act repealed the provisions to Title 10 USC 8549, which banned women from serving aboard combat aircraft engaged in combat missions. This became Public Law 102-190 on 5 December 1991. However, the law included an amendment sponsored by Senators Sam Nunn (D-GA), chairman of the Senate Armed Services Committee (SASC), John Warner (R-VA), the ranking minority member of the SASC, John McCain (R-AZ), and John Glenn (D-OH) to establish a commission to study the implications of amending the combat exclusion laws. This commission would become the 1992 Presidential Commission on the Assignment of Women in the Armed Forces; its report was delivered in November 1992. Since the combat air restriction had been dropped due to political pressure deriving from women's performance in the Gulf War, the commission offered a way to justify not dropping any further combat restrictions, and perhaps indeed to backtrack and reinstate the combat air exclusions as well.

In ethics, we are often told that it matters to do the right thing in the right way for the right reasons. In the 1990s, the right thing, far too often, got done in the wrong way and for the wrong reasons.

In many ways, the 1992 Presidential Commission on the Assignment of Women in the Armed Forces is little more than a historical footnote, and one that points in entirely the wrong direction, at that. It was an attempt by many of the commissioners to freeze military women in place. Yet at the time, it generated an enormous amount of cultural heat, for it was part of the military's often misguided response to changing cultural norms about the role of servicewomen, and to the Navy's crisis of leadership during the Tailhook crisis.

The Tailhook Association is a semiofficial association of Navy and Marine Corps aviators, and its yearly conferences fulfill the valid function of bringing junior officers, who do the majority of carrier flying, together with senior officers and industry representatives. Of course, as with many other conferences, some socializing usually goes on after hours. But for years prior to their infamous September 1991 convention, many of these junior officers had been working on a reputation surpassing the rowdy and escalating well into the criminal. According to legend, hotels that booked their convention might put off any remodeling plans until afterward, knowing how much damage would occur (and perhaps planning to use the compensation money to fund future improvements). As for the female attendees, military and civilian alike, the prevailing attitude seems to have been: "Presence denotes consent."

Some of the sexual cavorting that occurred at the 1991 convention was consensual, especially early in the evenings when people had had less to drink and the aviators behaved in a relatively civilized manner. But as the nights wore on, the behavior grew increasingly more egregious, culminating in a gauntlet that would form on the third floor of the Las Vegas Hilton. This gauntlet was orchestrated so that a woman would not realize she was walking into a gang assault until the men converged upon her. In general, the gentlemen in the group left early. Some did what they could to protect women or warn them to keep away from that floor of the hotel.

Suffice it to say that many of those on the third floor were not gentlemen. They manhandled women and worse. Some of the women enjoyed the attention, but others didn't; they cursed the men, resisted assault by using electronic devices and their bare hands, or ran away. Drunk as they were, the assailants nevertheless knew what they were doing was criminal assault: The more the women fought back, the more the men attacked them. When one of the women who was pushed and shoved through the gauntlet dropped her pager, the men stopped attacking her and looked for the pager.[12] The men got puking drunk. They got a teenager nearly dead drunk and passed her through the gauntlet of aviators, naked from her waist down. They hired strippers and prostitutes, went "ballwalking" (with their genitals hanging out of their flies), pressed their butts against windows, bit other people's butts, mooned yet others, went streaking, and barfed and peed on carpets.

This behavior should have gotten them cashiered from the service, but it was tolerated by the Navy's commissioned and civilian leadership. Worse, the behavior of junior aviators during the years leading up to the 1991 Tailhook Convention was becoming more and more extreme, and yet was condoned by the Navy leadership who attended. During those same years, the Navy's senior enlisted leadership was cleaning up enlisted celebrations so that they would be appropriate for participants and observers of both sexes, as well as their children. In 1991, the aviators had an attitude problem. They considered their behavior a legitimate unwinding after the Gulf War. They thought they were owed the preservation of combat aviation as an exclusively male domain, along with access to whatever female flesh happened by. A post–cold war, post–Gulf War force drawdown was getting under way. That meant fewer aircraft and therefore fewer flight hours. The entrance of women into combat aviation further threatened their access to both aircraft and training dollars (a problem presumably not posed by younger male aviators). Through it all, these aviators retained the sense of entitlement issuing from the idea that naval aviation constituted not only an elite profession, but a separate moral universe.

Had the Navy handled the excesses promptly and properly, this inappropriate behavior and the problems that ensued might have been an incident without deeper ramifications. Had the Navy prosecuted the worst offenders for assault, while reaffirming standards of behavior appropriate to officers and gentlemen, it might actually have used the media to present the 1991 Tailhook Convention as an example of the type of behavior the military would not tolerate. Instead, the Navy responded first with a "boys will be boys" shrug, and then with a cover-up. Its first mistake was its failure to heed the great truth that in political life the cover-up usually does more damage than the initial malfeasance. The scandal went public when Lieutenant Paula Coughlin appeared on *60 Minutes,* pushing the issue into the arena of high-stakes, high-drama politics. The Tailhook crisis would finally end with the resignation of the chief of naval operations, Admiral Frank Kelso, a man who did fine work restructuring the post–cold war Navy, but who would go down in history as the guy who didn't "get it" until far too late.

Then-president George Herbert Walker Bush was of the old school, a decorated naval aviator who wept when Lieutenant Coughlin recounted how she had been forced through the gauntlet of very drunken men, her professional comrades and peers, and brutally pawed and manhandled to the point that she was afraid she would be gang-raped. Bush Sr. came from a world where combat aviation was a man's job, but also from a world where gentlemen held their liquor. He understood very well that these were not inebriated gentlemen being silly. The commander in chief was far from approving of the Tailhook Convention's debased and degraded male sexuality, and for the same reasons, he refused to take steps to legalize women in combat aircraft.

While some of the women at Tailhook were, and considered themselves to be, victims, others did not see themselves as victims. A few individuals, such as Lieutenant Kara Hultgreen, took satisfaction in knowing that they had given worse than they got when attacked. But generally, the women's refusal to think of themselves as victims had nothing to do with what they had experienced and everything to do with how they thought they would be perceived. Some were servicewomen vulnerable to retaliation. Others felt they were responsible for being assaulted because they'd been warned, or should have known that something was wrong, or that the incident wasn't serious enough.

Tailhook and the Navy's subsequent handling of the affair was a disgrace, and it colored the way men felt about any easing of combat restrictions on women. The exercise in self-destructive self-protection began when the naval inspector general, Rear Admiral George W. Davis VI, chose to "differentiate" between criminal sexual assault and sexual assault—as though some forms of sexual assault could be noncriminal. He then failed to interview senior officers in order to assign personal responsibility, believing that what had happened was a cultural problem. "The naval IG [Admiral Davis] told [the Department of Defense inspector general] that he believed to do so would be perceived as a 'witch hunt' that would detract from fixing the cultural problem identified in the reports," said the report from the DOD. The DOD inspector general's office dimly understood this to be the wrong approach, but didn't quite understand why. The Navy had, after all, allowed the behavior at Tailhook to go on for many years, at least among aviators (it is impossible to imagine submariners behaving like this), by establishing a policy of "zero tolerance" for sexual harassment, then ignoring that policy in practice.

Admiral Davis's attempt at bureaucratic self-protection consisted of manufacturing spurious legal niceties and dismissing criminal activities vaguely as "cultural problems." The commander of the Naval Criminal Investigative Service (NCIS), Rear Admiral Duvall M. Williams Jr., further validated Admiral Davis's statements by concurring that "men" simply did not want women in the military. It was widely known that he was among those "men" he referenced, which his own statements made clear. At one point, he got into a screaming match with the assistant secretary of the Navy for manpower and reserve affairs, Barbara Pope, during which he characterized female naval aviators as topless dancers, go-go dancers, or prostitutes. When discussing Lieutenant Coughlin's statement with a female NCIS agent, he called attention to her use of profanity: "Any woman that would use the F-word on a regular basis would welcome this type of activity . . . " Rather than acknowledging that he interpreted a woman's use of profanity as an indication that she would enjoy being sexually assaulted, and that therefore it was consensual sex, not a criminal assault, he tried to convince the NCIS agent that she had misunderstood him. His attitudes about women's "proper" sphere are probably why he didn't want to question other admirals about their tolerance for criminal activity, and why he didn't want to pursue the investigation. Furthermore, he insisted on maintaining personal oversight of the investigation in order to control it.[13]

Amazingly, it got worse. The NCIS had to deal with widespread stonewalling in the aviation squadrons about who was at Tailhook and who had engaged in criminal behavior, to the point of resorting to mass polygraphing of squadrons. A different, more dignified approach was certainly possible. After all, a lot of people were at Tailhook, and a substantial minority of them engaged in sexual assault or other questionable activities. Certainly, they knew who was responsible. NCIS agents should have told the aviators they interviewed: "Fine, you don't want to talk to us, you don't have to. But crimes have been committed by a large number of naval aviators, and you can either tell us everything you know about who did what, or you can decide to be an accessory, thus no gentleman and so unfit to be a Navy officer. You have twenty-four hours to make up your mind, or put your wings on the table and resign your commission."

But such an approach would have had to have been sanctioned by the Navy's senior leadership, and it probably would have required some serious soul-searching on the part of that leadership.

The feminista, meanwhile, were watching naval aviation's meltdown with baffled delight and predatory fascination. It was, in fact, not the feminista, but the Navy's inspector general who first blamed the "culture," and who decided that since the culture was to blame, individuals weren't responsible for their actions. A more damning attitude would be hard to imagine. In fact, he was partially right. The culture *was* to blame. But culture doesn't come to be by itself. Individuals create culture, and they change culture, too. By attending Tailhook and choosing to look the other way, the Navy's senior officers, especially in aviation, had allowed many young naval aviators to defile themselves. Then, when the behavior became public knowledge, they left those young men twisting in the wind.[14] They said only, "We didn't know; certainly, we didn't know it was that bad; we left because we don't act that way." They never said, "We should have known, but we didn't want to. We allowed our young men to degrade themselves until they became criminals, rather than requiring that they act like the gentlemen the Republic has trusted them to be."

It is entirely fitting that Rear Admiral Jack Snyder, who refused to take seriously the attacks on his aide Lieutenant Coughlin (who was attacked precisely because she was a woman who was an admiral's aide), was relieved, ending his career. Rear Admiral Williams, who believed that if a woman used profanity to object to her mistreatment she must have liked it, retired. Admiral Kelso was forced—not unjustly—to retire even though he had had a genuine change of heart about sexual harassment and the professional humiliations of Navy women. He had been at Tailhook, but rather than intervene to stop a crowd of naval aviators surrounding a young woman and demanding that she strip, he'd left. He was disgusted, but he left, and when he did he abandoned the women he could have ordered his male subordinates to treat in a civilized manner. He also abandoned those few junior officers who risked the ostracism of their peers to warn women off from the gauntlet. And then he said he hadn't witnessed that misconduct. Vice Admiral Richard Dunleavy, the former head of naval aviation, his deputy Rear Admiral Wilson Flagg, and Rear Admiral Riley Mixson, director of the Air Warfare Division in the Office of the Chief of Naval Operations, were all censured.[15]

No one went to jail—not even one of the instigators of the gauntlet, Lieutenant Gregory Geiss. He ratted out his buddies in exchange for immunity. The files of 140 junior officers were reviewed for punishment, and more than half were discarded. Sexual assault charges are very difficult to try because there is a long-standing bias against the victim's (usually a woman's) perception of the incident. But even without that bias, many of the assaults at Tailhook involved gangs of men converging on women, who, even if they had been stone-cold sober, would have had a very difficult time identifying which man did what. Cases against the remaining officers were pursued legally and administratively; some charges were dropped, but forty-three officers received nonjudicial punishment consisting of fines, letters of reprimand, and orders to be counseled. Only six were court-martialed, five because they had demanded a trial rather than accept nonjudicial punishment; only one was tried, and the charges against him were dropped. But very few of these men would have any future in Navy aviation.[16]

The man who was tried and against whom charges were dropped was Robert Stumpf, commander of the Navy's Blue Angels demonstration squadron at the time of Tailhook. Before that, he had been commander of a fighter squadron during Desert Storm, where he had been awarded a Distinguished Flying Cross. For years after Tailhook, his promotion to captain was put on hold because some senators questioned his behavior there. He had attended a promotion party for one of his men; strippers performed, but he left before one of them performed oral sex. What happened to Stumpf was brutally unfair. Navy leadership should either have aggressively pushed for his timely promotion or asked him to resign for conduct unbecoming of an officer and a gentleman for tolerating the presence of a stripper at an official function. He said he witnessed none of the assaults and that furthermore it had never occurred to him that seeing previous secretaries of the Navy, previous chiefs of naval operations, and countless flag officers in the same room with exotic dancers was a problem. Yet Stumpf's own description of his actions also made his fate understandable: "It just . . . it didn't occur to me that that was . . . that behavior was not acceptable." As for dismissing the strippers before they could perform, he said, "That would have been bad form and certainly not in the spirit of the Tailhook that had been established by tradition over the decades preceding."[17]

The Navy's leadership couldn't be honest about Stumpf because they couldn't be honest about themselves—neither about what they may have done themselves when they were young men, nor about what they had tolerated as older men.

This is the real reason why the further integration of servicewomen after the Gulf War was such a political hot potato. The Navy leadership had proven itself untrustworthy in a very public way. Rather than standing up, explaining their contributions to the assaults at Tailhook 1991, and setting up an orderly, dignified, and serious prosecution of the perpetrators, they weaseled. They did their best to hang the junior officers out to dry, and when that did not work, they used administrative processes to remove the officers from naval aviation. They also violated a deeply moral tenet of sea service leadership: If it happens on the captain's ship, it is the captain's responsibility. Such an ethos demanded the willing resignation of Navy leadership for allowing a culture of profound denigration of women to develop in naval aviation. Some of those women were shipmates, after all, and all were citizens of the Republic. Instead, it would be the women, both in uniform and out, who would be blamed for the failures of the Navy leadership.

———————— ⊕ ————————

The feminista's role in all of this was to watch the house of cards fall and enjoy the wreckage. When the feminista spoke of changing military culture, it was because they wanted to humiliate the military and the men in it, not because they thought that as citizens of the Republic women, especially feminists, should be part of the military. In the 1990s, the Army would give the feminista ample opportunity because

:peat, over and over again, the Navy's pattern of bureaucratic
ng, toleration of crimes against women, and humiliation of
:d, though scandal after scandal would have the effect of
changing military culture, no credit is due to the feminista. At first,
women like Coughlin were the deviants, the outsiders (she resigned
from the Navy)—first for being women, then for being in the military,
then for being aviators, and finally for refusing to regard assault as the
price of military service. The military allowed too many servicemen to
view sexual assault and harassment as ways of male bonding, and Tailhook was a public expression of that criminal bonding. When brought
to light, it disgusted a lot of men who did not care for that behavior—
whether women were present or not.

Eventually, it would be their definition of masculinity that would
prevail, and that would begin the reshaping of the military as an institution inclusive of women as equals. Those who once thought themselves
the norm would become deviant—based upon their mistreatment of
others, not their conformity to gender roles.

Solicitor General Kenneth Starr swore in the fifteen members of the
1992 Presidential Commission on the Assignment of Women in the
Armed Forces on 25 March 1992.

Nine of them were male, including General Robert T. Herres, who
served for thirty-six years in the Air Force; Admiral James R. Hogg,
who retired from the Navy in 1991 after thirty-five years of service; and
Brigadier General Thomas Draude, a Marine who served three tours in
Vietnam. They were three men who would review the evidence of wom-
en's capabilities and become advocates for servicewomen's expanded
roles. By contrast, commissioner Ronald D. Ray was a Marine and Viet-

nam combat veteran who, in his personal statement, which the commissioners provided as part of the commission's final report, wrote, "As a military historian, and as a Christian, I sought direction from the Bible."[18] Amazingly, his failure to give precedence to standard research techniques over personal religious beliefs did not disqualify him.

Of the six women on the commission, we have already met Elaine Donnelly; she and Kate Walsh O'Beirne of the Heritage Foundation were the only two who hadn't served in the military. Along with commissioner Sarah F. White, a master sergeant in the Air Force Reserve, they opposed expanding the roles of women in the military. The other three women supported expanding roles. They were Meredith Neizer, a 1978 Merchant Marine Academy graduate and later a White House fellow to the secretary of defense; Captain Mary Finch, a West Point graduate and helicopter pilot; and retired major general Mary Elizabeth Clarke, the last director of the Women's Army Corps, who had made remedial weapons and physical training a priority for women recruits and officers.

The commission produced a laundry list of findings. Some of them were reasonable: opposing the use of quotas; retaining gender-specific physical fitness tests; encouraging the adoption of gender-neutral standards for military occupational specialties (MOSs) that require high levels of strength and endurance. (The methodology examining the disparity, real and potential, between male and female physical abilities is badly flawed, an issue to be dealt with in detail in Chapter Seven.)

Eight of the commissioners found that because military readiness should be the driving concern regarding assignment policies, there were circumstances in which women might be assigned to combat roles. They noted that one of the strongest sociological arguments for assigning women to combat positions was that a person ought to be picked regardless of gender, because he or she is the best-qualified person for that job, and that women should not be barred from military positions unless there is convincing evidence that they can't meet the occupational demands of those positions. Similar to the findings of the Gillem Board in their argument for black soldiers, the commission found that servicewomen should be treated as individuals. The commissioners distinguished between air, sea, and land direct combat roles. They also noted that it was their opinion that the American public actually encouraged and approved of the further integration of women into combat positions.

But as soon as it came to actually voting on which combat operations women should formally be allowed to participate in, that fragile consensus broke down. Eight commissioners voted to keep women out of combat aircraft, urging Congress to repeal Public Law 102-190, reenact the laws that prohibited women from flying combat aircraft for the Air Force and Navy, and extend them to prohibit women from flying Army aircraft (primarily helicopters) on combat missions.[19] In fact, public law had never *stopped* women from flying in combat when they were needed. Air Force women had flown tanker and transport aircraft in Operation Urgent Fury, the 1983 invasion of Grenada, and Operation El Dorado Canyon, the 1986 bombing raid on Libya. Female soldiers also flew Black Hawk helicopters in Operation Just Cause, the 1989 invasion of Panama. Navy women had flown reconnaissance missions over Iraq during the Gulf War.

The deciding vote against women in combat aviation was cast by retired general Maxwell Thurman, nicknamed Mad Max and Maxatollah for his aggressive style and his work habits. A master organizer, he did much to help turn the Army around after Vietnam. His reasoning was as blunt as it was based upon traditional notions of male protectiveness. "The idea that we would position women in the arena of being subjected to violence, death, depravity as prisoners is one I won't sign up to."[20]

The Gulf War experience of then-major Rhonda Cornum did not change his mind. Cornum was a flight surgeon on a search and rescue mission who became famous when her helicopter was shot down and she was wounded and taken prisoner. She viewed her experiences as a POW far less emotionally:

> *[B]eing raped in downtown DC or Peoria, Illinois, or*
> *somewhere like that is very different than getting raped in*
> *the military—you know, as a POW, just like getting shot.*
> *You know, you don't expect that to happen when you walk*
> *down the streets of your home town, but it is an occupational*
> *hazard of going to war, and you make the decision whether*
> *or not you are going to take that risk when you join the military.*[21]

Since the risk of capture was lower for naval combatants, eight commissioners found women should be allowed to serve on board combatant vessels, except for submarines and amphibious vessels, which carried Marines and engaged in land assaults. The commission voted unanimously to keep all special operations, even the aviation units, closed to women.

Cohesion was a major issue raised by the commission. Brigadier General Thomas Draude, the Marine who would advocate expanding opportunities for servicewomen, raised the legitimate concern of sexual tension that may be caused by women's presence in the intense and intimate environment of small ground combat units. His was a far from unique concern—that in a mixed-sex environment "the fabric of *unqualified* love necessary to hold men together in infantry combat would be torn by the sexual tension caused by the presence of women."[22] (This concern is often expressed by invoking the fact that the Greeks had different words for "love." *Eros* meant erotic love, while *philia* was nonsexual love that bound men together during war. That the Greek attitude toward homosexuality included the belief that lovers would fight better for each other, both to avoid shaming each other with fear and leaving each other in the lurch through weakness, we shall pass over in silence here.)

Other objections began with the silly and rapidly worsened. Navy Lieutenant Tom Downing protested that although he was certain women could fly combat aircraft, the real issue was: "It's how that woman affects the men that are doing that job, and that is—my personal feeling is that that is what is going to do it, and you can't grasp it, you can't put it on a piece of paper, you can't do a study about it."[23] Air Force Captain Dave Freaney said that he might be old-fashioned in his values, "but I cannot see myself running around with my flight of four, you know, doing the town in Song Tong City with—if one of them was a girl . . . I think it would affect, you know, the effectiveness of my flight squadron."[24] (Captain Freaney's implication that the presence of women would hinder the drinking and whoring by which men are thought to bond, we shall also pass over in silence.)

During the course of my research, I spoke or corresponded with several commissioners, including Elaine Donnelly, who refused to be interviewed. Brigadier General Draude spoke to me of his experience serving on the commission.

I naively went in thinking that, as we had all taken an oath,
that we were all going to go in with an open mind. But that

*was not the case, and there were very definitely agendas. From
both sides. I was on a committee with Admiral Hogg and Sarah
White and Kate O'Beirne. Here are two guys who are more
inclined to give women opportunities, and two women who were
absolutely opposed. And I thought this was so strange from what
outsiders would assume. I think we're all products of our
experience and our upbringing. I never sensed that women
in the service were held in low regard. I guess I felt conversely;
I held women in high regard. My daughter was in service, and
my wife was a Marine, and then in Desert Shield and Desert
Storm, I saw women do amazing things that caused me to
reexamine my conceptions of what women could and should
do, and the commission was an opportunity to reexamine
those conceptions.*

*The first thought was that I had seen more than my share of
combat—three times in Vietnam and Desert Storm—and the
grisly stuff. To translate that to anyone, male or female, is hard.*
It's hard. *"Not only no, but hell no, we can't have women do
these kinds of things."* But the second thought was the things my
daughter was doing amazed me. And it made me wonder if I had
shortchanged women and their capabilities.*

Brigadier General Samuel Cockerham, Elaine Donnelly, Sarah
White, Kate Walsh O'Beirne, and Ronald D. Ray became known as
the Gang of Five. They filed an Alternative View objecting to all combat roles for women. The document was loaded with conjecture and
misleading statistics, especially regarding women's physical capacity.
Their attitude may be summed up by their citation of Colonel Bryan D.

Brown, then commander of the U.S. Army's First Battalion, 160th Special Operations Aviation Regiment, at the time of this writing a four-star general in command of Special Operations Command: "I in no way doubt the female officers' and soldiers' bravery, dedication, or capability, but I do believe their assignment would not enhance the combat capability of the 160th."[25]

Why? Because That's the Way It Is. Why is that the way it is? Because We Say So.

Their arguments against women in combat as direct, voluntary combatants (as opposed to "noncombat" soldiers in whom the war has taken an interest, as it would have in cold war Europe and as it has in Iraq and Afghanistan) may be summarized thus: The military is not a corporation and women are not men. Since women "need" dual standards of physical fitness and lack the proud history as successful warriors that is shared by men of many races, servicewomen have no right to be treated as individuals. Instead, the burden was on women as a group to prove that they would not adversely affect the combat units that individual women would join. The Gang of Five quoted commissioner Charles Moskos telling Chairman General Herres (who believed that, all things being equal, equal opportunity should triumph) that mixed-gender units were not equal. They had lower deployment rates and less physical strength, cost more, and had more sex. The Gang then concluded that all of these problems would devastate combat readiness, unit cohesion, and military effectiveness. In short, the Gang concluded that since nothing servicewomen contributed could be worth their detrimental effect on the combat effectiveness of their unit, they should not be allowed to serve as combatants.[26]

As a signpost in the nation's larger culture wars, the commission was represented by the Gang of Five, with their position to exclude women from all combat specialties, retain the risk rule, and exclude women from any future draft registration, let alone conscription. As a solid voting bloc, they needed to add only three votes from other commissioners on any given issue to form a majority, and given the very emotional subject of women's participation in war as combatants, they often found those additional three votes. But it was a signpost ultimately pointing to a dead end, because it looked to the past instead of to a future defined by a civilian society ever more open to women's potential and advancement.

Brigadier General Draude was representative of the men who rejected the idea of facing the future by looking back at the past, and a rather mythologized past at that. "I really caused folks some difficulty when I raised the issue of excluding folks in uniform from assignments, positions, etc., based upon the *way* they were born, and I used the racial difference," he told me. "That raised a lot of hackles: 'This isn't the same at all.' I pointed out that we used a racially segregated force to defeat Nazi Germany and imperial Japan. And people asked, 'Why change something that works?' Because we can make it better. And we had it in Korea. [All the services formally integrated before the Korean War.] I saw lots of parallels. We were excluding the majority of the population, not because of lack of desire, or patriotism, or expertise, or character, but because of the way they were born. And it drove some people crazy. And I said, tell me what's different? Explain to me why it is right to exclude people because of the way they were born—when it's gender, but not race. And no one, to my satisfaction, could do so."

He has not changed his opinion over the years. In a follow-up to our interview, he wrote me, "Lifting the restrictions based on race provided us an even better military. Why is there such resistance to allowing women to demonstrate their full capabilities to provide us a still better military?"[27]

Within a few months, the Gang of Five's attempt to turn the clock back on servicewomen would be moot. On 20 January 1993, William Jefferson Clinton was sworn in as president of the United States. Shortly thereafter, the GAO issued a report entitled *Women in the Military: Deployment in the Persian Gulf War.* A total of 171 men and 147 women from ten units and all four services—Army, Navy, Air Force, and Marine Corps—participated in sixty-three group discussions.[28] It is a report that is short on conjecture and long on experience.

The report found that teamwork eliminated disparities in strength, which sounds like all the big, strong men covering for the little, weak women. But then you look at the assessment of women's actual job performance—by both men and women—and compare it to the expectations of how women perform. Both the men and the women who participated found that women performed better than they expected. Nearly 49% of men and women alike *expected* women to perform as well as or better than men; but 67.2% *found* women to perform as well as or better than men. This takes into account the fact that women made up 40% of those who expected, and 36.5% of those who found, women to do as well or better than men.[29]

While many men and women both noted that men felt the need to protect women, and that women needed protection from hostile fire, they also noted that men felt the need to protect women from other men—both outside and within the unit. Generally, the women were more worried about men inside the unit, and men about men from outside the unit.[30] As for cohesion, women were thought to make a positive or neutral contribution to interpersonal relations rather than a negative one. Sexual harassment was not thought to be a serious problem; at war, soldiers are often too busy for such activities. Most men are self-disciplined. And far more soldiers thought that mixed-sex units bonded at least as well as, if not better than, all-male units than otherwise; only a few thought that women harmed unit bonding.[31]

This report was issued at the beginning of the Clinton administration. The inclusion of women in combat aviation remained, and in January 1994, Secretary of Defense Les Aspin rescinded the risk rule. In its place, he established a new DOD-wide direct ground combat assignment rule. The explicit purpose of this change was to expand opportunities for servicewomen. As a corollary, he added that no units or positions that were open to women when the direct ground combat assignment rule was formulated could be closed thereafter.

Secretary Aspin's rule allowed all service members to be assigned to all positions for which they qualified, but excluded women from assignments to units below the brigade level, whose primary mission is direct ground combat.

The secretary also permitted the services to close positions to women if: (1) the units and positions were required to physically collocate and remain with direct ground combat units; (2) the service secretary attested that the cost of providing appropriate living arrangements for women was prohibitive; (3) the units were engaged in special operations forces' missions or long-range reconnaissance; or (4) job-related physical requirements would exclude the vast majority of women. The military services might propose additional exceptions, with justification to the secretary of defense.[32]

Aspin's assignment rule defined direct ground combat as taking place "well forward on the battlefield while locating and closing with the enemy to defeat them by fire, maneuver, or shock effect."[33] In other words, killing the enemy, maneuvering so that his formations were dislocated and he was unable to fight effectively, or forcing him to retreat precipitously. While these positions and units were closed to women, Aspin's rule greatly standardized assignment possibilities for servicewomen, expanded their career opportunities, and reduced the role subjective judgment might play in assigning women to particular units at any particular time.

Since the Army's brigades (generally a mix of infantry, armor, and artillery battalions with their service units, totaling about 3,000 to 5,000 troops) increasingly became its basic combat element after Desert Storm, this couldn't quite work as planned. Certain noncombat units, such as a medical company collocated with an infantry brigade, or combat correspondents with an infantry battalion, or MPs with the infantry at a forward operating base, were off-limits to women. But without women in these units, they increasingly couldn't function: I saw women serving in all of the above situations in Iraq and Afghanistan, and the barriers against women serving in smaller infantry units have eroded still further since then.

It was a Kafkaesque situation: Anyone with the wit to understand force structure knew women were becoming more and more involved in the real business of the military, which is combat. At the time, those generals and admirals who refused to cross the Clinton administration on the greater sexual integration of the military, or even supported that integration because of the evidence that women were good troops, were lambasted by the Right as dupes of the cowardly and decadent forces of political correctness. In hindsight, the greater sexual integration of the military has been a military blessing, although it came at far too high and unnecessary a price. In partisan political terms, it polarized the military, helping make it more and more Republican, and decreasing Democratic credibility on defense issues.

Part of the problem was the Army's endless dishonesty about what women were really doing (i.e., how the Army was really using them). The Army's regulations are its rules for how to run itself, and they have the force of law; AR 600-13 governs the assignment of women to their occupational specialties and units. AR 600-13 used a "direct combat position coding" system to classify units as P1, open only to male soldiers, and P2, open to female soldiers as well. (Gone were the old gradations of P1 through P7.) Female soldiers were allowed to serve in any officer or enlisted specialty or position except in those specialties, positions, or units of battalion size or smaller. Nor were they supposed to serve in units that were either routinely assigned direct combat mission or routinely collocated with direct ground combat units of battalion size or smaller. However, female soldiers were to remain with their units in the event of hostilities. Insofar as was possible, given their exclusion from combat and the combat arms, women were to be provided with full and equal opportunities to pursue careers in the Army.

Yet, even as the Army continued to oppose equality, and even as it resorted to idiotic games and anonymous accusation hotlines and puerile regulations (one order decreed male-female direct eye contact for more than five seconds to be "harassment") to protect itself against feminista harassment and lawsuits, it created loopholes to meet its own needs.

First were the loopholes for women in the Reserves and National Guard. As in the Regular Army, women in the Reserves and National Guard were not to be assessed, commissioned, appointed, or assigned to units that were either closed to women or going to be closed to women. However, if a woman's unit was going to be disbanded, reorganized, or moved, she could be assigned to a unit in her locale that was other-wise closed to her for up to one year. Women who were soldiers in the Active Guard Reserve (AGR) who would lose their positions because of unit reorganization or redesignation would have priority consideration for reassignment to vacant positions in open units. Until such time, they could remain in their old, now-closed positions for up to a year. In the AGR, female military technicians, who by law had to be assigned to open positions or be separated from the Army thirty days after losing such positions, would receive priority for assignment to open positions; again, they could serve in closed positions for up to a year. In the Reserves, female military technicians who were assigned to closed units, or whose positions were closed because of reorganization or redesignation, would be reassigned on a case-by-case basis. Women were permitted to serve in those closed positions under the Army's happy self-delusion that in case of call-up or mobilization, they would be reassigned.

Further—this is perhaps the greatest loophole, and also acknowledgement of reality—women were not prohibited from serving as individuals attached to direct ground combat arms battalions. Not in the Regular Army, the Reserves, or the National Guard. This included nurses, doctors, and medics, as well as intelligence specialists, MPs, cooks, clerks, and maintenance specialists. This was a deliberate oversight by the Army to allow women to be sent forward to combat units but never to be actually assigned. It was meant to cover predictable wartime contingencies. For example, perhaps units at the front need mechanics because all the men are casualties, but there are women in the rear. Move them forward as needed. Or perhaps a Special Forces or Ranger unit absolutely must have women to deal with the population of women in an area. Attachment is the perfect way to solve the problem, and it doesn't create a paper trail the way assignment of women in violation of AR 600-13 would. It is being widely used for this purpose today in Iraq and Afghanistan, while the collocation rule has been completely abandoned.

Finally, Army units come in two types, Table of Organization and Equipment (TOE) units and Table of Distribution and Allowances (TDA) units. A TOE unit is a tactical unit that operates in the field. A TDA unit exists to perform specific tasks for which there are no appropriate TOE units, and it's not "deployable"—even after it has set up shop in the middle of a combat zone. Their functions have ranged from the traditionally non-combatant work of medical care to the very combatant work of Ranger companies. Although AR 600-13 makes provision for TDA units to be gender-coded, such coding is discouraged. It's not hard to figure out why.

Essentially, the military has treated women as a married man treats his mistress, even as the number of women and the types of work they're doing have expanded beyond all possible expectations, and women have attained more and more rank, both as noncommissioned officers (NCOs) and officers. Something of a secret—but unlike a wife, even an acknowledged mistress has no social or legal claims unless so enforced by a court.

Servicewomen were deeply affected by this, but so were men. They were being told that women were equal while watching them being treated in profoundly unequal ways. In some cases, this was nothing more than the petty sadism of men demanding that women perform at a male level with utterly inadequate training, then refusing to provide adequate training as a remedial measure because it would constitute "special treatment." These men were probably the least disturbed: As far as they were concerned, the Army was just playing games to satisfy the feminista, because everyone knew the women would bail out when the going got tough, probably by getting pregnant, and they wouldn't mind being the sperm donors.

In other cases, men were concerned because they understood just how hard soldiering might end up being for female soldiers as they watched the Army ask far less of women physically than they might be capable of. By expecting less, the Army was not only doing women a disservice, it was putting women—as well as men and the service itself—at risk. For men who took war, the Army, and their female comrades seriously—and who tried to find a way to reconcile official Army doctrine about women, be it assignment or physical capacity, with real soldiers who happened to be women—the army's stance could be intellectually baffling and sometimes personally and professionally painful.

In my ongoing conversations with retired artillery officer Colonel Kurtz, he spoke with a candor that would have served the Army well during those early decades of integration: "I'm sure I'm just as big a troglodyte as anyone of my generation," he told me. "I had one child, a son, and I never thought about it. Sort of the yardstick I use now is my granddaughter. I don't want her to be a soldier—certainly I don't want her to be subjected to the environment I found when I joined the Army. But you can say that women shouldn't do this, and that's one thing. But telling my granddaughter she can't do what she wants to? Nobody ever better tell her what she can't do."

He had already begun applying this standard to women twenty years ago, as the Army, along with the women in it, was in the process of repairing the damage Vietnam had done to its soul. At that time, he began taking women, one and two at a time, into his artillery units as clerks. There was a surplus of women, and a shortage of men, with the right MOS, so if you needed a clerk the choice was to bring in a woman or try to cross-train a cannoneer to the job. Although the women didn't go to the field with his men, their work was essential to making the battalion run, and he and his sergeant major made sure

the men didn't bother them. Then there was the chemical
deployed to Germany with his field artillery battalion. '
female out of 399 guys. She was excited; she was getting to g
major exercise and do what she was trained to do. It was a miserably
cold, icebound winter. She bunked with the rest of us, and I never
regretted having her along for one second. We saw logistics units with
mixed male-female bunks in the same large areas, but they were a lot
more used to this than we were. I don't know that she took anything
from the guys, ever. Although we posted guards when she had to go to
the latrine. Had the proverbial balloon gone up, I wouldn't have sent
her away; I'd have wanted her to stay right where she was to do the job
she was doing. And she wouldn't have asked to be sent to 'the rear.'
I'm absolutely certain of that. She wanted to be a chemical officer and
she couldn't get the experience she needed at battalion level, except
this way, and she was grateful to get it."

Finally, one of his adjutants, like him a field artillery officer, was
a woman. "She was a captain, female, West Point, extremely sharp and
ambitious, athletic. It was awful watching her in a branch that she was
not going to be able to go anywhere—by then I was a lieutenant colonel
and I knew it was all BS. [Women] could go to Lance or Pershing [short-
range nuclear missiles that were a plum target for Soviet preemptive
attacks] but not cannon [field artillery], and so they couldn't compete on
an equal basis [with men]. The Army was just using women like her to
mollify those who wanted to see 'women in combat.'"

FEMINISTS

Chapter 6

DARKNESS
BEFORE
DAWN

In the aftermath of the Gulf War, Americans were far more polarized by the culture wars than they are now. One of the hot-button topics of those culture wars, not surprisingly, was women in the military. The Vietnam generation will go to their graves arguing about that war, and so many of the major issues from the 1970s through 2001 were just a way for those who went, or loved someone who did, and those who dodged the draft or loved someone who did, to get back at each other. Civil rights, the equal rights amendment and its defeat, gay rights, the environment, religion—none of these contentious social issues were really about the issues. They were about the conservatives and the liberals getting under each other's skin, to the frustration of those who actually wanted to solve a problem or two. The feminist movement, which was powerfully revitalized by the Vietnam protest movement, and with which U.S. servicewomen were closely identified, was part of this refighting of Vietnam. In the aftermath of Vietnam, servicewomen

een far more likely to *serve* in Vietnam than to *protest*

ampioned by an organized feminist leadership that

y to have been part of the peace movement.

lost on the military's institutional leadership. But if

g the military should have had its eyes on during the Clinton administration, it was the absolute certainty of danger to the security of the United States, a danger more diffuse and far harder to manage than the former Soviet Union. With women making up more and more of the military and serving in more and more career fields, the military should have made it a priority to weld the sexes into a cohesive team. After Desert Storm, servicewomen averaged one in eight of the military's strength—more in some services, such as the Air Force, less in others, such as the Marines. The Army matched up with the average. One in eight of its troops were women, and because women were increasingly deploying into difficult and dangerous situations with men, male-female cohesion was critical. But even though one in eight troops was a considerable proportion of the Army, because these troops were women, they were a minority—and you don't make major changes in institutional culture for a minority.

As for the organized feminist leadership that I've taken to calling the feminista, they didn't forget about the divisions of Vietnam, either. They were quite happy to pile on and "help" the serious women and men quietly working toward institutional changes in the status of military women through military and civilian channels. It was less a way of opening the military to citizens who were women than it was a way of refighting Vietnam. But as feminists, they should have had their eyes on the goal of reconciling "American woman" with "American citizen," and thereby making sure that military service was simply part of citizenship for all citizens—no more controversial for women than voting.

196

Until the end of the 1990s, U.S. servicewomen were generally considered tolerable peculiarities. It was often believed that, with the exception of nurses, women who entered the service were trying to get away from a man, looking to marry one, hoping to become one, or looking for love among each other. Women had to confront being labeled as whores, lesbians, or both, and they were sometimes viciously abused.

Nurses seem to have escaped this fate: partly because they were still practicing a nurturing and subservient art, and partly because no one with two active brain cells behaves abusively or offensively to someone who's trying to save his life.

At times, the abuse directed at servicewomen by their comrades seemed . . . normal. It was distasteful, yes, but it was also seen as the reasonable risk a woman assumed when entering a male-dominated profession. When the service academies opened their doors to women in 1976, General William Westmoreland held a press conference in which he stated, "Maybe you could find one woman in 10,000 who could lead in combat, but she would be a freak and we're not running the military academy for freaks."[1] In retrospect, it is incredible that this man, who, despite his Vietnam failings, had been a fine combat leader in previous wars, was cruelly dismissing fellow citizens who respected his calling enough to want it for their own. And it is even more astonishing that although General Westmoreland had presided over the profound moral disintegration of American forces in Vietnam, he was taken seriously.

From Westmoreland's perspective, it was servicewomen, not those who slandered and mauled them, who were the deviants. The men who attacked them were perceived as normal, respectable, even admirable. As integration intensified after the Gulf War, male attacks, often egged right-wing civilians, took on a new intensity. The attacks ranged ﹍ assertions that the men's standards were being lowered to accommodate women to what can only be called "fragging by rape": the deliberate use of violation to drive women out of the service.

Some service members of both sexes across the political spectrum considered these abuses inevitable. There was a syllogism of sorts: (A) Any woman who enters the service makes herself, if not fair game, certainly open to question, plus (B) All men exist along a continuum that ranges from criminality to piggishess to good-natured "boys will be boys," equals (C) Shit happens. What of it?

Those who accepted this syllogism shared a view of men as either overgrown children in need of testosterone detox or as monsters by nature and therefore always to be regarded as potential rapists. They also shared a view of servicewomen that amounted to: Nice girls (or at least smart ones) don't join a largely male institution, even an institution that has been central to citizenship throughout American and much of the Western republican tradition, even if women are more and more recognized as citizens. Contempt, and even abuse culminating in rape, was widely considered the price women should expect to pay for serving their country. It was an exceptionally limited view of what men and women can be, to themselves and to each other.

One thing should be clear. Toward the end of the 1990s, the feminista were clearly using the cause of servicewomen to goad the military's institutional leadership, and the leadership hurt the servicewomen and thus the institution itself by trying to appease the feminista rather than simply blowing them off and doing the right thing. The right thing would have been opening all units to women and a phased opening of all MOSs, combined with a thorough rethinking of the physical requirements for women and of relationships between men and women.

The military's mishandling of the further integration of servicewomen after Tailhook had driven a pretty good wedge between servicemen and -women until 9/11 refocused everyone's attention on war. And as it turned out, Westmoreland's "freaks" are pretty damn good soldiers.

Getting to this point, however, was hard and ugly. The feminist assault took the form it did because feminista scorned the military *and* the women who loved it. Indeed, the feminista cared little about what happened to military women after some barrier or other came down. Go to the website of the National Organization for Women (NOW) and you will search in vain for any mention of servicewomen that is not a recitation of victimization, or for any recognition of service-women's accomplishments as combatants in any war the United States is engaged in. In military parlance, the feminista regarded military women as "expendable." And military women, for their part, often had no choice but to accept the infrequent and often arbitrary support of the very women who scorned them. Meanwhile, the servicemen who served alongside their sisters-in-arms were reeling from bureaucratic game playing that neither covered Pentagon posteriors effectively nor contributed to the common defense.

Probably no issue did more damage than that of sexual harassment. An awful lot of people got hurt when the military first began to seriously tackle this problem in the rocky 1990s. Some of them were women who went public with crimes when the military institution refused to take those crimes seriously; others were men caught up in the search for scapegoats, or punished for doing something dumb, not nasty; others simply endured time-wasting efforts, such as being required to sit through idiotic sensitivity training on sexual harassment and assault and what became known as COO, "consideration of others." These were often just more examples of bureaucratic dodging. Sergeant Cooper or

:ker is being accused of harassing or raping Private Brown or t Black? That's odd. They've had sensitivity training. We've done our job. Case closed. Contrast this to the attitude on race: As a first lieutenant in the Marines, my partner Philip had the additional duty of serving as a human relations trainer. The Marine Corps took the simple attitude, "We don't care what you think, but we're going to control your behavior—and speech is behavior." The military could and should have taken the same approach to sex as it did to race.

As the era of scandals faded out after the 2000 elections, the advances toward women's equality under arms sloppily and painfully and hypocritically took hold. And by 9/11, it had become apparent to more and more men that the women were not the deviants; the men who demeaned and harassed and attacked servicewomen were.

Scandals, trials, and persecutions, according to those who study such things, can operate as a bonding mechanism, uniting a society against its deviants, whether they are real criminals or simply people outside the norm. But these scandals also become boundary markers when unity goes too far. Only when it's over do people look at what they've done—at the innocent women they've burned as witches, the innocent blacks they've lynched, the innocent teachers they've denounced as communists—and feel a shame that sticks. That shame is a necessary precondition for the rectification of past injustices and for the prevention of similar occurrences in the future. The military scandals of the last decade, from Tailhook to the horror of sustained sexual criminality at the service academies, have shone a glaring light upon how ready people were to excuse criminality within the military service. The military services have come a long way in how they deal with women, but as institutions, they have yet to integrate these changes into their perceptions of themselves as predominantly male institutions.

Forty-five years ago, women were still expected to devote themselves full-time to motherhood after they married. A married woman and mother with demanding work was an oxymoron. The career fields open to women in 1961 (just before Friedan published *The Feminine Mystique*) were very limited. Men were allowed to have fulfilling family lives *and* careers. It could be difficult, but they did not have to make the choice that most women did.

This was the background against which the women's movement, not yet self-obsessed and reflexively antimale, and the demands of the Vietnam War combined to influence Congress to lift the 2% ceiling on women's numbers in the armed services in 1967. From 1948 to 1969, women averaged 1.2% of military strength. The Gates Commission, established by President Nixon in 1969 to explore the feasibility of an all-volunteer force as an alternative to the draft, accepted that figure as a baseline. But by 1972, when the nation began moving toward the All-Volunteer Force, Secretary of Defense Melvin R. Laird began planning for the increased use of women to offset possible shortages of male recruits.[2]

For servicewomen to attain their civic birthright of equal protection under the law, they would have to take the military to court. Nothing was going to be given freely. In some instances servicewomen fought these battles on their own; in other cases, and often to forward their own agenda, the feminista helped. Occasionally, the military justice system worked as it should. No doubt, many servicewomen would have preferred not to have to go to court, but rather to simply be accepted as sisters and professional equals, not on a person-by-person, unit-by-unit basis, but by the institution they wanted so much to share in and to serve. But the exigencies and stridencies of those culture war years, coupled with the American love of tawdry scandal and the fact that nothing gets done in Washington, DC, unless it's a result of a scandal or a crisis, made that impossible. And the results, which saw both victory and defeat, ruined careers and embittered lives both female and male.

In 1969, U.S. Air Force Lieutenant Sharron Frontiero sought to obtain dependent's benefits for her husband, Joseph, a student receiving GI benefits: medical coverage and on-base housing. At the time, servicemen automatically received full benefits for their wives, regardless of their individual income and assets. Women, on the other hand, had to demonstrate that their husbands were in fact dependent upon them for more than half of their livelihood. Joseph Frontiero failed this test, prompting Lieutenant Frontiero to turn to the Southern Poverty Law Center and the Women's Rights Project of the American Civil Liberties Union.

In the case of *Frontiero v. Richardson* (1973), a plurality of the U.S. Supreme Court—which included Justice William J. Brennan, writing for William O. Douglas, Thurgood Marshall, and Byron R. White—would find in favor of Frontiero on the grounds of sex discrimination. Justice Lewis F. Powell wrote a concurrence for Chief Justice Warren E. Burger and Justice Harry A. Blackmun that found for Frontiero on the grounds that denying her husband benefits violated the due process clause of the Fifth Amendment. (Justice Potter Stewart wrote separately that the challenged laws worked an invidious discrimination in defiance of the Constitution.) Unlike Justice Brennan's opinion for the plurality of the court, which argued for treating sexual classifications as just as inherently suspect as racial ones, Powell's concurrence argued that defining sexual classifications as inherently suspect was best hammered out by the states during the ratification of the equal rights amendment. (Thirty of the necessary thirty-eight states had already ratified the ERA, which would have established the principle that sex, like race, is an inherently suspect category upon which to make legal distinctions.) The only dissenter was William H. Rehnquist.

Traditionally, the military granted waivers to women, especially to senior, trained women it wanted to keep, allowing children under eighteen to reside in their homes for more than thirty days a year. Pregnancy remained forbidden. It was the only temporary disability requiring discharge, and it was considered far worse for military efficiency than being drunk and disorderly or going absent without leave. A servicewoman's individual situation was irrelevant. If she became pregnant by rape; if she had an abortion or miscarried before her discharge; even if the father was married to her at the time of conception, or married her afterward, or was otherwise willing to assume all parental duties in case of the mother's deployment—all of these variations ensured the same outcome: goodbye. For decades the Army, Air Force, and Navy all played the game of waivers-of-convenience to avoid legal challenges to their policies. The Marine Corps refused their female members even that.

Marine Stephanie Crawford became pregnant in 1970; she was unmarried and promptly discharged. She applied for reenlistment and was refused because she had a child. (The Marines, as a matter of policy, denied enlistment to all mothers until 1976, even if the woman had formally surrendered all rights to her child's custody or if the child had been adopted by another family. As another matter of policy, they also notified the parents of the legally adult pregnant woman to inform them of their daughter's discharge and the reason for it.) *Reed v. Reed* (1971), the first landmark sex discrimination case, established that there only had to be a fair and substantial relationship between discriminating against a woman and the objective of any particular piece of legislation, for different treatments of different classes of people to meet the standard of the equal protection clause of the Fourteenth Amendment. This was a standard that women's rights activists had hoped to overturn in *Frontiero* with their attempt to achieve strict scrutiny for sexual classifications as well as racial ones. It was also a standard that allowed the Marines to discharge pregnant women and refuse enlistments to mothers. But by February 1976, the Department of Defense was already directing the military services to reduce attrition, and part of that attempt included new rules that allowed pregnant women to remain in the military. The Second Circuit Court ruled that the Marine Corps' discharge of Crawford violated her right both to due process and to equal treatment, and that she should be allowed to serve out the remaining months of her enlistment.[3]

Embedded in these policies toward pregnancy, motherhood, and marriage was a profound double standard, far less a statement about sexual morality than about human worth. The only men who might have been required to get the permission of their local commanders to marry were junior enlisted soldiers. It was never suggested that being a husband or a father, even a custodial single father, was fundamentally incompatible with military service. Nor were servicemen punished for fathering children out of wedlock, or even for abandoning those children in foreign countries where they would be despised as half-castes, their mothers as whores.

This systemic devaluation of women carried over to women's professional opportunities, as well. The officer candidate school (OCS) and Army ROTC, including Norwich University, the nation's oldest private military academy and the birthplace of ROTC, were considered good enough for women. The service academies, however, which produced a disproportionate share of the military's senior leadership, were to be kept for men only.[4] They were finally opened to women by an act of Congress in 1976, over the military's ferocious objections. Generals Matthew B. Ridgeway and Hal Moore, two of America's legendary soldiers, were among the most vocal opponents.[5]

The rationale behind the male-only policy was that the academies existed to produce future senior combat leaders. Never mind that West Point was founded to provide trained engineers, or that the vast majority of graduates of any service academy will never command large units in combat, and many leave after fulfilling their initial obligations. The anger and the arguments revolved around West Point's mystique. The participation of women in the profession of arms during peacetime was thought to dilute both the martial qualities of the military and the femininity of the women. However, there was also a widespread consensus that in the case of a national emergency, women could and would do everything the nation's survival demanded—including combat. In war, which is the raison d'être of the military, the greater the emergency, the less important mystique becomes. Even women and openly gay men can get permission to do for their country what they are denied during peace. As feminist political philosopher Judith Hicks Stiehm succinctly observed in 1981:

> *This meant, of course, what women were most excluded from,*
> *and what men were most closely guarding, was the peacetime*
> *military. In a sense, it was the role, the posture, the career,*
> *the profit—not the actual activity—that was being protected.*
> *Indeed, there is almost a correlation between barring females*
> *and a nonfighting military and including females and a fighting*

military. Yet women's exclusion had been justified on the
grounds of something not then existing—fighting! [6]

It's an observation that is still true today. Servicewomen, in this case sailors, had to sue to go to sea. In November 1976, three female officers and four enlisted women, including Navy electrician Yona Owens, sued to challenge Congress's prohibition of women on ships, except transports (the Navy had decommissioned its final transport ship in 1973) and hospital ships (the last decommissioned in 1975). Owens wanted to go to sea aboard the *Michelson,* a naval survey ship operated by civilians, which carried male Navy personnel and female civilians. The Navy said that if servicewomen were to be allowed on ships, it was only to be on tugs and other boats that did not actually reach blue water. Civilian women aboard seagoing Navy ships? Yes, *because* they were civilians. Female Navy personnel (not then thought of as sailors) at sea? No, because that would begin the process of admitting women to the seagoing brotherhood, which would precipitate the first step toward making the brotherhood not a brotherhood at all but something that there is still no word for—but that was then universally thought of as a lesser thing than a brotherhood because it contained women.

In July 1978, Judge John Sirica found for the plaintiffs in *Owens v. Brown.* The court ruled that the prohibition of women from sea service restricted their ability to enter trades with civilian applications and barred them from job and promotion opportunities; the limited and distorted career patterns open to women thus also limited their veterans' benefits and privileges. Furthermore, Sirica said, under the prohibition women were denied the opportunity to participate "in an 'essential national enterprise to the limits of their abilities.'" Based on this decision, the Navy slowly, reluctantly, began to put women aboard ships, although it would only begin to make its peace with seagoing female sailors after James Webb, Reagan's secretary of the Navy, resigned in 1988.[7]

The lawsuits didn't end until the admission of women to the Citadel and Virginia Military Institute (VMI). These two historic colleges have illustrious histories, and while they are not part of the military, they do contribute officers to it. In 1986, VMI's Board of Visitors reaffirmed their male-only policy. In 1989, the Justice Department brought suit against VMI on behalf of a female high school student who wished to attend; in 1990, VMI filed a countersuit asking that its all-male policy be declared constitutional. Of course, what these all-male policies were really about was keeping the prestige and the mystique for men. Because in fact, in order to pay the bills, VMI had begun allowing women to take summer and evening classes. And in order to attract more young men, VMI had dropped the requirement that its cadets be required to accept a post-graduation commission in the U.S. armed forces. In spite of this, Judge Jackson L. Kiser refused to follow gender discrimination law and held for VMI. In an appeal, the fourth circuit court ruled that VMI had three choices: integrate women; turn itself into a private college; or create a separate but equal institution for women. VMI responded by devising a plan, only briefly implemented, for a supposedly equivalent program—Virginia Women's Institute for Leadership (VWIL)—at nearby Mary Baldwin College. VWIL still exists; in fact, it is the only all-female military academy in the world. But VMI did not conceive of VWIL as a way to raise a corps of "Sister Rats" sharing almost everything with their brothers but barracks.

There were immediate, obvious disparities between the two institutions. Mary Baldwin was poor and in debt; VMI enjoyed lavish levels of public and private funding. Thanks to VMI's powerful alumni network,

VMI's athletic facilities, laboratories, classrooms, and faculty salaries were all markedly superior. The architecture of Mary Baldwin is that of a ladies' college, which is what it was founded to be; VMI is beautiful but stern and forbidding, self-consciously martial. Importantly, the curriculum at VWIL was to be far less mentally and physically demanding than that at VMI. The women would not be required to wear uniforms or be subject to military-style discipline on most days. Above all, they would not be subjected to a rigorous program of physical training or issued rifles and bayonets like VMI cadets, even though the very essence of the citizen, as affirmed in the Second Amendment to the Constitution, is the bearing of arms in the common defense—the "well-regulated militia" that covers the continuum from community self-defense to being the nation's trained and mobilized army during war.[8]

Inadequate funding for a rigorous academic program at VWIL was an issue far more difficult to tackle than the issues of physical training and arms. Much can be done with calisthenics and running, and free weights and weight machines are fairly cheap, especially compared to professional salaries. For that matter, so are arms and ammunition. In 2006, ten years after the VMI decision was handed down, M14 rifles are sold retail by private individuals for $1,200 to $1,600. Block purchases from the government would have resulted in a much lower cost per weapon. It was the refusal to institute a demanding physical training program, including the use of firearms, that made it very clear that VWIL as proposed was not a serious attempt to create a female military academy devised by women for women, borrowing from VMI's experiences and with VMI's assistance. It was proposed in an attempt to keep women out of VMI, a publicly funded institution that bestowed immense public and private prestige upon its male graduates and wielded very real power.

By 1996, the Supreme Court included Ruth Bader Ginsburg, who more than twenty years earlier, as the chief litigator for the ACLU's Women's Rights Project, had argued *Frontiero v. Richardson,* the court case that allowed servicewomen to claim dependents' benefits for their husbands without proving their husbands' dependency. Now, writing for a seven-justice majority in *United States v. Virginia et al.* (1996), Justice Ginsburg found VMI's refusal to admit women unconstitutional and subjected gender classifications to a heightened standard of skeptical scrutiny. Unfortunately, her opinion was far more about the diversity and equality of educational opportunities both VMI and VWIL offered than about citizenship and whether, in 1996, the equal protection clause of the Fourteenth Amendment included women.

The real heart of the case was contained in this clause of Justice Ginsburg's opinion: "Neither the goal of producing citizen soldiers nor VMI's implementing methodology is inherently unsuitable to women." As the feminist legal scholar Diane H. Mazur, herself a former captain in the U.S. Air Force, wrote:

> *The better analysis would have stopped instantly at the word "citizen" and inquired whether any circumstances can justify the exclusion of women from an institution that trains persons in their full range of responsibilities as citizens. . . . VMI represents the ideal of citizen responsibility for military service, and women cannot be excluded as a group from that responsibility.*[9]

Such an analysis would have done two things: It would have not threatened single-sex education per se (I hold no brief for either integrated or single-sex education, except to note that some young people of both sexes excel in one environment, some in the other), and it would have begun to establish as a matter of law that the equal protection clause may apply to women, in the context of military service. This would have pertained to VMI by determining that VMI could *not* meet its goal of producing citizen soldiers (and commissioned officers for the armed forces) if women were excluded. An opinion upholding women's rights to equal educational opportunities was much less radical than an opinion upholding their right (and responsibility) to equal participation in the common defense. Even though VMI was not the U.S. military, and therefore any decision about women's equality under arms would have had only tangential applicability to the military itself, neither Ginsburg, writing for the majority, nor Chief Justice Rehnquist, concurring separately, was willing to go there.

Curiously, VMI's alumni may have been. VMI is a *rich* institution, and not merely because the Commonwealth of Virginia has been so generous to it, but also because its alumni are. In her opinion, Justice Ginsburg noted that it had the largest endowment of any undergraduate institution in the nation. VMI had a choice: It did not have to integrate; it could have forgone state and federal money and remained all-male. And initially, there was strong alumni support to do just that. But when push came to shove, suddenly a lot of money wasn't there.

VMI is now coed, and is thus able to properly fulfill its mission of providing officers for the armed forces. When VMI went coed, the Citadel—the Military College of South Carolina—abandoned its attempts to remain all-male as well. The enduring image of its struggle to remain all-male is that of Shannon Faulkner, in August 1995, disconsolate and visibly out of shape, standing between two male marshals. Had her feminist legal advisors understood as much about the military as they did about the law of sexual discrimination, they would have ensured that Faulkner showed up in exceptionally good physical shape and avoided media attention like the plague. As Mazur noted, "If their client fails to make the most of the opportunity, their effort in litigation loses much of its satisfaction; even more significantly, her failure disadvantages the larger community of servicewomen."[10]

As the era of lawsuits drew to a close with the integration of VMI and the Citadel, scandals and trials involving sex took their place. Tailhook was the most infamous and the most telegenic, but it was far from the worst. Much of what went on at Tailhook was piggish and idiotic, but most of it fell into the category of "conduct unbecoming" and "prejudicial to good order and discipline" rather than criminal sexual assault.

That is not true of three more notorious cases—one at Aberdeen Proving Ground involving drill instructors having sex with their trainees; one involving Sergeant Major of the Army Gene C. McKinney, who took sexual advantage of a number of female soldiers; and a third case involving sexual misconduct by Major General Larry G. Smith. During this same era, in 1997, the Army released the findings of its *Senior Review Panel Report on Sexual Harassment,* which found that while sexual *harassment* crossed gender, rank, and racial lines, sexual *discrimination* was more prevalent. As a result, all these cases coalesced into one big scandal.

The case at Aberdeen Proving Ground found that some of the trainees either were not coerced or didn't consider themselves to be victims in their involvement with their drill instructors. One trainee did not consider herself to have been sexually harassed when her drill sergeant shoved his hand down her sweatpants when passing her on the stairs. She told him to stop, and because she thought she could handle his assault herself, she didn't report it to his superior.[11] Other accusations and revelations involved trainees seducing drill instructors, either because they only knew how to relate to men sexually, or because they expected favors and leniency in return for sexual favors. Sadly, instead of showing their trainees by their example that the way to succeed in the Army is to be a good soldier and a good person, the drill instructors opted to have sex with these trainees and later compare notes. Other instructors relied on their rank and the power they held over trainees to get what they wanted without overt force.

The worst of the misconduct was vicious. Delmar Simpson was far from the only offender punished for using his position to solicit sex, but he appeared to take a particular pleasure in the use of sex to cause pain and humiliation. To obtain sex from female trainees, he threatened to fail them. He punched and kicked and pulled them by the hair. He used his weight to pin them down so he could copulate with them, a tactic that is rarely determined by law to be force culminating in rape because it leaves no marks. One woman was raped on nine separate occasions. Her testimony showed the deliberate destruction of her will: "I felt like I was a puppet, that I had strings attached to me. . . . It got to a point where I gave up trying to resist."[12]

A mostly male jury of soldiers found Simpson guilty of fifty-seven criminal offenses, including eighteen out of nineteen charges of rape. He was sentenced to twenty-five years in prison; reduced to private, the lowest enlisted rank; and dishonorably discharged from the Army. His company commander, Captain Derrick Robertson, was sentenced to four months of imprisonment and was dismissed from the military for pleading guilty to adultery and sodomy. He had sex, described as consensual, with a soldier who had gone to his home to complain of being sexually harassed by her drill sergeant.

Like many plea bargains, Robertson's sentence bore little relationship to the gravity of what he had done and tolerated. And the Aberdeen scandal revalidated the principle that a little tolerance of such offenses inevitably leads to more.

The second high-profile case was that of Command Sergeant Major Gene C. McKinney, the sergeant major of the Army, the Army's senior enlisted soldier, who reports only to the chief of staff of the Army and advises him on enlisted matters. This case involved allegations against McKinney by six female soldiers, including one who accused him of befriending her and then betraying her by forcing unwanted sexual intercourse. McKinney was six feet, two inches tall, an infantry veteran of Vietnam, while the woman was seven and a half months pregnant at the time of the assault. McKinney's greater height, weight, and combat experience, combined with her advanced pregnancy and extreme vulnerability to miscarriage, meant that McKinney had no need to use the kind of force that the law recognized as force to perpetrate this violation. Since his having sex with her against her wishes wasn't seen as force, he was charged with adultery, not rape.

He was also accused of attempting to have sex with one of his aides, Sergeant Major Brenda Hoster. In this incident, he grabbed Hoster and kissed her. When she tried to escort him out of her room, he grabbed her by her waist, lifted her off her feet, and told her that he could "take her." He then tried to make her look at his groin, claiming she had aroused him. Hoster reported McKinney's assault to Colonel Robert Gaylord, deputy chief of public affairs, and asked for a transfer; Gaylord told her to confront McKinney instead. Rather than do so, Hoster, one of the Army's youngest sergeants major, retired from the Army. She made her charges public only when the Army failed its female soldiers by naming McKinney to the Army's Senior Review Panel on Sexual Harassment.[13]

McKinney ended up being acquitted of all but one of the charges against him, that of obstructing justice by trying to coach one of the women to say that their relationship had been a matter of discussing her professional development. As a punishment, he was reduced in rank one grade, which reduced his retirement pay. Of course, if no crimes had been committed and he had in fact only tried to mentor the woman, there would have been no obstruction of justice, and the court would have had no reason to demote him. The verdict was a tacit acknowledgment that McKinney's behavior was utterly unacceptable even if not criminal, and it could permanently shame him.[14]

The final case, in 2000, involved Lieutenant General Claudia J. Kennedy, the Army's deputy chief of staff for intelligence, who filed a formal sexual harassment complaint against Major General Larry G. Smith. She alleged that he had sexually assaulted her in her office in October 1996. She characterized the incident as unpleasant, less as deeply affecting her than as shocking and angering her: She liked Smith, and she liked his wife, and they'd helped each other out in the way Army families do. She did not report the incident when it happened because they were of the same rank, and she did not want to be discredited, or to discredit other women.[15] She had, however, referred to the incident in an open forum a few months after it happened, citing it as an example of how she had been sexually harassed during her career; later, Army investigators would use this as evidence in her favor.[16] When Smith was nominated for the Army's post of deputy inspector general in September 1999, which would have made him responsible for investigating accusations of misconduct and crimes, including sexual misconduct, Kennedy sought legal advice from an unnamed senior civilian lawyer in the Department of the Army. He told her that her initial impulse, which was to meet with Smith privately and suggest he withdraw from consideration, telling him that if he didn't, she would go to the Army leadership, would be extortion. After further consideration, the lawyer decided she should not go to the vice chief of staff of the Army but instead report the incident to the Army's inspector general, thereby ensuring that it would be handled through official channels. Kennedy took the lawyer's advice at the end of September 1999, and the ensuing inspector general's investigation found that she was telling the truth and that General Smith's conduct was not in line with that of the gentleman a male officer *must* be (just as a female officer must be a gentlewoman—a fine old word that has largely been forgotten). Reading the handwriting on the wall, General Smith retired early, a decision that probably cost him some money; the report about his conduct cost him his reputation.[17]

In a genuinely civilized military, the difference between soldiers of any rank and bullies (or worse) is an internalized code of significant personal restraint; soldiers who cannot manage that restraint are unfit to wear the uniform, much less supervise or command others.

The late 1990s were not a good time to be in the Army. Not for women, many of whom were *not* mistreated, and to a significant extent not for men, but not because they were losing rights or opportunities to women. The cold war was over and the forces were drawn down at a time when operations in the Balkans and in Africa were increasing. During this era of shrinking forces and intensified operational tempo, the forces were undergoing a sea change in how they thought about women. The Army's *Senior Review Panel Report on Sexual Harassment* shows an Army that was wounded in its soul, adrift, floating, and confused at a time of tremendous institutional change.

During the years from the end of the draft to the end of the messy, dangerous post–cold war peace on 9/11, the Army kept stepping on its institutional crank—to put it into appropriately macho language. The fuss about integrating West Point, and later VMI, was not about leadership, in combat or otherwise. The Army routinely commissions more officers from ROTC and OCS, both long open to women, than from West Point, let alone VMI and the Citadel. The career officer corps contains far more officers from these sources than from West Point; indeed, the propensity of West Pointers to leave the Army after serving their obligatory five years or so has long been a matter of concern. In times of war, the Army takes all it can get. Keeping West Point and the rest of the service academies male was about preserving male peacetime privilege and power, not providing junior (or senior) officers for combat in a sustained war.

Sometimes there was the callous belief that women who reported sexual harassment should have to accept ostracism and retaliation for reporting crimes. And sometimes the Army engaged in pure, bureaucratic self-protection stamped with the lack of imagination that is also typical of large bureaucracies.

A personal favorite example: In 1997, a high-level Army panel not otherwise identified, but almost certainly the Senior Review Panel, was reported to have removed six questions from its survey of sexual harassment. These questions were about patronizing strip clubs, watching pornographic movies, and bragging about sexual activities. Preliminary responses from male soldiers had shown a striking correlation between these activities and tendencies toward sexual harassment in units; but the Army found the questions irrelevant to sexual harassment and the habits they alluded to embarrassing.[18]

One of the reasons the Army kept stepping on its institutional crank was that the last group they expected to lead an assault against them were the professional feminista. Of course, the Army would never have been happy about outside criticism by women. The Army is supposed to be a man's world, despite the large numbers of women who serve in it. But the women leveling the criticism were not women who wished the Army well because it was an important institution, and they thought women should be part of it because they were American citizens. Rather, it was leveled by women who typically found the institution itself disgusting, who didn't think it should even exist, and who believed that the men who joined did so for sadomasochistic reasons and the women for mercenary ones.

In sum, the only thing that the feminist movement offered the military institution was humiliation. The only thing it offered military women was a cynical temporary alliance. And the only thing it offered military men was the opportunity to be squeezed between bureaucratic self-protection and feminist bile.

It didn't have to be that way. The very best early work on the sexually integrated military was done by feminist political philosopher Judith Hicks Stiehm. Her books *Bring Me Men and Women: Mandated Change at the U.S. Air Force Academy* and *Arms and the Enlisted Woman* have stood the test of time far better than almost anything else published on the subject. Stiehm seriously explored what the entry of relatively large numbers of women into the military might mean from a perspective that was both overtly feminist and respectful of the military's institutional purpose. Her military work has never received a fraction of the attention it deserves. In an interview with me, she spoke to the reasons behind this when she said that too many feminist academics do not "think the military itself is a valid and respectable and important institution. And the military itself just thinks that anyone writing about it from the outside doesn't really get it."

Most servicewomen are neither feminists nor academics. In particular, those servicewomen who served during the culture wars found themselves, like Stiehm, betwixt and between: between a military that culturally and institutionally did not welcome them and a feminist movement they embarrassed by their commitment to protect and defend the Republic. Academics had the academy. Military women didn't even have the backing of the institution they served. Which was one reason why Pat Schroeder supported them.

Congresswoman Schroeder's name runs like a bold thread through the tapestry of women's integration into the military—colored black or bright gold, depending on your perspective. To me, that thread is the brightest gold. A Democrat, Schroeder represented Colorado's First Congressional District from 1972 to 1996, serving on the House Armed Services Committee (HASC) her entire time in the House. As freshmen and newcomers to HASC, she and fellow Democrat Ron Dellums of California were humiliated by HASC Chairman F. Edward Hébert of Louisiana, who forced them to share a chair. In his view, a white woman and a black man were each worth only one half of a white man. She studied the war records of her fellow committee members, and when they questioned her ability to serve on the committee without ever having been in combat, she would reply, "Then you and I have a lot in common."[19] For twenty-four years, her entire time on the HASC, Schroeder pushed the integration of women into the military.

She was brutally caricatured by much of the cultural Right as an anti–Vietnam War feminist out to destroy the military by forcing it to admit women. Certainly, there were feminists who wanted the military to admit women in the hopes that they would destroy it by making it less masculine. But while Schroeder may have been against the Vietnam

War and a feminist, the Marine Corps took the time to educate her and found her to be a good friend. You don't spend twenty-four years on the HASC if you're not serious about defense.

Though Schroeder is hardly the only politician to have made enemies, she was one of the few women to do so deliberately rather than smiling at slights and insults. Which made her that much harder to take. She was also among the first wave of female politicians to win office in her own right, rather than "inherit" the position as a widow. Schroeder was prowoman—she worked to get military, CIA, and Foreign Service pensions declared joint property because she knew that those spouses, then almost entirely women, had forgone their own careers to help their husbands. She was also profamily. She understood marriage to be an economic partnership and she supported everything from family leave to allowing military couples to deduct adoption expenses. But even though there were those who wanted to paint her so, she was not antimale. Her friends from Harvard Law School tended to be ex-servicemen, usually pilots like herself. (She has a private pilot's license and put herself through college by salvaging wrecked aircraft.) Her husband, James, an ex-Navy man, was her greatest supporter and closest political advisor. And if she championed better childcare for military families, something considered a women's issue, she also championed higher hazardous duty pay for service members, which usually meant servicemen.

Congresswoman Schroeder's consistent advocacy for the personal and professional dignity of servicewomen probably cost her the chairmanship of the HASC in 1993, when Les Aspin became secretary of defense and Ron Dellums took over the HASC. Beltway pundits remarked that Dellums got the chairmanship because the leadership considered a communist to be less of a threat than a feminist. Never mind that they were allies. The pundits simply couldn't conceive of a promilitary feminist as chairman of the HASC. Schroeder paid another price as well. In 1992, she was the target of an obscene skit by Navy aviators during the "Tomcat Follies" at the Officers' Club at Miramar Naval Air Station. She was also physically attacked by a cameraman after he finished taping her for a TV appearance about the subject of women in the military and in combat; it took three people to pull him off her.

When I contacted Schroeder in the autumn of 2005 to ask her why, decade in and decade out, she had taken on the cause of servicewomen when she gained little benefit by doing so, she offered a very simple explanation:

"[The armed services] were educating them at the service academies, but they were not using them. And it was just crazy. The military was never interested in them; the situation was not for women like it was for black men; they were treated as a social experiment. And the feminist movement was very antiwar. 'Why do we need a defense establishment? Why do we need a military at all?' There were a lot of fights [between myself and other feminists]. And I thought the loneliest thing on the planet was to be a military woman. They were orphans."

Schroeder considered her fights with her feminist friends to be some of the most painful of the battles she waged on behalf of servicewomen. Military women, whatever their accomplishments, simply weren't their kind. Feminists could not understand Schroeder's efforts and concerns for them.[20] Sisterhood was indeed a powerful concept, but when push came to shove, not everybody could be a "real" sister.

Of course, only one label adequately describes the role Schroeder played in opening up the military to women: citizen. She left the military better than she found it, and the Republic ow

debt of gratitude.

––––––––––– ⊕ –––––––––––

In retrospect, though the movement toward equality under arms was hard and ugly, one might make the argument that it couldn't have been any other way. The real problem was not feminists like Schroeder or Stiehm, or servicewomen like Hoster and Kennedy. Nor was the problem that military men were barbarians or worse. In fact, the vast majority were decent, honorable, and well-behaved.

The problem, in essence, was twofold: First, the military simply could not imagine that servicewomen were worth the trouble of making fundamental institutional changes. A rule of marketing new products says that people do not make big changes for modest advantages. They have to see major value before they adapt. The military, an inherently conservative institution that was under sustained attack by a feminist movement that hated it, could not see any major benefits until very recently. Second, the military couldn't disaggregate the problem. It was unable to separate the defense of a masculine institution from the defense of traditionally male activities and attitudes that were ugly and sometimes criminal. The military knew that rape, prostitution, and pornography did not go hand in hand with the making of good combat soldiers, but it often chose to look the other way because of its inability to separate an attack against bad behavior from an attack on the institution as a whole.

Nor was it getting a lot of nonfeminist help. During the Aberdeen and McKinney scandals, Richard Rayner wrote an essay entitled "The Warrior Besieged" for *The New York Times Magazine* that tried to examine servicewomen's impact upon what it means to be a warrior. (The military often uses the word *warrior* to distinguish "warfighters" from bureaucrats in uniform. In actuality, a warrior is someone for whom combat is a means of individual self-expression; a soldier is someone for whom combat is a matter of discipline. Soldiers beat warriors almost every time, and when they lose, they inflict disproportionate damage on the victors, even when their numbers and arms are inferior, because of discipline.) In seven thousand words, Rayner never once got an experienced male soldier to talk about connections between military and criminal (including sexual) aggression. Had he done so, he might have found that these connections are fewer and weaker than is commonly supposed. He did quote strategic theorist Edward Luttwak, who was never a soldier, as saying: "Demasculinize an army and of course rape will stop. But is that what we want? Men who have that inadequacy join the armed forces. If you take away that motivation, you're in trouble."[21] I personally know of no instance of the feminista taking their antimilitary animus that far, let alone doing it that publicly, and yet Luttwak was considered a friend of the military.

Why did the military dig in on precisely the wrong issues, condoning or ignoring crimes and attitudes that they knew were both morally and militarily counterproductive? I suspect that it had something to do with a fundamental rule of politics. Who does something is as important as what gets done. The integration of the military wasn't being pushed by feminists who thought that as citizens, women, including feminist women, should be in the military because it is an honorable institution; it was being pushed by feminista who wanted to humiliate the men in it. Maternal feminist Sara Ruddick's essay "Pacifying the Forces: Drafting Women in the Interests of Peace," is a case in point. She writes:

> *Could we satisfy both feminists and antimilitarists by drafting*
> *women in the interests of peace? . . . Many people support*

a draft on the ground that conscripts are less eager for battle than self-selected volunteers. Women conscripts might be especially reluctant to fight, their families particularly appalled to see them on the battlefield.[22]

Ruddick's is an appalling proposal, barbaric in its reckless disregard for human life. You draft people for war: either to fight it or to deter it by being so strong no one wants to pick a fight with you. And the quickest way to lose people in combat is to not be wholeheartedly committed to the thorough, professional use of violence. No wonder the military resisted the feminista—but in doing so, they overlooked the fact that servicewomen were their military sisters.

———————— ⊕ ————————

So, what do the feminista who pushed the integration of women into the military think now, after more than three years of war?

I called the National Organization for Women to request an interview with Patricia Ireland (president of NOW from 1991 to 2001) and Karen Johnson, a retired Air Force lieutenant colonel who just ended her term as executive vice president. I wanted to talk to them about the roles they played in opening the military to servicewomen. I received messages saying my requests would be passed along to Ireland and Johnson. No one ever contacted me. The second time I called, I was told to send an email requesting interviews with them. Again, no response. I chose not to try a third time: The refusal to respond is also part of the story, and of the record.

At present, the feminista who still exist (there aren't many because they helped splinter and isolate a necessary movement) are largely silent. Approving of what servicewomen are doing in Iraq and

Afghanistan entails recognizing that there is a profound difference between the United States and the Arab/Muslim world in terms of the status of women. A serious feminist leadership would acknowledge that difference and accept the responsibility for taking sides in this war, rather than post (as NOW did) an online petition that calls for a peace process in Iraq. It was a pathetically sentimental document, not a serious appraisal of the enormous human and financial costs of a war that has resulted in no commensurate gain in security to this country. I'd sign *that* serious but sadly hypothetical petition after jumping for joy that a feminist organization had finally gotten it, and was encouraging women to think seriously about national security. I long for a feminist movement that tells American women that the polity that has largely accepted our equality as citizens and human beings requires our participation in this odd, twilight war for the survival of our republic. This is not a matter of waging some crusade into Muslim lands to liberate those who do not wish to be liberated, or make them be like us. This is a matter of quite simply saying that as American women are citizens of the republic, they have a role to play in its defense, a role in understanding and waging its wars, a role in sorting out the good ideas from the bad and helping execute the former. And serious feminists should be thinking about, doing, and encouraging other women to think about and do these things.

And what about the men who vocally opposed integration on the grounds that it would destroy combat effectiveness, unit cohesion, and the overall discipline of the military? I had no interest in rehashing their arguments, but I did have one question: Had anything, in their opinion, changed since 9/11?

To find out, I contacted three men who have published arguments against women's equality under arms.

The first was Brian Mitchell, a former U.S. infantry officer whom I once met at a retirement party several years ago. In 1989, he published *Weak Link: The Feminization of the American Military;* nine years later, he wrote an updated version, *Women in the Military: Flirting with Disaster.* He introduces the latter with the statement that his book

> *is the only in-depth treatment that offers an alternative view of the revolution that threatens to leave the American military no more disciplined, no more efficient, no more fearsome and no more military than the United States Postal Service.*[23]

In the book, he presents a laundry list of complaints against women, beginning with menstruation (sanitary supplies are an undue burden on the logistics system) and ending with the inability of female West Point cadets to draw back the bolt on the old M14 rifle, thus requiring them to be issued M16s. (Never mind that the M14, fine as it was, was removed from widespread use by the Army during the early years of the Vietnam War.) Mitchell rejects the ancient linkage between citizenship and military service as a "canard," which is perhaps a worthwhile exercise in free speech but contrary to political fact in the United States.[24] As for the value of citizenship for women, something that many feminists struggled long and hard for, Mitchell's interpretation is that its only function is to give women more personal power in the political arena. But, he argues, when men exercise power over others, that's not power, that's authority—because they acknowledge they are subordinate to others. After all, "Men who wield *power* answer to no one."[25]

Mitchell is now Washington bureau chief of *Investor's Business Daily*. I called *IBD* to request an interview. Kathleen Sherman, vice president and director of corporate communications, called me back and told me she had talked to Mitchell's editor, who thought there was simply too much of a time crunch for Mitchell to be interviewed by me. I sensed a clear embarrassment in her voice. I told her that I only needed to interview Mitchell briefly. She told me to send her an email; she couldn't get off the phone fast enough. My email included two questions: Have your thoughts on women in the military and in combat changed since 9/11, and particularly since the Iraq War? If so, how and why; if not, why not? I received a nice reply from Sherman saying that she had checked with the executive editor, and they had to pass on the interview request, but she wished me great success and would look for my work.

The next man I sought out was Martin van Creveld, an Israeli with a loyal American following. Dr. van Creveld is a serious military historian who has taught at many of the Western world's strategic institutes; some of his work is of seminal importance. But when it comes to women in the military, his usual incisiveness deserts him.

In his book *Men, Women, and War,* van Creveld posits that the real reason women seldom participate in war on a large scale is not their own inabilities but the psychological handicaps of men. He finds women biologically superior to men in many ways, most crucially in our ability to have children, an ability which he feels renders men disposable, and for which men compensate by excluding women from certain activities. It is this, even more than women's weaker bodies and life-cycle handicap of bearing children, that leads men to exclude them from war.[26] Thus, and somewhat illogically, he sees it as men's duty to protect women by fighting for the chance to violate them:

By demonstrating the domination of enemy women and the
ultimate humiliation of enemy men, rape is what war is all about.
Even if those among the victors who are guilty of it are
apprehended and punished and even if it never takes place.[27]

For a military historian of van Creveld's accomplishments to write this is simply tragic.

I emailed van Creveld in Germany and he agreed to talk to me in a telephone conversation. Again, I asked whether the performance of servicewomen in Iraq and Afghanistan had changed his thinking? Not really, he said. "I have seen this sort of thing before in Israel." He had read my *Seattle Weekly* article, "Lionesses of Iraq" (upon which the third chapter of this book is based). He told me, "As you know, we have Israeli women manning the roadblocks, and as far as I'm concerned all [the American servicewomen] do is to maltreat and abuse Iraqi women. Just as our female soldiers abuse Arab women. What you have here is Israeli women abusing Palestinian women, and American women abusing Iraqi women on behest of men. So where is the great gain for feminism? You tell me."

I asked Dr. van Creveld if it was abuse to search for weapons and papers of intelligence value, and he replied that it was. "I would argue that our entire presence in the territories, like your entire presence in Iraq, is one long story of abuse . . . because you are ten thousand times as strong as the enemy, so what you can do is only abuse." Most Arab women, of course, feel very differently about being searched by a woman than by a man. Furthermore, van Creveld's comments about Israeli presence in the territories being fundamentally abusive puts his comments about searching Iraqi women, or killing Iraqi men, into context.

I knew he was no more in favor of the Iraq War than I was, and I would have liked to discuss with him the ethical possibilities for defending oneself against a weaker enemy. But he turned the conversation back to my article. "As for your big lionesses—look at the figures. Do you know how many American women have died in Iraq?"

"Yes, I do," I replied. "Casualty rates are about—"

"Two percent," he interrupted. "That is only, as you know, one-seventh [of the total number of] women in the military. . . . So they're not lionesses. The great majority are sitting targets. It would be a very good idea for U.S. men if more women got themselves killed. That would mean that fewer men would be killed." If he was baiting me, I didn't bite. Having a background in military history myself, I understood his point: that the willingness to accept casualties is often a rough measure of combat motivation. But I also knew (and as a military historian, he should have, too) that the only way you would get such a remotely even distribution of casualties would be if women were evenly distributed throughout the military. And they're not.

As of October 2005, women made up approximately 11% (not 15%) of the troops deployed to Iraq and Afghanistan because they are overwhelmingly concentrated in noncombat positions. In the Marine Corps and the Army, which have borne the brunt of the fighting in Iraq, casualties have been concentrated in the infantry and in armor and artillery troops serving as dismounted infantry. At the same time, very few women go outside the wire on missions, partially due to the numbers, partially due to the reluctance of some commanders to send women when they could send men (about which I have heard far more complaining than rejoicing by women). So it is no wonder that female casualties run only 2%, rather than 11%, of total losses. And it's doubtful van Creveld would call the infantrymen who die in mortar attacks or suicide bombings sitting targets.

He finished our interview by making it clear that he though[t] war is to men what childbirth is to women, and that he simply cou[ld not] understand why women wished to serve in the military when they don't have to. "If I were [Freud] sitting in heaven watching all this, I would be holding my belly laughing my head off and saying, 'You see? I was perfectly right. This whole feminism is the biggest manifestation of penis envy.'" When I hung up the phone, I was saddened rather than angered by his comments. He had the serious scholar's ability to put the trend of American women participating in combat into historical perspective, yet he had chosen to indulge himself instead.

My conversation with Dr. van Creveld left me anxious for a less psychoanalytically informed assessment. I called Dr. Charles Moskos, professor emeritus of sociology at Northwestern University, dean of American military sociologists and a 1950s Army draftee. When he served on the Presidential Commission on the Assignment of Women in the Armed Forces in 1992, he voted against opening combat aviation; either voted against dropping the risk rule or abstained from voting on it (for he was not among those who dissented on keeping it closed); and voted against allowing women into both the direct ground combat arms and special operations troops. I asked him if women's performance since 9/11 had changed his views. He gave me a simple and revealing answer: "No. I'm an old codger."

Many people cannot change their views to reflect a changing reality, but few of them are honest enough to admit it.

In May 2005, 14.6% of the Army was female. By December 2005, the war in Iraq had begun to seriously harm the Army's recruiting efforts, and there appears to be no end to that damage in sight. Some blame declining numbers of recruits on the youth of the United States, as lamentably narcissistic and materialistic; others blame President Bush for not "selling the war" and pushing for volunteers. Some hold that young Americans of both sexes are passing judgment upon the necessity of the Iraq War by refusing to fight in it.

The truth is probably a mixture of all three of these explanations. But the effect is undeniable. The Army, despite and perhaps because of its game playing (lowering quotas and standards, especially), is pressed for personnel. Moreover, the Army must tread very carefully as it transforms from a structure of ten regular divisions (very large units are suitable for conventional wars) to about seventy small brigades that are lighter and more deployable. These are combat brigades that are supposed to contain their own support and service support elements in a forward support company (FSC), and the numbers of both the Army itself and of the FSCs dictate that many of those troops will be women. But since such a scenario would require collocation, the Army is still playing word games, promising that the women will be in separate brigade support battalions, to the rear of the combat brigades, and that any women who are where they shouldn't be will be evacuated any time their combat brigade is conducting combat operations.[28]

It's the same old game. The Army says it will evacuate women who find themselves in or near combat, but it won't, because it cannot fight without them; yet, institutionally, it cannot admit this reality to itself, let alone publicly. Moreover, the Army knows of the long and honorable tradition of male troops going AWOL in order to do such things as leave the hospital before they should to rejoin their units. Such incidents are part of legend. In previous wars and engagements, such as Grenada and Panama, servicewomen have made no secret of their rage at not being allowed to deploy with their units. As women have become less defensive about being soldiers, and men more accepting of them as soldiers, it is likely that such incidents will not be isolated if the Army tries to withdraw women wholesale from a combat zone. I suspect the Army's leadership has no desire to provoke the first female reverse mutiny—what the Germans called the *Flucht nach vorn* (flight to the front) in World War II—in U.S. history. And their male comrades would have every right to expect them to stay put in their areas of expertise because they *need* them there.

--------- ⊕ ---------

In May 2005, Congressman Duncan Hunter (R-CA), Vietnam veteran and chairman of the HASC, probably came close to precipitating just such a mutiny. On 11 May 2005, Military Personnel Subcommittee chairman Congressman John McHugh (R-NY) offered an amendment (now known as the Hunter/McHugh amendment) to the National Defense Authorization Act to remove women from all FSCs, regardless of name, that were providing support or service support to direct ground combat battalions. Taken seriously, this amendment would have meant removing the vast majority of female soldiers from Iraq.

The amendment passed a subcommittee vote along party lines, Republicans voting for it and Democrats against it. Opposition from the Democrats on the subcommittee and last-minute faxes from Dr. Francis J. Harvey, secretary of the Army, and General Richard A. Cody, vice chief of staff of the Army, could not prevent its passage. In a handwritten note, General Cody wrote that he had discussed the issue of women in FSCs with Chief of Staff of the Army General Peter J. Schoomaker, and that Schoomaker had concurred with Cody's assessment that Hunter's proposed amendment would only "cause confusion in the ranks."

Lieutenant General James L. Campbell, director of the Army staff, noted that passage of the amendment would mean that 21,925 slots currently open to female soldiers would be closed. Signing for the Association of the United States Army, General Gordon R. Sullivan, himself a former chief of staff of the Army, opposed the amendment. So did the National Guard Association of the United States, headed by Stephen M. Koper, a retired Air Force brigadier general.

On 18 May, the full HASC considered a watered-down version of the Hunter/McHugh amendment, legally freezing women in rear services units, and on 23 May, the House passed the amendment, which was yet a bit further diluted but still froze women in the positions they were currently serving in and mandated a study of what female soldiers were actually doing. While in many ways the Hunter/McHugh amendment codified Secretary of Defense Aspin's 1994 policy on the assignment of women, prohibiting them from being assigned to, or collocating with, direct ground combat units of brigade size and smaller, or serving in direct ground combat positions, there was a change. Aspin had issued that policy to *expand* servicewomen's opportunities. And even before Aspin issued his policy, the Army had issued its own regulation, AR 600-13, assigning and collocating women a whole echelon further forward than the Aspin policy would permit—outside combat arms battalions, not brigades.

In an attempt at damage control after the Hunter/McHugh amendment passed, Hunter's office put out a fact sheet stating that his attempted amendment would have closed no MOSs to women. True, as far as it went, keeping in mind that an MOS is a skill; assignment to a unit is a different matter. But Captain Lory Manning's excellent statistical report *Women in the Military: Where They Stand,* issued by the Women's Research and Education Institute in 2005, made it very clear that the Army had not been exaggerating when it estimated that Hunter's attempt to close FSCs to women would mean closing nearly 22,000 positions to women.[29]

The reaction of the organized feminist movement was limited: very few op-eds, a press release from NOW. They seemingly had nothing to contribute—though, given that their history and attitudes had only let servicewomen down, they weren't missed. The only women pushing the further integration of servicewomen and fighting the Hunter/McHugh amendment were either servicewomen or women who valued the military as an institution.

In fact, the only woman still trumpeting the old, and now very out-of-date, line "The feminists are out to destroy the military!" is Elaine Donnelly, president of the Center for Military Readiness. Donnelly's recommendations on barring women from combat aviation were dismissed long ago; for the past eleven years the military has ignored her agitation for the repeal of the Aspin policy and the reinstatement of the risk rule. The political landscape has changed. There's a war going on, although you wouldn't know it to read the Center for Military Readiness's *Notes* and *Reports*.

Donnelly and I crossed swords in June 2005, shortly after my piece, "All the Sisters and All the Brothers . . . " ran in the *Proceedings* of the U.S. Naval Institute. She sent an email to Philip and me to complain about our work. She wrote that she was disappointed in my writing about servicewomen in Iraq and that she had expected me to be more "objective." Philip and I responded in turns in the same email. I quoted Justice John Marshall Harlan's dissent in Plessy v. Ferguson that the Constitution neither knows nor tolerates classes of citizens.[30] Philip wrote that I had gone to Iraq and Afghanistan, spending two months embedded with combat troops, and asked if she would be going. She did not, she replied, have any plans to go to Iraq or Afghanistan, which was why she was hoping for an "objective" account from me. She also did not understand what my comments meant in the context of our conversation.

Congressman Hunter was within his constitutional purview to demand that the Army explain what it is doing with women troops, for the Army is clearly pushing the boundaries of policies governing the assignment of women soldiers. Perhaps he meant to protect his sisters, but he was once a soldier, and he should have known that his attempts to restrict their service dishonored them. The Army was caught off guard when it was called to provide this accountability. In point of fact, the Army (and the Marine Corps) fought Hunter hard, but they fought defensively, by defending women soldiers, rather than offensively, by stating forthrightly that it was time to expand women's roles, not decrease them.

Unfortunately, the Army (and the Marine Corps) views this as an issue not worth expending political capital on. They do not see it as a matter of keeping faith with their military sisters. They see it as a political issue with huge costs and little gain. Let it be decided at some later date by younger men who are more comfortable working with women as equals. They may be right. Many people, far from all of them chauvinist pigs, find the subject of women in combat very emotional. Yet it was a retired soldier, Colonel David Johnson, PhD, who summarized the slow, deep sea change running through the Army.

Johnson is a senior political scientist at Rand and the author of *Fast Tanks and Heavy Bombers: Innovation in the U.S. Army, 1917–1945.* His specialty is military transformation, and he is particularly interested in how institutions adapt to change. The son of an enlisted World War II paratrooper, he entered the Army in May 1972 as an ROTC graduate and retired as a full colonel in the field artillery in 1997. In the early 1980s, he knew two young female artillery officers serving in the

First Armored Division artillery, whom he described as West Pointers—hypercompetent, ambitious, dedicated women who wanted to be soldiers and who cared about soldiers.

In an interview he told me: "I understood, intellectually, that there was a cultural-generational issue about women in the military, but I quite frankly did not understand what people did not get about [those two women officers] doing the job as well or better than any men. The first classes of women who went through West Point went through conditions that were very similar to what blacks there went through, and anyone who can bear up under that, I want in my foxhole.

"What I see with combat exclusion is the domain of who's going to run the Army. Combat arms folks are the people who eventually run the Army. . . . And whether the exclusion of women from those branches is coincidental or what—they aren't going to run the Army."

Johnson spoke very directly about this common male attitude. "I have seen the role of women in the military change from this almost visceral inability to see that there was any role for [them] being forced on us, to a grudging acceptance, to a practical realization that [they] make up a substantial part of the force, to an individual inability to deny that they have made real contributions to the force."

Johnson knows full well the salient differences between integrating black men into the combat arms and integrating women into the Army at all, much less the combat arms. But he also believes that the real issue is neither skin color, nor sex, nor sexual orientation, but citizenship:

[It is] the obligation of all citizens to defend the Republic, not that of a select warrior caste. Rather than trying to find ways to exclude people who share this sense of how important the Republic is, and the necessity of defending it, we ought

*to be trying to find ways of including people who share this
sense of responsibility.*

*I just never got how we could put this warrior ethic in front
of the obligation to defend the Republic. It has always dumb-
founded me why we don't honor that more than we honor this
warrior tradition. The United States Army is not about war
fighting; it's about serving the Republic, and war fighting is a
dimension of that. Anyone who signs up for this life of service
should be cherished.*

*The criteria should be not who someone is, but what they believe
and what they can do. Any American—race, creed, color, gender,
sexual persuasion, orientation, whatever—should be welcomed. I
am very inclusive about* whatever. *We are all Americans.*

Johnson has always been bluntly outspoken on this issue, even
when he was on active duty, when it was an unpopular opinion. Now
his opinions are almost the norm. Throughout the research and writing of this book, I have received a great deal of cooperation from the
Army, virtually all of it on the record, and mostly by men with extensive experience in combat. (Some of it was with women.) In fact, many
times public affairs officers and sergeants would contribute their own
experiences and observations while I was interviewing other soldiers.
No woman, however leery, ever told me that she felt that my work or the
result of it would somehow force her into combat. Without exception,
every woman I have dealt with has understood that combat goes hand
in hand with being a soldier, even if she personally does not believe
she could hack it in combat, let alone in the infantry. Every woman has

understood that not only might she have to carry that burden, but that the Army has every right to expect it of her. Without exception, every woman I heard complain, complained about being restricted from combat service—again, even if she didn't think she could hack it. These women weren't Rambos. They understood the dangers involved, and it was simply very hard for them to watch men assume risks that they were forbidden to share.

Command Sergeant Major Lynette Harper, then of the Joint Logistics Command, put it best when I interviewed her at Bagram Airfield in February 2005. "The combat exclusion rule did not start becoming an issue until I realized that I could do anything the Army had to offer. . . . The reason I want to talk about this now is [because of] the great things I see and read about what women are doing with men: They're on patrols, they're out front. They're searching females. They're out with males on combat patrols here and in Iraq. Part of what bothers me is that I'm not sharing the risks of my male counterparts in those infantry battalions. When I hear [people] saying, 'Women shouldn't be killed or wounded or raped,' and mommies shouldn't be, I ask, 'What about men, what about daddies—is this okay for them?'"

———————— ⊕ ————————

It is time for the Army to end all restrictions against women in both occupational specialties and positions where women can be assigned. The simple fact is that as the demands of Iraq, Afghanistan, and future contingencies further stretch the Army, it will attach women wherever and in whatever capacities they are needed. Those women who for whatever reason are willing to take up the demanding service of being combat soldiers should be allowed to make that choice. It may be that there will be few of these women, but we have already learned that there are many more than have ever been expected. All in all, there are not that many men who choose combat voluntarily, either. Most do it out of a sense of duty, and a sense of honor, and a sense of responsibility for their country. As for those women who are willing to serve but who would prefer not to serve as combat soldiers per se, their wishes, just like the men's, should be accommodated insofar as the needs of the service permit.

It is time for the military to be as candid in their policies with women as they are with men. The hard truth of war is that even those who are neither combat soldiers nor in combat units may have to fight, and the Army has a moral obligation to its female soldiers, and to the nation, to train female soldiers to prevail. Support troops have always faced the possibility of combat, as we saw in the hard fate of the 507th Maintenance Company, but women seem not to take that to heart the same way men do. When the situation requires it, women will have to fight, and they should be physically and emotionally prepared for it.

In short, it is time for the military to treat women as they treat men: as intelligent, practical individuals who understand both their own capabilities and the needs of the service. These women have earned this equality. They will need courage and strength. Let the Army be as candid with them as it is with men, and it will not be disappointed.

Chapter 7

INDIVIDUALS BEING ALL THEY CAN ... AND MORE

⊕————————————————————

Well into the 1990s, reasonable men had reasonable concerns about women's performance in the armed services, and about how men would behave in the presence of women, as well as how both men and women would deal with the intimacy and emotional intensity of small combat units. Many of these men were older, and they simply had not had the experience that today's young men and women have—that of being friends and competitors in class and at play. As I researched this book, many of the men I talked to were shocked at how much the relationship between the sexes has changed since they were young, which in some cases was only about thirty years ago. For these older men (most of whom had little personal experience of roughhousing with female friends in soccer or volleyball, for example) the nearly five years since 9/11—a time of ever increasing numbers of women serving in austere and combat conditions—have greatly reduced legitimate concerns.

We now have a far larger database of women's capabilities as soldiers than we ever had before: between September 2001 and March 2006, more than 143,000 servicewomen rotated through Iraq, Afghanistan, and the ships in theater; by the time this book is published in August 2006, the number of women who have deployed to these theaters will have risen to approximately 170,000. Acceptance of women and recognition of their competence are the emerging norms; the long-term trends are extremely positive. The feared wave of combat failures, pregnancies, and sexual assaults simply hasn't happened, which is changing people's minds. And servicemen are growing accustomed to living with servicewomen as active equals rather than as lesser contributors or burdens.

But there's a difference between not having a theoretical problem with women in the combat arms and ignoring practical issues. There are still substantial differences in male and female capabilities that can be sharply narrowed by proper training, while sexual harassment and assault are still major problems, less in their incidence than in their handling. The military has just begun to face the serious underlying issue of what it has begun to understand is sexism. For the foreseeable future, the military will remain majority male, especially in the combat arms, but if you look you will see changes, both overt and subtle.

On 20 November 2005, *The New York Times* ran an article by Juliet Macur about some of the eight women attached to the First Battalion, Thirtieth Infantry Regiment, Third Infantry Division. Macur wrote that "one of the guys once" told Specialist Katherine Daronche, "I don't agree with you being here." *One* of the guys. *Once.* Specialist Daronche is a medic. There are three sorts of people infantryman should avoid pissing off: medics, cooks, and supply providers. Most soldiers are too smart, or at least sufficiently concerned with their comfort and survival, to have to be told this. The article does not address the response of this male soldier's male peers to his statement. I suspect, however, that his

buddies might have said something like, "Okay, then, if we're
don't we just tell her to treat you last?" But if you're a woma.
outnumbered by men, and you don't hear the jerk being ragged
"counseled") by his buddies, the guy who redefines the term "dumb
grunt" can seem a lot more representative than he actually is.

The fact is that women and men have changed. The culture at large
is more accepting of women's equality, and young men and women have
brought their attitudes toward each other into the military. Men have
changed their attitudes toward women, and, thanks to women's increasing participation in sports, women's capabilities are far greater than
they once were. The question, however, remains: Will the military as an
institution and a culture adapt and benefit from the social changes and
experiences its young men and women bring with them?

———————— ⊕ ————————

Women are not weak. Anyone who is aware of the amount of work
women do in the developing world, and is willing to accept that anyone
who can do that kind of work is not weak, knows that the notion of
inherent (as opposed to culturally derived) female weakness is a myth.
Throughout most of human history, and in much of the world still,
women do much hard agricultural and industrial labor, and in many
cultures the hardest work for the least pay. Throughout much of Africa,
most remunerative work is reserved for men; women work for food.
They often do it while pregnant, lactating, or recovering from a miscarriage, and almost always on less food than the men and boys in their
households. Given the virtual defenselessness of the human species (we
have two legs, not four; we have thin skin, rather than hide and fur;
we lack claws and our teeth are tactically useless), combined with our
long gestation periods and the prolonged helplessness of our young, our

species could not have survived if women were weak and nonaggressive. It bears remembering: Weakness, like poverty, is relative. It all depends on the task at hand.

Yet, the historically and culturally pervasive belief in women's inferiority almost automatically includes the words *weak* and *nonaggressive*. The fundamental reason for the belief in women's weakness lies less in muscle mass than in women's vulnerability to serious injury, even death, in pregnancy and childbirth. As for nonaggression, once the roles of the armed protectors and unarmed protected were allocated according to a sexual division of labor, for good or ill, the unarmed were at the mercy of the armed. Finally, especially in societies that still regard women as their husbands' property, nonworking women may serve as a sign of male economic achievement and prowess. The nonworking woman (who may only have to bear child after child while running the household) is a male status symbol. At best, she represents his ability to keep his part of the bargain to support his wife and children; at worst, she represents his wealth by her indulgence in conspicuous consumption. In nineteenth-century Europe and the United States—an era that saw the mass entry of not-so-lucky women into the industrial workforce—middle-class women often found themselves assigned to the former role, the women of the upper classes to the latter.

In the United States, ever since women stopped dying wholesale in childbirth, our belief in women's physical inferiority has generally taken the relatively benign form of men trying to protect women from physical exertion and risk. Even in the early twentieth century, when few people questioned patriarchal rule, many balked at the idea of women and children doing hard labor when the earnings they would make were meant for their husbands and fathers. If good work for good wages was a man's job, in cultures where male supremacy did not mean female and child slavery, hard labor was even more men's work. So was sport, by extension of its hard physical effort, even though sport is something that people do for themselves, for the pure pleasures of movement and competition.

Until the 1970s, women generally did not play sports after high school or college. Indeed, there is still a widespread belief that very hard training damages women through the combination of intense athletic activity and low body fat culminating in amenorrhea (cessation of menses) leading to osteoporosis. In fact, neither intense training nor low body fat have anything to do with amenorrhea. It is caused by inadequate calorie intake to meet the energy demands of training.

Surprisingly, female participation in sports is still a controversial topic. You can argue that Title IX, which mandates athletic opportunities for both sexes in substantial proportion to their representation in the student body, has harmed male collegiate sports. However, that is true only if you believe that every male wants to play football and so regard football as untouchable. Rather than cutting bloated football programs, many colleges cut non-revenue-producing sports, especially on the men's side of the house, while women's athletic programs are also often underfunded. Rather than fighting among themselves about whether women's sports harm men's sports, as some wrestling coaches have argued about female wrestlers, the solution is for smaller-sport college athletes of both sexes to challenge the preeminence of football and basketball, which have become far less about sport than about entertainment, and often coarse entertainment at that.

Title IX has done nothing less than revolutionize our understanding of women's physical capabilities, as athletic training and participation have proven that many supposedly biological limitations are in fact cultural. The increase in opportunities made available to women since its implementation in 1972 has resulted in an explosion in women's athletic participation. The United States sent a women's wrestling team to the 2004 Olympics. And so Title IX has also opened women's eyes to the advantages of strenuous athletics. When the duke of Wellington reportedly claimed, "The Battle of Waterloo was won on the playing fields of Eton," he was not talking about winning seasons in cricket or rugby. He meant the toughening and the hard lessons that athletics supplies.

But the military, and especially the Army, has not adequately internalized the lessons of women's athletics, even though military women are increasingly lifting weights and boxing. To better understand the Army's view of women's capabilities, it is worth turning to another sport, that of Thoroughbred racing on the flat (as opposed to "steeplechasing" over timber or furze jumps).

In the Army, both sexes are subject to weight control once they reach a certain weight for their height. For example, a male soldier, aged seventeen to twenty, with a height of sixty-one inches (five-foot-one) is permitted to weigh 136 pounds before being subject to weight control; a female soldier of the same age and height is permitted to weigh only 120 pounds. (Both sexes are permitted to exceed their weight if they pass their physical fitness tests, do not look visibly unfit, and do not carry an excessive proportion of body fat that varies by age and sex, of 20%–26% for men and 30%–36% for women.)

To put our five-foot-one female soldier's authorized weight of 120 pounds into perspective, it's instructive to look at Thoroughbred jockeys. The amount of weight carried by a racehorse is widely thought to affect the speed the horse can attain and the incidence of injuries to the horse's legs. Thus, the Jockey Club's scale of weights was created in order to equalize the chances of winning. The scale of weights is a table of weights horses must carry, depending upon the horse's age and the distance it will travel; it has not been revised in a century, despite the fact that even lean Americans are taller and thus heavier than they were a century ago. No other sport assumes such a constancy of physical size over decades, not to mention an entire century. Sportswriter Paul Daley noted the devastating effect of the scale on jockeys: "A 220-pound football player who was a lineman thirty years ago is a safety today. But in thoroughbred horse racing, then as now, let the scale register 120 pounds consistently and the jockey is out of a job."[1]

Daley assumed his reader would know that this is racing weight, not nude weight: The jockey must weigh in in his silks and boots, saddle and attachments. As the higher weights are reserved for older and more dominant horses, the only way jockeys can hope to ride those horses is by winning on younger and less dominant horses. So most jockeys who are male and quite small, no more than sixty-one or sixty-two inches tall, have virtually no body fat. The maximum body weight a journeyman jockey is permitted is 113 pounds, and the methods jockeys use to maintain that weight are famously unpleasant: anorexic levels of food intake, daily vomiting, hours spent running or in the sauna, even swallowing tapeworms. Such methods severely weaken their muscles and bones and reduce their stamina, greatly increasing both their risk for injuries and the severity of those injuries. Female jockeys who severely reduce increase the risk of birth defects in their potential children because limited food intake means limited nutrient intake, as well as obviously limited energy intake.

The only mitigating thing about the scale of weights is that jockeys (and even the mediocre ones are elite athletes) are expected to perform for no more than a few minutes at a time. Female soldiers, on the other hand, are not elite athletes, nor should they be expected to be. But they are increasingly expected to do physically demanding work for prolonged periods of time. Yet the Army expects a jockey-sized woman of five-foot-one to weigh just seven pounds more than a male jockey, who is not only short, but finely built and probably starving himself. While taller women soldiers are permitted to weigh more, they are scaled up from an unrealistically low base. These weight restrictions on women do not even begin to allow them to develop adequate lean muscle mass while still maintaining a realistic level of body fat. Any discussion of female physical abilities, then, must start with the unrealistically low weight expectations female soldiers are expected to meet.

If the difference in physical capability between men and women is one of the most contentious issues in the discussion of opening the ground combat arms to women, that difference is predicated upon and aggravated by the military's antiquated cultural assumptions about appropriate weights and body-fat levels for physically active women. In fact, these assumptions aren't even questioned, and they underpin the badly flawed analysis by the 1992 Presidential Commission on the Assignment of Women in the Armed Forces of the physiological differences between men and women. That analysis compared the body composition of the average male and female recruits. The figures in Table 7.1, were presented in the 1992 commission's report, and subsequently widely used to emphasize the difference between the capability of the average male and female soldier. (The percentages are mine.)

Table 7.1

AVERAGE HEIGHT OF MALE AND FEMALE RECRUITS[2]

Measure	Male (N=980) Mean	Female (N=1003) Mean	Change	Percentage Difference
Height (in)	68.9	64.1	-4.8	93%
Weight (lb)	160.4	128.7	-31.7	80%
Lean Mass (lb)	133.5	96.1	-37.4	72%
Fat Mass (lb)	26.9	32.6	5.7	
% Body Fat	16.8	25.3	8.5	

There is a significant discrepancy between these two individuals, especially in lean body mass. But the commission made a mistake in measuring the average female recruit against the average male recruit because, on average, height is a good indication of strength in both men and women. You would not compare a man who was sixty-four inches (five-foot-four) tall against another who was nearly sixty-nine inches (five-foot-nine) tall (or six-foot-one for that matter) and expect the smaller man to be as strong as the bigger man. (Although we all know of small men who compensate for strength with intestinal fortitude.) So why compare smaller women to bigger men? Since the average female recruit is 4.8 inches shorter than the average male recruit, I've scaled his height and weight down to match hers in order to compare body composition in individuals of like height.

Table 7.2

MALE RECRUIT SCALED TO AVERAGE FEMALE RECRUIT[3]

	Male	Female	Change	Percentage Difference
Measure	Mean (Scaled)	Mean		
Height (in)	64.1	64.1		
Weight (lb)	149.2	128.7	-20.5	86%
Lean Mass (lb)	124.2	96.1	-28	77%
Fat Mass (lb)	25.0	32.6	7.5	
% Body Fat	16.8	25.3	8.5	

As you can see from Table 7.2, the average woman's lean body mass has gone from 72%, and her weight from 80%, of the average man, to 77% of the lean mass and 86% of the total body weight of a male recruit of her height. This also assumes that, unlike a male recruit, the average female recruit will neither lose body fat nor gain muscle mass as she goes through military training. Both assumptions are false. And as men and women age, their body-fat percentage can be expected to increase.

Table 7.3 shows the maximum body-fat percentages men and women are allowed to carry, as established by the Army's Weight Control Program, AR 600-9. Incidentally, at a time when female soldiers are increasingly serving in combat, it's worth noting that the Army applies to women both the most liberal body-fat measurements and the most restrictive weight measurements of any service. This is precisely the wrong trend, even though it is notoriously hard to accurately measure women's body-fat percentages, especially in strong women, because women deposit fat very differently than men. Weight should be judged more liberally than body fat because weight can mean muscle mass and thick, dense bone, whereas, after a certain level, body fat is unhealthy dead weight one must simply haul around.

Table 7.3
Body Fat Levels[4]

Age Group	Male Maximum	Female Maximum
17–20	20%	30%
21–27	22%	32%
28–39	24%	34%
40+	26%	36%

The combined discrepancy in body weight *and* composition between the average-height man and the average-height woman explains much of the discrepancy between male and female standards on the Army Physical Fitness Test (APFT). Table 7.4 reproduces the scores from the Army's *Physical Fitness Training* field manual (FM21-20), dated 1 October 1998. Included are the raw numbers of push-ups, sit-ups, and run times needed to score 100% in each event on the APFT.

Table 7.4
Male and Female Raw Scores and Percentages to Max Each Event on the APFT[5]

Age Group	Male Pushups	Female Pushups	% of Male Raw Numbers	Male and Female Situps	Male Time (in seconds)	Female (in seconds)	% of Male Raw Numbers
17–21	71	42	59.15%	78	780	936	120.26%
22–26	75	46	61.33%	80	780	936	120.26%
27–31	77	50	64.94%	82	798	948	118.80%
32–36	75	45	60.00%	76	798	954	119.55%
37–41	73	40	54.79%	76	818	1020	124.69%
42–46	66	37	56.06%	72	846	1044	123.40%
47–51	59	34	57.63%	66	864	1056	122.11%
52–56	56	31	55.36%	66	882	1140	129.25%
57–61	53	28	52.83%	63	918	1182	128.76%
62+	50	25	50.00%	62	942	1200	127.39%

It is widely believed that it is much easier for a woman of any age to "max," or score 300 out of 300 points, on the APFT, than it is for a man, even though the Army has essentially imposed a massive disadvantage on women in terms of the lean body mass they are expected to carry. And although every soldier understands that the APFT has only limited applicability to performance in the field—there are plenty of soldiers who score high on the APFT but fade after a few days in the field—it is nevertheless widely and not unrealistically regarded as an indicator of physical performance and motivation.

The double standards on the APFT are widely understood by men and women alike to be an indicator of profound physical weakness in women. Women must do only 50–65% of the pushups men must, and they have 19–29% more time than men do to complete the run.

What is not frequently understood is how physical performance is adversely affected by the differences in the weight allowances the Army imposes on its male and female soldiers.

We all understand that both height and weight matter in men. Culturally, however, we have refused to apply that commonsense understanding to women.

It's time to start doing so.

Muscle is denser than fat. A cubic inch of muscle weighs about 22% more than a cubic inch of fat. A pound of muscle is about a fifth smaller than a pound of fat. Then there is bone. The greater its mineral density and the thicker the bone walls are, the heavier it is, and the fewer stress fractures and other bone injuries a person is liable to incur. A woman is expected to carry far less muscle mass than a man of her size, and to have far lighter and thinner bones. This is less a result of women's lower testosterone levels, or because women produce less estrogen than men do testosterone, than a result of cultural attitudes toward diet and exercise.

In other words, weight matters. Table 7.5 reproduces the weight-for-height tables from AR 600-9, the Army's Weight Control Program of 10 June 1987, a version that has not changed (except for maximum allowable body-fat percentages) since then. This despite a fitness revolution in American women that has made it more culturally acceptable for women to seriously pursue sports and athletic training, including weight lifting. Both men and women are allowed to exceed the weights for their heights if their body-fat percentages, determined through measuring the circumference of various points on their bodies (buttocks, forearm, wrist, and Adam's apple for women; Adam's apple and abdomen for men), are less than those specified by Table 7.3 (see page 249), the body fat table.

At no point are women allowed to weigh so much as 92% of the weight allowed men of their same height and of their same age group; the discrepancy is greatest for those women soldiers ages seventeen to twenty-seven, the age at which most women, like most men, will be doing the most physical work.

So let's return to our two hypothetical soldiers, both twenty, both jockey size, five-foot-one, one male, the other female. She's allowed to weigh, at most, 120 pounds before being subjected to weight control. Her male buddy, however, is expected to weigh no more than 136 pounds before being subjected to weight control. My use of "allowed" and "expected" is deliberate. It is not just the Army, but men and women in general who expect women to weigh less than men. Even presuming that these two soldiers have the same proportion of fat-free body mass, the woman has a sixteen-pound deficit in her fat-free body mass. But women don't carry the same amount of body fat that men do. They carry

Table 7.5

MALE AND FEMALE HEIGHT AND WEIGHT TABLES, AUTHORIZED WEIGHT BEFORE BEING SUBJECT TO WEIGHT CONTROL[6]

Height in Inches	Male 17-20	Female 17-20	Female Percentage of Male Weight	Male 21-27	Female 21-27
58	—	109		—	112
59	—	113		—	116
60	132	116	87.88%	136	120
61	136	120	88.24%	140	124
62	141	125	88.65%	144	129
63	145	129	88.97%	149	133
64	150	133	88.67%	154	137
65	155	137	88.39%	159	141
66	160	141	88.12%	163	146
67	165	145	87.88%	169	149
68	170	150	88.24%	174	154
69	175	154	88.00%	179	158
70	180	159	88.33%	185	163
71	185	163	88.11%	189	167
72	190	167	87.89%	195	172
73	195	172	88.21%	200	177
74	201	178	88.56%	206	183
75	206	183	88.83%	212	188
76	212	189	89.15%	217	194
77	218	193	88.53%	223	199
78	223	198	88.79%	229	204
79	229	203	88.65%	235	209
80	234	208	88.89%	240	214

Female Percentage of Male Weight	Male 28-39	Female 28-39	Female Percentage of Male Weight	Male 40+	Female 40+	Female Percentage of Male Weight
—				—	119	
—				—	123	
88.24%	139	123	88.49%	141	127	90.07%
88.57%	144	127	88.19%	146	131	89.73%
89.58%	148	132	89.19%	150	137	91.33%
89.26%	153	137	89.54%	155	141	90.97%
88.96%	158	141	89.24%	160	145	90.62%
88.68%	163	145	88.96%	165	149	90.30%
89.57%	168	150	89.29%	170	154	90.59%
88.17%	174	154	88.51%	176	159	90.34%
88.51%	179	159	88.83%	181	164	90.61%
88.27%	184	163	88.59%	186	168	90.32%
88.11%	189	168	88.89%	192	173	90.10%
88.36%	194	172	88.66%	197	177	89.85%
88.21%	200	177	88.50%	203	183	90.15%
88.50%	205	182	88.78%	208	188	90.38%
88.83%	211	189	89.57%	214	194	90.65%
88.68%	217	194	89.40%	220	200	90.91%
89.40%	223	200	89.69%	226	206	91.15%
89.24%	229	205	89.52%	232	211	90.95%
89.08%	235	210	89.36%	238	216	90.76%
88.94%	241	215	89.21%	244	222	90.98%
89.17%	247	220	89.07%	250	227	90.80%

more. In men and women, *minimum essential* body fat is that which is stored in the internal organs and bones, the central nervous system and the muscles. For men, that minimum is about 5% and it allows for little subcutaneous body fat. The minimum essential body fat for women is somewhat higher, depending on how much fat she is genetically disposed to carry in her breasts and hips.

We used to believe that women who did not carry at least 15% of their weight in body fat were risking amenorrhea due to the energy demands of pregnancy and lactation. The logic was simple. The young female body "knows" pregnancy and lactation are just around the corner. Pregnancy requires an *additional* 60,000 calories over its course to meet the woman's *increased* energy demands, while a woman who supplies most or all of her infant's nutritional needs by breastfeeding requires approximately 300 calories a day above her normal food requirements for the first three months of lactation, and an extra 500 or so calories a day after that until the child is weaned. A pound of human fat contains about 3,500 calories—thus the average female human body's desire to stockpile approximately 24 pounds of fat over the minimum essential 5%. These 24 pounds are 20% of the body weight of a 120-pound woman, 17.6% of the body weight of a 136-pound woman. These are emergency reserves that the young female body automatically tries to stockpile should she be unable to increase her food intake in the event of a pregnancy and a minimal nursing period of about three months after delivery. In a woman whose stockpiled fat reserves fall below that level, amenorrhea may result, a far from convenient form of birth control for a superfit or overly thin woman. It's the body telling her that she doesn't have the capacity to bear and nurse a child because a pregnancy would starve her. The consequences of disrupted menses include weakened bones—the body raids them for minerals it needs for more immediate tasks than long-term structural support.

In fact, however, amenorrhea does not result from low body fat. It results from energy intake that is too low to sustain the energy output of the woman's activities. When you combine a social expectation of low female body weight and the female body's biological tendency to store fat reserves, you erode women's physical capability. If our 136-pound, sixty-one-inch male has 10% body fat, and his 120-pound, 61-inch female buddy has 20%, he has 122 pounds of lean body mass, and she has 96 pounds. That is less lean muscle mass than a male jockey of her same height, and yet she is expected to do much more arduous work, and for far longer periods of time.

Men have often considered the solution to increasing women's physical capabilities to be simply a matter of raising the APFT requirements, and that is certainly part of it. But the real solution is one I have never heard raised by a man: Increase the weight women are permitted before subjecting them to weight control in order to accommodate changes in body composition produced by strength training. To expect a female soldier to have the same speed, strength, and stamina as a male soldier of her same height when she has 26 pounds less fat-free body mass with which to do it is both bizarre and cruel.

Yet for a time, the Marine Corps expected women Marines do just that. The Marine Corps once had the most restrictive weight standards for women of all the services, while expecting them to keep up with their male peers. The results were a disaster. A 2001 study by Captain Peggy Anne Fisher McNulty, Nursing Corps, U.S. Navy, entitled "Prevalence and Contributing Factors of Eating Disorder Behaviors in Active Duty Service Women in the Army, Navy, Air Force, and Marines," produced some disturbing findings. Yet, only 28% of the women she surveyed had normal eating habits: 1.1% were anorexic, 8.1% were bulimic, and 62.8% had eating disorders not otherwise specified (NOS)—a long list of extremely unpleasant behaviors that were not textbook bulimia or anorexia. These weren't fat women: Of the 3,613 women to whom she distributed her survey, 1,278 returned her questionnaire, and their body fat averaged 19.5%.

Among the female Marines she surveyed, 30.3% had 15% or lower body fat, although the Marines were also the most likely group of servicewomen to exceed the weight standards for their heights. Not surprisingly, female Marines had by far the highest incidence of eating disorders, with 4.9% anorexic, 15.9% bulimic, and 76.7% with NOS disorders. These results meant that only 2.5% of these women reported normal eating behaviors. Marines also had the highest rate of skipped menses among the women Captain McNulty surveyed—22.3%. The Marine Corps had put female Marines in the position of having to meet a profoundly unrealistic combination of weight and athletic performance standards. And those female Marines met their requirements, but the sacrifice for most of them was great—including normal eating, their health, and the health of their children or unborn children. Women Marines reported that breastfeeding, which confers irreplaceable immune benefits, was impossible after giving birth if they were to get back into required shape in the time allotted them.[7]

The solution to the inadequacy of the current APFT standards is to adjust the weight standards, and this must be broken down into two components: changing weight allowances and changing training. The first component, which the Air Force has already adopted, is to permit men and women of the same height the same maximum allowable weight, while limiting women's maximum allowable body fat to 32%. The Air Force has initiated a model that others might follow by having set "ideal"—which would be better termed "typical"—weights and body-fat levels by sex and age, based on the understanding that what is realistic, or even normal, for one individual may not be for another. This has two virtues. First, it allows women to weigh as much as men of their same height, and thus potentially to develop far more fat-free mass than they are currently permitted by the Army's current weight tables. Second, it keeps women's body fat in a healthy range, allowing for the effects of childbearing and breastfeeding—if those are choices women want to make during their service in the military. The Army should then move to reduce the maximum level of women's body fat to only about 5% more than what men of their age group are permitted. You don't have to think women should be skinny to think that 36% body fat, the Army's maximum allowable level for women, is too much body fat, especially for smaller women. Currently, our 120-pound female soldier is permitted 30% body fat as a seventeen- to twenty-one-year-old. That's 36 pounds of body fat. Raise her weight allowance to 136 pounds and reduce her allowed body fat to 25%, and she is permitted a maximum of 34 pounds of fat, but her total body weight has increased by 16 pounds, or 13%, and her fat-free body mass by 18 pounds. A much stronger soldier indeed.

The second component deals with training women effectively. After the weight standards are dealt with, the gap in APFT performance should be narrowed: The minimum number of repetitions of sit-ups and push-ups should be the same for both sexes, as should the maximum number of sit-ups. Maxing the push-ups (and for the Marine Corps, pull-ups) should be normed in favor of women based upon the actual difference of the percentage of body weight carried as upper body musculature between the average fit female soldier or Marine and the average fit male of the same height. Then, so that women are given the proper advantage to achieve a given score above the minimum, that difference should then be multiplied by the actual percentage of total body weight supported by the upper body in pull-ups (100%) and push-ups (60%). As for the run time, women's expected times should be somewhat slower than those for men, calculated according to a similar formula, based upon the difference of body fat percentages and stride length between the average fit female and the average fit male of the same height. However, because women are able to operate at higher levels of aerobic output than men, the cause of women's well-known capacity for endurance, women should have to run about twice as far as men have to. The logic behind this is simple. A minimum level of physical fitness is essential for everyone in the Army, and with women increasingly doing much of the same work men do in the same situations, they need the extra capacity provided by training for a higher level of physical fitness. Maximums, on the other hand, are by definition above and beyond what is necessary. They should be normed according to actual biological differences in male and female capacities rather than cultural beliefs about male athletic superiority.

With one exception, job standards should not be gender-normed, but the set standards must be rationally related to the work that is required. That one exception is special operations units, such as the Navy's SEALs, the Army's Rangers, and Special Forces. Although part of their peacetime status hinges on the fact that the standards are so high that few men can qualify for these units, physical standards in training units and garrison situations serve as a proxy for mental determination. These men do what they do not because they're muscle-bound gorillas, but because they are trained to reach deep within themselves for endurance. Moreover, special operations units make widespread use of women who are good soldiers, traditionally borrowing them from the Army's MP and intelligence branches. They are not taken along merely to interact with civilian women and children. If these women are capable enough to go on actual combat operations in extremely demanding terrain, a slight downward revision of peacetime training standards, particularly in the amount of brute weight an individual is expected to carry, might be in order. And if women are good enough to serve with special operations units in combat operations, they are good enough to go through selection and become part of those units.

Recall that the second part of the two-pronged solution to women's lesser physical capacity is training. While there is a point at which a legitimate concern with upper-body strength becomes an obsession, the fact is that many military jobs require significant upper-body strength and aerobic capacity. This is particularly true in the ground combat units, where women serve now and will continue to serve. Unfortunately, the discussion of training is too often a limited argument about whether integrated or segregated basic training works better, as defined by producing strong male soldiers. The issue of how to produce strong female soldiers is very rarely part of the argument.

As a rule, people who are not opposed to the idea of women in the military or in combat believe in gender-integrated basic training at the most basic military unit, the squad or platoon. Those who are opposed to women serving in combat units generally favor segregated basic training. The concerns of both are primarily cultural. The former hold that if men don't take basic training with women, they won't respect them as troops. The latter hold that if boot camp is integrated, men will not be pushed to their limits, and even if they are, that the women will suffer unacceptable injury rates trying to keep up with them. Additionally, there will be inappropriate relationships between trainees. These concerns are easily contradicted. No man in his right mind assumes that if a small man is excelling at something difficult that it must be easy, or that such serious injuries as stress fractures are legitimate prices for women to pay in the attempt to combat some men's chauvinism. And if trainees aren't too sore and too tired to have sex, then they're not being pushed hard enough.

The great debates of the 1970s and '80s and '90s—*Should women be in the military at all?* let alone, *Should they serve in combat?* and famously, *How many women does it take to degrade the performance of a military unit?*—were another generation's battle to fight. Fortunately, the side that opposed women's equality lost. The issue now is, how do we graduate women from basic training as strong, competent soldiers who are physically sound and who have a good foundation upon which to build a lot of physical capability?

Having gone through both enlisted boot camp and ROTC, I am mildly opposed to gender-integrated basic training, not because I think that men won't perform to their highest standards, but because I want hard, serious training for female recruits. The typical male recruit is in far better shape than his female counterpart due to greater muscle mass, ligament and tendon strength, aerobic capacity, and bone density. It takes years to develop the tendons, ligaments, and bones; and muscle that has been strong for years is very different than muscle that has been strong only for months. One thing men learn in basic training is that, all talk of the warrior ethos aside, the military does not need or want warriors for whom fighting is an act of individual self-expression. It needs and wants soldiers who fight as a disciplined team. And basic training is where women need to break the still very basic social connection between femininity and weakness. That is to say, by taking up military service, they have eschewed femininity for womanhood by choosing to be people their nation can count on in its time of need. As aggregate groups, men and women still tend to have very different physical backgrounds and social perspectives on aggression. Thus, as aggregate groups, they still need different training to achieve the same ends, a concept that is understood and valued in athletics.

Title IX notwithstanding, there is a marked difference in how boys and young men play and work out compared with girls and young women. The culture is far less censorious than it was when I was diagnosed as hyperactive and thereby drugged as a child, when my aunt forbade my cousin a trike, then a bike, because she did not want her to develop muscles in her legs. Nevertheless, when I interviewed Lieutenant Colonel Gillian Boice, an MP officer who graduated from West Point in 1989, and who is now professor of military science and department chair of Army ROTC at Pacific Lutheran University, she pointed out the obvious. "When most females hit initial entry, even physically fit women tend to struggle at first because most of their fitness prior was not generally focused on upper-body strength the way men tend to focus on it through weight lifting activities, or football training in high school. That said, we have found great success in developing fitness in our female cadets, and once women become fit in our program, I believe it is easier for females to achieve a 300 [maximum score] on the APFT than it is for males. With the generally poor fitness of today's youth, both sexes start out with serious physical limitations and that is mainly due to a very sedentary lifestyle. We are seeing, however, that it has become more acceptable for women to be athletic."

In short, anyone who lives a sedentary lifestyle, particularly as a youngster, will be weaker than they should be. All too many young men and women are far more sedentary than they should be, even though access to athletics has narrowed the gap between physically active young men and physically active young women.

This, too, is culture at work, just as it is at work in the differing ways young men and women struggle for social dominance. When young men wish to test their standing with each other, they are likely to ask, "How many push-ups can you do?" "Wanna arm wrestle?" Young women are more likely to compete on the basis of appearance, with questions that are internalized and judgmental, like, *Hmmm, those jeans are Wrangler, not Levi's,* or, *I wonder how much she weighs?* The overtly aggressive dominance posturing of young men is *far* healthier for everyone involved than the sublimated aggression of young women who are also struggling for dominance. Overt bullies can be dealt with by thumping them in the snout, and their victims should be encouraged to band together and do just that; it's much harder to confront the insidious backstabbing female bullies tend to indulge in.

The attitude among women of devaluing strength—*I'm not aggressive or muscular; I'm more feminine and slender than you because I "watch" what I eat*—has real consequences for female soldiers. When I interviewed Lieutenant Colonel Audrey Hudgins, a military intelligence officer and professor of military science at Seattle University, she spoke directly to this point. As I noted above, the Army permits soldiers, male and female alike, to be overweight, measuring them to make certain they are not overly fat in a process called "taping," which refers to the way they are measured with a measuring tape. "Since I was twenty-two, I've had to tape, and at first I was embarrassed. When males have to tape, they think it's manly: 'I'm Arnold Schwarzenegger.' When females have to tape, we think we have to go on a diet. It's very cultural, even though muscle [is denser] than fat, and I see a sharp difference between myself and my peers [in terms of strength and health]." Hudgins is a weight lifter and a triathlete, and of her female cadets who did very well on the APFT by male standards, all of them exceeded the weight for their height and so had to be taped to ensure they were within body-fat limits. Needless to say, most women don't consider themselves to have bragging rights if they're, say, five feet five inches tall, 160 pounds, and fit comfortably into a size 8 suit.

Combine the very divergent attitudes toward food and strength in young men and women, and then send them to basic training together (or even separately, depending on the training program), and the results are sharply elevated rates of injury in women. Generally, military women have a higher sick call rate than men, a reflection of both the female ability to have children and the female tendency to be more willing to engage in preventative medicine.[8]

But stress fractures are not about either childbearing or preventative medicine. Studies of military populations in different entry-level training programs consistently found higher injury rates among women than men. Estimates of stress fracture rates of 5% to 12% are reported for women in entry-level military training; this is 1.5 to 5 times higher than men in similar programs. More importantly, these stress fractures are particularly devastating for women because pelvic and femoral stress fractures are far more common among women than men; they take longer to heal and have a higher frequency of complications, such as delayed union or nonunion.[9]

There are three risk factors for stress fractures in women. The first is low aerobic fitness, meaning the ability of the body to process oxygen. This is generally measured by a person's ability to run a set distance, usually a mile, in a certain time. The easier it is for your blood to feed oxygen to your muscles, the easier it is for you to maintain your activity level. Military women seem to consume less than their minimum daily requirement of iron and calcium; the devastating effect of low

mbined with little or no weight-bearing exercise on bone-
nsity is well-known. Less well-known is that women who
deficiencies, even when they are not anemic, have reduced
aerobic fitness and endurance.[10] The second risk factor is amenorrhea
during the preceding year. The third factor is race—whites, including
people of Hispanic descent, are more susceptible to stress factures due
to the genetic component of bone-mineral density in women.

The fact that the risk factors in men are very similar, except for
the racial/ethnic component, indicates that cultural factors, such as
attitudes toward body image and physical activity, differ less among
men than among women. This fact also indicates that one's attitudes
toward eating and physical activity are far more important than the
genetic component of bone-mineral density. Muscle mass protects the
bones from stress by helping absorb shock. Light men with low muscle
mass and men who have low aerobic fitness levels both have a higher
risk for stress fractures, although their risk is still very low compared
to women. Heavy men, unlike heavy women, are not at increased risk
for stress fractures because they are more likely to be more muscular
and have denser bones with thicker walls. And unlike women, their
diet is not likely to be deficient in either calcium or iron. Men tend to
focus on lowering body fat, whether they are seeking greater muscle
definition or simply trying to reduce useless weight they have to carry.
Women tend to focus on lowering body weight per se, rather than trying to optimize their ability to carry themselves over a distance, a task
that is at odds with maintaining low body weight.

All of these factors are entirely cultural, and the contribution they
make to real female physical weakness bolsters the argument for segre-
gating basic training at the company level.

Basic training is not real military training for real war. It is a very well-thought-out process for determining if civilian trainees are suitable for military service and if they can think under pressure. Basic training is about assessment and acculturation. For female recruits, the most important thing basic training must do is break the civilian cultural connection between femininity and thinness and weakness. Even female athletes who ought to know better are less likely than men to use weight training, more likely to carry a higher percentage of body fat while weighing less than men of comparable height and build, and more likely to have diets deficient in calcium and iron. Any female recruit who needs to lose weight should do so before reporting to boot camp, as part of a general pre–boot camp conditioning program. For female recruits, especially, boot camp should be about gaining: gaining strength, stamina, endurance, and muscle mass, while beginning to slowly strengthen tendons and ligaments and build bone density and thickness. Drill instructors should be very clear that the Army does not want women to be thin or weak, and when male soldiers see female soldiers for the first time, they should see *women*—confident in their physical and mental strength and stamina, their own capacity for aggression, and their ability to do the things they will need to do as soldiers.

The answer to the question, *Are women as strong as men?* is always *No,* as an overall assessment of physical capacity. *On average,* men are taller and more heavily built than women, and a woman who is as strong as a man of her height will probably be slightly more heavily built because of her higher level of body fat, with her muscular strength distributed differently. Although ultralow body fat is not appropriate for soldiers because the body will not have a ready source of energy to be metabolized if the meal schedule is disrupted, and very lean soldiers tend to fade rapidly under field conditions, men can comfortably carry a bit less body fat than women. They have higher levels of testosterone than women do estrogen, which allows them to build more muscle mass. Even if the Army revises its weight standards to permit women to weigh what men of their height do, few muscular women will exceed those weights the way many muscular men do. Size matters. But ask the very different question, *Are women strong enough to do the things they have to do?* and you'll get a very different answer. Two studies showed what happens when you approach female physical capacity from the perspective of each of these two questions. You get a very different result if you insist on viewing women as inferior to men than you do if you simply try to find out what women can actually *do.*

The first study is by retired U.S. Army colonel William J. Gregor, who taught at the School for Advanced Military Studies at the Army's Command and General Staff College. He conducted a simple exercise, in which he graphed the run times, number of push-ups, and aerobic fitness for male and female Army ROTC cadets taking their APFTs at ROTC advanced camp between 1992 and 1998. As an example of obsessive number-crunching it's impressive. With the run times, he found that "only 2.5% of the women, 121 total, were able to attain the male average score (13.5 minutes) achieved by 11,226 of the men." Only 4.5% of the women achieved the male average of 60 push-ups. Only 19% of the female cadets achieved the minimum level of aerobic fitness set for men.[11]

It would have been helpful if Colonel Gregor had given us the raw numbers of women who were tested, but if 121 women totaled 2.5% of those tested, the base number of women was about 4,840. It is much harder to infer the number of male cadets, but there would have been about five times as many male cadets as female.

As analysis, Colonel Gregor's study was extremely poor because he only measured women meeting the standards the Army expected them to meet, not what they could actually do. Most of us, men and women alike, live up or down to what is expected of us. Earlier, I showed the discrepancy in male and female maximum scores for the APFT. Here, I will simply observe that the current minimum passing score for young women aged seventeen to twenty-one is nineteen push-ups; the minimum two-mile run time is 18:54. By comparison, men must do forty-two push-ups and run the two miles in 15:54. This expresses no confidence in women's physical abilities, and neither inspires women to confidence in their own abilities nor requires women to develop their abilities. In short, the Army asks for much less from women, and it gets much less.

The second study, published in 1997 in an unclassified report approved for unlimited distribution, was *Effects of a Specifically Designed Physical Conditioning Program on the Load Carriage and Lifting Performance of Female Soldiers.* This was done by a team of scientists in the military performance division of the U.S. Army Research Institute of Environmental Medicine (USARIEM), headed by Dr. Everett Harman. The goal was to develop a trial strength-training program to improve performance of common heavy military tasks (not performance on the APFT). The program was designed to qualify women to perform in "very heavy" MOSs that involved occasionally lifting one hundred pounds. It was a remedial strength-training program for women who were in poor shape. (They did not recruit women who were in good, or even average, shape, which is important to note because basic training did not do a good job of increasing female soldiers' physical strength at that time.)

The study included forty-five civilian women and one female soldier. Most of the volunteers participated because they wanted to get in better shape. Only one of the study volunteers appears to have been athletic—a competitive cyclist who, in fact, had to drop out of the study due to a breathing problem. The participants worked out an hour and a half a day, five times a week, lifting weights, running, and backpacking for twenty-four weeks—totaling a mere 180 hours—in a program designed to fit within the time allotted to physical training in Army units. Of the forty-six women who began the program, thirty-two completed it. This was a better completion rate than many studies of military women involving heavy physical exertion, where attrition is about 50%. Because the USARIEM researchers started slowly and increased the intensity gradually, attrition was closer to the male norm of 25%.

Of those who dropped out, two did so for motivational reasons, including a mother of four who had to drive fifty minutes each way to the training facility. Six withdrew for unanticipated reasons, including family situations, illness, and work constraints. The women bruised and blistered themselves, but only two dropped out for serious injuries—both of which were probably caused by preexisting conditions.

At the beginning of the program, only 24% of the women could lift more than one hundred pounds to a height of 52 inches, the height of a two-and-a-half-ton—"deuce-and-a-half," in Army slang—truck bed, a common military vehicle. After six months, 78% of the women could. They also averaged carrying seventy-five-pound backpacks for two miles at a pace of 4.4 miles an hour, considerably faster than the Army's normal march speed of 2.5 miles an hour, suggesting that they could have sustained the lower speed for long distances. (Their weekly training hikes were five miles long at a pace of four miles an hour.) Their ability to tow a 110-pound trailer, to complete jumping exercises, and to do squats with a hundred-pound barbell all increased; they almost quadrupled the number of squats they could do. Their aerobic ability increased approximately 14%, to the average of men in their age group.

The average height for the volunteers was 64.61 inches, a little taller than our mythical average female recruit. But their average weight was higher: 152.9 pounds. Their chests expanded, their arms grew thinner and more muscular, and their waists and hips slimmed, while their thighs grew larger thanks to the exercise. On average, they lost only 3.08 pounds of body weight, which amounted to an average loss of 6.16 pounds of body fat and a gain of 1.98 pounds of muscle. Their bone-mineral density increased by less than 1%, and their lean body mass rose from an average of 60% to 62.5%, which was still less than that of the slightly shorter average female recruit shown in Table 7.1, who also carried a great deal less dead weight in the form of body fat. Which made their performance all the more impressive.

Cultural linkages between femininity and physical strength suggest that the women had become less stereotypically feminine. However, friends, family, and the researchers themselves all noted that the training had made the women markedly more attractive. The participants also liked their appearances better. They were more confident, felt more peaceful and more socially adept; they liked themselves and other women better, and they not only felt stronger, they felt other women were stronger, too.[12]

These were not results many would attempt to dispute. Personally, I find it hard to believe anyone who *likes* women could dispute them. Yet, an attempt was made. Rowan Scarborough of *The Washington Times,* who has long been friendly to Elaine Donnelly, ran a 1995 article denouncing the study while it was in progress. "Why Can't a Woman Be More Like a Man?" featured Robert Maginnis, a 1973 West Point graduate and retired Army infantry officer who opposed women in combat, and who was then with the Family Research Council, a right-wing advocacy group:

"It doesn't make any sense financially, because we can hire men off the street now who already have the physical strength.

"It is not about equal opportunity, it is about military readiness. Underline. Exclamation point," he said. "We cannot afford social experiments with the military forces of this country."[13]

In fact, as reported by Scarborough, the entire study to develop a strength-training program for female soldiers cost just $140,000, about the cost of reassigning and retraining just nine female soldiers if they were unable to perform the MOSs they had been trained for. Those costs do not include the medical and disability costs to, or the physical pain and emotional frustration of, women who seriously injure themselves doing work they like but aren't strong enough to handle, but could be with proper training. Such training builds muscle mass in women (even if not to the same degree it does in men) and both bone-mineral density and bone-wall thickness, and increases a woman's weight. Combined with aerobic training, weight lifting increases a person's base metabolic rate and reduces body-fat levels. The net result of such training is stronger, faster, and, yes, often heavier women who suffer fewer injuries. Weight training has long been used by men to strengthen themselves, and if it may be something of a social experiment to encourage women to take advantage of it on a large scale for the same purposes, where is the harm?

This was precisely why the Army's attitude toward this program was very different from that of people who had a vested interest in denouncing female soldiers. I interviewed Colonel Karl Friedl, commander of USARIEM, who oversaw the Harman study and who had this to say: "One thing to consider is how much strength requirements are related to poorly designed equipment that would injure anyone—especially if they're fatigued. The biggest, fattest people are going to have the greatest strength: They're power lifters. For people who aren't thinking about their appearance, they can eat to requirements. Fat and lean go together." As Colonel Friedl notes, power lifters are enormously strong, but they tend to not only have the muscle mass that enables their strength, but are often fat from eating to sustain their workouts. It is a body build that is not only unattractive but impractical for service members, who need to balance speed, strength, stamina, flexibility, and endurance.

"Some of the standards have been absolutely unrealistic," Colonel Friedl said. "We've weeded out a lot of anachronistic standards. All MOSs require more than one set of strength requirements. You need a mix of abilities. There are several aspects to strength requirements. Strength training reduces injury risk, reduces lower back pain . . . Marilyn [Sharp, the Army's expert on MOS-specific physical requirements] is the authority [on what] MOS-specific strength standards [we can set], and we've never been able to set standards. Everyone needs a minimal level of strength."

I asked Colonel Friedl how Dr. Harman's study had been perceived, and he told me that it had received an enormous amount of attention, some of it very sensationalistic, even more sensationalistic than Maginnis's declaration that weight training is social engineering when women do it. Ultimately, he summed up his thoughts with a bit of wry humor. "The Army seemed to like it, but generally, the smart people understood that we needed to know how to train women—and we needed more of that—and it filled a key gap area."

The widespread assumption that women are smaller, inferior versions of men has rarely extended to the idea that weight training would benefit women as it has men. But then, for some people, the real issue is not what particular women can do, or would like to do, but what *they* feel is proper for women to do. In Chapter Six, I included part of my interview with Dr. Moskos, in which I asked him if women's increasing participation in direct ground combat had changed his mind on whether they should serve in ground combat units. No, he replied. Dr. Moskos also raised the issue not only of double standards in the APFT, but of higher injury rates for women, telling me that he had seen a press release noting that when the British went to a single standard of basic training, injury rates for women were nine times that of men. I told him the press release probably referred to the May 2002 Ministry of Defence report *Women in the Armed Forces*. The British noted in that report that if they corrected for fitness levels, the difference in injury rates then disappeared.[14] "I don't believe it," he told me. I did not offer to send him the report.

Risk is associated with everything we do, and yet people do what is important to them. I've seen infantrymen with wrecked feet, lower backs, knees, and hips from a lifetime of carrying heavy rucksacks long distances; I've known men who broke their arms or backs or cracked their vertebrae in parachuting accidents; and this is all just the minor aches and pains of soldiering, not combat wounds. And yet they keep doing the work that got them hurt for the simple reason that it's important to them.

We met Lieutenant Colonel Gillian Boice earlier in this chapter. As a young woman, she was a competitive diver, and she is now an MP officer. Over the course of her career, she has lost about an inch of height and has had to have two disc surgeries due to the impact of weight on a spine already stressed by tower diving. "I declined bat-

WOMEN IN THE LINE OF FIRE

talion command because of two back surgeries," she told me when I interviewed her in her office. "I thought it was because I'm weak, a female; but I asked, and it turns out that there have been four declines for battalion command recently—all male, all for backs." I asked her if she would still have been a soldier had she known the physical price she was going to pay. "I love what I've done. The pinnacle of my career was in Iraq, and getting the Baghdad Police Department back on the streets. Where could I do that in the United States? I have incredible memories of the Iraqi Police."

————————— ⊕ —————————

If approaching the issue of female physical capacity means treating individuals as individuals (after all, we do not size all-male infantry battalions by height, which is the best proxy for strength), pregnancy must be addressed in a similar way. Ten to fifteen years ago, pregnancy was a radioactive issue: Women, especially junior enlisted women, were reputedly getting pregnant by any means available to get out of everything from APFTs to combat zones. Therefore, the reasoning went, they should not be in the military, or on ships, or in deployed units. Rumor held that Pat Schroeder suppressed a study of pregnancy in the Gulf War. But I suspect that's all it was—rumor—just like all the other mud people threw at her.

The flagship military medical journal *Military Medicine* published a study that included partial pregnancy rates for female soldiers deployed during the Gulf War relatively shortly after the findings were announced at the thirtieth annual meeting of the Armed Forces District at the American College of Obstetricians and Gynecologists in October 1991. "Ambulatory Health Care Needs of Women Deployed with a Heavy Armor Division During the Persian Gulf War," by Captain Jeffrey Hines, was published in the May 1992 issue. Captain Hines noted

24 pregnancies out of the 1,065 women assigned to the First Cavalry Division, with a crude pregnancy rate of 22.7 per 1,000 women, from which he extrapolated some 900 pregnancies among approximately 40,000 women deployed to the Gulf.[15]

Those 24 pregnancies were not good news: A woman who becomes pregnant on deployment must be evacuated, and that leaves her buddies, male and female, to pick up the slack. If you extrapolate them, as Hines did, they look even worse, and worse still if you consider that the time period was from 27 October 1990 to 20 March 1991. (If you were to extrapolate out to a year, that would mean that 4.5%, or about one out of every twenty female soldiers who deployed to the Gulf War, would have been evacuated from the theater due to pregnancy.)

However, extrapolation from small samples to large populations is extremely risky. When you are extrapolating from such a small data set to more than 40,000 women, one or two knuckleheads or dirtbags in a unit can badly skew your numbers.

Good units, which in mixed-sex units means making few distinctions between men and women, have little disciplinary trouble. A woman having to be evacuated because she's pregnant in an operational situation is a problem. Even if she hid her pregnancy to deploy with her unit because she couldn't bear to be left behind (and wasn't going to get an abortion to deploy for the duration) she would get an A+ for fidelity and a D- for common sense. If she went off birth control because she fully intended to be celibate in a field environment, then fell off the wagon, she still gets a D- for common sense, but stupidity is not the same thing as malingering. The woman who gets pregnant to get out of a deployment is a disciplinary problem—as is the father, if he is a serviceman. Especially since the male partner in the equation doesn't need an exam or prescription to use condoms.

Without comprehensive statistics, there is no way to tell whether Captain Hines's projections were accurate, a little off, or very badly skewed. And the Department of Defense does not keep comprehensive statistics about pregnancies because the Department of Defense considers pregnancies to be an administrative, not medical, matter (even though these officials recall the deliveries in their own families as having taken place under medical supervision). Compiling comprehensive statistics would establish what the overall pregnancy rate for women is and determine whether or not there were or are any spikes in pregnancy to avoid deployment, and in which units, if any, those spikes might be concentrated.

Disciplinary statistics can be misleading: A good unit may have few disciplinary problems because its officers and sergeants use peer pressure to stop small problems before they get to the stage of requiring formal disciplinary action. A bad unit can have low statistics because its leadership doesn't want to generate statistics.

A unit with high pregnancy statistics might indicate a unit just back from deployment, experiencing a baby boom among its soldiers. It might also indicate a unit about to go on deployment whose female soldiers did not, for whatever reason, feel the need to deploy with it. And while the women requesting pregnancy discharges might be junior enlisted women, who are often said to get pregnant to get out of anything they don't want to do, from unit physical training to deploying to a war zone, they might also be women making the transition to being midcareer professionals who feel they can't combine family and the military, and get out to avoid slighting either. The point is, without comprehensive statistics, you can't get an accurate reflection of the reality of the women's circumstances. And if you deliberately choose not to know that your experienced women are leaving because it is much harder for them to combine work and family than it is for men (and it is *hard* for servicemen), you don't have to reevaluate your career progression pattern, which was developed for men with wives who generally did not have careers (the case for ever fewer servicemen).

What I do know is this: I was told by a Department of the Army spokeswoman, without any hard numbers to back it up, that there had been no spike in pregnancies since 9/11. This is contrary to all the dire predictions of waves of women getting pregnant to avoid arduous service. A public affairs officer for the Office of the Secretary of Defense promised me a Defense Manpower Data Center (DMDC) run for pregnancies. What I wanted, in addition to raw numbers of pregnancies, was to compare those rates with rates among civilian employed women, as well as with pregnancy evacuations from Central Command's area of operations: Iraq, Afghanistan, the austere bases in Central Asia, the Philippines. And I wanted a breakout by rank. The officer agreed to my request. I was psyched. To my knowledge, such numbers had never been made public before. When push came to shove, however, the public affairs officer could not provide the DMDC run on pregnancy statistics, and he sounded far more uncomfortable in our follow-up call than I remembered him being in our first conversation. His excuse was that the statistics were held at the unit level. True, many statistics are held at the unit level: vehicles that don't work, casualties, disciplinary actions, ammunition on hand. But they are reported up so that military managers have a statistical picture of what the service has to work with, people included.

One might surmise that if servicewomen's pregnancies seriously impinged upon readiness, the military would track those numbers, and that if it does not track those numbers, it is because pregnancies do not

present any significant readiness problem. You'd think that would
good news that the military wants to get out.

As far as I have been able to determine, it is fact, not supposition, that pregnancies do not constitute a readiness problem for the services, and certainly not a widespread disciplinary problem in deployed units. A military medical officer who was in a position to know said he had seen an incredibly low number of women evacuated from Iraq because of pregnancies, far lower than he had been led to expect would be the case. Those few pregnancies he did see, he said, seemed to be a matter of contraceptive failure by both parties rather than a woman malingering by getting pregnant, or a man helping her to by getting her pregnant.

The few statistics that I have been able to obtain verify this officer's observations. I have been told that in the Army, since 9/11, about 2,500 to 3,500 women are pregnant at any given time, roughly between 3.4% and 4.8% of the Army's female strength—comparable with 4.62% of employed civilian women in 2004, according to the U.S. Census Bureau's Statistical Abstract of the United States, 2006. I was provided with pregnancy discharge statistics by fiscal year from 1994 through the first half of 2005, and a breakout by service from 2004 on. In 2004, there were 1,573 pregnancy discharges from the Army, and 744 in the first half of 2005. (The Army provided me with updated pregnancy discharge numbers from 2005 and the first quarter of 2006, which totaled 1,632. This indicates, but does not prove, a further drop in the pregnancy discharge rate: The Army refused to break those numbers out through the end of 2005 and the first quarter of 2006.) All but three of the women who requested pregnancy discharges between 2004 and the first half of 2005 were enlisted. I compared these pregnancy discharge numbers to a statistical breakout the Army gave me of the women who had left the *regular* Army due to pregnancy after deployment to either Iraq or Afghanistan, shown below in Table 7.6.

Table 7.6

NUMBER OF ARMY PERSONNEL WHO HAVE LEFT THE ACTIVE DUTY DUE TO PREGNANCY AND WHO WERE PREVIOUSLY DEPLOYED TO OEF/OIF[16]

Separation Date Due to Pregnancy	Deployment End Date				
	FY 2005	FY 2004	FY 2003	FY 2002	Total
FY 2005	53	292	81	1	427
FY 2004		156	197	5	358
FY 2003			49	34	83
FY 2002				12	12
Total	**53**	**448**	**327**	**52**	**880**

As of December 2005, 75% of the Army has served in Iraq or Afghanistan, some troops more than once, and nearly 11% of those soldiers are female. As can be seen from the number of pregnancy discharges among women who deployed to Iraq and Afghanistan versus the total number of pregnancy discharges, the vast majority of such discharges were requested by women who did *not* deploy to Iraq and Afghanistan.

But what about those pregnancy discharges? Whether they occurred before or after, or to get out of deployment, shouldn't they be indicative of women unwilling to serve out their contracts?

The answer: not necessarily.

Some of these women discharged for pregnancy may have done their bit and perhaps more in the Balkans and elsewhere, and then faced the fact that if they were to do another deployment they might neve. have a family, or a chance to have another child. The Army deploys personnel for a year; the other services prefer six-month rotations. The Marines I spoke to in Ramadi were flabbergasted by the policy; an Air Force friend of mine told me he could do a six-month deployment standing on his head, but he was a lieutenant colonel with a wife who had a master's degree. He could not fathom how junior enlisted soldiers, some of them married with children, or even custodial single parents, could maintain their families through a year's separation. Yet many have, and do.

As for enlisted women, I never met a female soldier who regarded being required to participate in combat operations, no matter how much she disliked the idea, as a breach of contract, let alone a breach of the Army's faith in her. But the yearlong deployment is widely regarded as an unnecessary hardship for their families. Men and women voice their dislike of this policy with similar intensity. As reported by Donna Miles of the American Forces Press Service in 2005, "Army officials reported 10,477 divorces among the active-duty force in fiscal 2004, a number that's climbed steadily over the past five years. In fiscal 2003, the Army reported fewer than 7,500 divorces; in 2002, just over 7,000; and in 2001, about 5,600." For 2004 and 2003, the divorce rate was higher among Army officers than enlisted, an unusual trend.[17] The Army's very high pregnancy discharge and divorce rates are very likely related, and have the same cause: too many deployments for too long.

But what about those women who are not putting their families first because they are in an impossible situation? What about the pregnancy discharges that really are the weeding out of women who never expected or wanted to go to war in the first place? Recruiting women by overtly appealing to them for the same qualities of disciplined physical courage, desire to dare and to risk, and drive to ›mething larger than oneself, all of which have tradition- ›r good soldiers in men, would be a cheaper and more .uuuane way of doing the same thing. Especially when you consider that men generally find less onerous ways to avoid deployment. Dropping a fifteen-pound barbell on your foot pales in comparison to having an abortion or raising a child to adulthood. Now, without reviving the old comparison of time off for pregnancies and gynecological complaints—i.e., real medical issues—to time in the brig for drugs, drunk and disorderly conduct, assault, etc., how might the Army deal with pregnancies institutionally?

They might do what female, and, to a lesser extent, male soldiers do about them. Differentiate. Most men draw an instinctive distinction between the woman who tries to plan her pregnancy and perform her duties and physical training until she can't, and the woman who gets pregnant to get out of those duties. By the same token, the many women I know who handled their sexuality and fertility responsibly resented men who used the malingering of a few women as a stick to beat on all servicewomen. And while military women tend to excuse pregnancies resulting from lack of contraception more than men do, they also tend to be less tolerant of malingering and more sympathetic to the idea of the military adopting a disciplinary article in the Uniform Code of Military Justice that deals with pregnancies.

All military pregnancies, save those occasioned by the crime and tragedy of rape, fall into one of three categories: (1) *Congratulations!* (2) *Oops!* and (3) *Get Me Out of Here!*

Congratulations! pregnancies are those planned by a woman, and usually her husband, during her career. Many women "schedule" their pregnancies during their nondeployable assignments. Not everyone, male or female, can be "good to go" all the time, and wars are generally long. Walk the halls of the services' war colleges and command and staff schools and you're likely to see a lot of maternity uniforms. It's harder for enlisted women, especially if they work with hazardous materials, but the same principle of attempting to minimize disruption applies. No further action need be taken, because life is going pretty much according to plan.

Oops! pregnancies are just that. Sometimes they impact unit readiness; sometimes they don't. They tend to cluster among the more junior enlisted women who are overwhelmed by a certain tonnage of male attention that they have no idea how to cope with; others are senior women who may have been trying to get pregnant without success. Sometimes deployments make planning moot, and a long-hoped-for pregnancy is not quite as happy as it should be because the unit has to leave the female soldier behind, and she has to watch them go. These women should be treated on a case-by-case basis, with attention given to circumstances, including her prior service record and her desire to remain in the military. Each service should set up high-level boards to handle these cases; this is not a matter properly left to a woman's immediate superior or unit commander. The goal should be to minimize present disruption while hanging on to good women for the long term. As for punishing mistakes, if you're a good soldier, it's penalty enough to be evacuated for a mistake shared between you and the father.

Get Me Out of Here! pregnancies constitute deliberate malingering and worse, and should be handled by the military justice system. It should be hard, very hard, to get a court-martial conviction: as hard, perhaps, as trying to prove desertion. But in flagrant cases, the servicewoman (and the father, if a military member) should receive, at the very least, discharge under other than honorable conditions. And yes, *Get Me Out of Here!* pregnancies do occur, although they happen primarily before deployment, when some women openly say, "I'm not going—sorry, I'm pregnant." I met one soldier who was being evacuated for pregnancy at Al Asad Airbase when I was leaving Iraq. I expressed my sympathy for her, and she told me, "That's okay. The father is my fiancé. I was tired of being deployed." Disgusted, I turned and walked away from her without another word.

Her behavior was qualitatively different from that of another soldier I heard about from her battalion commander: She'd gotten pregnant, and although he was sorry to lose her, he tried to be supportive because she was terribly upset. She was evacuated and had an abortion stateside so she could return to her unit in Iraq as soon as possible, an outcome that rather stunned her commander. A board might have been able to help her find another solution.

The real problem, that of losing good soldiers—chiefly women but also men—who have to choose between their families and the military institution, is not a problem the military can solve alone, because it does not affect the military alone. American society has made it very hard to combine the two things that most people need in various proportions: meaningful work and a family. People are still generally forced to develop career patterns around the mythology of the male breadwinner and the female homemaker, which is now based upon the assumption that double-income, no-kids couples are just having fun rather than wondering how they can balance the work they do with the family they might like to have. The only long-term solution is to develop what I call a "parenthood phase," when both parents are expected to sharply reduce their workload in order to care for young children while still being allowed to remain active in their fields. This solution requires a total rethinking of career patterns and insurance access outside the military as well as within the military, where a wholesale overhaul of its personnel system is necessary, including allowing personnel to move far more freely between the Reserves and National Guard and the active forces than they currently can.

$$\oplus$$

Like physical strength and pregnancy, post-traumatic stress disorder (PTSD) is both physically real and culturally mediated. Just as a culture can make it more or less difficult for women to be strong, it can also make it more or less difficult for people to reintegrate their personalities following their experience of what is sanitized by the term *trauma*.

PTSD has been around for a long time. In nineteenth-century England, it was called *railway spine* or *railway hysteria* because it was so often seen in the survivors of the horrific railroad accidents of the period. Sometimes the effects were physical, sometimes emotional—as if the two were easily separated. During the Civil War in the United States, it was called *soldier's heart*—a term that stuck into the first years of World War I. Later, it would be called *shell shock* by the British, and then in World War II we called it *battle fatigue,* or *combat fatigue.* After the Vietnam War, PTSD was called *post-Vietnam syndrome,* and classified as an anxiety disorder in Vietnam veterans who needed help readjusting to civilian society after an abrupt return to the United States, compounded by an often hostile reaction from the American public.

The National Center for PTSD (NCPTSD), part of the U.S. Department of Veterans Affairs, defines PTSD as a psychiatric disorder that can occur after one has been involved in or witnessed such life-threatening events as military combat, natural disasters, terrorist incidents, serious accidents, or violent personal assaults like rape. People with PTSD often have nightmares and flashbacks about the events they were involved in or witnessed. They may be afraid or unable to sleep. And they may be detached or estranged even from the people they love the most. These symptoms are often severe enough and last long enough to damage not only a person's daily life, but his or her future as well. Although PTSD research has far to go, we know this much. The condition is marked by clear neurobiological changes in how the sufferer's memory is stored and processed in the brain. Thyroid functions seem to be enhanced; cortisol levels seem to decrease, while levels of epinephrine and norepinephrine and natural opiates seem to be elevated. Moreover, neurohormonal levels are the opposite of those seen in people with depression, even when the person with PTSD also has depression.[18]

In other words, something very physical is going on, as we all know from stories of the rape survivor who has to detach herself from the ceiling when a coworker walks into her office, or the combat vet who has to come out of hiding after something has gone *bang*. Enhanced startle reflexes, sometimes violent, are extremely common, as is anger and an inability to handle it appropriately.

Yet to accept the medical definition of PTSD as an anxiety disorder is to define it as an aberrant reaction to trauma wherein the chief symptom is anxiety. And that is wrong. Here I have been strongly influenced by Richard B. Ulman and Doris Brothers's work *The Shattered Self: A Psychoanalytic Study of Trauma,* in which they define PTSD not as an anxiety disorder, but as a dissociative disorder that can lead to traumatic neurosis.

In layperson's terms, this means that certain events derange our sense of ourselves, and of the world and our place in it. For women, sexual trauma through rape and incest is a primary trauma. Women are regarded throughout their lives as easy targets, not only because of their smaller size and lighter weight but because of their general cultural socialization to passivity and prohibition against adequate (i.e., violent) self-defense or retaliation. Girls who have been assaulted do not often "outgrow" their vulnerability to further assaults the way boys often seem to. While any particular statistic or set of statistics on sexual assault (for the sake of consistency, I have used the NCPTSD's statistics on both PTSD and sexual victimization) is open to questions about methodology, the different sexual assault rates of men and women reflect this difference. Women suffer about a 27% rate of childhood sexual abuse,[19] a 13% to 17% rate of completed rape, and a 14% rate of other sorts of sexual assault,[20,21] while men suffer at least a 10% sexual assault rate.[22] Even though there is likely to be a large overlap between childhood and adult female sexual victimization, sexual assault up to and including rape is a much more normative experience for females than it is for males.

For men, combat, not rape, is the paradigmatic trauma. Men are expected to be dominant and aggressive, even violent. The soldier's role is theirs. Yet combat has a way of chastening even the most mature man's assessment of his physical strength and mental stamina. The man who believes that the profession of arms is noble can find his moral compass—his definition of himself as a good man and good soldier who can be counted upon—deranged by what he has seen and done. It is little consolation to a man who has witnessed or participated in the deaths of women and children that the insurgents who deliberately used these innocents as cover when opening fire on uniformed soldiers bear all moral responsibility for their deaths.

Not everyone who is raped or survives combat develops a traumatic neurosis. People differ widely in how their bodies produce and process neurotransmitters and hormones such as cortisol, adrenaline, testosterone, estrogen, and progesterone. They also differ widely in their personal and family backgrounds, which can either be a source of great strength or have already inflicted profound wounds upon their souls. Everyone who survives trauma has horrifying memories, but the ability to function in the trauma's aftermath varies greatly. Some people are able to integrate what they have seen and done into their self-image as a good person and their image of the world as a sensible place in which most people are humane. Others are not.

Severe PTSD in men has often been understood to be a matter of traumatic neurosis. The very real physical aftereffects of trauma were often compounded by what was understood to be the sufferer's failed attempt to restore his self-image as a worthwhile man. In women, the combination of physical symptoms and inability to reconcile trauma with a positive self-image were often diagnosed as hysteria, resulting from a woman's inability to cope with "rape fantasies"; Freud gets most of the blame for this, but he had plenty of company. The genius of Ulman and Brothers in their book was to make clear that whether it resulted from rape, incest, or other trauma, in men or in women, disabling PTSD resulted from a profoundly negative and largely unconscious meaning assigned to that event. This was compounded by the individual's subsequent unsuccessful attempt to repair his or her self-definition as a worthwhile human being and ability to trust in the world as a just place after those definitions had been shattered. They do not discuss the use of psychoactive drugs, helpful as they may be in managing the physical effects of trauma. Instead, they treated their patients by helping them restore—in some cases, develop for the first time in their lives—their belief in their human worth and dignity.

The issues of sexual trauma and combat trauma can fuse for female soldiers. American women are estimated to be twice as likely as American men to suffer from PTSD (10.4% of women versus 5% of men) at some point in their lives, even though the rates of traumatic experience are lower for women than men (51.2% for women compared to 60.7% for men).[23] This is because rape is much more likely to cause PTSD than combat (45% of women reported their PTSD to have originated from experiencing a rape, while 38.8% of men reported its cause to be their experience of combat).[24] Female service members and veterans are more likely than the general female population to have experienced sexual assault before they join the military. Like men, women are often drawn to the military to improve their situations. Joining a respected institution can provide enormous scope to a woman of spirit and ambition; the military also represents an honorable way to become physically strong and aggressive, and honorable employment for those qualities.

Does this mean that servicewomen are more vulnerable to combat trauma than servicemen? We don't know. There is a real possibility that combat trauma can build upon sexual trauma to produce more serious PTSD. Given the fact that the military is still overwhelmingly male, in raw numbers more men may have been exposed to the combination of sexual and combat trauma than women, although the proportion of women may be higher. On the other hand, the National Vietnam Veterans Readjustment Study surveyed 1,632 veterans about their exposure to trauma and their adjustment to civilian life. Of these veterans, 432 (26.4%) were women. Women were vastly oversampled according to their proportion in the military, let alone of Vietnam veterans. This was done to obtain more accurate data. Had the female sample been representative of the Vietnam-era military's sex ratio, about twenty women would have been included. Had the female sample been representative of Vietnam veterans' sex ratio, it would have included about four women. These tiny numbers would have produced grossly distorted findings about women's vulnerability to combat stress.

None of the women who were surveyed were combat soldiers; most were registered nurses and 90% of them were commissioned officers. In short, the proportion of those women who dealt with incredible suffering was probably also heavily oversampled, not only among women, but among the military in general. Approximately 27% of the women veterans developed PTSD, a substantially lower percentage than male combat veterans generally.[25] This despite the fact that nurses are often exposed to far more horror than infantrymen, and that their response to it is necessarily passive, in the way an infantryman's is not.

It will take years of research, which includes asking the right questions, to provide a trustworthy answer to the question of whether servicewomen are more vulnerable to combat trauma than servicemen. Until then, we can simply give those who suffer from PTSD the help they need, whether they're men or women, whether they suffer a little or a lot. This begins with reducing our tolerance for sexual abuse and ends with the acceptance of women as combat veterans. Just as we think of men as sexual aggressors and not victims, no matter how much damage has been done to individual men by assault, when we think of women and war we still think of women as victims. There is a cultural dissonance that goes with being a soldier and a combat veteran on the one hand, and with being a woman on the other.

Female combat veterans can be very lonely people, not merely because there are so few of them, but because they do not get the validation male veterans can expect as a matter of course. Other women, especially civilians, often withdraw from them because opportunities are still scarce for women; female veterans are often regarded as passing some kind of judgment on the lives of other women. Even men who are not chauvinists are often intimidated by female combat veterans because these women have done things that only men are supposed to do and to be able to do. If women often regard female combat veterans as passing judgment on choices, men regard those same veterans as judging, a wanting, their manhood. And this is not only outside th... but inside it as well. There are a great many servicemen who do not wish to assume the risks of combat, yet nevertheless wish to be thought of as bearing those risks in ways that servicewomen, in the same or similar units and MOSs, do not.

Yet physical strength, courage, and aggression are not intrinsically male attributes, no more than kindness and gentleness are inherently female attributes. Ideology aside, most men do not wish to live with a weak, helpless, and timid woman. They are too much trouble! No more than most women wish to live with men who are coarse, callous, and cruel. And the minute things get the least bit intimate or difficult, the minute we actually have to rely on someone when the going gets tough, or trust them in our personal lives, we learn anew that both sexes need strength *and* gentleness. In this, as in the issue of physical strength, the Army can recognize this ancient truth, and make it clear to men and women alike that it wants women who are serious soldiers, who will be treated as personal and professional equals.

Or it can have the grace to admit that what it really wants is for women to be second-class and that it intends to keep treating them as such.

Chapter 8

A Changing
Institution

ϕ ————————————————————————

In the military's lexicon of institutional self-excusal, the word *culture*
carries almost as much baggage as the word *policy*. When bad things
happen, the military exonerates itself by saying, Well, yes, it happened,
but it wasn't *policy*. When that no longer works, the problem becomes
a matter of *culture,* as in, "We must change the institutional culture."
Some institutional changes are matters of policy, such as determining
that criminal and boorish behavior toward one's comrades will no longer be tolerated, condoned, or ignored—and then making it stick. Other
changes are cultural, such as the consequences of women's movement
toward full equality under arms. Let me suggest one such change: It's
time for the military to accept that one of its favorite notions, the vital
importance of "small unit cohesion" to success in combat, must be
broadened to include women. The need for this expansion is not based
on theory, but on the reality of 143,000 servicewomen this nation sent
to war between September 2001 and March 2006. By the time this book

ppears in August 2006, the true number will be closer to 175,000. This means that the military, and especially the Army, must finally come to terms with the fact that, for too many decades, they've used supposed threats to "cohesion" to justify exclusion and criminality.

This is a cultural change that is, in fact, happening; it's been under way for quite some time. But it must be recognized and legitimized in a policy change. It's often said, "If the people lead, eventually the leaders will follow." Today, the troops and younger officers in the field are leading. It's time for the institution to follow.

———————— ⊕ ————————

John Kuehn is a retired Navy commander who is now wrapping up his PhD in history and teaches military history at the U.S. Army's Command and General Staff College. From time to time, we've discussed the issue of servicewomen, and over the past six years, I've watched his attitude change from, "Well, they're here," to "They're here and get over it" (which I've toned down from his self-described ranting and raving about the subject). In a three-hour long-distance phone conversation in late 2005, he led me through the Navy's extraordinary cultural changes, which he himself lived though from 1982 until his retirement in 2004.

Kuehn joined the Navy in 1980. The Iranian hostage crisis was still in the news, the Soviet invasion of Afghanistan a year old. Kuehn had a degree in zoology, but he'd also read Solzhenitsyn and been to Berlin, coming back with a small piece of the wall *before* it was torn down. He thought the United States was losing the cold war, so he joined the Navy to make his contribution to victory.

Since he had a college degree, a semester of graduate school, and good grades, the recruiter suggested Kuehn attempt to become a Navy pilot. His eyes weren't quite good enough, so he opted to become a naval flight officer. First, however, he had to make it through Aviation Officer Candidate School (AOCS), a curriculum made famous by the movie *An Officer and a Gentleman.* "Here's where women start to come into the picture," he told me.

My AOCS class did not have women in it, [but] three classes prior, the first class with women had graduated four gals. Subsequent to our class, they had women coming in. There was a lot of resentment by some of the real hardcore gunnery sergeants about that. The Marine drill instructor and the Navy officer—of the two, the gunnery sergeant ran the show and the officer was just a figurehead; at the time, the Navy did not send their best— and some of the Marines were very vehemently against women attending AOCS. Not [my drill instructor]. Mine was enlightened. Black guy, Vietnam veteran.

The norm was,"What are you doing here? We're going to make life miserable, we're going to get you to [drop on request]." If they couldn't get [the women] legally, they were going to get them some other way. One of the gunnies had his conquest wall in his closet— and some of the women were aviation officer candidates [AOCs], and he said they knew the only way they could graduate was to sleep with him. This was not sanctioned—there was a code of silence, and it was not all the gunnies. But it happened. . . . It was a different time: Most of us were disgusted with the Neanderthals, but not outraged. There was sort of a code of brotherhood that you didn't violate. I thought, What a joke, to think this impresses people, never mind the moral poverty. I was not the person I am today, but I thought it was a disgusting abuse of power—but not enough

*to throw down the flag and wash out of AOCS, because my goal
was to get a commission and become a Navy officer.*

Kuehn's first operational assignment would be at VQ-1, Fleet
Reconnaissance Squadron 1, on Guam.

*There were women in VC-5 [another squadron]; they flew
straight-up aggressor aircraft. They were not allowed to do
combat missions, but they came out to do exercises at Guam.
What was the real difference? They weren't flying off carriers near
Vietnam, China, or Russia, but they were close enough. Most of
us, we knew what the Navy's policy was, and that it was no big
deal. And I think most of us thought that women would go into
the operational squadrons eventually. In fact, illegally, we would
sometimes take our female intelligence officers with us on actual
missions so they could better support us. This wasn't regular, it
was totally against regulations, but it happened. We had no
operational female aircrew, but we had female ground crew, intel,
data processors. There were people—the old chiefs, who didn't
think there should be that many women in the Navy. No need for
women in the Navy, biggest mistake the Navy ever made. Okay,
Chief, your Navy—my Navy's going to be different. But you'd
never accost a chief, not in public—even in private. But they were
going to retire and die out.*

When Kuehn entered the Navy in 1980, the military tolerated, and
sometimes even encouraged, the widespread use and abuse of prostitutes and pornography as a means of male bonding. Up until the late
1990s, the use of prostitutes by servicemen on liberty was simply con-

sidered a reward for military service. Ships are not nice places to spend several months on, and people work very, very hard. However, many millions of people in the developing world also work hard, and often what poor people have to work with is their bodies, and those of their children, especially their daughters.

In 1995, Admiral Richard Macke, the commander of U.S. forces in the Pacific, was forced to retire when an Okinawan girl was kidnapped, beaten, and raped by three U.S. troops, two Marines and a sailor. Macke's statement was that the servicemen were stupid for doing what they'd done because they could have hired a prostitute for what they'd paid to rent the car they used to commit the crime. The Okinawans reasonably understood him to have said that it would have been okay to have beaten and raped a prostitute. After his apology failed to calm the furor, Macke announced his retirement.

Macke's forced retirement was not a matter of his failure to be politically correct. A great many servicemen confronted with wide-spread prostitution in places like South Korea, Okinawa, the Philippines, or Thailand understood, then and now, that their actions would tell them about what kind of men they were, and walked away. Undoubtedly, a great many other men, less strong-willed or more naive, indulged once or twice before they decided that they were revolted by what they were doing to themselves and to the women they were using. But not enough men. The ugly fact remains that, for half a century, the United States military regarded the Far East as its private brothel. Although prostitution flourished around military bases in Europe, it was not a way of life as it was in the Pacific. Without dismissing larger issues of national sovereignty, the brutalization of women and crimes committed against them were major factors in the loss of U.S. basing rights in the Philippines, and in the ongoing tension in Okinawa and South Korea.

But as the culture changes, so do opinions. It has always been illegal for a servicewoman (or man) to be a prostitute, but in January 2006, President Bush signed into law a new provision of Article 134 of the Uniform Code of Military Justice that makes the patronizing of a prostitute by service members a crime, punishable by dishonorable discharge, forfeiture of all pay and allowances, and imprisonment for one year. This provision was passed in an effort to end the complicity of U.S. troops in human trafficking by providing a market for slave dealers who rent out women, girls, and boys for sex. The military's recognition that it needed to end any possibility that service members might be involved in such activities was a radical and progressive move.

In a relatively short time, from 1973 to 2006, the U.S. military has undergone a major change in how it thinks about women; in some ways, it has come further in a shorter period of time than civilian society has. Until the 1990s, prostitution was considered to be part of soldiers' liberty, or the R&R experience; now the serviceman who participates in it is expected to understand he is participating in a slave trade, and that he will be punished for doing so—even if it is a legal slave trade. And yet, the U.S. military could not have come this far, this fast, if it were not reflecting changes in the larger society, at least that portion of it that doesn't buy into Madison Avenue's ever coarser advertising campaigns.

When I interviewed him, John Kuehn talked about how that change happened in the Navy. "Right after Desert Shield, I got stationed out in Japan, and I went down to a change of command with my old squadron, VQ-1 in Guam . . . and they had female EP-3 fliers. This was in 1991, and I'd left in 1986. This happened in five short years [and despite the still-extant ban on women flying combat missions]. Not a lot of people knew what these squadrons did—out of sight, out of mind. They were shore-based, not ship-based, but they were flying reconnaissance mission sometimes in Iraq itself. They were in combat. There was a big folderol about these women getting air medals when they weren't in combat, because 'women aren't in combat.' But any reasonable person who knew where they flew and what they did knew they had been in combat! It was a done deal before Tailhook and Clinton. You can't let females start flying operational missions, then limit the operations they're going to fly. From that point on, in 1991 or 1992, when people said, 'Women aren't in combat,' I'd laugh and say, 'They already are.' When they'd say, 'That's not combat,' I'd say, 'Flying reconnaissance over Iraq in the middle of a war isn't combat? We need to have a discussion.'

"The bottom line is, women came into the fleet, and by the time I got to the USS *Stennis,* this 'no women in combat' line was bullcrap. I know mothers with children flying F-18s into triple-A [anti-aircraft artillery] fire and dropping bombs. And when I spent time on a ship with five hundred women, watching them flying helos, working chocks and chains, heavy work, light work, major brain work, standing watch—it's a done deal. Get the best out of these people so they can develop personally and professionally, and get on with it."

The single biggest issue in integrating women into the military, much less into the combat arms, has been held to be cohesion: the emotional bonds between members of a unit. These bonds have been deemed absolutely crucial to combat effectiveness. The presence of women in combat units has long been thought to preclude the development of those bonds because, to put it coarsely, cohesion was understood to be male bonding, and the exclusion, and often the denigration, of women was thought to be central to male bonding.

Strength can be dealt with: You can train people. Pregnancy is not an issue if people are responsible about their fertility. But how do you argue with people's emotions? An awful lot of white people were violently and dehumanizingly racist in the 1940s and '50s and '60s. But white infantrymen got over it (very quickly, too) when combat took an interest in them and black men were the only infantry replacements available. But sex isn't race, so we've been told. As though that three-word mantra, "Sex isn't race," explains everything. The idea that it might be easier to integrate women into a culture where many men like and respect women, even if they don't think of them as military equals, than it was to integrate black men into the white army of a segregated nation, rarely made it past the shouting. Too many people, whether the social conservatives or the feminista, had too much emotionally invested in their positions to ask those kinds of questions, let alone face the answers. There was also another mistake, a fundamental one. In the military mind, cohesion had become more than just a contributor to combat effectiveness. It was now synonymous with it. And you have to wonder how men who had been there and done that could believe, first, that friendship between men was more important to combat power than the numbers of troops, and second, that that friendship depended upon the absence of women, even their denigration.

For decades now, the U.S. Army has tied itself up in a philosophical debate with vital real-world consequences. The issue was: Should the Army replace its combat losses by unit or by individual? That is, should the Army keep units in the field until they fall below some percentage of effective troops, then rotate the units out for refitting? Or should the Army keep the same outfits in the field indefinitely, replacing casualties with individuals whose relationship with those units began when they got off the replacement truck?

In World War II, the Army found that an infantryman's effectiveness peaked at about four months' experience for privates and seven months' for sergeants, after which both tended to become less effective in combat and more likely to become casualties, the noncommissioned officers precipitously so.[1] For Army GIs during World War II, especially in the European theater of operations, there was only one way off the line, and that was to be killed, or wounded, or to break under the mental strain. This is why in Vietnam the Army replaced soldiers after one year: to give them some hope of survival that was not predicated upon their suffering an incapacitating wound, illness, or nervous breakdown.

After Vietnam, the replacement of casualties by individual, rather than the rotation of whole units, came to be derided as the symbol of waging war as if it were an exercise in industrial management. In the aftermath of the Army's destruction in Vietnam, some military reformers came to take seriously the post–World War II excuse of German generals blaming their defeat on their material and numeric inferiority. Had they not been overwhelmed on the eastern front by hordes of godless Slavic subhumans, Eastern Europe would have been saved from Communism. On the western front, the Germans were overwhelmed by the lavish use of Allied firepower. In their historical studies and memoirs, the German generals disparaged the actual combat value of American troops, ignoring their performance in places like the *bocage* country of Normandy, where every densely hedged field was its own little fortress, or the Vosges Mountains, where terrain and weather gave the Germans all the advantages. Those German generals were trying to avoid being hung, and during the early cold war, exaggerating the combat power of German troops against the Allies seemed one way to do it. In the aftermath of the Vietnam War, General William Westmoreland, the same man who attacked female aspirants to West Point as "freaks," had come to symbolize the use of attrition as the dumb use of firepower to trade American casualties for Vietnamese lives until the enemy was bled to death. That both the North Vietnamese and the Vietcong had a different calculus of acceptable losses was not factored into his algorithms, or those of his boss, Secretary of Defense Robert McNamara, who forced his indiscriminate obsession with statistics onto the Pentagon.

For the United States, the Vietnam War was a war of policy, and wars of policy can be fought. But when such wars are wise, they should be fought by professionals for limited, attainable ends. For the northern and southern Vietnamese, the Vietnam War was anything but limited. Yet Westmoreland and McNamara tried to fight a very hot war with American draftees, who were expected to be committed in cold blood. Theirs was a managerial approach to war that removed the human element from combat. In the aftermath of Vietnam, cohesion came to symbolize the human element in combat, and so of course it became a focal point—both wisely and unwisely—to those who rebuilt the Army after Vietnam. The only problem was that too many of the reformers tended to look in the wrong place for an understanding of its importance. The German Army between 1914 and 1945 may have had a genius for *combat,* but they provided an object lesson in how not to wage *war.*

I knew of Martin van Creveld long before I asked to interview him for this book. His own book, *Fighting Power: German and U.S. Army Performance, 1939–1945*, is perhaps the single most influential work on the idea that cohesion is the critical element in combat effectiveness. Van Creveld believed that one of the keys to the effectiveness of the Wehrmacht, or the World War II–era German armed forces (accurately understood, this includes the SS, Hitler's private army), was its system of withdrawing units from the line to reconstitute them with troops from their home regions. This practice was aggravated by Hitler's personal preference for creating new divisions rather than reinforcing depleted ones. Disregarding the administrative and logistical overhead involved, van Creveld also described the widespread German use of specialist troops (radar, or intelligence technicians, or mechanics) as infantry as a means of eliminating organizational waste.[2] Rather, it was a waste of the specialists who could, if properly utilized, have enormously increased the effectiveness of the combat units by sustaining and supporting them.

Of course, throughout much of World War II, only elite units in the German military had their losses routinely replaced; the others were ground down to embers, to the point that when German troops deserted or surrendered, it was in extremely cohesive groups. German troops fought not only to defend their homeland (from an invasion and revenge that it had deliberately provoked), but also because of threats that their families would be punished if they surrendered or deserted to the Western Allies. And German military authorities made liberal use of the death penalty to impose combat discipline on the *Landser,* the ordinary German soldier. Thus, in the spring of 1945, with the war clearly lost, trees bloomed all over Germany with hanged men.

In van Creveld's view, the U.S. Army saw war not so much as a struggle between men as one between machines. In other words, individual replacement of casualties enabled the U.S. Army to throw men and material at the Wehrmacht until the Germans were defeated. Meanwhile, the Wehrmacht fought well at the small unit level because men "suffered, fought, and died together."[3] Van Creveld's view evinces a profound misunderstanding of war as a struggle between "warriors" rather than between entire societies, with all their intellectual, agricultural, industrial, and demographic resources. However, his view resonated in the U.S. Army, which had overvalued the "managerial" mentality in Vietnam.

Van Creveld confined his analysis largely to bureaucratic documents, rather than studying engagements in which weather and terrain nullified American logistical advantages, such as in airpower. Such engagements, and they do exist, would have offered an ideal way to compare the actual performance of units that did not receive replacements to those that did.

Personnel specialists and historians who favored individual replacement invariably based their arguments on the American experience in World War II, of replacing losses in rifle companies on an almost daily basis, in regular as well as elite units, and the effect of this policy upon actual engagements. Whenever possible, new soldiers would be given a few days of orientation, often by handling ammunition and other supplies, before being paired with more experienced soldiers—the "old men" who would teach them how to survive. Often these "old men" would actually *lead* replacements into combat until these inexperienced soldiers knew enough to do the same for the replacements coming after them. It very rarely took more than a few days before a man became part of his unit's family. The U.S. Army's institutional experience, then, is that of sharing the hard world of war, which matters more to soldiers than how they feel about each other, or would feel about each other under different circumstances. Which is why, despite all the bad press about the "fucking new guy syndrome," a syndrome that exists more in Hollywood's imagination than in any decent rifle company, the U.S. Army still replaces casualties by individual, even as it rotates entire units in and out of Iraq and Afghanistan.

In war, as soon as you learn you can count on someone, you become very close. General Matthew Ridgeway, a soldier of immense physical and moral courage who salvaged the U.S. Eighth Army from disaster during the Korean War, knew he could drive home the integration of black

302

soldiers in Korea in a way that formal peacetime Army policy could not. He knew that whites who learned they could count on blacks to stand shoulder to shoulder with them would never think about them the same way again. He also knew that blacks who had proven their worth in combat would never think of themselves as inferior again.

And because I had studied all these things, I surmised it would happen with women as well, in Iraq and Afghanistan.

This issue's hold on me was what led me to do my master's thesis on cohesion and combat effectiveness. But my fascination was more than academic. By the summer of 2000, you could practically smell looming war, and without a draft, a war of any duration would render the existing exclusion of women from ground combat untenable. I knew that the cohesion argument, however flawed, would be a major obstacle to ending that exclusion. I also knew that the Army, still reeling from the feminista assault, didn't need to have the issue defined, once again, as Us Against Them. And while I wanted to help end that exclusion for profoundly political reasons concerning the right and requirement of citizens to participate in the common defense, I certainly did not want to write my master's thesis on women in the military.

Part of my reluctance was personal. I remembered the culture wars of the 1990s too well. Feminism, which should have been about the establishment and integration of women as full citizens in American society, and conservatism, which should have been about modifying traditional values (rather than prejudices) for a modern era, became ways of refighting Vietnam. I had no desire whatsoever to revisit that era. I also had more long-term goals in mind than obtaining a master's thesis, and had no wish to be academically pigeonholed or written off as a "women in the military" specialist. I wanted to write seriously, and I was aware that many of the women who wrote about servicewomen knew little about the military, cared to know less, and often regarded the military as evil and servicewomen as dupes. I thought that, on the contrary, servicewomen should be written about by someone who knew a little about the institution, its values, and its history.

So I looked around for a campaign in which a U.S. Army infantry unit had not received replacements. I already knew how those that had received replacements had performed against German units that hadn't, so I wanted to study the units that hadn't received replacements at all. The campaign I settled on was Buna in Papua New Guinea. *Bloody Buna,* as Lida Mayo, then the senior military historian of the U.S. Army Center of Military History, titled her book. There were two early campaigns in World War II that checked the Japanese drive to establish their breathtakingly mislabeled Greater East Asia Co-Prosperity Sphere. Guadalcanal was one; Buna was the other. They both lasted about six months. The Marines would get the publicity, but Buna was the bloodier victory. Mayo summarized the losses: "At Guadalcanal, of some 60,000 Americans committed, about 1,600 were killed and 4,245 were wounded. At Buna, of a total of about 40,000 Australians and Americans, 3,095 were killed and 5,451 were wounded, not counting losses from illness."[4]

The American troops at Buna—the Thirty-second Infantry Division, a Michigan- and Wisconsin-based National Guard infantry division—were green. I chose to study the 127th Infantry Regiment. It was an ideal unit for two reasons. First, it received almost no replacements, and second, it was a National Guard unit based near Chicago, an area of the country I was familiar with. There were two questions I needed to answer. Was the 127th a cohesive unit? If so, how did that cohesion affect its combat effectiveness? Although there obviously were no women in the infantry regiment, I believed that lessons on the combat value of cohesion in segregated units could be applied to integrated units.

To answer my questions, I built a demographic profile of the 127th from three sources. Edward Lauer's *32d Infantry Division, World War II*[5] provided unit rosters including the names and hometowns of every man in the division when it was mobilized on 15 October 1940. From the regimental adjutant's records on file at the National Archives, I compiled a list of the regiment's battle casualties by name, service number, and hometown. Some of these would be draftees, not prewar volunteers. Then, from the U.S. Army's personnel records center in St. Louis, I got the morning reports for the 127th, and I compiled the names and service numbers of every soldier of the regiment who was killed, wounded, or missing in action, or who was evacuated because of shell shock, immersion (trench) foot, or malaria. My database was 3,200 lines long and building it was a major obsession, but when I was done, I could track losses by cause on any given date, whether they were battle losses or disease nonbattle injuries, by rank and company. And since service numbers were based on the soldier's geographic origin, I used a color-coding system that allowed me to see at a glance who came from what region of the United States. Then, using unit diaries, I correlated losses to what happened on the ground. In short, there was not a lot of room for guesswork or abstract theorizing.

There was no question that the 127th and the rest of the Thirty-second soldiers were combat effective, even though they were appallingly green and inadequately prepared for the shock of combat. Their training had been repeatedly interrupted as they were shuttled from one location to the next, from their hometowns all the way to Australia and finally on to Papua New Guinea. At Buna, the soldiers of the 127th overcame an enemy entrenched in well-constructed, networked, camouflaged bunkers, foxholes, and sniper nests. The 127th had no tanks, and there was only a single 105-millimeter howitzer to provide artillery support on the entire Buna front. "Dusty," as this howitzer was called, had only a limited supply of ammunition, and there was no air support to replace the missing artillery. The soldiers of the 127th attacked covered and concealed troops with little more protection than their herringbone twills and personal weapons: mortars, machine guns, rifles, and grenades, as well as some flamethrowers.

From 11 December 1942 to 2 January 1943, when they cleared the bunkers of Buna itself, the 127th would lose 34% of its starting strength of 2,734 soldiers; 26% of its losses were combat casualties. The infantry companies themselves, which did the bulk of the fighting and the physical labor incidental to actual combat, were ground down to less than two-thirds of their starting strength. One battalion could muster no more than seventy-six men in each infantry company, and half of the remaining infantry companies in the regiment could muster no more than one hundred soldiers.

My findings led me to conclude that these were indeed cohesive units. In Lida Mayo's words, "The division had a great deal of esprit de corps, proud of the name it had won in World War I, 'Les Terribles.'"[6] According to my database, at least 20% of the prewar volunteers fought at Buna, a figure that is probably low, even with the weeding out of unfit and inapt troops since the division was mobilized two years earlier. I have hometown information for almost 800 soldiers, half of whom were from the division's traditional cantonment area of Michigan and Wisconsin. Many of them shared last names: in all likelihood brothers, cousins, even fathers and sons. But even if they had only been neighbors, they had grown up together in those small northern counties: Milwaukee, Font du Lac, Manitowoc, Oconto, Sheboygan, Waupaca—except for Milwaukee, none of those counties had more than 77,000 people in them when the 1940 census was taken. They'd farmed and cut timber, hunted and fished and played together all their lives, and they had very good reason to prove themselves good soldiers, for their battlefield reputations would follow them home.

Once these soldiers cleared Buna itself, if cohesion had translated to combat effectiveness, you would have expected them to mop up the surviving Japanese fairly quickly so they could get themselves cleaned up and treat their sicknesses in austere but reasonably comfortable conditions. Especially since the Japanese were a broken collection of stragglers lacking unit cohesion, armed only with rifles, pistols, grenades, the occasional machine gun, and the very occasional mortar. They were also starving, eating grass and roots and raw crabs. Some would resort to cannibalism.

But some of the GIs were simply too worn out to take care of themselves; others were determined to become sick to get off the firing line. Operational tempo slowed to a crawl. The 127th finished clearing the entire Buna combat area, in some cases rescuing Japanese soldiers who had been disabled by hunger, on 25 January 1943. When they left the area on 2 February, there were 914 men of the regiment's original 2,734 present for duty; of these 914 men, the nine rifle companies that had borne the brunt of the fighting could muster only 373 soldiers out of a starting strength of 1,474: 25%. The strongest rifle company, Baker, had 59 of its original 171 soldiers left, and the weakest, King, only 26 of its original 157; the strongest rifle battalion had fewer infantrymen at the end of the campaign than the weakest infantry company had at the beginning of the campaign. By contrast, the regimental headquarters, the antitank and cannon companies and medical detachments, and even the battalions' headquarters and heavy weapons companies, had suffered less than the rifle companies on the line.

THESIS

The losses in this second phase of the campaign were overwhelmingly due to disease and nonbattle injuries. Caution, prudence, and the desire to make it home alive rather than aggressively pursuing the enemy meant that the 127th stayed in those swamps until disease and fever and fatigue broke the regiment. In short, the 127th was a band of brothers who had become vastly more cohesive during the Buna campaign. Yet their cohesion was oriented not toward defeating the enemy, but toward personal survival. Since there were no replacements, there were no green soldiers whose presence forced them out front to lead them into combat. It was very clear that cohesion per se did not equal combat effectiveness; in fact, in this case it had detracted from it.

Once you accept that cohesion does not equal combat effectiveness, you adopt a different way of thinking about both. It's not that cohesion is not an ingredient in combat effectiveness; it's just that the interpersonal relationships that can contribute to combat effectiveness are not the combat effectiveness itself. And, in fact, the relationships that contribute to combat effectiveness grow out of what makes a unit combat effective: shared training and shared living experiences, including some recreation, in an environment where people can trust each other. But drinking until you puke, sharing a prostitute, and running people out of your unit because they don't look like you does not ensure combat effectiveness. These behaviors do not even contribute to it, and so to define them as cohesion is a perversion of the word in its military context.

Military cohesion is what happens when new replacements team up with veterans, and when the combination of energetic ignorance, fieldcraft, and experience keeps a unit functioning. Cohesion is what happened when black men volunteered to take off their sergeants'

stripes and join the infantry as privates in the winter of 1944, even thou they were fighting in a segregated army. It's what happened when their white counterparts looked them over and said, Welcome to the family. Cohesion is when seven women join an infantry battalion somewhere in Iraq and each suddenly discovers she's got an overwhelming number of guys (in addition those trying to hit on her) who regard her as a sister and look out for her as a soldier who happens to be a woman.

Cohesion is what happened when a female medic, Sergeant Misty Frazier of the U.S. Army's 194th Military Police Company, whom I interviewed for this book, ran through enemy fire to treat wounded soldier after wounded soldier on the streets of the Iraqi city of Karbala. While Frazier was treating the wounded, another soldier in her company, Private Teresa Broadwell, covered other soldiers with aimed bursts from her machine gun. Cohesion is what happened when Staff Sergeant Timothy Nein and Sergeant Leigh Ann Hester of the Kentucky National Guard's 617th Military Police Company helped clear a trench of insurgents outside the Iraqi town of Salman Pak, south of Baghdad. Broadwell and Frazier were both awarded the Bronze Star with valor device, while Staff Sergeant Nein and Sergeant Hester were both awarded the Silver Star. Also for the day's fighting at Salman Pak, Specialist Jason Mike, a medic, was awarded the Silver Star, while Specialist William Haynes II and Specialist Ashley Pullen were awarded the Bronze Star with valor device. And while Broadwell, Frazier, Hester, and Pullen are all women (Hester was the first woman since World War II to be awarded the Silver Star and the first woman ever to be awarded it for engaging in close combat), it didn't matter to the men they were fighting alongside that they were women, just as it didn't matter to the women that their comrades were men.

Social cohesion may or may not contribute to mission cohesion.

st, social cohesion adds another layer of trust to that built by ~~ogether. But you're certainly not going to care how fun a guy~~ ~~is to go drinking with if the enemy is coming through the wire and you~~ ~~find him hunkered down by an unopened box of grenades~~. At its worst, social cohesion among men can become a matter of acting in a way that is an exaggerated, even criminal, version of stereotypical masculinity. Charles Bronson once defined true machismo as "the art of manhood." If so, then the caricatured, perverse version of manhood might be called by the sociological term "hypermasculinity." And it has about as much to do with manhood as *Vogue*'s emaciated hothouse version of femininity has to do with womanhood.

A 2003 study, "Cohesion and the Culture of Hypermasculinity in U.S. Army Units," by Leora N. Rosen, Kathryn H. Knudson, and Peggy Fancher, published by *Armed Forces and Society,* discovered something very interesting. In male-only units, hypermasculinity had a positive relationship with cohesion, but in mixed-sex units it had a negative relationship. Not surprising. What does surprise, but should not, is this:

> . . . *at the* individual *level, group hypermasculinity was significantly negatively correlated with cohesion and readiness . . . those who rated their groups high on hypermasculinity also tended to give them low ratings on cohesion and readiness. Meanwhile, others in these same groups rated their groups high on cohesion and readiness.*[7]

Stripped of social science jargon, the study holds that men who are members of hypermasculine groups rate their groups as highly cohesive. At the same time, many of the members dislike the hypermasculine activities by which this cohesion is achieved. In short, they

WOMEN IN THE LINE OF FIRE

go along to get along, then justify their participation, to borrow a base-ball phrase, as "taking one for the team."

This happens for various reasons. First, scumbags can emerge to set the tone in any group setting. (We can also consider this a command and leadership failure.) Second, many of these men lack plausible grounds for refusal. Unless they are married, in serious relationships, or chaste for religious reasons, "Not tonight, Mac, I've got a headache," doesn't cut it. They do what they do in order to avoid appearing "unmanly." Finally, many young men are simply unaware of other ways of achieving intense cohesion short of shared hardship and combat. When women are added to the unit, hypermasculine cohesion loses a great deal of its attractiveness. Indeed, those who might be allowed to set the tone in all-male units often find themselves shunned or relegated to marginal status in integrated units.

Not mentioned in the study, but well known to anyone who has ever worn a uniform, is the "buddy system." Within the group, individual soldiers will form intense, nonsexual personal relationships based upon shared backgrounds and characteristics: the "hillbillies," the college guys, the jocks, the evangelicals, et cetera. Very seldom do these affinity relationships negatively impact overall unit cohesion in a good outfit. In Iraq and Afghanistan, I saw a new kind of buddy system. Married men and women, as well as those in committed relationships back home, would band together and keep each other faithful. I did not observe any lessening of unit cohesion because these people were keeping their vows . . . and their self-respect.

Another study, by Leora Rosen and Lee Martin, called "Psychological Effects of Sexual Harassment, Appraisal of Harassment, and Organizational Climate Among U.S. Army Soldiers," published by *Military Medicine,* found that a lack of acceptance of women as soldiers was a chronic, severe stressor for female soldiers. This was to be expected, but what the researchers also found was that *male* soldiers who worked with female soldiers *also* suffered psychologically from the lack of their female peers' acceptance as soldiers. They theorized that this was because "aggressors against women are characterized by intimacy deficits, loneliness, and depression."[8] That may be true, but the *aggressors* do not suffer from aggressing against women. The ones who suffer are those men who do not enjoy such aggression, but nevertheless cannot bring themselves to take a woman's side, even when it is the right thing to do, because they are men and they fear transgressing the group norms of hypermasculinity. Nevertheless, their consciences do not give them peace.

Social cohesion gone bad is a matter of letting the jerks set the unit tone. No unit is without jerks, of course, and in mixed-sex units some of those jerks will be female. But when jerky behavior breaks down along gender lines, it can be very hard for men to call a halt to it. Violating group norms is hard enough in civilian society, much less in an institution that is male by demographic and masculine by ethos. And this holds whether the issue is just a trivial slight or cruel behavior, whether or not it rises to the level of a crime.

Then, of course, there is the issue of guilt, real and imagined. Plenty of young men together overseas and alone for the first time in their lives have done things, such as patronizing prostitutes, that they would never have done had they been back home in the States, or overseas in a mixed-sex group. Whether the behavior is genuinely uncharacteristic or not, regretted or not, and regardless of whether it is entirely civilized, it allows the real jerks to say: Everyone does it. Therefore, any man who's been part of that grotesquely caricatured masculinity, even briefly, does not feel entitled to criticize it. He's heard it's all a slippery slope, and the people who are most in favor of slippery slopes perpetrators. If you're only a little less guilty, you can't pass jud now, can you?

——————— ⊕ ———————

The presence of women in any units, but especially in combat units, was thought to pose a threat to cohesion for several reasons. The first, legitimate concern was that women's lesser physical capabilities meant that they simply wouldn't be able to keep up. That would threaten combat effectiveness, and thus *military* cohesion. The second threat was to *social* cohesion. There were two subsets to this second threat: that of favoritism or the appearance of favoritism; and that of women having consensual sexual relationships that were not a matter of trading sex for preferential treatment.

We have dealt with the first, military threat in detail in Chapter Seven. My argument stands: Adjust the weight standards and train women effectively to take advantage of the increased capacity for muscle and bone, and see what happens. The second threat's two different components raised questions. Would women deliberately trade sex for promotions, or trade sex to get out of heavy or dirty work? What if men fell in lust (or in love) and had their good military judgment clouded by a woman's sexuality? All organizations have their 10% who cause 90% of the problems, and some women do willingly (at least attempt to) trade sex for favors. Some of the time. To some men. Who accept some offers some of the time. As I argued in the last chapter about pregnancy, the military would do well to adopt a policy of differentiation. Here it would mean assuming that neither most men nor most women in a unit would jump at the chance to trade favoritism for sex, and hammering those few willing to make that trade.

But, of course, the threat that women might use sex to get ahead or distract men from their work was not considered merely as an aberration and to be fairly and sensibly dealt with as such. Instead it was feared that women would be so inherently distracting and manipulative that their presence would threaten the very integrity of the military institution. It's an unrealized worry, which, because it is unrealized, says a lot about the quality of the average man or woman in the institution, and even more about the worriers' opinions of those men and women—perhaps especially about their own personal motivations and weaknesses.

As for the more common scenario of women having sexual relationships with men that were in no way attempts to curry favor, the worry there was that other men in their units would be consumed with jealousy over the idea that some man, somewhere, was getting something they weren't. It is generally not a good idea to have a sexual relationship with someone in your immediate unit, for the same very obvious reasons, vastly intensified, that you should not have an affair with a coworker. People who realize that they are serious about each other, and ask their superiors for reassignment, however, are in a different category. But the concerns often went far beyond that. As one soldier with a postgraduate education told me, "'Who's she fucking now?' will be what every man in her company would want to know." His face was straight. He wasn't joking—just giving me great insight into his own preoccupations. Fortunately, this was a vocal but not exactly representative subset of the Army, much of which, in fact, is married—including quite a few young men in the infantry. Presumably, most of them love their wives and are faithful to their marriage vows, or they wouldn't have gone to the trouble of getting married in the first place. A good many of the single men have lovers, civilian or military, female and occasionally male, whom they care for deeply. A lot of men never get credit for their chastity, including the chastity of their thoughts.

The fact is that fraternization, or personal relationships that threaten the integrity of professional relationships, can be a hard problem to solve. In sexual terms, fraternization means everything from trading sex for favors to indiscriminate screwing around to an officer and an enlisted person realizing they love each other and want to get married. The Army's fraternization policy prohibits shared living accommodations among officers and enlisted personnel, except when they must live together due to operational requirements: a battalion commander and his sergeant major, for example, or a company commander and his first sergeant sharing a barracks room in Iraq. The policy also prohibits all dating and intimate or sexual relationships between officers and enlisted soldiers, or even soldiers of different ranks when there is impropriety or the appearance of impropriety. On deployment in Iraq and Afghanistan, that is being interpreted as: Don't have sex with someone you're not married to, and don't develop a romantic relationship with such a person, either. The penalty is an Article 15, or nonjudicial punishment, which, though not a court-martial, is also not a good thing to have on your record. I've known commanders to give Article 15s to both of the parties involved in an improper sexual relationship.

If the traditional concern, developed in a largely single (i.e., conscript) military tolerant of prostitution and pornography, has always been one woman's influence or impact on many men, then this concern is a backhanded recognition of the fact that most men are apt to be jealous of the man who has a girlfriend or wife who is geographically close to him. Even if they're celibate for operational reasons. But the real reason that fraternization can be such a tough problem to solve is that personal relationships are natural. It's not so much that men and women may have sexual feelings for each other. It's that people have a tendency to like and associate with each other in all kinds of ways, and military units tend to be very close organizations. One of the most important reasons that the military is such a hierarchical institution is because of the need to preserve professional integrity between people who are personally close.

Indeed, most of the Army's guidance on avoiding fraternization in AR 600-20 has *nothing* to do with sex. Virtually all of it has to do with preventing nonsexual relationships between soldiers that might threaten professional relationships. Just as the Army does not want soldiers owing their officers or sergeants gambling debts, or vice versa, it does not want a company commander and first sergeant renting a house together (although people of different ranks may do such things as rent or buy property from each other), or running a business together, unless they are in the Reserves or National Guard. And for good reason. It is prejudicial to good order and discipline to mix the personal and professional between people who may have to order or be ordered by each other into danger, and possibly to their deaths.

Ironically, though, one reason sexual relationships between men and women have not undermined the professional relations upon which good military order and discipline rely is that men and women like each other too much. Many men have always liked each other too much to jeopardize their friendships by gambling or making loans to each other. Not that they're saints or angels, but for many men and women their self-respect and their lives are more important than fucking around. This isn't true of everyone all the time, but most of us have higher priorities and other values than just sex; those of us who don't fall somewhere between pathetic and predatory.

It is time for the Army to recognize the fact that men and women can live and work together civilly without indulging their sexual

316

impulses. There is a distressing tendency in some deployed prohibit female and male soldiers from spending time in eac quarters, and to require women to be escorted at all times. For the women, this means isolation, extreme isolation if they are one of only a handful of women in their units. The assumption is that men and women will get together for only one thing: sex. In reality, this isn't true. A more humane, and practical, solution to prevent people on deployment from screwing around is to set a policy of no sex between soldiers who aren't married to each other. Then firmly and strictly enforce it without assuming that every card game is a potential orgy. This is kinder to the women, certainly; but anecdotally, units that assume their soldiers are adults and deal with the individuals who aren't as exceptions have fewer problems with people screwing around than units that assume adults cannot control their sexuality. Policies that require men and women to treat each other as forbidden fruit sexualize their relationship and make it that much harder for them to develop a nonsexual relationship.

As for requiring women to be escorted to ensure their safety, that's a cop-out. If a commander is that worried about female soldiers being attacked by male soldiers, that commander should issue pistols and ammunition to every woman who does not carry one, starting with the smallest woman. The commander should then encourage the women to make vigorous use of their arms if they need to defend themselves, stating that the command will view any such shooting as a clear-cut act of self-defense.

For the real, corrosive threat to cohesion among mixed-sex units is the presence of men who like to prey upon women, and the reluctance of some men to break ranks with their "brothers" and take the side of the injured woman, whom far too few understand to be their sister. There is no nice way to say this: The military has a serious institutional problem with sexual assault—with inadequately punishing it, with some units tolerating behaviors that are precursors to rape. A 2003 Veterans Affairs survey found that women who had experienced unwanted sexual advances or remarks either on duty or in their sleeping quarters were four times as likely to be raped as women who hadn't. In the absence of harassment, mixed-gender sleeping quarters was not a major risk factor.[9]

Men who rape do so deliberately and because they like it, not because, as one myth has it, they can't control their desire to have sex with a willing but not-quite-ready partner, or, as the other myth has it, that it is an act of dominance divorced from sex. They also work themselves up to it in order to suppress the natural instinct not to rape, and they are more likely to do so in an environment that denigrates women, especially sexually. Anecdotally, units based in South Korea, where human trafficking is practiced openly and lucratively, have worse problems with sexual violence than units that come from the United States, where human trafficking is far less prominent and acceptable. Such anecdotes are no substitute for analysis, but they make enormous sense: Like individuals, units are the products of their cultures, and while good leadership makes a huge difference, it also can't do everything.

Unfortunately, all too often people ignore the warning signs of incipient rapists. These men are often shrugged off, perhaps even slightly shunned, as men who have trouble dealing with women. The other guys think they're assholes, but they don't confront them and warn them that they can't talk about their sisters that way, and that if they do they will not be tolerated.

It's not the case that most men (or even most servicemen) are rapists. Even though most sexual assaults, including rapes, on women and men alike, are not reported, most women—and even more men—

are never sexually assaulted. This makes society's failure (for sexual assault is a social, not a military, problem) to aggressively punish rape reprehensible.

The military's failure to do so is even more heinous, because service members must have special confidence in one another, must be able to trust each other with their lives. Most perpetrators are repeat predators. A small number of men and a minuscule number of women do tremendous damage to the institution by directly attacking the women and men who are a part of that institution. And yet too many people compound the damage by actively collaborating with the rapist after the fact—by choosing to ignore the pain such people inflict or by buying into the myths about victim culpability: She was drunk or careless or trusted him or "really" wanted it. Some of these bystanders are active collaborators, others have suffered themselves, and so they believe that other people should suffer as they have. In the military, all of this too frequently takes the form of the attitude: *The women wanted to be here, and they knew the risks of working with soldiers, so let them take what comes with the territory.* As if these women were not soldiers themselves, pursuing a profession that is not only legal, but widely honored.

And though it's mostly true that men in the military genuinely revile rape as a crime, the military has traditionally valued the men who do rape and their bonds with other men more than the men and the women they rape. So it is the victim, trying to halt the predator by reporting, who is seen as violating cohesion, not the predator. It is as if the military, as an institution, has assumed that rape unfits the victims to serve, that if you have been personally and intimately victimized you cannot protect others. And so many women and men keep their rapes secret for years, even decades, choosing to remain loyal to and serve in the institution they love.

There have been many findings on sexual harassment and assault within the services, starting with *Sexual Harassment in the Military: 1988,* which found that 5% of women and 1% of men had reported actual or attempted rape or sexual assault,[10] and ending with *2004 Sexual Harassment Survey of Reserve Component Members,* which found that the sexual assault rate was 2% for women overall, and 3% for women in the Army National Guard, Army Reserve, and Marine Reserve components; the sexual assault rate for men was between 1% and 0%.[11] In the crisis at the service academies, 6% of female and 1% of male cadets at the Military Academy, 5% and 1% of midshipmen at the Naval Academy, and 4% and 1% of cadets at the Air Force Academy experienced sexual assault during the 2004–2005 academic year.[12]

For present purposes, however, it makes sense to concentrate on a hearing held by the Total Force Subcommittee of the House Armed Services Committee (Duncan Hunter's committee) on 3 June 2004, called "Sexual Assault Prevention and Response in the Armed Forces." Less important than what came out of the hearing is how it was conducted: that is, how this nation's defense officials, legislators, and experts discussed the matter.

Michael Dominguez, assistant secretary of the Air Force for manpower and reserve affairs, cited a 2000 Justice Department study that found that one in four college-age women had experienced some form of attempted or completed rape, then approvingly quoted Dr. David Lisak, a nationally recognized expert on rape, as saying, "Sexual violence on that scale can only exist in a culture that facilitates it."[13] Here was an assistant secretary of the Air Force saying, in essence, that the United States tolerated the widespread rape of its young women.

John M. McHugh (R-NY), the Total Force Subcommittee chairman, who a year later would help HASC chairman Hunter attempt to restrict the service of military women in Iraq, told Dr. David S. C. Chu, undersecretary of defense for personnel and readiness, that over the past fifteen years, there had been eighteen major studies on sexual assault within the military, and yet the military has a long way to go before adequate prosecution, prevention, and response programs were in place. McHugh stressed that he was being kind and he told Chu that he believed "we are at a crisis point here. I happen to believe we are at a juncture . . . I think we are in real danger of losing the faith and trust of the female contingent in the United States military."[14]

He then turned Chu over to Vic Snyder (D-AK), who told Chu and William Navas, assistant secretary of the Navy for manpower and reserve affairs, that a 2003 survey found that 4% of servicewomen had been subjected to sexual assault or abuse over a twelve-month period, which meant that sexual assault was not the aberration that Navas characterized it as. Snyder also told Navas that the services should not be looking at the incidence of sexual assault in a single year, but during a servicewoman's entire tenure in uniformed service, because that would produce a more accurate incidence rate: "If you took a four-year career and add that up, at the end of the career, it would be a significant number." Snyder then told Navas, "You can fool yourself a little bit by coming up with an over-twelve-month number when those are additive. I mean, the same four percent in 2003 is very likely not going to be the same four percent in 2004 or 2005 or 2006."[15]

Frances M. Murphy, undersecretary for health policy coordination for the Veterans Health Administration of the Department of Veterans Affairs, testified that of the veterans screened for what is now called military sexual trauma (MST), or sexual assault suffered during military service, about 20% of women and 1% of men reported to the department that they had experienced sexual trauma. Very few of these assaults were reported to law-enforcement agencies for prosecution. And considering that the military is overwhelmingly male, the 1% assault rate for men rivals the women's 20% assault rate in terms of the raw numbers of those reporting military sexual trauma. Moreover, the Department of Veterans Affairs also found that the rates of rape across the services, beginning with the Vietnam era all the way forward to 2002, were consistent. In short, this means that previous efforts to reduce rape have not worked.[16] Furthermore, this estimate of MST may be very low, by nearly half again as many men and a third as many women. When the Department of Veterans Affairs surveyed three million veterans to arrive at the prevalence of men and women suffering MST, more than 33,000 men and almost 29,000 women said they had experienced it. However, about 3,000 women declined to answer the question, as did more than 34,000 men, which prompted Murphy to say in her testimony: "They did not say no. They just would not answer. And I think that is very telling."[17]

With the exception of Dr. Murphy, everyone quoted above is a man. They are no more the man-hating radical feminists of legend than Pat Schroeder was. Republican or Democrat, whether they think women should serve in combat positions or not, they are following in Schroeder's footsteps by trying to leave the military better than they found it. And they are cognizant of two factors that make it very difficult to measure the incidence of sexual assault, including rape. The first is the military's traditional, and extremely narrow, definition of rape. The second is the widespread tendency in American society to assign responsibility to a victim.

Until recently, and like civilian law before it, military law has not recognized anything short of rape as a serious crime. This definition of rape included conventional penile-vaginal intercourse only, clearly against the woman's will, and by force. The kind of force that had to be proven was the type of force that *men* usually recognize as force, even though the average disparities in size, weight, physical strength, and especially training and socialization mean that force is perceived differently by women than by men. Unlike victims of all other crimes, the victim of a rape had to prove both force and lack of consent. Military law began to recognize male victims or female perpetrators of rape in the 1990s, while still defining oral and anal rape as forcible sodomy. Since all oral and anal sex, defined as sodomy, was illegal, and since forcible sodomy was thought not to be as serious as rape, it was generally not prosecuted as aggressively. Nor did military law recognize penetration with a hand or an object as rape. In short, the law didn't view sexual assault from the perspective of the people who experienced it.

Military law on sexual assault is in flux and being modernized; section 552 of 1815, the National Defense Authorization Act for Fiscal Year 2006, which takes effect on 1 October 2007, completely rewrites Article 120 of the Uniform Code of Military Justice, which governs rape. As a precursor to the change of law, the U.S. Army's Sexual Assault Prevention and Response Program, at www.sexualassault.army.mil, now defines sexual assault as

> *intentional sexual contact, characterized by use of force, physical threat or abuse of authority or when the victim does not or cannot consent. Sexual assault includes rape, non-consensual sodomy (oral or anal sex), indecent assault (unwanted, inappropriate sexual contact or fondling), or attempts to commit these acts. Sexual assault can occur*

without regard to gender or spousal relationship or age of victim. "Consent" shall not be deemed or construed to mean the failure by the victim to offer physical resistance. Consent is not given when a person uses force, threat of force, coercion or when the victim is asleep, incapacitated, or unconscious.

This is an excellent working definition of sexual assault—provided that it is enforced. Because even the statutory limitations of the old laws would not have been insurmountable problems had the culture believed the following: When people, including women, say no, they mean it. Due to their different socialization and their different physiological characteristics, men and women perceive force and the threat of force differently. And as terrifying as stranger rape can be, acquaintance rape can utterly corrode one's sense of trust and have even more harmful ramifications. In the case of service members preying upon other troops, the damage is doubly egregious, since even a stranger in such a tight community is presumed to be a comrade you can trust with your life and your honor.

Unfortunately, it is still very difficult to get convictions for sexual assaults when there exists any kind of previous relationship between victim and assailant, including even casual acquaintanceship, or any kind of "contributory" or "provocative" behavior by the victim, such as having had anything to drink prior to the incident. The failure to prosecute perpetrators is compounded by the widespread belief that rape under these types of circumstances is largely a he-said, she-said issue, resulting in far too much emphasis being placed upon the victim's word rather than forensic and other evidence.

The pure ugliness of a rape exam, even when it is administered by a humane and compassionate examiner, means that even people who have reason to lie are usually telling the truth when they report a rape and submit themselves to the exam. In the civilian world, less than 4% of all felony allegations are ultimately discovered to be unfounded.[18] Compared to civilian America, the military has a lower crime rate; for this reason, it's probably even less likely that servicewomen lie by falsely reporting rape than civilian women do. A review of more than eighty-five reported sexual assault cases at the Military and Naval Academies from 1995 to 2005 found only two, or 2.4%, that *suggested* fabricated allegations. Most victims who recanted their accusations did so because they did not want to endure the investigative and judicial process.[19]

The number of reported incidents is, in fact, surprisingly low when you look at the numbers. Chu's figure indicated that 4% of servicewomen were sexually assaulted. In 2005, there were 209,912 women and 1,202,237 men on active duty alone.[20] A 4% sexual assault rate for woman and a 1% rate for men would have translated to 8,396 assaults on women and 12,022 on men in the active component alone. However, DoD's Sexual Assault Prevention and Response Program reported 2,374 sexual assaults in all components for fiscal year 2005—less than 12% of the expected incidence in the active component. In other words, when people claim sexual assault, they are almost always telling the truth, and they should be treated with respect and compassion. Conversely, when people lie about sexual assault, it is more often than not a lie of omission, a refusal that is sadly reasonable in people who have assumed the burden of the common defense to describe themselves as victims.

Survivors, a term most men and women who've endured violations prefer to the term *victims*, are still widely blamed for being raped. Overt blame has generally gone out of style, but whenever a woman is raped, there is an undue emphasis on what she was doing to expose herself to the criminal. This emphasis far exceeds an attempt to warn other women about the common tactics of perpetrators. And of course, perpetrators want the focus on the victim. So let's talk about the perpetrators.

Dr. David Lisak, cited earlier, is a forensic psychologist at the University of Massachusetts and a nationally recognized expert in rape as it is most often committed: by an unarmed rapist who knows his victim and reoffends repeatedly. The typical weapons these perpetrators use are psychological, such as power, control, emotional manipulation, and threats of physical force. The last thing they want is to leave marks. Alcohol is often deliberately used to render a victim more vulnerable to attack, even to the point of unconsciousness.[21] This level of control and planning serves the violator's interests, as many people still widely believe myths about rape, especially the "We both had too much to drink" myth. In fact, that line ought to be understood as the confession of the premeditation it almost always is. Because this type of manipulative behavior is so commonplace among predators, it makes reporting and responding adequately to sexual assault particularly difficult in the military because—and this cannot be overemphasized—the military is a culture where people are regarded less as strangers than as comrades you haven't yet met. It's also a culture in which the use of alcohol is widely (and far from always unwisely or excessively) used as an aid in dealing with difficult experiences and memories.

Dr. Lisak has consulted with the U.S. military, particularly the Air Force, about preventing and responding to sexual assault, and in a phone interview he spoke with me at length about the perpetrators. "The comparison I make is to child molesters. They [serial, undetected rapists] become very good at identifying women who are good targets, and they groom their victims very effectively. Their activities can span hours, days, or weeks. There is a tremendous amount of planning and premeditation.

WOMEN IN THE LINE OF FIRE

"Most of these men do not perceive what they've done as rape," he told me. "They do not express remorse. I have almost never heard remorse, over twenty years of research, whether from a repeat offender or a single offender."

I asked him about the common perception that misunderstandings between men and women can lead to rape. "There is a firm distinction between mistakes in sexual communication and offenders working themselves up to rape," he answered. "Rapists say, it was all a misunderstanding, we were both drunk, and investigators are so prone to believing this that they don't investigate the guy's background; if there are one, two, three other incidents, is it really a misunderstanding?

"From listening to predators think and talk over many, many years, I am struck by their proclivity for controlling, taking advantage of, and dominating people."

Predators. He called them that over and over again. I never once heard him call sexual offenders "aggressors," or describe them as aggressive, or their acts as aggression. *Predators* was the word he consistently used. And *prey* and *predation.*

And these predators rely on two things: the shame of their victims, and other people—the predators' unindicted collaborators. According to the June 2004 HASC report, these collaborators include people who took down the confessions of perpetrators who acknowledged that they had raped servicewomen, and yet did not charge those perpetrators.[22] One such instance was an Army Criminal Investigation Command (CID) officer who told a major who did not remember certain details of her attack that she had lied about being raped, despite the forensic evidence proving that she had been. After being attacked and strangled in a latrine, she had no memory of her perpetrator vaginally penetrating her; she thought he had masturbated onto her backside.[23] Another case involved an Air Force judge advocate general who told an Air Force officer she did not have a rape case because, as she later recounted: "He went on to tell me that if he were a defense attorney he would tell me I gave the officer mixed signals, and 'No' was not enough." In her testimony, she made it clear that she hadn't just said no; she'd also said, "I don't want to do this yet," and had clung to her underwear as the perpetrator forcibly undressed her.[24] In yet another instance, an Army sergeant who was raped in Afghanistan reported the incident only to confront the accusations of her fellow soldiers. She testified: "Some male soldiers accused me of being at fault for the rape to include making a false allegation."[25] So, first she was accused of having collaborated in her own rape, and then she was accused of making everything up. This is a far step beyond the failure of common sense that leads people to accept the rapists' everlasting claims of consent, rather than asking, "If she wanted sex with you, why is she filing charges rather than sending you flowers and a thank you note?"

It was proactive on the part of the Department of Defense to create a modern definition of sexual assault and establish a sexual assault prevention response website, which, at the time of this writing, is headed up by Brigadier General K. C. McClain. It's significant, as well, that the DOD is now authorizing confidential reporting by victims, with the eventual goal of bringing them into the military justice system in order to prosecute their perpetrators.

But it is not enough.

The Department of Defense also needs to establish an Office of the Victim Advocate, which has been proposed by Congresswoman Louise Slaughter (D-NY). However, this Office of the Victim Advocate should not, as proposed, do any sensitivity training. We met Colonel Kurtz in

Chapter Five, when he discussed his experiences working with service-women during the early years of integration on the inter-German border, and he made clear how little he thought women's location in rear areas would have mattered had the cold war gone hot. In that interview, he also talked about the cultural aspects of working with women: "Stuff that the Army leadership thought would be a big deal, like sharing sleeping spaces and latrines, isn't for this new generation. It's almost as if the Army leadership attributed to their subordinates all the evil stuff going through their own minds. One thing that really must have intimidated women was "jodies" [running chants—then often profane—that troops sing]. But it was my generation that did that, that taught the troops those jodies, and we sang them running through housing areas. I look back and I'm appalled. I'm appalled at what I thought was funny then, that now is so clearly boorish behavior. The only time I remember talking to people about sexual harassment was during race relations training. No one ever talked to us about how to work with women, about how not to offend them, about how to lead units with women in them; and for my generation, it would have helped."

Sensitivity training, as it's commonly understood, works for men who are boors only because they think their boorishness is funny, not because they wish to be boorish, let alone intimidating. Colonel Kurtz felt his generation needed formal instruction on how to work with women for the simple reason that they had little experience with women as friends and peers. The culture has changed a great deal since then. Young men are apt to have female friends, and can do so without the burden of sexual pressure.

The current generation of service members doesn't need sensitivity training. They need to be dealt with directly and informally. One word, "Enough," should suffice. Those who don't get it don't get it because they choose not to. And each separate service should handle those men, who are probably going to make up the hard core of the troublemakers and their hangers-on. I have heard of local, small-scale initiatives, such as male Marines talking to other male Marines about their sexual responsibilities, or white male combat arms soldiers as well as, more commonly, black female soldiers, serving as equal opportunity officers. These are promising developments, and it should be the norm in all services for men to talk to other men about harassment and assault. Men with shaved heads, chests like tables, and combat action ribbons or combat infantry badges telling other men, "You disrespect or mistreat our sisters or betray their trust, you are not our brother," will make more of an impression on would-be thugs than all the sensitivity training in the world.

By the same token, any Office of the Victim Advocate should operate across the Department of Defense. It should have real authority to follow up on rape and sexual assault charges, and real authority to prosecute accessories after the fact, as well as superiors who engage in cruelty toward and oppression and maltreatment of their subordinates, which is a crime according to the UCMJ. Such cruelty and maltreatment includes, for example, refusing to take a survivor's report of rape, or assigning a survivor to work with her perpetrator, or telling a survivor she put herself at risk by drinking with her perpetrator. The best way to "sensitize" people to rape is to punish the perpetrators and their collaborators; as punishment rates go up, more victims will report and more perpetrators will be punished sooner, which is what seems to have happened in civilian America over the past three decades. The DOD also needs to collect data on the perpetrators in a timely manner, and share it with law-enforcement agencies across the department, as well as with civilian law-enforcement agencies, because most perpetrators are repeat offenders.

330

But these are all attempts by one institution, and a hierarchical one at that, to find a solution to a problem that is endemic in our society. One of the most pernicious legacies of the high maternal mortality rates I discussed in Chapter Four is the widespread belief that, since a woman's cross to bear is the inevitable pain, serious injury, and even death associated with childbirth, sex at women's expense is . . . normal. Normal for men to do to women, and normal for women to suffer. And even when such behavior is judged as improper and wrong, it has often been regarded as certainly not worth jailing or shunning a man over doing what comes "naturally, " especially if the rape is not considered to be overtly violent.

"Our whole society has trouble dealing with this issue," Dr. Lisak told me. "The only solution is long-term cultural change."

I hear the reader agreeing with me, saying, *Yes, American society needs to change.* But that's civilian society. Can the military overhaul its culture and promote an unequivocal intolerance of rape and still be effective? Isn't this a price "we" have to pay for an effective military? Aren't Martin van Creveld—with his contention that war is always about rape, even, he says, if it is punished, even if it never occurs—and Edward Luttwak—with his contention that the Army must be demasculinized to deal effectively with sexual assault and serious harassment because men who like to rape join the Army—right?

Everything I've experienced in writing this book leads me to believe *no.* But I needed to talk to an expert about this; one Marine led to another, which led to Jon Rider (who in turn led me to Brigadier General Thomas Draude). Rider was commissioned as a Marine infantry officer in 1963. During twenty-seven years in the Marine Corps, his assignments included command of rifle, mortar, and sniper platoons and two rifle companies during ground tours in Vietnam in 1965–66 and 1969–70, and commands of a force reconnaissance battalion and the School of Infantry at Camp Pendleton from 1988 through 1990; he has since retired to work in nuclear nonproliferation.

Rider was intrigued by what I was doing, especially because I said very bluntly that I thought the real key to integrating women into the combat arms was to draw a clear distinction between military aggression and criminal aggression. He agreed to examine any linkage between the two from his perspective as an infantryman who had been responsible not only for operational Marines, but also as the commanding officer of the Marine Corps' School of Infantry at Camp Pendleton. He cautioned me that while he still keeps up with active-duty Marines, and works in a "joint" environment with former servicemen from the Army and the Air Force, his observations were drawn from his time as a Marine on active service.

"What the military needs in combat troops is cohesion," he said.

The idea of taking untrained civilians and in a very short period of time turning them into Marines who are capable of going into combat and either destroying the enemy or destroying their will to fight is an onerous task. And there are two primary components: the training regimen, which has to be as close to actual combat as you can actually get it and still keeping a margin of safety. Training is key. And the other thing . . . [is to] establish [a] team identity.

These two areas are what we really strive for: the intense, realistic training and the forging of the strong team identity.

Because the result is that people are thinking less about themselves and their fear than their team and their responsibilities to that team. Integrity is vital to this training and the success of the team. You have to trust people, and be able to trust and know what they will do in a particular situation. What makes a particular organization strong is the ability to trust their leaders. When you have perpetrators of any type, if they are unofficially condoned by the leaders, that will destroy the cohesion of any type of unit. Not only can you not trust the criminal in your midst, you can't trust your leaders to do the right thing! There is no such thing as someone being so valuable to a unit that, even though they're a criminal, they will not face punishment for their crimes. And a unit that feels it cannot lose a such person is a weak unit.

You mentioned the implicit bargain between parents and the Marine Corps. I don't know that anyone writes about this, but we all understand it. There is an unwritten contract—but it's sealed in blood—that we're going to take your son or daughter, and we can't guarantee that they won't be harmed in combat, we're going to do everything possible to take care of them and train them so that they are the ones who will come out of a fray as victors. We take that literally as a sacred oath: We will do everything we can to assure that they are trained well and led well. If my daughter were a Marine, I would want her focused on the mission and, if need be, the enemy. Not on a threat from her fellow Marines.

He then squarely addressed the possible relationship between military aggression and culture and crime, and he found it virtually impossible to make that connection. Criminals, after all, are not aggressive in the sense of being willing to fight. The number of those willing to fight decreases as the perceived risk increases, and combat is a very high-risk environment. But predators, no matter how violent and cruel, are looking for the weakest among those they regard as vulnerable. By its nature, however, military aggression requires both discipline and daring.

There are people who come into the Marine Corps because they know they can be violent. But the vast number of men and women I have known who come into the service do so for altruistic reasons. And I believe they'd be disturbed to know there are people who come into the service for a chance to be violent toward their fellow Marines. But there are. And I believe that the units that are strongest either weed them out, or they put so much pressure on those individuals that they do not do those things that will tear them away from the team. Peer pressure and command pressure can bring people who might wander back onto the straight and narrow. And every time we make the excuse that I really need this person, that even though this person has confessed or been found guilty of a crime against his or her fellow Marine, this person has done well in their duties and has a CAR [combat action ribbon], that "we can't turn them in even though they've raped someone"—that's weak, and it creates a weakened unit.

If the commander uses excuses not to prosecute rapists, he has essentially broken his people into men and women and

*is using different standards to judge them by. I can think of
no situation in which this enhances combat effectiveness—
it's inexcusable.*

*We do teach people to overpower the enemy, but there
should be no equation between overpowering the enemy
and overpowering someone in my unit. The only thing
that is similar in those two situations is the word power.
We tout that we hold ourselves to a higher standard, but
it should be in deed, not in word. There is no justification
for winking at criminals.*

So many of the broader cultural excuses for criminal predation
as the logical outgrowth of military aggression have been made by
men who, as civilians, were not responsible for other people's sons,
and as men did not expect to endure victimization by servicemen. It
was women, in and out of uniform, whom these men defined as the
natural targets of criminals wearing the uniform. But because women
were women, these men deemed them incapable of participation in the
common defense, which eliminates any need to tolerate male predation upon women as the price women "need" to pay for their defense.
The logic of such men was at best circular; it was also disconnected
from any genuine military ethic. In the many conversations with servicemen I have had on this subject, I rarely encountered excuses for
crime; I did occasionally, however, encounter the belief that crimes
against women were a matter of misplaced military aggression. Yet
whenever I spoke of the behavior combat units train for, and how that
differs from sexual predation, I got a look that said, *Why hasn't anyone said this before?*

On 4 April 2004, I published an article, "Prosecution Should Be Automatic in Cases of Sexual Assault, Harassment in the Military," in the *Seattle Post-Intelligencer*. It was a harsh critique that said that the military's institutional mishandling of sexual assaults dishonored the institution, and that "[i]n extreme cases, the flags of units with such a history should be retired. Battle honors earned against a valiant enemy should not be sullied by cowards who prey upon comrades." This article was read in Iraq by some of the soldiers of the First Brigade. I confess, it made me nervous, knowing that the public affairs soldiers and the unit leadership would read it in order to get some background on me before I visited. I was afraid they'd think, *She's looking to make her reputation by putting someone in jail.* And yet I never heard a bad thing about that article. And it wasn't just female soldiers who liked it; quite a few male soldiers did, too.

The Romans had a saying: "Of all our laws, some are written, others are unwritten." And it is the enforcement of unwritten laws that can make the written laws so effective, especially in the military, which is a shame culture, not a guilt culture.

Congressman McHugh was right. The military and—since this book is primarily written about the U.S. Army—the Army are at a crisis point. The military has a decision to make, and its soul is at stake.

Approximately 15% of the Army is female. With retention and recruiting slipping, women will be more and more important as raw recruits and seasoned veterans, and as combat soldiers. There is so far little indication that women are put off from the Army by the risk of combat, even if they are not combat soldiers per se. In 2004, 17.5% of active-duty recruits were female, a number disproportionate to their presence on active service.[26] Perhaps the growing number of women may be explained by the fact that women are not recruited for the infantry, for which the Army, like the Marine Corps, has a great need. However, women are recruited for the military police, who often operate as infantry, and for which the Army and Marine Corps also have a need. It is reasonable to assume that many of these young women are enlisting in a time of war for the same reasons many young men do: to do something difficult and dangerous and to see just how far they can push themselves mentally and physically while being a part of something far greater than themselves, and to accept the burden of the common defense.

As for the Army itself, it is time it recognized that the traditional martial virtues of strength and courage, disciplined aggression and stamina, while generally thought to be masculine, are also women's common human heritage. *Feminine,* if you like, though I prefer *womanly.* The military is capable of being overwhelmingly masculine in numbers and ethos, and yet welcoming and respectful of women. The military may make the collective decision that those men who don't think women should be in the military—especially not as combat troops—and therefore refuse to treat them with professional respect, are not men worthy of bearing arms. Finally, the military may openly regard men who use their military training to hurt women, be the women civilians or military, as a perversion of what the United States has raised its military to do: to protect and defend the larger society and its values. It may regard such men as dishonoring their arms and the military services, and, because the military is a shame society and not a guilt society, treat them as such, ostracizing them when the law is too blunt an instrument for proper punishment.

There are those who will not like these solutions, but "I don't like it" is not a legally or constitutionally adequate argument to oppose the citizen's traditional right and responsibility to bear arms in the common defense.

There will be those who will say, "God doesn't like it," but even

were the god of every American, neither their god nor any
izen.

, there are those who say that it is a new thing under the sun,
to let American women choose to bear the risks of war and the hard-
ships of providing for the common defense. And they are right. But to
borrow ineptly from the great historian Bernard Bailyn, the American
Republic also began the world anew.

We Americans, with fits and starts, slowly, imperfectly, sometimes reluctantly, sometimes with great resolution and clarity, have
for a century and a half now been engaged in creating a society where
women are both fully human and full citizens. From the first married
women's property acts after the Civil War to women's generations-long
struggle to vote, that they might have a say in the laws they are subject
to. From opening up education and employment to women based upon
their potential, not what others thought suitable for them, to our halting
efforts to redefine rape as a crime against the woman from her perspective. To redefine strength and courage and aggression to include the
strength and courage and aggression women have always had to have,
without which we humans could never have survived. To allow women
to develop their virtues and choose their risks for themselves, rather than
having them imposed upon them by biology and the decisions of men,
who often loved them, but to whom they were not equals. To reshape
foreign policy so that we look at how we affect half the population of
the countries we are dealing with. In short, to eliminate so much of the
pain and sorrow between men and women because it is not biologically
necessary, even though that pain and sorrow derived from all those millennia in which childbirth was a virtual death sentence.

Normalizing the position of American servicewomen is just one of the
steps in that long journey. Perhaps it is time to take that step with grace.

Civic Feminism and the Wars of the 21st Century

Jim Bartlett is a freelance military affairs correspondent and photographer who has been covering conflict areas since the Bosnian War in 1992. In 2003, he accompanied the 101st Airborne to Baghdad, and he was embedded for almost six months with a U.S. Army civil affairs detachment during 2004. All told, he was in Iraq for almost a year.

"During my time with the civil affairs unit, one of their female staff sergeants was involved in a project to establish shelters for battered women around Baghdad," Bartlett told me.

The project was being led by Women for Women International and several other organizations. "Our" sergeant was a nurse and medical specialist whose expertise proved useful because each shelter has an emergency room. The locations of these shelters are a closely guarded secret because Iraq is seeing a resurgence of "traditional Islamic values" in a culture that accepts wife abuse as the norm. Wives who flee abusive situations are in deadly danger.

At the same time, the CA unit I was embedded with befriended a pair of civilian contractors responsible for running a pool of translators in Fallujah, and the contractors would visit a couple times a week to socialize. One night, however, the soldiers heard banging on the door at midnight and they opened it to find the two contractors in a panic, carrying a small woman in their arms. The woman was one of their interpreters. We rushed them inside and immediately hung two bags of fluids, one into each arm of the unconscious woman. She was almost gone, but one of the CA docs had done his intern work in a Chicago emergency room, and together they managed to save her life.

It turned out that the interpreter's family had seen something on Al Jazeera or such and had been talking about the Americans and how terrible they were. The interpreter had disagreed: She worked with Americans every day and she knew more about how they behaved than her husband. She had openly contradicted him in front of members of his family. For this affront, he had beaten her savagely and then left her tied up on the floor of the bathroom to die of thirst. She had been kept like that for almost five days.

The contractors knew she had a contentious marriage, and so they were immediately suspicious when she didn't show up for work. She'd never missed a day of work. They drove by themselves through Fallujah to her home. Her husband first told them she was out shopping, but it was clear he was lying. So they drove back to their compound and grabbed the first armed Americans they could find, in this case a group of security contractors they knew. They returned after dark and the mercenaries broke down the door and that's when they found the interpreter. The contractors knew that her only hope was to vanish, so they made the snap decision to run the Fallujah road to Baghdad at night and get her to the CA team I was embedded with. When the interpreter recovered enough to travel, she was spirited out of Iraq on the underground railroad.

We heard stories like this in the shelter circle over and over again. Worse, neither the police nor local hospital staff seemed to have any compassion for the victims, whom they thought had "got what was coming to her." Hence the need for emergency rooms in women's shelters, and the need for total secrecy, lest the women's husbands arrive with the police and demand "their" women back, or fundamentalists attack the shelters with deadly force.

In 1973, when American women first began to be integrated into the military, such an attempted murder would have been more than likely thought to be the private business of the man and his wife. U.S. troops would not have been involved in setting up battered women's shelters. The attitude would have been, *Too bad.*

When people imagine the ending of servicewomen's exclusion from combat (at least combat they are allowed to choose by selecting a combat-oriented MOS, as opposed to combat the enemy visits upon them), they probably imagine a Supreme Court case, perhaps triggered by the award of a Medal of Honor for gallantry above and beyond the call of duty. But the most easily foreseeable end of the combat exclusion is that it will come from the sheer need for combat troops, coupled with the increasingly obvious stake American women have in the survival of the Republic. Even more than the need for troops capable of interacting with Afghan and Iraqi women, the need for combat troops has already led the Army to gradually abandon the combat restriction in practice, if not in law. The Marine Corps has followed suit, less by loosening the restrictions on female Marines than by borrowing female soldiers from the Army. Now, of course, the only thing needed is to change the laws to reflect not only the existing military reality and necessity, but also women's accomplishments. As is so often the case, formal law lags behind informal cultural change.

But one issue needs to be addressed before the law can be changed, and it's one that goes to the heart of the changes in American women's lives that feminism has brought about. It's not a matter of whether female combat soldiers are extraordinary and whether they should be treated as exceptions: In fact, given women's historic stoicism in the face of maternal mortality and often brute physical labor, female combat soldiers are probably closer to the female norm than otherwise. The issue is, in fact, a clear-cut matter of citizenship and what an American citizen's responsibilities are to her polity.

That issue is the draft. The Army and Marine Corps adamantly opposed a draft until it was too late for conscripted troops to have an impact in Iraq. But a draft at some future date, in some future large war, needs to remain a viable option. The possibility of drafting women is not only a highly emotional issue, it's an issue that must be dealt with legally: section 541 of HR 1815, the National Defense Authorization Act for Fiscal Year 2006, requires the secretary of defense to give thirty days' notice of continuous session of Congress of any proposed change that:

> *(A) closes to female members of the armed forces any*
> *category of unit or position that at that time is open*
> *to service by such members;*

> *(B) opens to service by female members of the armed forces*
> *any category of unit or position that at that time is closed*
> *to service by such members; or*

> *(C) opens or closes to the assignment of female members of*
> *the armed forces any military career designator.*

Just to be clear, the military is not seriously contemplating closing anything to women, only wondering how to get away with locating women wherever they are needed, including in small infantry units, where, as always, there is the greatest need for soldiers. The secretary of defense is also required to provide

> *(A) a detailed description of, and justification for,*
> *the proposed change; and*

> *(B) a detailed analysis of legal implication of the proposed*
> *change with respect to the constitutionality of the application*
> *of the Military Selective Service Act (50 App. U.S.C. 451 et seq.)*
> *to males only.*

In this book, I have advocated that all restrictions on women's combat service be ended, specifically in the ground combat arms, where the casualties have traditionally been heaviest. I also believe that militant fundamentalist Islam is only the tip of the iceberg in terms of real threats to this country. Thus, it is right that I deal with the issue of conscription, even though neither Iraq nor Iran, nor, for that matter, Syria, pose such great threats to the United States that they justify a draft.

In 1981, the Supreme Court upheld the constitutionality of male-only draft registration, and by implication the male-only draft, in *Rostker v. Goldberg* (1981). Writing for the majority, Chief Justice Rehnquist explained:

> *The existence of the combat restrictions clearly indicates the basis for Congress's decision to exempt women from registration. The purpose of registration was to prepare for a draft of combat troops. Since women are excluded from combat, Congress concluded that they would not be needed in the event of a draft, and therefore decided not to register them.*[1]

The constitutionality of a male-only draft was based upon judicial deference to Congress, based in turn on congressional deference to the military, which had never really been forthright about women's vulnerability to combat. For the Army and the Marine Corps, ending the formal restrictions on women's assignments and jobs will entail being forthright about their need for women as combat troops, as well as women's ability to make good combat troops. By the logic of *Rostker v. Goldberg,* ending women's legal *exclusion* from the combat arms strips women of their traditional *exemption* from the draft.

But the political legitimacy of a male-only draft rests upon something else, and that is morality. This is deeper than the military's evaluation of its own needs, an evaluation that even in 1980 was carefully tailored to skirt the reality of its dependence on women. The legitimacy of female exemption from the draft rests upon the moral balance between men and women I spoke of in Chapter Four.

The reader will recall the Tables 4.1 and 4.2 (pages 135 and 138), and my estimates that 840,429 American women died from complications of live births from 1900 to 1960, while the official Pentagon estimate of battle and nonbattle deaths in the major American wars from the Revolution to Korea totals 1,079,245. The reader will also recall that 41% of those deaths, from World War II and Korea, occurred after 1940, when a woman's lifetime risk of maternal mortality dropped below 1% and even the most fragile of women had a fighting chance to survive her reproductive years. Year in and year out, then, for centuries, childbirth had been more dangerous for women than soldiering was for men; the years when soldiering was more dangerous for men were exceptions, stunning in their devastation, but exceptions that nevertheless proved the rule.

The exemption of American women from conscription and the draft was as much a function of female reproductive vulnerability as of female legal and social disabilities. The latter culminated in the Anglo-Saxon tradition of coverture, which meant that a married woman was "covered" by her husband. (It was to her husband, not the state, that a woman owed responsibilities, including the responsibility to have sex with him and bear his children, even at the cost of her life. The state guaranteed her few rights against him.) Full citizenship and human regard for women is theoretically compatible with high maternal mortality rates. In practice, most people, especially men who had to live with the responsibility of having been the agent of a woman's death, could not make the sustained and intense effort to sufficiently suppress their fear and shame and value women as equals. The denigration of women was almost essential to maintaining a society's sanity, especially that of men, but to a significant, if much lesser extent, the sanity of women, too. What was never morally compatible with high maternal mortality rates was deliberately exposing women to combat when there was any choice about doing so, let alone exposing women to combat involuntarily, as draftees.

Large-scale military, especially combat, service for women would do more than give women weapons and the sanction to use them to deadly effect. Neither men with clean consciences nor self-respecting women can reasonably object to women bearing arms in defense of themselves or their communities. But until about 1960, when the daughters of the first women who could reasonably expect to survive childbearing came of age both for motherhood and for military service, for women to serve in combat except in utter desperation would have violated a fundamental moral compact as old as our species. Women who, because of their sex, risked their lives and health bearing children should not also have to bear the burden of defending those children when men were available.

I believe this to be the real root of the deep emotional revulsion that many people—especially older men but also older women—feel about women, especially mothers, and particularly *young* mothers, serving in combat. The revulsion is fundamentally not about women killing, even though we think of women as giving and sustaining life: The female of any species is commonly reputed to be far deadlier in defense of her young than the male. It is not that men, especially young, unmarried men, are reproductively expendable: Any society that reduces fatherhood to a squirt of semen is going to have a very tough time raising men who are *men,* who meet Aristotle's definition of a man as someone who meets his obligations and demands his just due. And many societies have attempted to allay their serious concerns about how exposure to combat affects returning (male) veterans—to the point of possibly endangering their families and the larger society—through a variety of rituals meant to purify the men of the violence they had suffered and seen and inflicted. Rather, I believe this revulsion results from the idea that this serious moral bargain, which has been upheld throughout most of human history as a part of everyday life, is being violated. The problem, however, is that that old bargain was politically and morally legitimate only so long as women were not citizens in their own right and routinely died in childbirth. Once American women were recognized to be citizens in their own right, it should have been reasonable and proper to begin to claim participation in the common defense because the bearing of arms has historically been rightly central to citizenship in the American political tradition. That it took so long to make this final claim is understandable; attitudes and practices often take generations to catch up with reality.

Now that reproduction only very rarely costs women their lives and health, their blanket exemption from mandatory service, including in combat, should the nation decide it needs a draft, is no longer moral, and so it should cease to be politically tenable. We are only about two generations into a society where American women have become citizens and no longer die with any frequency during childbirth. But we still have the moral reflexes, and the older of us have the memories, of a time when women did. Our moral emotions, if you will, have not caught up with the moral fact that to expect young men to bear the overwhelming burden of military service, especially of ground combat, because they are men is now as morally revolting as expecting women to bear the twin burdens of maternal mortality and combat.

This is not to call for reversing the all-male quota of men in the combat arms with a hard quota of women into those arms. It is simply to say that men are no longer expendable in huge numbers for the purpose of defending women, who ran monstrous risks their entire reproductive lives, during wartime. The moral balance must be recalibrated to account for women's vastly diminished reproductive vulnerability. In the developed world, because human reproductive biology is no longer a common tragedy, women not only need not be, but should not be shielded from the risks of citizenship.

Women must be in the military, and in increasing numbers, as volunteers or as conscripts. I refuse to dodge that by arguing about any future draft. My partner, Philip Gold, has written an excellent book on the draft, *The Coming Draft: The Crisis in Our Military and Why Selective Service is Wrong for America,* that deals both with the bad faith of previous drafts and with the connection between citizenship and service in the twenty-first century. Suffice it to say that we both regard it as the unalienable responsibility and right of every citizen to participate in the military according to the limits of force structure, individual desire, and ability—and as imposed by necessity. Both women and gay people are citizens and thus this responsibility and right should apply to them as it does to straight males. And neither the right nor the responsibility is a blank check to be imposed on the body politic of the Republic, whether those bodies are straight or gay, men or women.

I write this as a civic feminist, a term Philip and I coined in the fall of 2002, when I was an angry radical feminist and he had no patience for angry feminists. He actually told me that I was the angriest woman he'd ever met. The thing that saved our friendship was that he understood quite clearly that I was angry because I was frustrated by a life that was far too small. The cure for my frustration was work. He placed two articles on my thinking about the future development of feminism, one in *The Washington Times* (then conservative, now right-wing) and one in the *Seattle Post-Intelligencer* (liberal), as well as talking a friend of his into interviewing me for NewsMax.com (right-wing). We mutually decided that I needed to call myself something other than a radical feminist, a label I had proudly worn for years. What I was saying was radical, was in fact a return to the roots of feminism, but "radical feminist" left a bad taste in people's mouths, thanks to sexual politics and consciousness-raising. Those ideas had been distorted from useful tools of analysis into something that evoked man-hating extremists motivated by a desire for unearned moral authority. The antifeminists were more than happy to take advantage of, even attempt to provoke, some of these distortions. But feminists are solely responsible for the sloppiness modern feminism descended into. The first rule of politics is that you never make enemies you don't need to make, because why something gets done is often more important than what needs to be done. When you are working to end something as intimate and profound as male supremacy, your physical, intellectual, moral, and emotional seriousness and dignity is crucial. Feminists, not the antifeminists, were responsible for their own self-indulgence, the more so because this self-indulgence was so rarely a personal or momentary lapse. Without a feminist movement that had deliberately chosen an undignified, deeply unserious style, the antifeminists would have had a lot less traction and been shown up as the bigots and misogynists and opportunists most of them were. As a movement, contemporary feminism chose a personal and intellectual style that meant they accomplished less than they could have, or should have.

Yet, feminism also made possible many essential changes to American women's lives that had been put off for far too long, and it took a lot of incredibly tough-minded people to initiate those changes and see them through. The World War II generation, which had seen so much suffering between the Depression and Korea, was one group of women. But it would have been expecting too much of human nature to expect the younger women to take on their forebears' hard-earned gravitas as their own, any more than we expected the sons of the men of that generation to carry their fathers' dignity. Some of the younger second-wave feminists were reacting less to the diminishing restrictions on their own lives than to the restrictions that had warped their mothers' lives. And a lot of men in the 1960s and '70s reacted to women's absolute *need* for a life beyond the home by saying, *I've done a lot of things I didn't want to all my life, and I've been a good provider; I've always been a kind father and loving husband. So what's the problem?* It was simply unthinkable for people to willingly work collectively to deliberately restructure society along the lines of the shared pleasures and responsibilities of work and family.

But if I had to put my finger on the single biggest culprit for the disintegration of feminism in the aftermath of Vietnam, it would be the movement's reflexive insistence on women's "natural" pacifism and nonviolence: I believe that this was an attempt to have equality for rights, but not for responsibilities, which has included avoiding conscription. The pacifism of the early-twentieth-century feminists was that of women who ran their own risks of dying in childbed, and who didn't want any more of their men dying in ill-advised wars. Naive, maybe, but promale, and antimilitarist far more than antimilitary.

For those second-wave feminists to deal with conscription on its merits—within the context of the Constitution and a particular war, not as a blank check—would have entailed admitting that conscription could be a necessary tool and that at certain times citizens, including women, would be subject to it. It didn't help that the U.S. government almost destroyed its credibility on war, defense, and foreign policy during the Vietnam War. For those who wanted rights without the responsibilities that preserve them, women's supposedly nonviolent and pacifist nature was an ideal excuse. Embracing nonviolence and pacifism as a political platform made it extremely hard for organized feminism to deal with the real violence that women are subjected to. The insistence on pacifism as an inherent feminine virtue also made it nearly impossible for the feminist movement to face the hard choices that are commonplace in foreign and defense policy, much less contribute to those policy decisions with any kind of credibility.

I used to argue with this sort of feminist, the type who missed the last helicopter out of the 1970s, as well as with the men who ranted about them as if they were all there was to feminist thought. They weren't even representative of feminism's long history, I'd attempt to explain. Then I realized I needed to stop complaining and create something. That's when I decided to make up my own feminism, rooted in the early movement that had both incubated and been incubated by the abolitionist movement. The feminists of the 1860s were always about a woman's right to live her life freely; they worked to articulate that women had a place in society and a right to contribute to their polity as free citizens. These were women who understood that pacifism was not necessarily a virtue, and though almost none of them expected to serve as line infantry, they knew they might well die bearing the sons who might have to fight and die as infantry. This was a fact that they used to counter those men who said women should not be allowed to vote because they would never be soldiers. They balanced risk for risk to do the things that needed to be done, even at the cost of human life, and accepted that they might have to pay part of that price.

I chose to envision a feminism based upon citizenship because, at the simplest and most basic level, I thought that women had contributions to make to the worlds of defense, military, and foreign policy. I thought we shouldn't have to be defensive about being women. Those were our policies and our institutions, too. They were ours because we were citizens; some of us were in them, and more of us had husbands, fathers, sons, brothers in them. Why should we not be taken as seriously on military issues as on childcare issues? Why should we not take foreign policy as seriously as education? If anything, military issues are even more important to us and our families. Like those early feminists, I thought that American women had not just a physical stake in the survival of our society, but a political stake as well. If all you have is a physical stake, survival is your highest good; if you believe you have a political stake—political from participating in the public life of the polis, which encompasses more than partisan divisions or ranting about capitalist oppression—then you believe that your physical life is less important than the kind of life you wish to live. Or the kind of woman you wish to be.

---------------- ⊕ ----------------

Underneath all the talk about women's right to serve, in places like *Ms.* magazine's now defunct online boards, there has never been any real sense that women *should* serve. For all the talk of women's equality, there was little consensus on the idea that it is acceptable for women to take the lives of the enemies, domestic and foreign, who are a mortal threat to the United States—a society that recognizes women's freedom and dignity. Those women who served in the military (and also law enforcement) were regarded at best as fools and dupes of the patriarchy, at worst as fascists or racists. And while I have always thought that women *should* serve, I did more than take servicewomen, and thus the military itself, seriously. I thought that women should serve not only because we paid for these institutions, not even only because we are citizens, but because the United States has made our lives possible.

I wanted a feminism that spoke to men about "women's issues" as central to a society, just as "men's issues" are; a feminism that also spoke to women as citizens of the Republic. I did not wish to waste my time arguing with people who couldn't even disagree civilly. I wanted to create an alternative, and with Philip's help, I did.

To the Founding Fathers, citizenship was composed of an enabling civic triad that was as old as the Greek city-states and the Roman republic. The first leg was a solid education, both liberal and practical, that prepared boys and young men for the other two legs of that triad. The second leg, meaningful work that enabled an economically dignified life for a man (and his family) as more than just a wage slave, was epitomized by Thomas Jefferson as the yeoman farmer, but also included craftsmen and merchants. And the third leg, participation in the polity—a continuum stretching from defining the polity by voting to enforcing the boundaries of that polity through jury service, and defending that polity by participation in the common defense—entailed participation from the individual level of self-defense to militia service to expeditionary warfare. Feminism has long since claimed the first two legs of that triad for women, but it stopped at the common defense. Which is precisely why it's time to claim participation in the common defense for women as an unalienable right and immutable responsibility, limited only by individual will, ability, and trustworthiness, and coerced only by necessity. It's time to claim the entire civic triad for American women as American citizens.

For the horror of contemporary American civilization is that it needs taxpayers and consumers—not citizens, of either sex. Simply put, it needs our money. It does not need all the things that make us individuals: our intellects and our energies, our individual talents, an aristocratic sense of regard and responsibility for our civilization and the Republic. It needs us to buy, not to create. It needs us to work cheaply, not to take pleasure in mastering a craft or a trade. It needs poll numbers, not public conversation between citizens.

Civic feminism means restructuring our society so that balancing work and family is not an individual juggling act, which means accommodating both as a natural part of the lives of both men and women. It means revamping our educational system so that our children come out literate, numerate, and socialized as Americans who honor the values of this Republic and treat each other with dignity and respect. It means educating our young people to pursue skills leading to dignified employment and a basis for lifelong learning. It also means ending our wholesale exportation of manufacturing to China, India, Mexico, Canada, and every other country we can think of, while importing workers—most of them illegal, underpaid, and exploited—to do much of what remains. It's wrong to siphon off the brightest and most industrious from some countries, while paying pathetic sums to others to make products they themselves can't afford to buy. I don't care what economists say about comparative advantage, it's wrong to make nothing but software, weapons, and porn masquerading as entertainment, while entertainment pretends to be politics. Walk into any Wal-Mart and you see the price we have set on our nation's soul. For me, civic feminism means demanding an end to living beyond our means and passing the bills down to our children, bills that we owe not to ourselves, but to the Chinese. It means requiring a fundamental change in the way American companies do business so that they recognize that they have a responsibility to more than just their shareholders.

And, critically, it means changing how women think about defense and foreign policy, the military and law enforcement professions, and the legitimate use of force.

By the winter of 2005–2006, global warming has become an undeniable reality; we witnessed our first loss of a city, although no one is saying so publicly. Yet some of New Orleans will be rebuilt because it's a place where the United States must have a city. New Orleans is as far inland as ships can navigate up the Mississippi channel, which drains the American heartland. Inevitably, more Category 5 storms are on the way.

Where I live, in rural Washington State, we risk earthquakes and a massive mudslide off Mount Rainier, and we know that the Olympic Peninsula is overdue for a tsunami. In the winter of 2005–2006, we had a colder-than-average December, followed by thirty straight days of rain; meanwhile, wildfires burned in Texas and Oklahoma. Seattle is also within range of North Korean missiles. North Korea, in addition to killing its own people by the millions with failed economic and agricultural policies, blackmails South Korea and the United States into providing them food and energy, while infiltrating South Korea, counterfeiting U.S. currency, and dealing in nuclear technology. Furthermore, terrorist strikes in Madrid and London have revealed the vulnerability of mass transit systems in every major or even midsized city in this country and throughout Europe. The absolute certainty of random violence and great destruction from converging sources promises a future of natural and man-made catastrophes.

As a nation, we are utterly unprepared for this future, still hoping the horror will pass us by. Above all, we are unprepared for the immense harm that small but organized minorities of violent predators can do to a decent but unorganized or apathetic majority, whether they are the thugs of al-Qaeda or the thugs of New Orleans. We need to be *increasing* the National Guard, which has unlimited liability for domestic disturbances and disasters, as well as the regular services: The

Regular Army alone could stand another 200,000 to 300,000 soldiers. Yet the military, especially the Army, has given up on recruiting people for *any* component—National Guard, Reserves, or Regulars—in favor of buying equipment that takes ridiculously long to procure. This places a premium on citizen response to disturbances and disasters.

How to prepare for disaster without depending upon the National Guard and Regular Army? How about supplementing law-enforcement and emergency relief services with revitalized militias—something as old as the Republic itself, and still part of contemporary American law? It's already happening in some places. I'm not talking about the survivalist, often white-supremacist, and sometimes violent militia movement of the 1980s and '90s, but the militia of the American founders. The founders knew that the common defense was the responsibility of every citizen capable of bearing arms; that the common defense started with the constant necessity of individual and community self-defense. Americans are rediscovering this truth, although it hasn't quite been articulated yet. In essence, this new militia is composed of all those who understand themselves to be exactly what the founders intended them to be: members of the "universal" or "unorganized" militia by virtue of their citizenship— citizens who then participate according to their abilities and opportunities. The beauty of the unorganized militia is that taking the idea seriously means that every citizen has the legal standing to participate in enforcing the law. This does not mean an end to deputizing law-enforcement professionals to act for us, and it certainly is not a call for "vigilantism." It does mean that responsibility for enforcing the law inheres in the citizenry at large, and while the citizenry as a whole may delegate law-enforcement authority to a discrete group of public servants, they can never delegate away their civic responsibility for enforcing and upholding the law.

Consider, for example, search and rescue (SAR) volunteer work.

This is highly specialized work. People invest thousands of dollars and hundreds of hours in training and equipment for themselves and their animals. We don't think of them as part of the militia, but they are. The Minuteman Project, forming not only on our Mexican border, but also on the Canadian, provides nonviolent assistance to the border patrol. The many and diverse individuals in these different groups share the citizen's response to danger, and to the formal power of the state breaking down: Do what you can to provide security, not just for yourself and your own need for a life that is about more than physical comfort, but for your society—or, as the SAR motto puts it, so that others may live.

Section 311, Chapter 13 of Title 10 of the United States Code currently defines the militia as all able-bodied males aged seventeen to forty-five who are or who have declared their intention to become citizens, and all female citizens who are members of the National Guard. The organized militia includes the naval militias of Alaska, California, New Jersey, New York, and Ohio and the National Guard. The unorganized militia includes those members of the militia who are in neither the National Guard nor naval militias. Only a nucleus of the unorganized militia exists, in the form of state guards and state self-defense forces. A complete listing can be found at the State Guard Association of the United States, and there are now about fourteen thousand members of these state-sponsored organizations. That nucleus can and should be expanded far beyond the vision of the State Defense Force Improvement Act of 2005, HR 3401, which would regularize the position of these forces to finesse cooperation between them and the Departments of Defense and Homeland Security. HR 3401 is bottled up in the House Armed Services Committee, and it's not going to go anywhere until there's a catastrophe calling for lots of smart, mature citizens with guns, not professional soldiers with heavy weapons, on the street.

These state guards are volunteers who are paid only if called to active duty; they cannot be sent outside the state. As the National Guard continues to be deployed abroad, the need for state guards will only grow. Very few members of the unorganized militia—those males between seventeen and forty-five who are either citizens or intend to become citizens, but are not part of the National Guard or naval militias—know they are part of it. They should know it, and this knowledge should become a normal part of civic life, especially in our hugely complex cities, with their vast human needs. The idea is not to militarize the United States, but to reduce the need for a military response to domestic emergencies, including a federalized Guard. We should each know someone we can rely upon in case of a natural disaster or terrorist attack, and we should each, in our own ways, also be such a person.

Especially women. Once, the unorganized militia was considered to be made up of males of an age and fitness to bear arms. First it was made up of whites only, then of all such males. Now it is time to modify Chapter 13 of Title 10 to so that the unorganized militia is composed of all such *citizens* and those who have declared their intention to become citizens, female as well as male, and up to age sixty, not forty-five. Precisely *because* most women are smaller and lighter, and thus usually weaker than most men, we must participate in the common defense. Hiding behind walls destroys our human dignity; moreover, predators study their intended victims, looking for those who will run and hide rather than those who will face them. Not only does a woman's human dignity depend upon her participation in the common defense; so does her safety, as some unarmed women in New Orleans found to their sorrow.

As for American foreign policy, it must be our goal to bring as much of the developing world into the twenty-first century as possible. We and our children will inherit a violent era, an era Philip and I call the Wars of the Ways, to distinguish it from the wars of ideology that stretched from the end of the cold war all the way back to Lexington and Concord, and the French Wars of Religion, which raged between Protestants and Catholics from 1562 to 1598, until Henry IV, a Protestant, converted to Catholicism and brokered a permanent truce between the warring religions. With the end of the Thirty Years' War in Germany in 1648, Europeans decided they were no longer going to kill each other over religion.

All eras are violent, but some are far more violent than others. Our future holds a unique potential for violence because very small groups and individuals can access weapons of mass destruction (nukes and major conventional explosives, gassed-up airplanes), of mass death (chemical and biological weapons), and of mass disruption (radiological, cyberwar, electromagnetic pulse). Further, in previous violent eras, when people ceased destruction, destruction ended. But new weapons, coupled with the effects of climate change and possible natural pandemics, lead to an almost limitless potential for uncontrolled violence.

The Wars of the Ways are fought over the meaning of what it is to be human, a status that women in much of the developing world barely share. And while these Wars of the Ways will be about a great deal more than simply the human and civic status of women, their human and civic dignity will be one of the central issues. In his essay "To Guard an Era," for the September 2005 issue of the *Proceedings* of the U.S. Naval Institute, Philip divides the participants in these Wars of the Ways into three categories:

> *Those nations, peoples, regions, groups, and movements who partake of the twenty-first century, its freedoms and diversities and possibilities: those whose ways are those of prosperity, tolerance, and humane aspiration.*

Those who want out of the twenty-first century: jihadi, political extremists, violent racial and ethnic separatists, terrorists of other ilk (animal rights, ecological, etc.), male supremacists, leftover Marxist and traditional tyrants, and the gurus and gauleiters of philosophies and movements yet to be espoused—those whose ways would bring upon us new Dark Ages of hate, intolerance, oppression, and worse.

Those who can't get into the twenty-first century: the three billion of us who live on under two dollars a day, amid conditions of overpopulation, disease, and starvation, havoc, degradation, despair; most of the women of this planet; youth with no sense of opportunity and place—in sum, all those who may choose to live by the motto, "When you've got nothing, you've got nothing to lose."[2]

We believe that the Wars of the Ways will pit those of us who are part of the twenty-first century (much of America and Europe and parts of Asia) or want to be part of it against those who want out of modernity and into a fantasy of a past that wasn't nearly as good as they think it was. Those who want out will deliberately ally themselves with those who can't become part of this century (much of Asia and Latin America and most of the Middle East and Africa), who will in turn accept their help in order to destroy what they can't be a part of. Thanks to modern media, even relatively isolated people in underdeveloped nations know that a life that is short and full of despair and suffering is no life. Some of those who want into the modern world want our Declaration of Independence and Constitution to make their lives and polities more humane. Others will want into the modern world for the porn we produce in ever larger quantities. Very few of the people wanting into the modern world will know how to create what they want, especially the good things, or how to protect themselves, or the good things they wish to create. And these wars will play out against serious climate change, pandemics, and shortages of oil and water.

Philip and I hold that the United States should never make the assumption, as it did in Iraq and to a lesser extent in Afghanistan, that the people we deal with want what we want. We do, however, believe that the foreign policy of the United States must be focused on doing all we can to bring as many people into the twenty-first century, with its promise of a decent and dignified life, as we can. But we cannot save these people, and we should not try. What we can do is give them the tools to save themselves.

For the foreseeable future, this effort will remain focused on what I call the enabling civic triad. It should be absolutely central to our foreign policy in the developing world, especially in the Middle East and Africa, and our attitude should be, *You don't have to take it if you don't want it— but it's all or nothing.* American foreign aid should be oriented toward helping these societies develop free primary education, both liberal and practical, through high school to prepare children for the world of work and ideas that they will inherit as adults. If the United States needs to redevelop and reconstruct its industrial and manufacturing base, part of that policy should be directed toward diverting some low-tech manufacturing and light industry from China to various Asian and African countries. The adults need remunerative work in humane conditions that enables them to support their children and lead a dignified life. To protect those adults' families and enable them to keep what is theirs, American military missions, including private military corporations such as Military Professional Resources Incorporated, should develop ground-up participation of those adults in the common defense. They need to be able to resist thugs, whether they are "police officers" robbing them at blockades, or "politicians" selling their countries' wealth for personal gain.

People in most developing countries need to vote less than they need to establish the rule of law and respect for property rights. They need high-level engineers less than they need blacksmiths; they need brain surgeons less than they need general practitioners, physicians' assistants, nurses, and skilled midwives. The children need to be educated as children; the adults need to have confidence that their children will survive to adulthood. In some cases, pressing environmental problems must be solved before they explode into monstrous violence, as happened in Rwanda. But one thing holds true: People can't share power until they learn how to trust each other and know that such trust will be affirmed, not betrayed. Such trust is very, very thin on the ground in much of the developing world. Elections under such circumstances can be a recipe for authoritarian dictatorship at best, massacre at worst.

And the role of American women, of feminists if you will, is to make sure that women are included from the very beginning, as is their right, in all three legs of that enabling civic triad. Girls need to be educated, women need not suffer fistulas or die in childbirth. Women raped in war need to be reintegrated into their communities, and there needs to be an absolute ban on all forms of child labor, domestic slavery, and human trafficking. Women with firearms need to be able to face down men with machetes. Women's property rights, and their right to physical self-determination—their right to not have to hide their hair or faces or bodies; to not be married off or beaten; to be educated; to work and be paid; to not be raped, mutilated, or murdered; to not become impoverished upon abandonment, divorce, or widowhood—all need to be enforced, and even developed as points of law, in large parts of the world. In short, American feminism needs to be a feminism the world can use.

Marriage and motherhood should not be forms of slavery any more than men should be slaves. Freedom, dignity, and equal justice before the law are universal human aspirations. Not everyone shares them, but they know no cultural or intellectual boundaries. They may be identified with the West, particularly when applied to women, but, like courage and strength, they are our universal human heritage. And no society in which men live at the expense of women, to the point that children are routinely born at the very cost of women's lives, can prosper. It has nothing to do with competitive advantage and everything to do with the fact that we are born from each other and cannot be opposites. Male supremacy and widespread maternal injury and mortality establish the principle that power is always at the most intimate expense of another, often among those who should be dearest to each other. And I say this knowing that men are by nature no more monsters than women are saints. We do not make cultural excuses for the mistreatment, torture, and slavery of men; we should not make any for the mistreatment of women, either, even when it occurs in the home or when it's committed in the name of religion or culture.

These broad changes in American foreign and domestic policy will not occur if American women are not part of the military or foreign policy establishments. It isn't that men don't know or care about these things; it's not even that most men lack the experience to know how to support women without endangering them, especially in the Middle East. Rather, it's that women should not be excluded from participating in the defense of the United States and its values, any more than American women should expect American men to bear the entire moral, physical, and emotional burden of these Wars of the Ways alone.

The founders of this country were smart men. They left us a republic—if we could keep it, as Ben Franklin famously told Mrs. Powel. The founders understood that this republic would depend upon each of us being smart enough to weigh ideas and arguments, and civil enough to persuade each other with facts and in turn be persuaded by facts. The republic would also depend on each of us being willing to sacrifice private wealth and comfort for the safety of the community and the welfare of the nation. The founders were pessimistic enough to know that many would not do these things, would turn their brains over to demagogues, would prefer to indulge their fears with cowardice rather than cultivate their own courage, choose private indulgence and ease over the rigors and pleasures of public life. But they were optimistic enough to believe that enough of us would do what was necessary to preserve, consolidate, extend, and defend the republic. Among those who have proven their commitment have been women.

I believe that the founders' instincts were right, that our Republic can endure, even in this violent era now upon us. I believe that we are strong enough, smart enough, and good enough, and that we as a people can help steer a safe course for the world through these wars. But it depends on us. The founders did not include women as citizens, and it has been one of the great triumphs of the United States that women are now widely understood to be citizens. The Republic depends on what each of us do, and none of us can know what others will do. We can only rely on ourselves and our willingness to hold others—men and women—accountable. Together, we who choose to guard our Republic as citizens, civilian and military, and to help guard our world, might be sufficient.

In mythology, gods walk among mortals. Two gods, Athena and Poseidon, once asked a band of settlers to name a city they were founding at the mouth of a harbor after them. The settlers had to pick which god to offend, and whose gifts to accept. Some say Poseidon offered a gift of salt water; others that he offered a white horse. Since I'm fond of our equine friends and Poseidon is lord of horses as well as the sea, I say it was the horse. But the settlers accepted Athena's gift of the olive tree. Ever after, Athens was said to have trouble from Poseidon in the form of lost naval battles and earthquakes; and though they bred, rode, and drove horses, the Greeks were never known for their cavalry as much as for their infantry.

But here's another interpretation: Athens is at one end of the European land mass. Trade between Greeks and the grasslands peoples surrounding the Black Sea goes back time out of mind. And while some of the most beautiful jewelry ever to survive combines grasslands themes with Greek workmanship, the nomadic horse peoples were not civilized. Living as nomads with a very thin margin of survival made them extremely hardened. When they waged war, it was with absolute ferocity; *Mongol* is still a byword for horror. In offering the horse to the Athenians, Poseidon had offered them a life of war.

Athena's olive tree, which provides both fruit and oil, was an offer of civilization. Olive trees can grow to be fifty feet tall, spread their branches thirty feet, and live for five hundred years. One plants an olive tree for one's children and one's children's children, for they will survive even wars. Chop them to the ground, fire their stumps, and they will resprout. Their branches serve as a windbreak; their roots hold soil. When they chose Athena's olive, those settlers chose civilization.

Athena is a war goddess, but she is no friend to the warrior or the raider, only to the hoplite, the heavy-armed Greek infantryman who defended his polis, and his *strategos,* or general. She knew very well that what you make—create with time and skill from raw materials—you must guard with force from those who wish to take it from you rather than trade with you: fair value for fair value. For she is not only the Greek goddess of wisdom, of science and mathematics. Hers are the domestic arts of spinning and weaving, as well as the arts of agriculture and animal husbandry, the building of ships and chariots and the training of horses. Athena's symbol is commonly the owl, but it is also the pomegranate, which is the symbol of mature and fertile womanhood. And although Athena is never *gyne,* a young girl, only very rarely *kore,* a maiden, but almost always *parthenos,* an unmarried woman, she was lovely enough to ask the Trojan prince Paris whether she or Aphrodite herself was more beautiful.

The Greeks endlessly proclaimed Athena no friend to woman, and the favorite child of Zeus. But in truth, Athena's mother was Metis, the wisest of all, and Zeus swallowed her so that her child would not surpass him. And the Greeks left Athena her womanhood. Beneath her armor, she wore her peplos, or her woman's long chiton; she retained her skill with the spindle and the loom. She was equally skilled with arms in the field and as a strategist; her beauty and her fertility were revered, although she took no lovers and bore no children. Athena's heirs, the Athenians, left to her what they took from her heiresses, their own sisters: all the arts and learning of the public and private worlds, a public presence in the civilization such work created, and the means to defend both.

The Athenians knew, but could not face, what we are just beginning to accept: that despite all the many and significant differences between men and women, the only ineluctable one is the difference between the biological act of impregnation and the process of bearing children. And if the ability of women to control their own fertility and the vastly diminished reproductive risks women now face have greatly diminished the meaning of that difference, that is right, and proper, and just.

The only civilization the United States should cherish is nothing less than that which men and women create together, intellectually and physically, and together defend, as equals in public and private.

ACKNOWLEDGMENTS

One of the great pleasures of finishing a solitary task is realizing how many people, and how many different kinds of people, offered help and encouragement and shared their insights and experiences. When combat-hardened infantrymen encourage a self-identified feminist to write about their profession and their lives; when you sign a contract with an old-line feminist press while also publishing in the *Marine Corps Gazette* and Naval Institute *Proceedings*; when military men and women let you know that what you're doing needs to be done—the reasons to say "thank you" pile up.

Although women's involvement in the military has fascinated me since childhood, this book began in the spring of 2002 at an Army War College conference. I was a graduate student at the time, working a day job as a secretary: no one to take too seriously in that setting. Troubled by the remarks of one distinguished speaker, I made a comment from the audience, suggesting that military service was and should be recognized as an inherent part of citizenship for all. Carl Bernard, a retired Army colonel and decorated three-war veteran, grabbed my notebook and scrawled, "You must write about this." There have been many others who told me, in effect, "I may never agree with you, but press on."

Two years after that conference, Kimberly Mills of the *Seattle Post-Intelligencer* took a chance on a secretary with a few book reviews and op-eds to her name; she accredited me, sight unseen, for Iraq. My then employer, The National Society of The Colonial Dames of America, administered my research grant for Iraq, and many of the Dames also encouraged me. There truly is nothing like a Dame! The Washington Council on International Trade handled my grant to Afghanistan. Thank you, Bill Center (a retired admiral, another tough old vet who encouraged me mightily) and Julie Sardo. Many thanks to Ed Tracy and Jane Feerer of the Tawani Foundation, which provided the funding.

From the beginning, my goal was to write a book. After Iraq, I started looking for an agent. In a year, I learned a lot about agents: I went through five, ranging from a pathological liar to a pathological perfectionist. The sixth agent, Jonathan Lyons of McIntosh & Otis, sold this book in a month, in the summer, to Seal Press. My editor there, Brooke Warner, is simply wonderful, and I learned a great deal from her about the craft of writing.

When you are a freelancer schlepping your own gear, you remember kindness. In Iraq and Afghanistan, a lot of people were very kind to me. I would like to thank them for their kindness.

In Al Anbar Province, Iraq: the men and women of the U.S. Army's First Brigade Combat Team, First Infantry Division. In particular, Colonel Arthur Connor, Lieutenant Colonels David W. Brinkley and Michael Cabrey; Captains Joseph Jasper, Anastasia Breslow, Drew Hettich, and Moses Scheinfeld; Lieutenant Doran Strauss and First Sergeant Michael

Greenwalt; Sergeant Clark and his scouts; and PFC McIntosh. I'd also like to thank some Marines. Of the First Force Services Support Group, Captain Kristin Lasica, Chief Warrant Officer Andrews, and Sergeant Epright, and of 2/4 Marines, Colonel Paul Kennedy, Captains Dominic Harris and Kelly Royer, and Staff Sergeant Callaway.

Finally, the Marines at Camp Junction City who let me decoy their military working dogs for them. I once trained dogs professionally, and never miss a chance to get back in the game, even for a little while.

In Afghanistan: the advisors and de-miners of two private military corporations. These are often derided as "mercenary"; nothing could be further from the truth. Of the U.S. Air Force, Lieutenant Colonel Kevin Cole, Captain Katie Hague, and Airman Brandy Quioce (which I am quite certain is a misspelling, but there it is). Of the U.S. Army—Regulars, Reserves and Guard alike—Lieutenant Colonels Lisa Bailey and Dr. Alan Towne, Major Hoss, Lieutenant Gonzalez, Command Sergeant Major Lynette Harper, Sergeant First Class Cochran, Sergeant Valerie Bolejack, and Specialists Koenig and Jasmine Smith. Also, Drew Adams, Alex Johnson, and Bob Smith, all of the USDA.

In the United States: Lieutenant Colonels Gillian Boice and Audrey Hudgins, both professors of military science, at Pacific Lutheran University and Seattle University, respectively, and Lieutenant Colonel George Abbott and Sergeant Kristine Turley of the Washington National Guard. Major Joel Graham deserves my thanks not only for serving as my escort at ROTC Advanced Camp at Fort Lewis, but also for contributing his own experiences and insights (as so many public affairs officers will do, if a journalist will only ask). Of the U.S. Military Academy at West Point, first, Mike D'Aquino, public affairs; Colonel Gregory Daniel and Lieutenant Colonel Thomas Kolditz, Majors Samantha Breton and Jason Dempsey, Dr. Eugenia Kiesling, and Kelli

Kidd. Of the U.S. Army Research Institute of Environmental Medicine, Colonel Karl Friedl, Dr. Everett Harman, and Marilyn Sharp. Of Fort Jackson, Colonel Jay W. Chambers.

Lory Manning, Captain, U.S. Navy, ret., of WREI, the Women's Research and Education Institute, and Teresa Scalzo, director of the National Center for the Prosecution of Violence Against Women at the American Prosecutors Research Institute, were particularly helpful; Dr. David Lisak offered invaluable insights into sexual predation.

Several men provided the interviews that anchor much of this book: retired Marine Corps brigadier general Thomas Draude; retired Army colonels John Collins, David Johnson, and Jim Kurtz; retired Marine colonel Jon Rider; and retired Navy commander John Kuehn. Former congresswoman Pat Schroeder deserves my thanks for her interview, and the Republic's thanks for her role in opening the military and protecting its women.

On my way to West Point, independent filmmaker Meg McLagan of Room 11 Productions, who is at work on the documentary *This Woman's Army,* was the kindest of hosts when I stayed in New York.

Now to the standard disclaimers. The persons mentioned in these acknowledgments should not be assumed to agree with this book, in full or in part. Except for a very few formal interviews, I never asked people what their opinions about servicewomen were, and very few people shared their opinions with me. Most people, however, offered their perspectives and personal experiences, research leads, and ideas on a wide variety of issues that they thought I should address—most of which had nothing to do with "women in the military" or "women in combat." For example, when I left for Afghanistan on rather short notice, I needed good cold weather advice. Retired Army infantryman Lieutenant

Colonel Lewis Higginbotham (four Vietnam tours) responded promptly with good guidance and some excellent waterproof leather dressing.

Any errors and omissions of fact are mine alone.

Finally, I should like to thank some special teachers. Horses and dogs have been important to me all my life. Carol Knock, a great dog breeder and judge, was my mentor when I trained dogs professionally. She and her husband, Frank, a retired Navy captain, are now old friends. Charlie Anderson of Timepiece Arabians and Stacey Gesell of Catherine Coats' Griffinwood Stables, both in Olympia, got me back into riding after a lapse of several decades. Thanks for the excellent instruction. And patience. Thanks also to Gwen, Emily, Jack, Jason, and Elizabeth: five wild deer who adopted Philip and me during the winter of 2005–2006 when we had moved for a few months to a small cottage in the woods. Feeding them was great fun. Deer, we have learned, like a corn-oats-barley mix with molasses, and prefer their apples sliced into wedges.

TABLE OF RANKS, ALL SERVICES

Enlisted	Army	Navy	Marine Corps	Air Force
E1	Private	Seaman Recruit	Private	Airman Basic
E2	Private E-2	Seaman Apprentice	Private First Class	Airman
E3	Private First Class	Seaman	Lance Corporal	Airman First Class
E4	Corporal or Specialist	Petty Officer Third Class	Corporal	Senior Airman
E5	Sergeant Second Class	Petty Officer	Sergeant	Staff Sergeant
E6	Staff Sergeant	Petty Officer First Class	Staff Sergeant	Technical Sergeant
E7	Sergeant First Class	Chief Petty Officer	Gunnery Sergeant	Master Sergeant or First Sergeant
E8	Master Sergeant or First Sergeant	Senior Chief Petty Officer	Master Sergeant or First Sergeant	Senior Master Sergeant or First Sergeant
E9	Sergeant Major or Command Sergeant Major and the Sergeant Major of the Army	Master Chief Petty Officer or Fleet/Command Master Chief Petty Officer or Master Chief Petty Officer of the Navy and Coast Guard	Sergeant Major or Master Gunnery Sergeant or Sergeant Major of the Marine Corps	Chief Master Sergeant or First Sergeant or Command Chief Master Sergeant or Chief Master Sergeant of the Air Force

Warrant Officer Rank	Army	Navy	Marine Corps	Air Force
W1	Warrant Officer 1	USN Warrant Officer 1	Warrant Officer 1	No Warrant
W2	Chief Warrant Officer 2	USN and USCG Warrant Officer 2	Chief Warrant Officer 2	No Warrant
W3	Chief Warrant Officer 3	USN and USCG Chief Warrant Officer 3	Chief Warrant Officer 3	No Warrant
W4	Chief Warrant Officer 4	USN & USCG Warrant Officer 4	Chief Warrant Officer 4	No Warrant
W5	Chief Warrant Officer 4	USN Chief Warrant Officer 5	Chief Warrant Officer 5	No Warrant

Officer Rank	Army	Navy	Marine Corps	Air Force
O1	Second Lietenant	Ensign	Second Lieutenant	Second Lieutenant
O2	First Lieutenant	Lieutenant Junior Grade	First Lieutenant	First Lieutenant
O3	Captain	Lieutenant	Captain	Captain
O4	Major	Lieutenant Commander	Major	Major
O5	Lieutenant Colonel	Commander	Lieutenant Colonel	Lieutenant Colonel
O6	Colonel	Captain	Colonel	Colonel
O7	Brigadier General	Real Admiral Lower Half	Brigadier General	Brigadier General
O8	Major General	Rear Admiral Upper Half	Major General	Major General
O9	Lieutenant General	Vice Admiral	Lieutenant General	Lieutenant General
O10	General Army Chief of Staff	Admiral Chief of Naval Operations and Commandant of the Coast Guard	General Commandant of the Marine Corps	General Air Force Chief of Staff
	General of the Army (Reserved for wartime only)	Fleet Admiral (Reserved for wartime only)	N/A	General of the Air Force (Reserved for wartime only)

NOTES

General Fred C. Weyand, quoted in *Armor,* September–October 1976.

Akhil Reed Amar and Alan Hirsch, *For the People: What the Constitution Really Says About Your Rights* (New York: Free Press, 1998), 135.

INTRODUCTION

1. David Fraser, *Knight's Cross: A Life of Field Marshal Erwin Rommel* (New York: Harper Collins, 1993), 5–6.
2. Linda K. Kerber, *No Constitutional Right to Be Ladies: Women and the Obligations of Citizenship* (New York: Hill and Wang, 1998), 261–62.
3. Ibid., 263.
4. Lory Manning, *Women in the Military: Where They Stand,* 5th ed. (Washington, DC: Women's Research and Education Institute, 2005), 4.
5. Ibid., 3.
6. Ibid., 12.

Chapter 1 A KNIFE UNDER MY PILLOW

1. You can find these locations on maps at www.GlobalSecurity.org, but to give you an idea of the time involved to transit these distances in a combat zone, my memory is that Al Taquaddum is about an hour's flight by helicopter from Camp Blue Diamond, headquarters of the First Marine Division, across the Euphrates from Camp Hurricane Point. Alternatively, it is about three hours by Humvee with Army scouts from Camp Junction City to Al Taqaddum.
2. Captain Randall Baucom, email message to author, August 7, 2004.

Chapter 2 CHOOSING SIDES

1. Alan Bullock, *Hitler and Stalin: Parallel Lives* (New York: Alfred A. Knopf, 1992), 987.
2. Jean Bethke Elshtain, *Women and War* (New York: Basic Books, 1987), x.
3. Cynthia Enloe, "What Is NATO—and Why Should Women Care?" in *Loaded Questions: Women in the Military,* ed. Wendy Chapkis (Washington, DC: Transnational Institute, 1981), 61.
4. Ilene Rose Feinman, *Citizenship Rites: Feminist Soldiers and Feminist Antimilitarists* (New York: New York University Press, 2000), 30.
5. Department of Defense, Department of the Army, "Attack on the 507th Maintenance Company," at www.army.mil/features/507thMaintCmpy/.

6. *See Center for Military Readiness Notes,* no. 75, March 2004, 1; and Notes, no. 76, June 2004, 2; along with *Center for Military Readiness Report,* no. 16, April 2003, 1. You can also go to the "Issues" section of the website and peruse the essays on "Women in Combat." Hereafter, Center for Military Readiness will be abbreviated as CMR.

7. I have consulted *CMR Notes,* no. 75, March 2004; no. 76, June 2004; no. 77, September 2004; no. 78, March 2005; no. 79, June 2005; and no. 80, November 2005, as well as *CMR Report,* no. 17, December 2004, and the "Women in Combat" 2004 subsection of the "Issues" section of the website.

8. *CMR Notes,* no. 65, May–June 2001, 4; Defense Advisory Committee on Women in the Services, *2001 Spring Conference Issue Book: Equality Management,* located at www.dtic.mil/dacowits/issue_books/Spr2001-IssueBk-EqMgt.html.

Chapter 3 THE LIONESSES OF IRAQ

1. Philip Gold, *Take Back the Right* (New York: Carroll and Graf, 2004).

2. Gordon Lubold, "Band of Sisters: Army 'Lionesses' Hit Streets with Marines on Combat Ops," *Marine Corps Times,* August 9, 2004, at www.marinecorpstimes.com/story.php?f=1-MARINEPAPER-280274.php.

3. James Glanz and John F. Burns, "Suicide Car Bomb Kills 4 American Women in Iraq," *The New York Times,* June 25, 2005.

4. Michael Moss, "Hard Look at Mission That Ended in Inferno for 3 Women," *The New York Times,* December 20, 2005.

Chapter 4 AFGHANISTAN AND THE TRAGEDY OF BIOLOGY

1. Because of their work as advisors, these men are identified with false names to protect them and their families.

2. The names of the de-miners, their boss, and my Afghan friend have been changed out of respect for their security and to protect their privacy.

3. In order to protect them and their families, special operations troops are usually identified only by their first names; since these were women with unusual names, I have taken that precaution a step further and fully masked their names.

4. These rates are a little lower according to the newer, 2006 edition of the CIA *World Factbook,* located at www.cia.gov/cia/publications/factbook/geos/af.html#People.

5. World Health Organization, *Maternal Mortality in 2000* (Geneva: World Health Organization, 2004), 22, 26, 27, at www.who.int/reproductive-health/publications/maternal_mortality_2000/mme.pdf. It should be noted that the American rates are drawn from a 1984 article (*Maternal Mortality in 2000,* 29), and that in 1998, the Centers for Disease Control reported an average of 7.5 maternal deaths per hundred thousand live births between 1982 and 1996.

6. Salima Ghafari and Mari Nabard, "A Life for a Life," Afghan Recovery Report, 186, 12 September 2005, Institute for War and Peace Reporting, www.iwpr.net/?p=arr&s=f&o=254844&apc_state=heniarr2005.

7. This chart is a concatenation of statistics from two sources, expressed in decimal terms and then combined in various ways to arrive at lifetime risk of maternal mortality and estimated numbers of maternal deaths in the United States from 1915 to 1960. It is important to note that these statistics are based upon all races, because maternal mortality rates are generally much higher for blacks than for whites. Column 1, Maternal Deaths per 100,000 Live Births, is drawn from Department of Health and Human

Services, Public Health Service, *Vital Statistics of the United States: 1992,* vol. 2, *Mortality: Part A* (Hyattsville, MD: National Center for Health Statistics, 1996), 69. It may be accessed online at www.cdc.gov/nchs/data/vsus/mort92_2a.pdf; go to page 86 of the PDF document. Column 2, Risks per Live Birth, divides the number in Column 1 by one hundred thousand, then expresses it as a percentage. Column 3, Fertility Rate, is the number of children born per thousand women, ages fifteen to forty-four. The source for this is Centers for Disease Control, National Center for Health Statistics, "Live Births, Birth Rates, and Fertility Rates, by Race: United States, 1909–2000"; it may be accessed online at www.cdc.gov/nchs/data/statab/t001x01.pdf. Column 4, Children Born to the Average Woman, is derived by dividing the fertility rate by one thousand, then multiplying it by thirty, the average woman's childbearing years from fifteen to forty-four. Column 5, Risk of Maternal Mortality, multiplies the average woman's children by the average risk per live birth, to find the average woman's risk of dying in childbirth. Column 6, Children Born, is expressed in hundreds of thousands, and the source is also "Live Births, Birth Rates, and Fertility Rates." Column 7, Maternal Deaths, multiplies the maternal deaths per hundred thousand live births by the number of live births in hundreds of thousands, then rounds to the nearest whole number. *It is very important to understand that the fertility rate is a straight calculation per thousand women. No attempt has been made to correct any of the calculations based upon the fertility rate for the percentage of women who actually bore children in that year, because until women had widespread access to safe and reliable contraception, neither a woman nor her family really knew how many she would bear children until she reached menopause. Until 1940, this meant that the woman and her family lived in substantial uncertainty as to whether or not she would survive her reproductive career. For this reason, the lifetime risk of maternal mortality is a lifetime risk per average woman only, regardless of race, not the risk ran by women who actually bore children. These are rough calculations written to indicate a profound trend, not scientific analysis by a trained statistician.*

8. Department of Defense, Directorate for Information Operations and Reports, Statistical Information Analysis Division, Personnel, "Principal Wars in Which the United States Participated, U.S. Military Personnel Serving and Casualties," at http://web1. whs.osd.mil/mmid/casualty/WCPRINCIPAL.pdf. The Civil War numbers include Confederate battle and nonbattle deaths, but not Confederate POW deaths because the range, between twenty-six thousand and thirty-one thousand, is only an estimate, and I have tried to minimize estimates.

9. Genesis 3:16, found online at www.sacred-texts.com/bib/jps/gen003.htm#016. This is the 1917 public domain translation by the Jewish Publication Society.

10. "Faces of the Fallen" can be found at www.washingtonpost.com/wp-srv/world/iraq/ casualties/facesofthefallen.htm.

Chapter 5 PRETENDING TO INTEGRATE THE MILITARY

1. Bettie J. Morden, *The Women's Army Corps, 1945–1978* (Washington, DC: U.S. Army Center of Military History, 1990), at www.army.mil/cmh-pg/books/wac/index.htm, 233–34. The footnotes in the original have been omitted here.

2. Eli Ginzberg and James K. Anderson, *The Ineffective Soldier: Lessons for Management and the Nation,* vol. 1, *The Lost Divisions* (New York: Columbia University Press, 1959), 121–22.

3. Morris J. MacGregor Jr., *Integration of the Armed Forces, 1940–1965* (Washington,

DC: U.S. Army Center of Military History, 1985), at www.army.mil/cmh-pg/books/integration/IAF-FM.htm, chapter 6.

4. Ibid., chapter 8. The footnote in the original has been omitted here.

5. Office of Management and Budget, *Historical Tables, Budget of the United States Government, Fiscal Year 2007* (Washington, DC: Government Printing Office, 2006), table 4.1, 75, at www.whitehouse.gov/omb/budget/fy2007/pdf/hist.pdf.

6. *CMR Notes,* no. 78, March 2005, 5.

7. Arthur T. Hadley Jr., *The Straw Giant: Triumph and Failure: America's Armed Forces: A Report from the Field* (New York: Random House, 1986), 258.

8. Ibid.

9. A brigade is an organization of about three thousand to five thousand soldiers, divided into smaller units. A battalion is an organization of five hundred to one thousand soldiers, divided into companies, generally between one hundred and two hundred soldiers in strength. Direct combat is defined as "engaging an enemy with individual or crew-served weapons while being exposed to direct enemy fire, a high probability of direct physical contact with the enemy, and a substantial risk of capture." Direct combat occurs while closing with the enemy in order to destroy or capture, or while repelling assault by fire, close combat, or counterattack.

10. General Accounting Office (GAO), National Security and International Affairs Division, *Combat Exclusion Laws for Women in the Military* (Washington, DC: GAO, 1987), 7–10.

11. *The All Volunteer Force After a Decade: Retrospect and Prospect,* ed. William Bowman, Roger Little, and G. Thomas Sicilia (Washington, DC: Pergamon-Brassey's, 1986), 111.

12. Department of Defense, Office of the Inspector General, *The Tailhook Report: The Official Inquiry into the Events of Tailhook '91* (New York: St. Martin's Press, 1993), 45–6, 52–3.

13. Department of Defense, Office of the Inspector General, *Tailhook 91: Part 1—Review of the Navy Investigations* (Arlington, VA: Department of Defense, 1992), at www. mith2.umd.edu/WomensStudies/GenderIssues/SexualHarassment/tailhook-91.

14. I am indebted to Captain Lory Manning for this insight, as well as for information about the change in enlisted Navy celebrations.

15. Jean Zimmerman, *Tailspin: Women at War in the Wake of Tailhook* (New York: Doubleday, 1995), 270–73.

16. Ibid., 257–58, 264.

17. PBS *Frontline,* "The Navy Blues," show no. 1502, October 15, 1996, transcript accessed at www.pbs.org/wgbh/pages/frontline/shows/navy/script.html.

18. Presidential Commission on the Assignment of Women in the Armed Forces, *Women in Combat: Report to the President* (Washington, DC: Government Printing Office, 1992), 116.

19. Ibid., 28–29.

20. Ibid., 87.

21. Ibid., 89.

22. Ibid., 104. Emphasis in the original.

23. Ibid., 86.

24. Ibid., 86.

25. Ibid., 43–44.

26. Ibid., 45, 47–48.

27. General Thomas Draude, personal communication via his assistant, Jennifer Butler, December 15, 2005.
28. GAO, National Security and International Affairs Division, *Women in the Military: Deployment in the Persian Gulf War* (Washington, DC: Government Accounting Office, 1993), 12–13.
29. Ibid., 21–22.
30. Ibid., 25.
31. Ibid., 40–43.
32. GAO, National Security and International Affairs Division, *Gender Issues: Information on DOD's Assignment Policy and Direct Ground Combat Definition* (Washington, DC: GAO, 1998), 2–3. Footnotes in the original have been omitted.
33. Ibid., 7.

Chapter 6 DARKNESS BEFORE DAWN
1. "Women at West Point?' 'Silly' to Westmoreland," *The New York Times,* May 31, 1976.
2. Martin Binkin and Mark J. Eitelberg, "Women and Minorities in the All-Volunteer Force," *The All Volunteer Force After a Decade: Retrospect and Prospect,* ed. William Bowman, Roger Little, and G. Thomas Sicilia (Washington, DC: Pergamon-Brassey's, 1986), 82-3.
3. Judith Hicks Stiehm, *Arms and the Enlisted Woman* (Philadelphia, PA: Temple University Press, 1989), 117–18. Judith Hicks Stiehm teaches political science at Florida International University and has been visiting professor at the U.S. Army Peacekeeping Institute and the Strategic Studies Institute at Carlisle Barracks, Pennsylvania. (Both institutions are part of the U.S. Army's War College.)
4. Judith Hicks Stiehm, *Bring Me Men and Women: Mandated Change at the U.S. Air Force Academy* (Berkeley: University of California Press, 1981), 18.
5. Ironically, General Ridgeway loathed the way segregation corrupted both black men, by requiring them to behave as if they were inferior, and white men, by giving them a sense of unwarranted superiority. Also ironically, the second superintendent of West Point was Alden Partridge, founder of Norwich and a lifelong advocate of women's education in a time when it was thought folly to educate women for much more than their household duties.
6. Stiehm, *Bring Me Men and Women,* 39. Emphasis in the original.
7. Stiehm, *Arms and the Enlisted Woman,* 119–22.
8. Philippa Strum, *Women in the Barracks: The VMI Case and Equal Rights* (Lawrence: University Press of Kansas, 2002), 201–6.
9. Diane H. Mazur, "A Call to Arms," *Harvard Journal of Law and Gender* 22 (Spring 1999): 79. Emphasis in the original.
10. Ibid., 76., May 4, 1997.
11. Elaine Sciolino, "The Army's Problems with Sex and Power," *The New York Times,* May 4, 1997.
12. Fred L. Borch III, "Military Law and the Treatment of Women Soldiers: Sexual Harassment and Fraternization in the U.S. Army," in *A Soldier and a Woman: Sexual Integration in the Military,* ed. Gerard J. DeGroot and Corinna Peniston-Bird (Harlow, Essex, U.K.: Pearson Education, 2000), 348.
13. Eric Schmitt, "Top Enlisted Man in the Army Stands Accused of Sex Assault," *The New York Times,* February 4, 1997.

14. Elaine Sciolino, "Top Army Sergeant Was Secretly Taped in Sex Investigation," *The New York Times,* June 28, 1997.

15. Claudia Kennedy, with Malcolm McConnell, *Generally Speaking* (New York: Warner Books, 2001), 165–68.

16. Christopher Marquis, "General Seeks to Retire as Charges Are Supported," *The New York Times,* July 8, 2000.

17. Kennedy, *Generally Speaking,* 186–90, 200.

18. Eric Schmitt, "Army Is Criticized on Harassment Survey," *The New York Times,* June 27, 1997.

19. Pat Schroeder, *Champion of the Great American Family* (New York: Random House, 1989), 25.

20. Pat Schroeder, *24 Years of House Work . . . and the Place Is Still a Mess* (Kansas City, MO: Andrews McNeel, 1998), 203.

21. Richard Rayner, "The Warrior Besieged," *The New York Times Magazine,* June 22, 1997.

22. Sara Ruddick, "Pacifying the Forces: Drafting Women in the Interests of Peace," *Signs* 8, no. 3 (Spring 1983): 476–77.

23. Brian Mitchell, *Women in the Military: Flirting with Disaster* (Washington, DC: Regnery, 1998), xvii.

24. Ibid., 346.

25. Ibid., 193–4.

26. Martin van Creveld, Men, *Women and War: Do Women Belong in the Front Line?* (Bodmin, Cornwall, U.K.: Cassell, 2001), 229–30.

27. Ibid., 34.

28. GAO, *Gender Issues,* 2, 3, 7; Mackubin Thomas Owens, "A Man's Job," *National Review Online,* May 12, 2005, at www.nationalreview.com/owens/owens200505120814.asp.

29. Manning, *Women in the Military,* 17, 19, 25.

30. For the purposes of this book, it is worth noting that Justice Marshall—himself a former slave owner, and the only dissenter in *Plessy v. Ferguson* (1910)—which found racial segregation legal—also wrote the dissent in *Thompson v. Thompson,* 163 U.S. 537 (1896), which found that a wife could sue her husband for damages against her property but not her person—in other words, for damaging or disposing of her property, but not for beating her (as Mr. Thompson had repeatedly and brutally done to his wife, and while she was pregnant).

Chapter 7 INDIVIDUALS BEING ALL THEY CAN . . . AND MORE

1. Paul Daley, "Jockeys: Racing in the Danger Zone," *The Lowell Sun,* July 22, 2000.

2. Presidential Commission on the Assignment of Women in the Armed Forces, *Women in Combat, C-3.*

3. Ibid., female data only.

4. Ibid., AR 600-9, Interim Change, 4 March 1994.

5. Ibid., FM21-20, 30 September 1992, Change 1, 1 October 1998.

6. Ibid., AR 600-9, 10 June 1987.

7. Peggy Anne Fisher McNulty, "Prevalence and Contributing Factors of Eating Disorder Behaviors in Active Duty Service Women in the Army, Navy, Air Force, and Marines," *Military Medicine* 166, no. 1 (January 2001): 53–58.

8. CMR, "Army Gender Integrated Training, Report Appendices," at www.crmlink.org, Appendix B.

9. Richard A. Shaffer, Mitchell J. Rauh, et al., "Predictors of Stress Fracture Susceptibility in Young Female Recruits," *The American Journal of Sports Medicine* 34, no. 10 (September 2005): 1.

10. Institute of Medicine, *Assessing Readiness in Military Women: The Relationship of Body Composition, Nutrition, and Health* (Washington, DC: National Academies Press, 1998), 116–19.

11. CMR, "Army Gender Integrated Basic Training, Report Appendices," Appendix C.

12. Everett Harman, Peter Frykman, et al., *Effects of a Specifically Designed Physical Conditioning Program on the Load Carriage and Lifting Performance of Female Soldiers* (Natick, MA: U.S. Army Research Institute of Environmental Medicine, 1997).

13. Rowan Scarborough, "Why Can't a Woman Be More Like a Man?" *The Washington Times,* February 14, 1995.

14. Ministry of Defence (U.K.), *Women in the Armed Forces,* a report by the Employment of Women in the Armed Forces Steering Group (May 2002), 4.

15. Jeffrey F. Hines, "Ambulatory Health Care Needs of Women Deployed with a Heavy Armor Division During the Persian Gulf War," *Military Medicine* 157, no. 5 (May 1992): 219–21.

16. The figures in the table were provided in email by Ms. Martha Rudd, Department of the Army Public Affairs, November 23, 2005. Pregnancy discharge statistics were provided in email by Lieutenant Colonel Richard Joseph, Department of Defense Public Affairs, May 11, 2005, and updated by Ms. Cynthia Smith, December 20, 2005.

17. Donna Miles, "Programs Aim to Reduce Military Divorce Rates," American Forces Press Service, June 9, 2005, at www.defenselink.mil/news/Jun2005/20050609_1666. html.

18. National Center for PTSD, "What Is Post-Traumatic Stress Disorder?" a National Center for PTSD fact sheet, at www.ncptsd.va.gov/facts/general/fs_what_is_ptsd. html.

19. Erica Scharansky, "PTSD Information for Women's Medical Providers," a National Center for PTSD fact sheet, at www.ncptsd.va.gov/facts/specific/fs_female_primary. html.

20. The distinction is that legal codes often specify rape as penile-vaginal penetration, and sexual assault as penetration of the body in other ways, whether with the penis, the hands, or objects; legal codes also define degrees of sexual assault according to the level of force the offender used, although men and women differ sharply in their perceptions of force due to average differences in size, strength, and socialization.

21. Sue Orsillo, "Sexual Assault Against Females," a National Center for PTSD fact sheet, at www.ncptsd.va.gov/facts/specific/fs_female_sex_assault.html.

22. Julia M. Whealin, "Men and Sexual Trauma," a National Center for PTSD fact sheet, at www.ncptsd.va.gov/facts/specific/fs_male_sexual_assault.html.

23. National Center for PTSD, "What Is Post-Traumatic Stress Disorder?"

24. Scharansky, "PTSD Information for Women's Medical Providers."

25. Lynda A. King and Daniel W. King, "Traumatic Stress in Female Veterans," a National Center for PTSD fact sheet, at www.ncptsd.va.gov/facts/veterans/fs_women_vets. html.

Chapter 8 A CHANGING INSTITUTION

1. Samuel A. Stouffer et al., *The American Soldier: Combat and Its Aftermath,* vol . 2 (New York: John Wiley and Sons, 1965), 285.

2. Martin van Creveld, *Fighting Power: German and U.S. Army Performance, 1939–1945* (Westport, CT: Greenwood Press, 1982), 45.
3. Ibid., 45, 167. Footnotes omitted.
4. Lida Mayo, *Bloody Buna* (New York: Doubleday, 1974), 170.
5. Edward Lauer, *32d Infantry Division, World War II* (Madison, WI: 32d Historical Commission, 1957).
6. Mayo, *Bloody Buna,* 54.
7. Leora N. Rosen, Kathryn H. Knudson, and Peggy Fancher, "Cohesion and the Culture of Hypermasculinity in U.S. Army Units," *Armed Forces and Society* 29, no. 3 (Spring 2003): 344.
8. Leora Rosen and Lee Martin, "Psychological Effects of Sexual Harassment, Appraisal of Harassment, and Organizational Climate Among U.S. Army Soldiers," *Military Medicine* 163, no. 2 (February 1998): 67, footnotes omitted.
9. University of Iowa, "UI, VAMC Researchers Study Women's Risk of Rape in Military," news release, March 11, 2003.
10. Melanie Martindale, *Sexual Harassment in the Military: 1988* (Arlington, VA: Defense Manpower Data Center [DMDC], 1990), xiii.
11. Rachel N. Lipari, Anita R. Lancaster, and Alan M. Jones, *2004 Sexual Harassment Survey of Reserve Component Members* (Arlington, VA: DMDC, 2005), iv, 42.
12. Paul J. Cook et al., *Service Academy 2005 Sexual Harassment and Assault Survey* (Arlington, VA: DMDC, December 2005), iv–vi.
13. House Armed Services Committee, *Sexual Assault Prevention and Response in the Armed Forces,* H. R. Hearing, 108th Cong., 2nd sess., June 3, 2004, 13.
14. Ibid., 14–15.
15. Ibid., 16–17.
16. Ibid., 38.
17. Ibid., 49.
18. Ibid., 41.
19. Department of Defense, Defense Task Force on Sexual Harassment and Violence at the Military Service Academies, *Report of the Defense Task Force on Sexual Harassment and Violence at the Military Service Academies* (Washington, DC: Department of Defense, June 2005), 34.
20. Manning, *Women in the Military,* 12, 23.
21. Dr. David Lisak, "Rape Fact Sheet," U.S. Army, March 2002, at www.sexualassault.army.mil/files/RAPE_FACT_SHEET.pdf, 3.
22. HASC, *Sexual Assault Prevention and Response in the Armed Forces,* 102.
23. Ibid., 137.
24. Ibid., 141.
25. Ibid., 139.
26. Department of Defense, Department of the Army, *Army Profile, FY04,* at www.armyg1.army.mil/hr/demographics/FY04%20Army%20profile.pdf, 3.

Conclusion CIVIC FEMINISM AND THE WARS OF THE 21ST CENTURY

1. Justice William H. Rehnquist, *Rostker v. Goldberg,* 453 U.S. 57 (1981).
2. Philip Gold, "To Guard an Era: American Purpose After Iraq," *Proceedings* of the U.S. Naval Institute (September 2005): 19–20.

BIBLIOGRAPHY

Books

1. Amar, Akhil Reed, and Alan Hirsch. *For the People: What the Constitution Really Says About Your Rights.* New York: Free Press, 1998.
2. Bachetta, Paoloa, and Margaret Power. *Right Wing Women: From Conservatives to Extremists Around the World.* New York: Routledge, 2002.
3. Bailyn, Bernard. *The Ideological Origins of the American Revolution.* Cambridge, MA: Belknap Press of Harvard University Press, 1967.
4. ————. *To Begin the World Anew: The Genius and Ambiguities of the American Founders.* New York: Alfred A. Knopf, 2003.
5. Binkin, Martin, and Shirley J. Bach. *Women and the Military.* Washington, DC: Brookings Institution, 1977.
6. Blackman, E. A., ed. *The Reference Shelf: Women in the Military.* Vol. 64, No. 5. New York: H. W. Wilson, 1992.
7. Blanton, DeAnne, and Lauren M. Cook. *They Fought Like Demons: Women Soldiers in the American Civil War.* Baton Rouge: Louisiana University Press, 2002.
8. Bowman, William, Roger Little, and G. Thomas Sicilia, eds. *The All-Volunteer Force After a Decade: Retrospect and Prospect.* Washington, DC: Pergamon-Brassey's, 1986.
9. Bragg, Rick. *I Am a Soldier, Too: The Jessica Lynch Story.* New York: Alfred A. Knopf, 2003.
10. Breuer, William B. *War and American Women: Heroism, Deeds, and Controversy.* Westport, CT: Praeger, 1997.
11. Bonn, Keith E. *When the Odds Were Even: The Vosges Mountain Campaign, October 1944–January 1945.* Novato, CA: Presidio Press, 1994.
12. Bullock, Alan. *Hitler and Stalin: Parallel Lives.* New York: Alfred A. Knopf, 1992.
13. Chapkis, Wendy, ed. *Loaded Questions: Women in the Military.* Washington, DC: Transnational Institute, 1981.
14. Chesler, Phyllis. *The Death of Feminism.* New York: Palgrave MacMillan, 2005.
15. Clausewitz, Carl von. *On War.* Princeton, NJ: Princeton University Press, 1989.
16. Creveld, Martin van. *Fighting Power: German and U.S. Army Performance, 1939–1945.* Westport, CT: Greenwood Press, 1982.
17. ————. *Men, Women and War: Do Women Belong in the Front Line?* Bodmin, Cornwall, U.K.: Cassell, 2001.
18. Daly, Lois K., ed. *Feminist Theological Ethics: A Reader.* Louisville, KY: Westminster John Knox Press, 1994.
19. DeGroot, Gerard J., and Corinna Peniston-Bird, eds. *A Soldier and a Woman: Sexual Integration in the Military.* Harlow, Essex, U.K.: Pearson Education, 2000.

20. Dever, John P., and Maria C. Dever. *Women and the Military: Over 100 Notable Contributors, Historic to Contemporary.* Jefferson, NC: McFarland, 1995.
21. Doubler, Michael. *Closing with the Enemy: How GIs Fought the War in Europe, 1944–1945.* Lawrence: University Press of Kansas, 1994.
22. D'Amico, Francine, and Laurie Weinstein, eds. *Gender Camouflage: Women and the U.S. Military.* New York: New York University Press, 1999.
23. Ellis, John. *The Sharp End: The Fighting Man in World War II.* New York: Charles Scribner's Sons, 1980.
24. Elshtain, Jean Bethke. *Women and War.* New York: Basic Books, 1987.
25. Elshtain, Jean Bethke, and Sheila Tobias, eds. *Women, Militarism, and War: Essays in History, Politics, and Social Theory.* Savage, MD: Rowman and Littlefield, 1990.
26. Embser-Herbert, Melissa Sheridan. *Camouflage Isn't Only for Combat: Gender, Sexuality, and Women in the Military.* New York: New York University Press, 1998.
27. Enloe, Cynthia. *The Curious Feminist: Searching for Women in a New Age of Empire.* London, U.K.: University of California Press, 2004.
28. ———. *Does Khaki Become You? The Militarization of Women's Lives.* London, U.K.: Pandora Press, 1983.
29. ———. *Maneuvers: The International Politics of Militarizing Women's Lives.* London, U.K.: University of California Press, 2000.
30. Feinman, Ilene Rose. *Citizenship Rites: Feminist Soldiers and Feminist Antimilitarists.* New York: New York University Press, 2000.
31. Fenner, Lorry M., and Marie E. deYoung. *Women in Combat: Civic Duty or Military Liability?* Washington, DC: Georgetown University Press, 2001.
32. Fields, Sarah K. *Female Gladiators: Gender, Law, and Contact Sport in America.* Urbana and Chicago: University of Illinois Press, 2005.
33. Fraser, David. *Knight's Cross: A Life of Field Marshal Erwin Rommel.* New York: Harper Collins, 1993.
34. Friedan, Betty. *The Feminine Mystique.* 1963. Reprint with a new introduction, New York: W. W. Norton, 1997.
35. ———. *Life So Far: A Memoir.* New York: Simon and Schuster, 2000.
36. ———. *The Second Stage.* 1981. 2nd ed. with a new introduction, Cambridge, MA: Harvard University Press, 1998.
37. Ginzberg, Eli, and James K. Anderson. *The Ineffective Soldier: Lessons for Management and the Nation.* Vol. 1, *The Lost Divisions.* New York: Columbia University Press, 1959.
38. Goldman, Nancy Loring, ed. *Female Soldiers—Combatants or Noncombatants?: Historical and Contemporary Perspectives.* Westport, CT: Greenwood Press, 1982.
39. Gruber, James E., and Phoebe Morgan, eds. *In the Company of Men: Male Dominance and Sexual Harassment.* Boston, MA: Northeastern University Press, 2005.
40. Gruhzit-Hoyt, Olga. *A Time Remembered: American Women in the Vietnam War.* Novato, CA: Presidio Press, 1999.
41. Gutman, Stephanie. *The Kinder, Gentler Military: Can America's Gender-Neutral Fighting Force Still Win Wars?* New York: Scribner, 2000.
42. Hadley, Arthur T., Jr. *The Straw Giant: Triumph and Failure: America's Armed Forces: A Report from the Field.* New York: Random House, 1986.
43. Harrell, Margaret C., Megan K. Beckett, et al. *The Status of Gender Integration in the Military: Analysis of Selected Occupations.* Santa Monica, CA: RAND, 2002.
44. Harrell, Margaret C., and Laura Miller. *New Opportunities for Military Women:*

Effects Upon Cohesion, Readiness and Morale. Santa Monica, CA: RAND, 1997.

45. Hayward, Steven, ed. *Foreign Entanglements: An Institutional Critique of U.S. Foreign Policy.* San Francisco: Pacific Research Institute for Public Policy, 2001.

46. Henderson, William Darryl. *Cohesion: The Human Element in Combat.* Washington, DC: National Defense University Press, 1985.

47. Hischman, Loree Draude, with Dave Hirschman. *She's Just Another Navy Pilot: An Aviator's Sea Journal.* Annapolis, MD: Naval Institute Press, 2000.

48. Holm, Jeanne. *Women in the Military: An Unfinished Revolution.* Novato, CA: Presidio Press, 1982.

49. Institute of Medicine. *Assessing Readiness in Military Women: The Relationship of Body Composition, Nutrition, and Health.* Washington, DC: National Academies Press, 1998.

50. Johns, Dr. John H. *Cohesion in the U.S. Military: Defense Management Study Group on Military Cohesion.* Washington, DC: National Defense University, 1984.

51. Kann, Mark E. *On the Man Question: Gender and Civic Virtue in America.* Philadelphia, PA: Temple University Press, 1991.

52. Karpinski, Janis, with Steven Strasser. *One Woman's Army: The Commanding General of Abu Ghraib Tells Her Story.* New York: Hyperion, 2005.

53. Katzenstein, Mary Fainsod, and Judith Reppy, eds. *Beyond Zero Tolerance: Discrimination in Military Culture.* New York: Rowman and Littlefield, 1999.

54. Keegan, John. *Fields of Battle: The Wars for North America.* New York: Vintage Books, 1997.

55. Kennedy, Claudia, with Malcolm McConnell. *Generally Speaking.* New York: Warner Books, 2001.

56. Kennedy, Kathleen. *Disloyal Mothers and Scurrilous Citizens: Women and Subversion During World War I.* Bloomington: Indiana University Press, 1999.

57. Kerber, Linda K. *No Constitutional Right to Be Ladies: Women and the Obligations of Citizenship.* New York: Hill and Wang, 1998.

58. Krause, Sharon R. *Liberalism with Honor.* Cambridge, MA: Harvard University Press, 2002.

59. Lasch, Christopher. *Haven in a Heartless World: The Family Besieged.* New York: Basic Books, 1977.

60. Leebaert, Derek. *The Fifty Year Wound: The True Price of America's Cold War Victory.* New York: Little, Brown, 2002.

61. Manning, Lory. *Women in the Military: Where They Stand.* 5th ed. Washington, DC: Women's Research and Education Institute, 2005.

62. Mansoor, Peter R. *The GI Offensive in Europe: The Triumph of American Infantry Divisions, 1941–1945.* Lawrence: University Press of Kansas, 1999.

63. Marmion, Harry A. *The Case Against a Volunteer Army: Should America's Wars Be Fought Only by the Poor and the Black?* Chicago, IL: Quadrangle, 1971.

64. Marshall, Kathryn. *In the Combat Zone: An Oral History of American Women in Vietnam, 1966–1975.* Boston, MA: Little, Brown, 1987.

65. Mayo, Lida. *Bloody Buna.* New York: Doubleday, 1974.

66. Meyer, Leisa D. *Creating GI Jane: Sexuality and Power in the Women's Army Corps During World War II.* New York: Columbia University Press, 1996.

67. Mitchell, Brian. *Women in the Military: Flirting with Disaster.* Washington, DC: Regnery, 1998.

68. Monahan, Evelyn M., and Rosemary Neidel-Greenlee. *And If I Perish: Frontline*

U.S. Army Nurses in World War II. New York: Alfred A. Knopf, 2003.

69. Moore, Brenda L. *To Serve My Country, To Serve My Race: The Story of the Only African American WACs Stationed Overseas During World War II.* New York: New York University Press, 1996.

70. Nelson, T. S. *For Love of Country: Confronting Rape and Sexual Harassment in the U.S. Military.* Binghampton, NY: Haworth Press, 2002.

71. Ortega y Gasset, Jose. *The Revolt of the Masses.* 1930. Translated by Anonymous. 25th anniversary edition, 1957. New York: W. W. Norton, 1960.

72. Overy, Richard. *Why the Allies Won.* New York: W. W. Norton, 1996.

73. Palmer, Robert R., Bell I. Wiley, and William R. Keast. *United States Army in World War II: The Army Ground Forces: The Procurement and Training of Ground Combat Troops.* Washington, DC: U.S. Army Center of Military History, 1991.

74. Parker, Alison M., and Stephanie Cole, eds. *Women and the Unstable State in Nineteenth Century America.* College Station: Texas A & M University Press, 2000.

75. Peckham, Howard H, ed. *The Toll of Independence: Engagements and Battle Casualties of the American Revolution.* Chicago: University of Chicago Press, 1974.

76. Pogue, C. Forrest. *George C. Marshall: Education of a General, 1880–1939.* New York: Viking Press, 1963.

77. Rosenau, Pauline Marie. *Post-Modernism and the Social Sciences: Insights, Inroads, and Intrusions.* Princeton, NJ: Princeton University Press, 1992.

78. Schneider, Dorothy, and Carl J. Schneider. *Sound Off! American Military Women Speak Out.* New York: E. P. Dutton, 1988.

79. Schroeder, Pat. *24 Years of House Work . . . and the Place Is Still a Mess.* Kansas City, MO: Andrews McNeel, 1998.

80. Schroeder, Pat, with Andrea Camp and Robyn Lipner. *Champion of the Great American Family.* New York: Random House, 1989.

81. Shepherd, Ben. *A War of Nerves: Soldiers and Psychiatrists in the Twentieth Century.* Cambridge, MA: Harvard University Press, 2001.

82. Skaine, Rosemarie. *Women at War: Gender Issues of Americans in Combat.* Jefferson, NC: McFarland, 1999.

83. Smirnova-Medevedeva, Zoia Matveevna. *On the Road to Stalingrad: Memoirs of a Woman Machine Gunner.* Edited and translated by Kazimiera Janina Cottam. Nepean, ON, Canada: New Military, 1997.

84. Stewart, Dr. Nora Kinzer. *Mates and Muchachos: Unit Cohesion in the Falklands/ Malvinas War.* New York: Brassey's, 1991.

85. Stiehm, Judith Hicks. *Arms and the Enlisted Woman.* Philadelphia, PA: Temple University Press, 1989.

86. ———. *Bring Me Men and Women: Mandated Change at the Air Force Academy.* Berkeley: University of California Press, 1981.

87. ———, ed. *It's Our Military, Too!* Philadelphia, PA: Temple University Press, 1996.

88. Stouffer, Samuel A., et al. *The American Soldier: Combat and Its Aftermath.* Vol. 2. New York: John Wiley and Sons, 1965.

89. Strum, Philippa. *Women in the Barracks: The VMI Case and Equal Rights.* Lawrence: University Press of Kansas, 2002.

90. Ulman, Richard B., and Doris Brothers. *The Shattered Self: A Psychoanalytic Study of Trauma.* Hillsdale, NJ: Analytic Press, 1988.

91. Weinstein, Laurie, and Christie C. White. *Wives and Warriors: Women in the Military in the United States and Canada.* Westport, CT: Bergin and Garvey, 1997.

92. Willenz, Julie A. *Women Veterans: America's Forgotten Heroines.* New York: Continuum Press, 1983.
93. Williams, Kayla, with Michael E. Staub. *Love My Rifle More Than You: Young and Female in the U.S. Army.* New York: W. W. Norton, 2005.
94. Witt, Linda, and Judith Bellafaire. *"A Defense Weapon Known to Be of Value": Servicewomen of the Korean War Era.* Hanover, NH: University Press of New England, in association with the Military Women's Press of the Women in Military Service for America Memorial Foundation, 2005.
95. World Health Organization. *Maternal Mortality in 2000.* Geneva, Switzerland: World Health Organization, 2004. Located at www.who.int/reproductive-health/publications/maternal_mortality_2000/mme.pdf.
96. Young, Alfred F. *Masquerade: The Life and Times of Deborah Sampson, Continental Soldier.* New York: Alfred A. Knopf, 2004.
97. Zimmerman, Jean. *Tailspin: Women at War in the Wake of Tailhook.* New York: Doubleday, 1995.

GOVERNMENT DOCUMENTS

1. Centers for Disease Control, National Center for Health Statistics. "Live Births, Birth Rates, and Fertility Rates, by Race: United States, 1909–2000." Located at www.cdc.gov/nchs/data/statab/t001x01.pdf.
2. Congressional Research Service. *Women in the Armed Forces: Proceedings of a CRS Seminar Held on November 2, 1979 and Selected Readings.* February 14, 1980.
3. Cook, Paul J., et al. *Service Academy 2005 Sexual Harassment and Assault Survey.* Arlington, VA: Defense Manpower Data Center, December 2005.
4. Defense Advisory Committee on Women in the Services. *2001 Spring Conference Issue Book: Equality Management.* Located at www.dtic.mil/dacowits/issue_books/Spr2001-IssueBk-EqMgt.html.
5. Department of Defense, Defense Task Force on Sexual Harassment and Violence at the Military Service Academies. *Report of the Defense Task Force on Sexual Harassment and Violence at the Military Service Academies.* Washington, DC: Department of Defense, June 2005.
6. Department of Defense, Department of the Army. *Senior Review Panel Report on Sexual Harassment.* Vols. I and II. 1997.
7. ———. "AR 600-13, Army Policy for the Assignment of Female Soldiers." March 27, 1992. Located at www.army.mil/usapa/epubs/pdf/r600_13.pdf.
8. ———. "AR 600-9, the Army Weight Control Program." June 10, 1987. Located at www.usapa.army.mil/pdffiles/r600_9.pdf.
9. ———. "AR 600-9, the Army Weight Control Program, Interim Change." March 4, 1994. Located at www.armyg1.army.mil/hr/weight/600-9_I01.pdf.
10. ———. *Army Profile, FY04.* Located at www.armyg1.army.mil/hr/demographics/FY04%20Army%20Profile.pdf.
11. ———. "Attack on the 507th Maintenance Company." Located at www.army.mil/features/507thMaintCmpy/.
12. ———. "FM 21-20, Physical Fitness Training." October 1, 1998. Located at www.hooah4health.com/4You/FM2021-20.pdf.
13. Department of Defense, Directorate for Information Operations and Reports, Statistical Information Analysis Division, Personnel. "Military Casualty Information." Located at http://web1.whs.osd.mil/mmid/casualty/castop.htm.

14. ———. "Principal Wars in Which the United States Participated, U.S. Military Personnel Serving and Casualties." Located at http://web1.whs.osd.mil/mmid/casualty/WCPRINCIPAL.pdf.
15. Department of Defense, Office of the Inspector General. *Report on the Service Academy Sexual Assault and Leadership Survey, Executive Summary.* Washington, DC: Department of Defense, March 2005.
16. ———. *Tailhook 91: Part 1—Review of the Navy Investigations.* Arlington, VA: Department of Defense, 1992. Located at www.mith2.umd.edu/WomensStudies/GenderIssues/SexualHarassment/tailhook-91.
17. ———. *The Tailhook Report: The Official Inquiry into the Events of Tailhook '91.* New York: St. Martin's Press, 1993.
18. Department of Health and Human Services, Public Health Service. *Vital Statistics of the United States: 1992.* Vol. 2, *Mortality: Part A.* Hyattsville, MD: National Center for Health Statistics, 1996. Located at www.cdc.gov/nchs/data/vsus/mort92_2a.pdf.
19. General Accounting Office, National Security and International Affairs Division. *Combat Exclusion Laws for Women in the Military.* Washington, DC: General Accounting Office, 1987.
20. ———. *Gender Issues: Information on DOD's Assignment Policy and Direct Ground Combat Definition.* Washington, DC: General Accounting Office, 1998.
21. ———. *Medical Support for Female Soldiers Deployed to Bosnia.* Washington, DC: General Accounting Office, 1999.
22. ———. *Operation Desert Storm: War Highlights Need to Address Problem of Nondeployable Personnel.* Washington, DC: General Accounting Office, 1992.
23. ———. *Women in the Military: Deployment in the Persian Gulf War.* Washington, DC: General Accounting Office, 1993.
24. Harman, Everett, Peter Frykman, et al. *Effects of a Specifically Designed Physical Conditioning Program on the Load Carriage and Lifting Performance of Female Soldiers.* Natick, MA: U.S. Army Research Institute of Environmental Medicine, 1997.
25. House Armed Services Committee. *Sexual Assault Prevention and Response in the Armed Forces.* H.R. Hearing. 108th Cong., 2nd sess., June 3, 2004.
26. Kochanek, Kenneth A., and Sherry L. Murphy. "National Vital Statistics Report: Final Data for 2002." *National Vital Statistics Reports* 53, no. 5 (October 2004). Located at www.cdc.gov/nchs/data/nvsr/nvsr53/nvsr53_05.pdf.
27. Lipari, Rachel N., Anita R. Lancaster, and Alan M. Jones. *2004 Sexual Harassment Survey of Reserve Component Members.* Arlington, VA: Defense Manpower Data Center, June 2005.
28. Lisak, Dr. David. "Rape Fact Sheet." U.S. Army, March 2002. Located at www.sexualassault.army.mil/files/RAPE_FACT_SHEET.pdf.
29. MacGregor, Morris J. *Integration of the Armed Forces, 1940–1965.* Washington, DC: U.S. Army Center of Military History, 1985. Located at www.army.mil/cmh-pg/books/integration/IAF-FM.htm.
30. Martindale, Melanie. *Sexual Harassment in the Military: 1988.* Arlington, VA: Defense Manpower Data Center, 1990.
31. Ministry of Defence (U.K.). *Women in the Armed Forces.* Employment of Women in the Armed Forces Steering Group, May 2002.
32. Morden, Bettie J. *The Women's Army Corps, 1945 1978.* Washington, DC: U.S. Army Center of Military History, 1990. Located at www.army.mil/cmh-pg/books/wac/index.htm.

33. Office of Management and Budget. *Historical Tables, Budget of the United States Government, Fiscal Year 2007.* Washington, DC: Government Printing Office, 2006. Located at www.whitehouse.gov/omb/budget/fy2007/pdf/hist.pdf.

34. Presidential Commission on the Assignment of Women in the Armed Forces. *Women in Combat: Report to the President.* Washington, DC: Government Printing Office, 1992.

35. Rice, Condoleezza. "Remarks." 104th National Convention of the Veterans of Foreign Wars, August 25, 2003. Located at www.whitehouse.gov/news/releases/2003/0 8/20030825-1.html.

36. Sharp, M. A., and J. J. Knapik. *Physical Fitness of Soldiers Entering and Leaving Basic Combat Training.* Natick, MA: U.S. Army Research Institute of Environmental Medicine, 2000.

POPULAR PRESS

1. "Army Judge, in Disputed Ruling, Refuses to Drop Rape Charges." *The New York Times,* April 19, 1997.

2. "Army Says No Bias Was Found in Sexual Misconduct Inquiries." *The New York Times,* January 16, 1999.

3. Bull, Chris. "The Quiet Crusader." *The Advocate,* July 23, 2002.

4. "Captain Enters Guilty Plea in Sexual Abuse of Private." *The New York Times,* March 21, 1997.

5. Daley, Paul. "Call for Change in Racing Long Overdue." *The Lowell Sun,* July 25, 2000.

6. ———. "Chris McKenzie: A Jockey Dies for His Dream." *The Lowell Sun,* July 24, 2000.

7. ———. "Jockeys: Racing in the Danger Zone." *The Lowell Sun,* July 22, 2000.

8. Dotinga, Randy. "Military Women Can Hack It." Wired, January 13, 2006. Located at www.wired.com/news/technology/0,70006-0.html?tw=wn_tophead_1.

9. Eberhart, Dave. "Women in Combat." *NewsMax,* February 2005.

10. Ferraro, Susan. "The Prime of Pat Schroeder." *The New York Times Magazine,* July 1, 1990.

11. Ghafari, Salima, and Mari Nabard. "Afghanistan: A Life for a Life." *Afghan Recovery Report,* 186 (September 12, 2005). Institute for War and Peace Reporting. Located at www.iwpr.net/?p=arr&s=f&o=254844&apc_state=heniarr2005.

12. Glanz, James, and John F. Burns. "Suicide Car Bomb Kills 4 American Women in Iraq." *The New York Times,* June 25, 2005.

13. Gordon, Michael R. "Panel Opposes Allowing Women to Choose Combat Voluntarily." *The New York Times,* November 3, 1992.

14. Gross, Jane. "Sergeant Major's Accusers Fault Excess Army Loyalty." *The New York Times,* March 16, 1998.

15. ———. "Service Women's Families Speak Out on Abuse." *The New York Times,* July 26, 1992.

16. ———. "When Character Counts." *The New York Times,* March 15, 1998.

17. "The Harassment of Female Troops." *The New York Times,* September 13, 1997.

18. Kilborn, Peter T. "Sex Abuse Cases Sting Pentagon, But the Problem Has Deep Roots." *The New York Times,* February 10, 1997.

19. Landesman, Peter. "A Woman's Work." *The New York Times Magazine,* September 15, 2002.

20. Levy, Nathan. "The Reach of War: Detainees; Private England Pleads Guilty to Abuses." *The New York Times,* May 3, 2005.

21. Lubold, Gordon. "Band of Sisters: Army 'Lionesses' Hit Streets with Marines on Combat Ops." *Marine Corps Times,* August 9, 2004. Located at www.marinecorps-stimes.com/story.php?f=1-MARINEPAPER-280274.php.

22. Macur, Juliet. "In the Line of Fire." *The New York Times,* November 20, 2005.

23. Marquis, Christopher. "General Seeks to Retire as Charges Are Supported." *The New York Times,* July 8, 2000.

24. Miles, Donna. "Programs Aim to Reduce Military Divorce Rates." American Forces Press Service, June 9, 2005. Located at www.defenselink.mil/news/Jun2005/20050609_1666.html.

25. Moss, Michael. "Hard Look at Mission That Ended in Inferno for 3 Women." *The New York Times,* December 20, 2005.

26. Myers, Steven Lee. "Female General in Army Alleges Sex Harassment." *The New York Times,* March 31, 2000.

27. ———. "General Accused of Sex Harassment Had Won Key Post." *The New York Times,* April 6, 2000.

28. Owens, Mackubin Thomas. "A Man's Job." *National Review Online,* May 12, 2005. Located at www.nationalreview.com/owens/owens200505120814.asp.

29. Pruden, Wesley. "When a Cold Reality Quiets the Henhouse." *The Washington Times,* March 12, 2002.

30. Ratnesar, Romesh, and Michael Weisskopf. "Person of the Year: The American Soldier: Portrait of a Platoon." *Time,* December 29, 2003, 58–81.

31. Rayner, Richard. "The Warrior Besieged." *The New York Times Magazine,* June 22, 1997.

32. Reed, Cheryl L. "War Stress Heavier on Women." *Chicago Sun-Times,* May 8, 2005.

33. Scarborough, Rowan. "Iraq War Muddles Role of Women." *The Washington Times,* October 17, 2005.

34. ———. "Why Can't a Woman Be More Like a Man?" *The Washington Times,* February 14, 1995.

35. Scharnberg, Kirsten. "Stresses of Battle Hit Female GIs Hard." *Chicago Tribune,* March 20, 2005.

36. Schlafly, Phyllis. "Challenge to Rumsfeld." *The Washington Times,* November 20, 2005.

37. Schmidt, Susan, and Vernon Loeb. "She Was Fighting to the Death," *The Washington Post,* April 3, 2003.

38. Schmitt, Eric. "Air Force Sergeant in a Sex Complaint Tells of Reprisals." *The New York Times,* June 10, 1994.

39. ———. "Army Inquiries Find a Wide Bias Against Women." *The New York Times,* July 31, 1997.

40. ———. "Army Is Criticized on Harassment Survey." *The New York Times,* June 27, 1997.

41. ———. "Role of Women in the Military Is Again Bringing Debate." *The New York Times,* December 29, 1996.

42. ———. "Sex Harassment Case Polarizes Soldiers." *The New York Times,* February 16, 1997.

43. ———. "Top Enlisted Man in the Army Stands Accused of Sex Assault." *The New*

York Times, February 4, 1997.
44. ———. "War Is Hell. So Is Regulating Sex." *The New York Times*, November 17, 1996.
45. Sciolino, Elaine. "Accuser of Army's Senior Soldier Says He Should Face More Serious Charges." *The New York Times*, June 27, 1997.
46. ———. "The Army's Problems with Sex and Power." *The New York Times*, May 4, 1997.
47. ———. "From a Love Affair to a Court-Martial." *The New York Times*, May 11, 1997.
48. ———. "Harassment Charges Detailed in Hearing." *The New York Times*, July 26, 1997.
49. ———. "In Limbo, a Soldier's Soldier Reviews His Rise and Fall." *The New York Times*, June 16, 1997.
50. ———. "Military Women Are Vulnerable to Abuse, Psychiatrist Says." *The New York Times*, April 16, 1997.
51. ———. "Rape Witnesses Tell of Base Out of Control." *The New York Times*, April 15, 1997.
52. ———. "Sergeant Convicted of 18 Counts of Raping Female Subordinates." *The New York Times*, April 30, 1997.
53. ———. "Sexual-Harassment Hearing for Top Enlisted Man." *The New York Times*, June 26, 1997.
54. ———. "Top Army Sergeant Was Secretly Taped in Sex Investigation," *The New York Times*, June 28, 1997.
55. "Sergeant Gets 25-Year Term for 18 Rapes of Recruits." *The New York Times*, May 7, 1997.
56. "Sergeant in Sex Case Dishonorably Discharged." *The New York Times*, September 1, 1997.
57. Shenon, Philip. "Army's Leadership Blamed in Report on Sexual Abuses." *The New York Times*, September 12, 1997.
58. ———. "Hearings Against Sergeant Major Conclude." *The New York Times*, August 27, 1997.
59. "Soldier Tells About Threat After Rape." *The New York Times*, April 18, 1997.
60. "Trials Over, Army Faces Issues of Sex." *The New York Times*, November 9, 1997.
61. Weiner, Tim. "One Sergeant Pleads Guilty as Army Widens Sex Inquiry." *The New York Times*, November 13, 1996.
62. "Women at West Point? 'Silly' to Westmoreland." *The New York Times*, May 31, 1976.

SCHOLARLY JOURNALS
1. Adler, Amy B., and Ann H. Huffman. "The Impact of Deployment Length and Experience on the Well-Being of Male and Female Soldiers." *Journal of Occupational Health Psychology* 10, no. 2 (April 2005): 121–37.
2. Araneta, Maria Rosario G., Deborah R. Kamens, et al. "Conception and Pregnancy during the Persian Gulf War: The Risk to Women Veterans." *Annals of Epidemiology* 14, no. 2 (February 2004).
3. Baier, Annette C. "What Do Women Want in a Moral Theory?" *Noûs* 19, no. 1 (March 1985): 53–63.
4. Bailey, Joanna. "Favoured or Oppressed? Married Women, Property and 'Coverture'

in England, 1660–1800." *Continuity and Change* 17, no. 3 (December 2002): 351–72.

5. Belkin, Aaron, and Melissa Sheridan Embser-Herbert. "A Modest Proposal: Privacy as a Flawed Rationale for the Exclusion of Gays and Lesbians from the U.S. Military." *International Security* 27, no. 2 (2002): 178–97.

6. Bray, Robert M., Carol S. Camlin, et al. "The Effects of Stress on Job Functioning of Military Men and Women." *Armed Forces and Society* 27, no. 3 (Spring 2001): 397–417.

7. Calhoun, Byron C., Bonnie M. Jennings, et al. "Focused Obstetrical Clinic for Active Duty Junior Enlisted Service Women: Model for Improved Outcomes." *Military Medicine* 165, no. 1 (January 2000): 45–48.

8. Carlton, Janis R., Gail H. Manos, and John A. van Slyke. "Anxiety and Abnormal Eating Behaviors Associated with Cyclical Readiness Testing in a Naval Hospital Active Duty Population." *Military Medicine* 170, no. 8 (August 2005): 663–67.

9. Centers for Disease Control. "CDC on Infant and Maternal Mortality in the United States: 1900–99." *Population and Development Review* 25, no. 4 (December 1999): 821–26.

10. Cott, Nancy F. "Marriage and Women's Citizenship in the United States, 1830–1934." *The American Historical Review* 103, no. 5 (December 1998): 1440–74.

11. Creveld, Martin van. "Less Than We Can Be: Men, Women, and the Modern Military." *The Journal of Strategic Studies* 23, no. 4 (December 2000): 1–20.

12. Dietz, Mary G. "Citizenship with a Feminist Face: The Problem with Maternal Thinking." *Political Theory* 13, no. 1 (February 1985): 19–37.

13. Friedl, Karl E. "Biomedical Research on Health and Performance of Military Women: Accomplishments of the Defense Women's Health Research Program." *Journal of Women's Health* 14, no. 9 (November 2005): 764–802.

14. ———. "Can You Be Large and Not Obese? The Distinction Between Body Weight, Body Fat, and Abdominal Fat in Occupational Standards." *Diabetes Technology and Therapeutics* 6, no. 5 (October 2004): 732–49.

15. Gat, Azar. "Female Participation in War: Bio-Cultural Interactions." *The Journal of Strategic Studies* 23, no. 4 (December 2000): 21–31.

16. Gemmell, Ian M. M. "Injuries Among Female Army Recruits: A Conflict of Legislation." *Royal Society of Medicine* 95, no. 1 (January 2002): 23–27.

17. Gold, Philip. "To Guard an Era: American Purpose After Iraq." *Proceedings of the U.S. Naval Institute* (September 2005): 18–22.

18. Hanna, John Harvey. "An Analysis of Gynecological Problems Presenting to an Evacuation Hospital During Operation Desert Storm." *Military Medicine* 157, no. 5 (May 1992): 222–24.

19. Hauret, Keith G., Dana L. Shippey, and Joseph J. Knapik. "The Physical Training and Rehabilitation Program: Duration of Rehabilitation and Final Outcome of Injuries in Basic Combat Training." *Military Medicine* 166, no. 9 (September 2001): 820–26.

20. Henderson, Nancy E., Joseph Knapik, et al. "Injuries and Injury Risk Factors Among Men and Women in U.S. Army Combat Medic Advanced Individual Training." *Military Medicine* 165, no. 9 (September 2000): 647–52.

21. Hines, Jeffrey F. "Ambulatory Health Care Needs of Women Deployed with a Heavy Armor Division During the Persian Gulf War." *Military Medicine* 157, no. 5 (May 1992): 219–21.

22. Hoge, Charles W., Carl A. Castro, et al. "Combat Duty in Iraq and Afghanistan, Mental Health Problems, and Barriers to Care." *The New England Journal of Medicine* 351, no. 1 (July 2004): 13–22.

23. Hoiberg, Anne, and Jack F. White. "Health Status of Women in the Armed Forces." *Armed Forces and Society* 18, no. 4 (Summer 1992): 514–33.
24. Hughes, Thomas C., and Deborah Staren-Doby. "Reducing Unintended Pregnancy in Young, Single Active Duty Women in an Overseas Environment." *Military Medicine* 168, no. 1 (January 2003): 11–14.
25. Jones, Kathleen B. "Citizenship in a Woman-Friendly Polity." *Signs* 14, no. 4 (Summer 1990): 781–812.
26. Kelly, Edward W., Scott R. Jonson, et al. "Stress Fractures of the Pelvis in Female Navy Recruits: An Analysis of Possible Mechanisms of Injury." *Military Medicine* 165, no. 2 (February 2000): 142–146.
27. Kennedy-Pipe, Caroline. "Women and the Military." *The Journal of Strategic Studies* 23, no. 4 (December 2000): 32–50.
28. Kerber, Linda K. "The Meanings of Citizenship." *The Journal of American History* 84, no. 3 (December 1997): 833–54.
29. Knapik, Joseph, Michelle Canham-Chervak, et al. "Discharges During U.S. Army Basic Training: Injury Rates and Risk Factors." *Military Medicine* 166, no. 7 (July 2001): 641–47.
30. ———. "The Fitness Training Unit in U.S. Army Basic Combat Training: Physical Fitness, Training Outcomes, and Injuries." *Military Medicine* 166, no. 4 (April 2001): 356–61.
31. Kramer, Karen M. "Rule by Myth: The Social and Legal Dynamics Governing Alcohol-Related Acquaintance Rapes." *Stanford Law Review* 47, no. 1 (November 1994): 115–60.
32. Lauder, Tamara D., and Carol S. Campbell. "Abnormal Eating Behaviors in Female Reserve Officer Training Corps Cadets." *Military Medicine* 166, no. 3 (March 2001): 264–68.
33. Lauder, Tamara D., Marc V. Williams, et al. "The Female Athlete Triad: Prevalence in Military Women." *Military Medicine* 164, no. 9 (September 1999): 630–35.
34. Leu, John R., and Karl E. Friedl. "Body Fat Standards and Individual Physical Readiness in a Randomized Army Sample: Screening Weights, Methods of Fat Assessment, and Linkage to Physical Fitness." *Military Medicine* 167, no. 12 (December 2002): 994–1000.
35. Ling, Wen, Vern Houston, et al. "Women's Load Carriage Performance Using Modular Lightweight Load-Carrying Equipment." *Military Medicine* 169, no. 11 (November 2004): 914–19.
36. MacLeod, M. A., A. S. Houston, et al. "Incidence of Trauma-Related Stress Fractures and Shin Splints in Male and Female Army Recruits: Retrospective Case Study." *British Medical Journal* 318, no. 7175 (January 1999): 29.
37. Mazur, Diane H. "A Call to Arms." *Harvard Women's Law Journal* (now *Harvard Journal of Law and Gender*) 22 (Spring 1999): 39–88.
38. McDermott, Michael T., Reed S. Christensen, and Joan Lattimer. "The Effects of Region-Specific Resistance and Aerobic Exercises on Bone Mineral Density in Premenopausal Women." *Military Medicine* 166, no. 4 (April 2001): 318–321.
39. McKnight, James G. "Women in the Army: Experiences of a Battalion Commander." *Parameters* 9, no. 2 (June 1979): 20–26.
40. McNulty, Peggy Anne Fisher. "Prevalence and Contributing Factors of Eating Disorder Behaviors in Active Duty Service Women in the Army, Navy, Air Force, and Marines." *Military Medicine* 166, no. 1 (January 2001): 53–58.

41. Miller, Laura L. "Not Just Weapons of the Weak: Gender Harassment as a Form of Protest for Army Men." *Social Psychology Quarterly* 60, no. 1 (March 1997): 32–51.

42. Miller, Laura L., and Charles Moskos. "Humanitarians or Warriors? Race, Gender, and Combat Status in Operation Restore Hope." *Armed Forces and Society* 21, no. 4 (Summer 1995): 615–637.

43. Nantais, Cynthia, and Marsha F. Lee. "Women in the United States Military: Protectors or Protected? The Case of Prisoner of War Melissa Rathbun-Nealy." *Journal of Gender Studies* 8, no. 2 (July 1999): 181–91.

44. Nindl, Bradley C., Everett A. Harman, et al. "Regional Body Composition Changes in Women after 6 Months of Periodized Physical Training." *Journal of Applied Physiology* 88, no. 6 (June 2000): 2251–59.

45. Oberwetter, Ellen. "Rethinking Military Deference: Male-Only Draft Registration and the Intersection of Military Need with Civilian Rights." *Texas Law Review* 78, no. 1 (November 1999): 173–209.

46. Pierce, Penny F., Cathy Antonakos, and Barbara A. Deroba. "Health Care Utilization and Satisfaction Concerning Gender-Specific Health Problems Among Military Women." *Military Medicine* 164, no. 2 (February 1999): 98–102.

47. Pope, Rodney P. "Prevention of Pelvic Stress Fractures in Female Army Recruits." *Military Medicine* 164, no. 5 (May 1999): 370–73.

48. Reynolds, Katy T., Everett A. Harman, et al. "Injuries in Women Associated with a Periodized Strength Training and Running Program." *Journal of Strength and Conditioning Research* 15, no. 1 (2001): 136–143.

49. Robbins, Anthony S., Susan Y. Chao, et al. "Costs of Excess Body Weight Among Active Duty Personnel, U.S. Air Force, 1997." *Military Medicine* 167, no. 5 (May 2002): 393–97.

50. ———. "Unplanned Pregnancy Among Active Duty Servicewomen, U.S. Air Force, 2001." Military Medicine 170, no. 1 (January 2005): 38–43.

51. Rosen, Leora N., and Paul D. Bliese. "Gender Composition and Group Cohesion in U.S. Army Units: A Comparison Across Five Studies." *Armed Forces and Society* 25, no. 3 (Spring 1999): 365–86.

52. Rosen, Leora N., Doris B. Durand, et al. "Cohesion and Readiness in Gender-Integrated Combat Service Support Units: The Impact of Acceptance of Women and Gender Ratio." *Armed Forces and Society* 22, no. 4 (Summer 1996): 537–53.

53. Rosen, Leora N., Kathryn H. Knudson, and Peggy Fancher. "Cohesion and the Culture of Hypermasculinity in U.S. Army Units." *Armed Forces and Society* 29, no. 3 (Spring 2003): 325–51.

54. Rosen, Leora N., and Lee Martin. "Personality Characteristics That Increase Vulnerability to Sexual Harassment Among U.S. Army Soldiers." *Military Medicine* 165, no. 10 (October 2000): 709–13.

55. ———. "Predictors of Tolerance of Sexual Harassment Among Male U.S. Army Soldiers." *Violence Against Women* 4, no. 4 (August 1998): 491–504.

56. ———. "Psychological Effects of Sexual Harassment, Appraisal of Harassment, and Organizational Climate Among U.S. Army Soldiers." *Military Medicine* 163, no. 2 (February 1998): 63–67.

57. ———. "Sexual Harassment, Cohesion, and Combat Readiness in U.S. Army Support Units." *Armed Forces and Society* 24, no. 2 (Winter 1997): 221–44.

58. Ruddick, Sara. "Pacifying the Forces: Drafting Women in the Interests of Peace."

Signs 8, no. 3 (Spring 1983): 471–489.

59. Shaffer, Richard A., Mitchell J. Rauh, et al. "Predictors of Stress Fracture Suscepti-bility in Young Female Recruits." The American Journal of Sports Medicine 34, no. 10 (September 2005): 1–8.

60. Sheehan, Kathleen M., Michelle M. Murphy, et al. "The Response of a Bone Resorp-tion Marker to Marine Recruit Training." Military Medicine 168, no. 10 (October 2003): 797–801.

61. Shils, Edward A., and Morris Janowitz. "Cohesion and Disintegration in the Weh-rmacht in World War II." Public Opinion Quarterly 12, no. 2 (Summer 1948): 280–315.

62. Simpson, Mark, Jay Earles, et al. "The Tripler Army Medical Center's LE3AN Pro-gram: A Six-Month Retrospective Analysis of Program Effectiveness for African-American and European-American Females." Journal of the National Medical Asso-ciation 96, no. 10 (October 2004): 1332–36.

63. Snyder, R. Claire. "The Citizen Soldier Tradition and the Gender Integration of the U.S. Military." Armed Forces and Society 26, no. 2 (Winter 2003): 185–204.

64. Titunik, Regina F. "The First Wave: Gender Integration and Military Culture." Armed Forces and Society 26, no. 2 (Winter 2000): 229–57.

65. Wiesen, Andrew R., and Jeffrey D. Gunzenhauser. "Laboratory-Measured Preg-nancy Rates and Their Determinants in a Large, Well-Described Adult Cohort." Military Medicine 169, no. 7 (July 2004): 518–21.

66. Zellman, Gail L., and Anne S. Johansen. "Military Child Care: Toward an Integrated Delivery System." Armed Forces and Society 21, no. 4 (Summer 1995): 639–59.

MISCELLANEOUS

1. Baucom, Randall. "Re: Return to Kuwait." Email message to author. August 7, 2004.

2. Center for Military Readiness. CMR Notes 1, 16–18, 20, 22–27, 29–31, 33, 35. 36, 40, 45–47, 49–52, 55–81; CMR Reports 1, 3–14, 16, 17; "Army Gender-Integrated Basic Train-ing (GIBT): Summary of Relevant Findings and Recommendations: 1993–2002," and "Army Gender Integrated Training," 22 March 2002. Located at www.cmrlink.org.

3. Miller, Laura. "Feminism and the Exclusion of Army Women from Combat." Project on U.S. Post–Cold War Civil-Military Relations. John M. Olin Institute for Strategic Stud-ies. December 1995. Located at www.wcfia.harvard.edu/olin/publications/workingpa-pers/civil_military/no2.htm.

4. PBS Frontline. "The Navy Blues." Show no.1502. October 15, 1996. Located at www.pbs.org/wgbh/pages/frontline/shows/navy/script.html.

5. Solaro, Erin. "Casualties and Combat Effectiveness: The 127th Infantry During the Buna, Papua New Guinea Campaign." Master's Thesis. Diplomacy and Military Sci-ence, Norwich University, November 2003. Unbound, and in author's personal collec-tion.

6. University of Iowa. "UI, VAMC Researchers Study Women's Risk of Rape in Military." News release. March 11, 2003.

7. U.S. Census Bureau, Statistical Abstract of the United States, 2006. Located at www.census.gov/prod/2005pubs/06statab/vitstat.pdf.

8. U.S. Department of Veterans Affairs, National Center for Post-Traumatic Stress Disor-der. Located at www.ncptsd.va.gov/.

9. Women in Military Service for America Memorial Foundation. "Do You Know That . . . ?" Located at http://womensmemorial.org/historyandcollections/historysplash2.html.

INDEX

Broadwell, Teresa, 309
Bronson, Charles, 310
Brothers, Doris, 284, 286
Brown, Bryan D., 183–184
buddy systems, 311
Buna, Papua New Guinea, 304–308
Burger, Warren E., 202
Burns, John F., 102
Bush, George Herbert Walker,
    171–172
Bush, George W., 124, 141–142, 295
Bu Zhyahb, Iraq, 84–85

C

Cabrey, Michael, 86–96, 101
calcium and iron deficiencies,
    263–265
Campbell, James L., 232
Camp Blue Diamond, 32, 80
Camp Doha, 32, 44–45, 79
Camp Hurricane Point, 31–32, 36
Camp Junction City, 31, 32, 33, 48,
    79–100
career opportunities, 14, 160, 181,
    187–189, 204–206, 232
Carlson, Dudley, 72
Carlson, Tucker, 160
Carter, Jimmy, 59
casualties
    Buna, Papua New Guinea, 304–
        308
    civilians, 56–57
    major American wars, 138–139
    Marine Corps, 92–93, 102, 228
    servicewomen, 26, 102, 148, 228
    U.S. Army, 228, 298–301
    war casualties, 345
Center for Military Readiness, 72, 233
Chicken Street, 125–126
childbirth
    See maternal mortality; pregnancy
Chu, David S. C., 320–321, 325
Citadel, 207, 210–211, 216
citizenship

basic attitudes, 353, 356–358,
    363–364
equal rights issues, 8, 24, 209,
    348–352
and feminism, 351–354
military service, 196, 225, 235–
    236, 347–348
civic feminism, 348, 353–354
civic triad, 361–362
Civil Affairs units, 114
civilians
    battered women's shelters, 339–
        341
    casualties, 56–57
    female civilians, 117–119,
        130–132
    Protocol 1 (Geneva Conventions),
        98–99
Civil War, 10
Clarke, Mary Elizabeth, 179
Clark, Sergeant, 33–34
Clinton, William Jefferson, 186–188
Coalition Joint Civil-Military Opera-
    tions Task Force (CJCMOTF), 112
Cockerham, Samuel, 183
Cody, Richard A., 231
cohesion, 20, 182, 186–187, 196,
    297–319, 331–335
Coldsteel "C" Company, 83
Cold War, 148
Collins, John, 156–158
collocation, 187–189, 191, 230, 232
combat
    assignment versus attachment,
        69–70, 73, 162–164, 189–191
    combat aviation, 169–178, 180–
        182, 187, 229, 233, 296–297
    combat effectiveness, 20, 186–
        188, 298–314
    equal rights issues, 159–165
    government legislation, 168, 187–
        188
    individuals versus unit replace-
        ment, 298–302, 304, 308

and the feminist movement, 199

gender inequalities, 288

post-traumatic stress disorder
(PTSD), 285

sexual assaults, 211–215, 326–331

sexual predators, 317–319, 326–328, 330, 333–335

Tailhook crisis, 172, 175

victims of war, 56–58, 141

See also sexism and harassment

Vietnam War, 12, 195, 299–300

Virginia Military Institute (VMI), 207–211, 216

Virginia Women's Institute for Leadership (VWIL), 207–209

W

Walters, Donald, 69

warhead search, 83–85

Warner, John, 168

warrior versus soldier, 221–222, 236, 301

Wars of the Ways, 358–363

wartime roles, 56–57

weakness in women, perceived, 241–242, 261–262, 264–267

See also physiological differences

Webb, James, 67, 207

Wehrmacht
See German armed forces

weight control, 244–246, 251, 254–258, 262–265

weight/strength training, 255, 265, 267, 270, 271

Weisskopf, Michael, 70–71

Westmoreland, William, 197, 299–300

West Point, 205, 216, 235

White, Byron R., 202

White, Sarah F., 179, 183

Will, 107–109

Williams, Duvall M., Jr., 173, 175

Williams, Kayla, 18

Women in the Military: Deployment in the Persian Gulf War (GAO), 186–187

Women's Army Corps (WAC), 145–147

women's movement
See feminism

World War I, 10

World War II, 10, 63–64, 298–302, 304–308

Z

Zinni, Anthony, 67

CREDITS

Table of Ranks, public information available from the Department of Defense, ©
DefenseLINK.

Excerpt from *Bring Me Men and Women: Mandated Change at the Air Force Academy,*
by Judith Stiehm, © 1981. Reprinted by permission of the Regents of the University of
California, University of California Press.

Excerpt from *The All-Volunteer Force After a Decade: Retrospect and Prospect,* ed.
William Bowman, Roger Little, and G. Thomas Sicilia, © 1986. Reprinted by permission
of Potomac Books, Inc.

Excerpt from "A Call to Arms," by Diana H. Mazur. © 1999 *Harvard Journal of Law
and Gender* 22, spring. Reprinted by permission of the President and Fellows of Harvard
College and the Harvard Women's Law Journal.

Excerpt from *The Women's Army Corps, 1945–1978,* by Bettie J. Morden, is made available
by the U.S. Army Center of Military History. © 1990.

Material from *The Straw Giant: Triumph and Failure, America's Armed Forces: A
Report from the Field,* by Arthur T. Hadley, © 1986. Reprinted with permission of Random
dom House, Inc.

Material from Philip Gold's "To Guard an Era: American Purpose After Iraq,"
reprinted from *Proceedings* with permission; Copyright © 2005 U.S. Naval Institute/
www.usni.org.

Material from *For the People: What the Constitution Really Says About Your Rights,* by
Akhil Reed Amar and Alan Hirsch is reprinted wit the permission of The Free Press, a
Division of Simon & Schuster. Copyright © 1998 by Akhil Reed Amar and Paul Hirsch.
All rights reserved.

ABOUT THE AUTHOR

© BRAD KEVELIN, www.adonisphotos.com

Erin Solaro has been a radical feminist, Army reserve officer, defense analyst and historian, professional dog trainer, overeducated secretary, and journalist. She has appeared on public and network television and talk radio, and published more than twenty articles on military affairs, including two series from Iraq and Afghanistan in the *Seattle Post-Intelligencer, The Baltimore Sun, The Christian Science Monitor,* the Naval Institute's *Proceedings,* and the *Marine Corps Gazette.* Since 2004, Solaro has become a major national voice on women in the military and the new civic feminism. She lives in Seattle with her partner, writer Philip Gold, and assorted animals.

For more than thirty years, Seal Press has published groundbreaking books. By women. For women. Visit our website at www.sealpress.com.

The F-Word: Feminism in Jeopardy by Kristin Rowe-Finkbeiner. $14.95, 1-58005-114-6. An astonishing look at the tenuous state of women's rights and issues in America, and a call to action for the young women who have the power to change their situation.

Pissed Off: On Women and Anger by Spike Gillespie. $14.95, 1-58005-162-6. An amped up and personal self-help book that encourages women to go ahead and use that middle finger without being closed off to the notion of forgiveness.

Voices of Resistance: Muslim Women on War, Faith, and Sexuality edited by Sarah Husain. $16.95, 1-58005-181-2. A collection of essays and poetry on war, faith, suicide bombing, and sexuality, this book reveals the anger, pride and pain of Muslim women.

Reckless: The Outrageous Lives of Nine Kick-Ass Women by Gloria Mattioni. $14.95, 1-58005-148-0. An entertaining collection of profiles which explores the lives of nine women who took unconventional life paths to achieve extraordinary results.

A Matter of Choice: 25 People Who Have Transformed Their Lives edited by Joan Chatfield-Taylor. $14.95, 1-58005-118-9. An inspiring collection of essays by people who made profound changes in their work, personal life, location, or lifestyle, proving that it is indeed never too late to take the road less traveled.

Without a Net: The Female Experience of Growing Up Working Class edited by Michelle Tea. $14.95, 1-58005-103-0. A collection of essays "so raw, so fresh, and so riveting, that I read them compulsively, with one hand alternately covering my mouth, my heart, and my stomach, while the other hand turned the page. *Without a Net* is an important book for any woman who's grown up—or is growing up—in America."—Vendela Vida, *And Now You Can Go*